Communications
in Computer and Information Science 263

Tai-hoon Kim Hojjat Adeli
William I. Grosky Niki Pissinou
Timothy K. Shih Edward J. Rothwell
Byeong-Ho Kang Seung-Jung Shin (Eds.)

Multimedia, Computer Graphics and Broadcasting

International Conference, MulGraB 2011
Held as Part of the Future Generation
Information Technology Conference, FGIT 2011
in Conjunction with GDC 2011
Jeju Island, Korea, December 8-10, 2011
Proceedings, Part II

Springer

Volume Editors

Tai-hoon Kim
Hannam University, Daejeon, Korea
E-mail: taihoonn@hannam.ac.kr

Hojjat Adeli
The Ohio State University, Columbus, OH, USA
E-mail: adeli.1@osu.edu

William I. Grosky
University of Michigan, Dearborn, MI, USA
E-mail: wgrosky@umich.edu

Niki Pissinou
Florida International University, Miami, FL, USA
E-mail: pissinou@fiu.edu

Timothy K. Shih
National Taipei University of Education, Taipei City, Taiwan, R.O.C.
E-mail: tshih@cs.tku.edu.tw

Edward J. Rothwell
Michigan State University, East Lansing, MI, USA
E-mail: rothwell@egr.msu.edu

Byeong-Ho Kang
University of Tasmania, Hobart, TAS, Australia
E-mail: byeong.kang@utas.edu.au

Seung-Jung Shin
Hansei University, Gyeonggi-do, Korea
E-mail: sshin@ncsu.edu

ISSN 1865-0929 e-ISSN 1865-0937
ISBN 978-3-642-27185-4 e-ISBN 978-3-642-27186-1
DOI 10.1007/978-3-642-27186-1
Springer Heidelberg Dordrecht London New York

Library of Congress Control Number: Applied for

CR Subject Classification (1998): C.2, H.4, I.2, H.3, D.2, H.5

Typesetting: Camera-ready by author, data conversion by Scientific Publishing Services, Chennai, India

Printed on acid-free paper

Springer is part of Springer Science+Business Media (www.springer.com)

Foreword

Multimedia, computer graphics and broadcasting are areas that attract many professionals from academia and industry for research and development. The goal of the MulGraB conference is to bring together researchers from academia and industry as well as practitioners to share ideas, problems and solutions relating to the multifaceted aspects of multimedia, computer graphics and broadcasting.

We would like to express our gratitude to all of the authors of submitted papers and to all attendees for their contributions and participation.

We acknowledge the great effort of all the Chairs and the members of Advisory Boards and Program Committees of the above-listed event. Special thanks go to SERSC (Science and Engineering Research Support Society) for supporting this conference.

We are grateful in particular to the speakers who kindly accepted our invitation and, in this way, helped to meet the objectives of the conference.

December 2011 Chairs of MulGraB 2011

Preface

We would like to welcome you to the proceedings of the 2011 International Conference on Multimedia, Computer Graphics and Broadcasting (MulGraB 2011) — the partnering event of the Third International Mega-Conference on Future-Generation Information Technology (FGIT 2011) held during December 8–10, 2011, at Jeju Grand Hotel, Jeju Island, Korea

MulGraB 2011 focused on various aspects of advances in multimedia, computer graphics and broadcasting. It provided a chance for academic and industry professionals to discuss recent progress in the related areas. We expect that the conference and its publications will be a trigger for further related research and technology improvements in this important subject.

We would like to acknowledge the great effort of the MulGrab 2011 Chairs, Committees, International Advisory Board, Special Session Organizers, as well as all the organizations and individuals who supported the idea of publishing this volume of proceedings, including the SERSC and Springer.

We are grateful to the following keynote, plenary and tutorial speakers who kindly accepted our invitation: Hsiao-Hwa Chen (National Cheng Kung University, Taiwan), Hamid R. Arabnia (University of Georgia, USA), Sabah Mohammed (Lakehead University, Canada), Ruay-Shiung Chang (National Dong Hwa University, Taiwan), Lei Li (Hosei University, Japan), Tadashi Dohi (Hiroshima University, Japan), Carlos Ramos (Polytechnic of Porto, Portugal), Marcin Szczuka (The University of Warsaw, Poland), Gerald Schaefer (Loughborough University, UK), Jinan Fiaidhi (Lakehead University, Canada) and Peter L. Stanchev (Kettering University, USA), Shusaku Tsumoto (Shimane University, Japan), Jemal H. Abawajy (Deakin University, Australia).

We would like to express our gratitude to all of the authors and reviewers of submitted papers and to all attendees, for their contributions and participation, and for believing in the need to continue this undertaking in the future.

December 2011

Tai-hoon Kim
Hojjat Adeli
William I. Grosky
Niki Pissinou
Timothy K. Shih
Ed. Rothwell
Byeongho Kang
Seung-Jung Shin

Organization

Honorary Chair

Jeong-Jin Kang	Dong Seoul University, Korea

General Co-chairs

William I. Grosky	University of Michigan-Dearborn, USA
Niki Pissinou	Florida International University, USA
Timothy K. Shih	National Taipei University of Education, Taiwan
Ed Rothwell	Michigan State University, USA

Program Co-chairs

Tai-hoon Kim	GVSA and University of Tasmania, Australia
Byeongho Kang	University of Tasmania, Australia
Seung-Jung Shin	Hansei University, Korea

Workshop Chair

Byungjoo Park	Hannam University, Korea

Publication Chair

Yongho Choi	Jungwon University, Korea

International Advisory Board

Aboul Ella Hassanien	Cairo University, Egypt
Andrea Omicini	DEIS, Università di Bologna, Italy
Bozena Kostek	Gdansk University of Technology, Poland
Cao Jiannong	Hong Kong Polytechnic University, Hong Kong
Cas Apanowicz	Ministry of Education, Canada
Ching-Hsien Hsu	Chung Hua University, Taiwan
Claudia Linnhoff-Popien	Ludwig-Maximilians-Universität München, Germany
Daqing Zhang	Institute for Infocomm Research (I2R), Singapore
Diane J. Cook	University of Texas at Arlington, USA
Frode Eika Sandnes	Oslo University College, Norway

Guoyin Wang	CQUPT, Chongqing, China
Hamid R. Arabnia	The University of Georgia, USA
Han-Chieh Chao	National Ilan University, Taiwan
Ing-Ray Chen	Virginia Polytechnic Institute and State University, USA
Jae-Sang Cha	Seoul National University of Science and Technology, Korea
Jian-Nong Cao	Hong Kong Polytechnic University, Hong Kong
Krzysztof Pawlikowski	University of Canterbury, New Zealand
Krzysztof Marasek	PJIIT, Warsaw, Poland
Lionel Ni	The Hong Kong University of Science and Technology, Hong Kong
Mahmut Kandemir	Pennsylvania State University, USA
Matt Mutka	Michigan State University, USA
Mei-Ling Shyu	University of Miami, USA
Rajkumar Buyya	The University of Melbourne, Australia
Robert Young Chul Kim	Hongik University, Korea
Sajal K. Das	University Texas at Arlington, USA
Sajid Hussain	Acadia University, Canada
Sankar K. Pal	Indian Statistical Institute, India
Schahram Dustdar	Vienna University of Technology, Austria
Seng W. Loke	La Trobe University, Australia
Stefanos Gritzalis	University of the Aegean, Greece
Yang Xiao	University of Alabama, USA
Yong-Gyu Jung	Eulji University, Korea
Zbigniew W. Ras	University of North Carolina, USA
Aboul Ella Hassanien	Cairo University, Egypt

Program Committee

Abdelwahab Hamou-Lhadj
Ahmet Koltuksuz
Alexander Loui
Alexei Sourin
Alicja Wieczorkowska
Andrew Kusiak
Andrzej Dzielinski
Anthony Lewis Brooks
Atsuko Miyaji
Biplab K. Sarker
Ch. Z. Patrikakis
Chantana Chantrapornchai
Chao-Tung Yang
Chengcui Zhang
Chi Sung Laih
Ching-Hsien Hsu
Christine F. Maloigne
Dae-Hyun Ryu
Daniel Thalmann
Dieter Gollmann
Dimitris Iakovidis
Doo-Hyun Kim
Do-Hyeun Kim
Eung-Nam Ko
Fabrice Mériaudeau
Fangguo Zhang
Francesco Masulli
Federica Landolfi
Gérard Medioni
Hae-Duck Joshua Jeong
Hai Jin Huazhong
Hiroaki Kikuchi
Hironori Washizaki
Hongji Yang
Hoon Jin
Hyun-Sung Kim
Hyun-Tae Kim
Jacques Blanc-Talon
Jalal Al-Muhtadi
Jang Sik Park
Javier Garcia-Villalba
Jean-Luc Dugelay
Jemal H. Abawajy

Ji-Hoon Yang
Jin Kwak
Jiyoung Lim
Jocelyn Chanussot
Jong-Wook Jang
Joonsang Baek
Junzhong Gu
Karl Leung
Kee-Hong Um
Kenneth Lam
Khaled El-Maleh
Khalil Drira
Ki-Young Lee
Kouichi Sakurai
Kyung-Soo Jang
Larbi Esmahi
Lejla Batina
Lukas Ruf
MalRey Lee
Marco Roccetti
Mark Manulis
Maytham Safar
Mei-Ling Shyu
Min Hong
Miroslaw Swiercz
Mohan S Kankanhalli
Mototaka Suzuki
Myung-Jae Lim
Nadia Magnenat-Thalmann
Neungsoo Park
Nicoletta Sala
Nikitas Assimakopoulos
Nikos Komodakis
Olga Sourina
Pablo de Heras Ciechomski
Pao-Ann Hsiung
Paolo D'Arco
Paolo Remagnino
Rainer Malaka
Raphael C.-W. Phan
Robert G. Reynolds
Robert G. Rittenhouse
Rodrigo Mello
Roman Neruda
Rui Zhang
Ryszard Tadeusiewicz
Sagarmay Deb
Salah Bourennane
Seenith Siva
Serap Atay
Seung-Hyun Seo
Shin Jin Kang
Shingo Ichii
Shu-Ching Chen
Sidhi Kulkarni
Stefan Katzenbeisser
Stuart J. Barnes
Sun-Jeong Kim
Swapna Gokhale
Swee-Huay Heng
Taenam Cho
Tony Shan
Umberto Villano
Wasfi G. Al-Khatib
Yao-Chung Chang
Yi Mu
Yong-Ho Seo
Yong-Kap Kim
Yong-Soon Im
Yoo-Sik Hong
Young-Dae Lee
Young-Hwa An
Yo-Sung Ho
Young Ik Eom
You-Jin Song

Special Session Organizers

YangSun Lee
Kwan-Hee Yoo
Nakhoon Baek

Table of Contents – Part II

Table of Contents – Part I

Logical User Interface Modeling for Multimedia Embedded Systems*

Saehwa Kim

Hankuk University of Foreign Studies, Yongin-si, Gyeonggi-do, 449-791 Korea
ksaehwa@hufs.ac.kr

Abstract. Multimedia embedded systems such as smart phones, tablets, and smart TVs are ever proliferating. One of the major hurdles for reusing applications for multiple multimedia embedded systems is user interfaces (UIs) cannot be the same for the target embedded systems. While there have been many research activities regarding model-based UI development environments, they are focused on web of desk-top based systems and not suitable for embedded systems. This paper proposes logical user interface modeling for multimedia embedded systems (LUMME). LUMME incorporates the notions of reference containers and multimedia instance presentations. While conventional approaches model only visible UI components, LUMME incorporate events as a first-class modeling entity, which is essential to model UIs for embedded systems. Moreover, LUMME does not employ the task model, which is widely employed in conventional approaches, but incorporates events as navigators. We have fully implemented a modeling tool for LUMME as Eclipse rich-client platform (RCP) using Eclipse Graphical Modeling Framework (GMF). We have also performed a case study with a gallery application in Android targeted for multiple embedded systems with various resolutions from HVGA to XGA. The case study clearly shows how LUMME makes the modeling of UIs for multimedia embedded systems concise and allows reusing UIs for multiple multimedia embedded systems.

Keywords: User interface modeling, model-driven architecture (MDA), embedded systems, pattern-based transformational UI development, multimedia embedded applications.

1 Introduction

Multimedia embedded systems such as smart phones, tablets, navigators, and smart TVs are ever becoming diverse. This has lead to the increasing needs for applications that are adaptable for multiple devices. One of the major hurdles for increasing such reusability is that the user interfaces (UIs) for multiple devices cannot be the same for the target systems. This is because different kinds of embedded devices have different screen sizes and diverse sensors such as buttons, touch panel, and accelerometer. This

* This work was supported by the Hankuk University of Foreign Studies Research Fund of 2011.

T.-h. Kim et al. (Eds.): MulGraB 2011, Part II, CCIS 263, pp. 1–8, 2011.

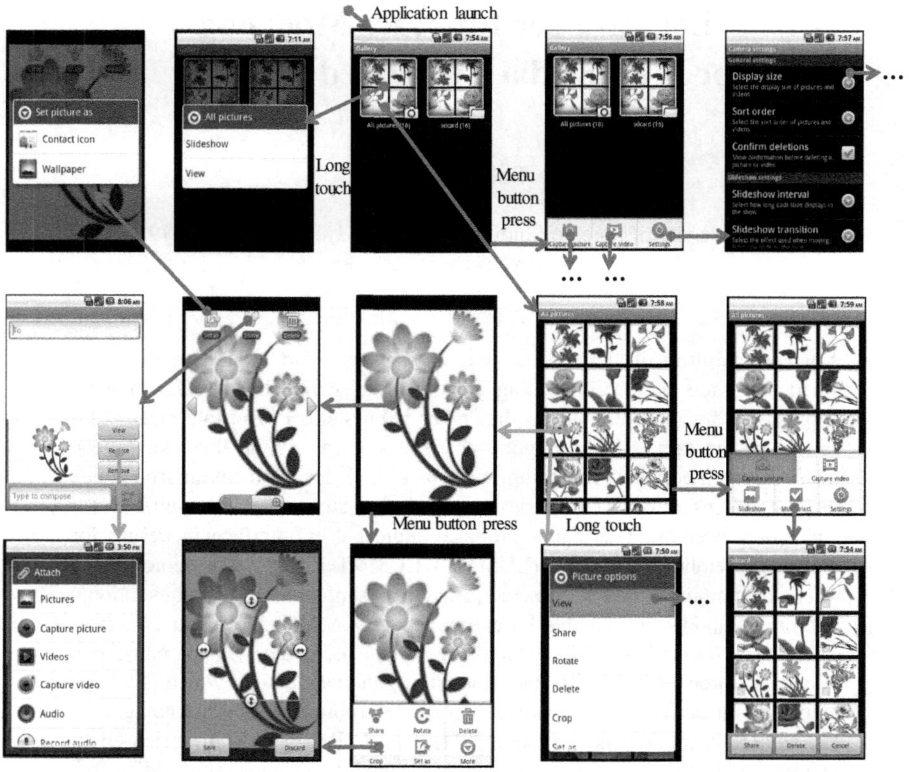

Fig. 1. A walk-through example: An Android gallery application targeted for a cell phone of HVGA with 160 ppi

makes it very difficult to reuse multimedia embedded applications for multiple embedded systems.

To solve such difficulties, there have been many research activities to provide a model-based user-interface development environment (MB-UIDE) or model-driven engineering (MDE) of user interfaces for multiple devices. They are listed in some survey work [4, 5]. However, these previous research activities received criticisms about their practicality as addressed in [3, 6, 7]. In [8], we identified some dominant limitations of these approaches and proposed a Pattern and Event based Logical UI Modeling framework (PELUM) to model UIs targeted for multiple embedded systems.

In this paper, we extend PELUM by proposing logical UI Modeling for multimedia embedded systems (LUMME) so that PELUM can support multimedia embedded applications. Specifically, we extend logical UI model (LUM) of PELUM by incorporating the notions of (1) reference containers and (2) multimedia instance presentations. First, we extend LUM containers so that they can refer to other applications. Such an extension is similar to the notion of *ref* scenario in UML 2.0 [9]. Second, while logical UI modeling intentionally ignores graphical UI modeling, there are some exceptions in multimedia applications. In multimedia applications, instance presentations themselves may be sorts of graphical resources while there are inherent differences with common graphical resources in UI implementations. Details will be explained in Section 2.

We fully implemented the modeling tool for LUMME as an Eclipse rich client platform (RCP) using the Eclipse Graphical Modeling Framework (GMF). We also performed a case study with a gallery application in Android targeted for multiple embedded systems, such as a cell phone of HVGA with 160 ppi that is the same as that of Apple iPhone 3G, a 7 inch tablet device with 170 ppi that is the same as that of Samsung galaxy tab, and XGA with 130 ppi, the same as that of Apple iPad. We use an Android gallery application for HVGA with 160 ppi, as a walk-through example shown in Fig. 1.

The remainder of this paper is organized as follows. Section 2 describes the background of this paper, which is PELUM. Section 3 explains the proposed extended logical UI model for multimedia embedded systems. Section 4 presents our tool support. Section 5 concludes the paper.

2 Background: Pattern and Event-Based Logical UI Modeling (PELUM)

Conventional research activities regarding model-based user-interface development environment (MB-UIDE) or model-driven engineering (MDE) of user interfaces for multiple devices [4, 5] share a hierarchical model-driven architecture as shown in the first row in Table 1. However, some recent work [3, 6, 7] has made criticisms about their practicality. In [8], we identified some dominant limitations of these approaches. First of all, conventional approaches are based on the task model [3] and this makes the whole hierarchical model unstable. The instability and unpredictability of the task model was well addressed in [6] and [10]. Moreover, conventional approaches have basically optimized for modeling UIs for web on desk-top environments [11, 12]. While events of desk-top based web applications are usually coupled with any kind of visible UI components, embedded systems, especially mobile multimedia embedded devices, have various events that are not associated visible UI components. This is because embedded systems are coupled with events from various sensors, such as gyroscope, accelerometer, compass, proximity sensor, ambient light sensor. Conventional approaches have not modeled such invisible UI components.

To overcome such limitations of conventional approaches, we have proposed a Pattern and Event based Logical UI Modeling framework (PELUM) to model UIs targeted for multiple embedded systems in [8]. PELUM incorporates events as a first-class modeling entity. This enables modeling events that do not have visible UI components, which is essential for embedded systems. PELUM also incorporates events as navigators, which enables abstract UI model implicitly cover the task model. The second row of Table 1 shows the hierarchical models of PELUM comparing with those of conventional MB-UIDE approaches. As shown, PELUM merges the Abstract UI and the task model into the Logical UI Model (LUM), while the names of other models are changed to explicitly emphasize the modeling entities in each specific modeling layer. Each UI component in LUM can be incorporated with a specific type that corresponds to a specific UI pattern [13]. We prepare graphical resource model (GRM) and UI controls and layout model (CLM) templates for each target device for each pattern in LUM. We can easily derive run-time flexible UI targeted for multi-devices, applying the template-based UI transformation method in [14] to this.

3 Extended Logical User Interface Model for Multimedia Embedded Systems (LUMME)

LUMME adopts the graphical modeling language for logical UI model (LUM) of PELUM [8] and extends it for multimedia embedded systems. Specifically, we extend LUM by incorporating the notions of (1) reference containers and (2) multimedia instance presentations. First, we extend LUM containers so that they can refer to other

Table 1. Comparison of model-driven architecture for UI modelling: (a) conventional approaches such as TERESA [1], CAMELEON [2], etc. The screen shots were taken from [3]. (b) pattern and event based logical UI modeling (PELUM). The left-most model is the lowest layer and the right-most model is the highest model. The left-most models, the observed model an programming interface model, are not the part of UI models but play the role of base model for UI modelling.

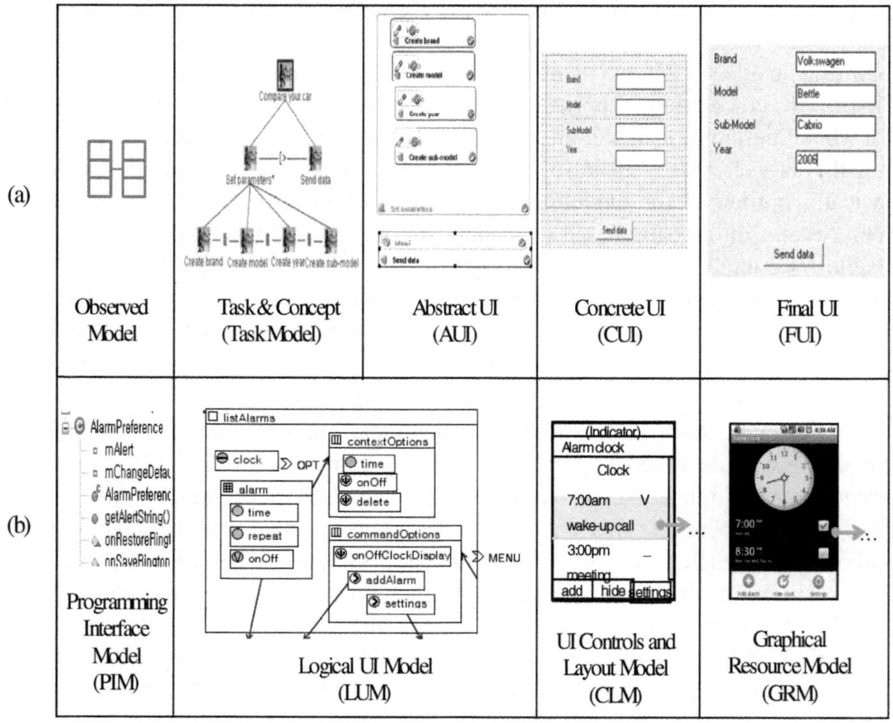

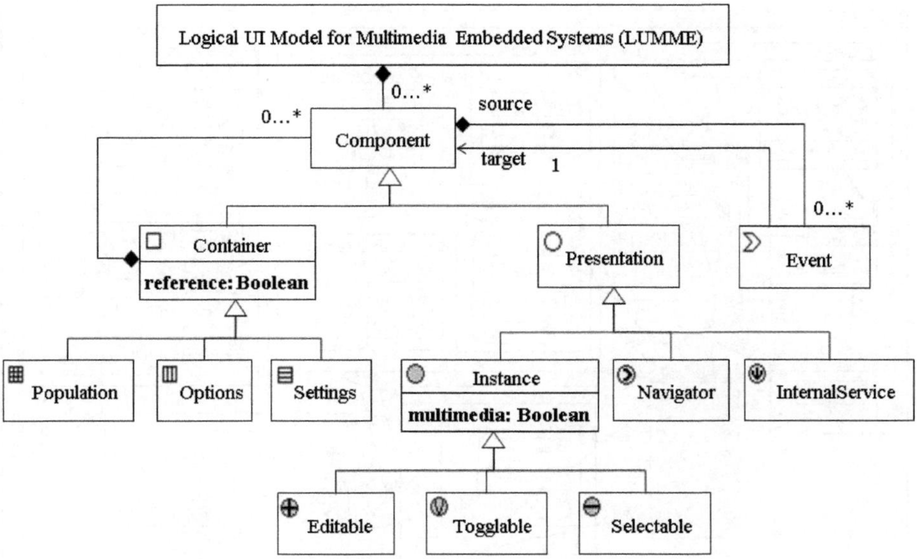

(a)

(b)

Fig. 2. (a) Meta-model of Logical UI Model for multimedia embedded systems (LUMME). Attributes of bold fonts are added to LUM component for LUMME. (b) Graphical notation for added attributes.

applications. Such an extension is similar to *ref* scenario in UML 2.0 [9]. Second, we extend LUM instances so that they can denote multimedia presentations. Logical UI modeling intentionally ignores graphical UI modeling that is covered in GRM where graphical resources are modeled as templates. However, in multimedia applications, instance presentations themselves may be sorts of graphical resources such as image, video, and sound. Note that there are inherent differences between graphical resources in GRM and multimedia instance presentation. Graphical resources in GRM should not be accompanied with API in the programming interface model (PIM). On the contrary, multimedia instance presentations should be accompanied with APIs in PIM.

Fig. 2 (a) shows the meta-model of LUMME where bold-font attributes represent extended parts to the original LUM of PELUM. Fig. 2 (b) shows graphical notations for LUMME components when corresponding attributes are true. Specifically, `Container` with attribute `reference` is true, that is reference container, is represented as a blue node while `Instance` with attribute `multimedia` is true, that is multimedia instance presentation, is represented as a red node.

Fig. 3 shows an example LUMME for the walk-through example of Fig. 1. While it is hard to figure out which screen shots are related together in Fig. 1, container boundaries and navigations or arrows with events in Fig. 3 make it easy to catch

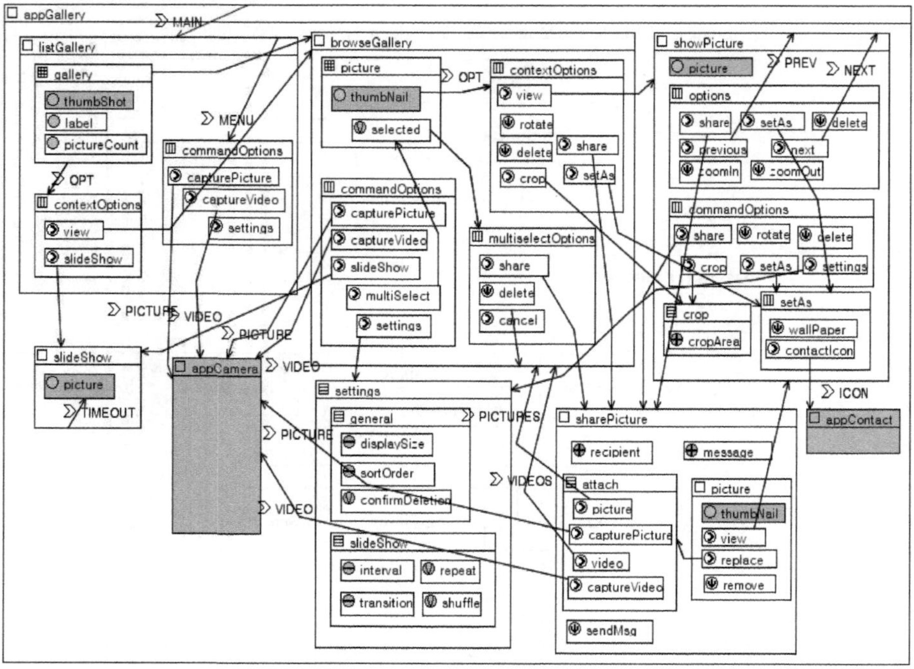

Fig. 3. LUMME examples for the walk-through example of Fig. 1. As shown in Fig. 2 (b), blue nodes are reference containers and red nodes are multimedia instance presentations. Note that an event name to a reference container means argument passing for invoking another application.

which dialogues are related together and how they are navigated. Containers `appCamera` and `appContact` are reference containers and the event names in navigation arrow into these containers represent arguments to the target containers. Red nodes including `thumbShot` in container population `gallery` are multimedia instance presentations whose images should be retrieved from some APIs of programming interface model (PIM). Note that container `slideShow` contains only multimedia instance presentation `picture` and this is triggered by an event `TIMEOUT`. As such, invisible UI components that are important in modeling UIs for embedded multimedia systems can be easily modeled in LUMME.

4 Tool Support

LUMME provides a graphical modeling tool that enables modeling logical UI model extended for multimedia application support. This tool is based on Eclipse graphical modeling framework (GMF). GMF enables users to build a tool binary from user-defined models based on it framework. [15] describes the architecture of this tool.

Fig. 4 shows a screen shot for our tool that supports LUMME. As shown, there are only three tools for modeling nodes while there are many nodes as shown in the Fig. 2 (a).

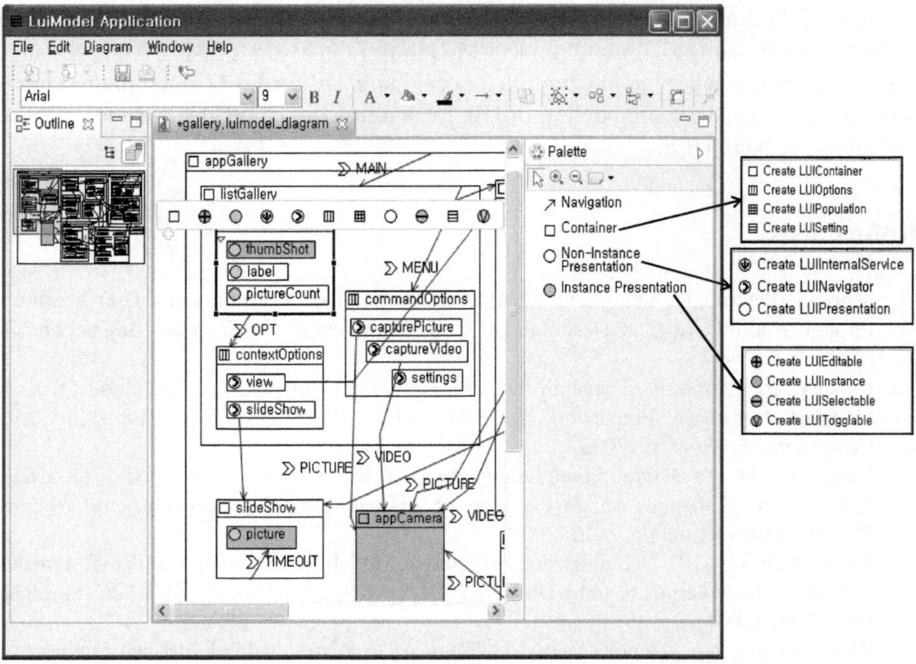

Fig. 4. Supporting tool for LUMME based on Eclipse GMF

The reason why we provide such a small set of tools in the tool palette is to simplify the interface for developers. If there are too many tools in the tool palette, it is annoying for developers to use our modeling environment. However, we made all nodes required to be directly modeled by grouping nodes and then mapping the grouped nodes into specific tools. For example, if we click tool 'Non-Instance Presentation', a popup window appears for developers to select one of 'Create LUIInternalService', 'Create LUINavigator', and 'Create LUIPresentation'.

5 Conclusions

We have proposed logical UI modeling for multimedia embedded systems (LUMME). LUMME first incorporates the notions of reference containers, which enables containers to refer to other applications. This is similar to the notion of ref scenario in UML 2.0 [9]. It also incorporates the notion of multimedia instance presentations. While logical UI modeling intentionally ignores graphical UI modeling, there are some exceptions in multimedia applications. In multimedia applications, instance presentations themselves may be sorts of graphical resources while there are inherent differences with common graphical resources in UI implementations.

While conventional approaches model only visible UI components, LUMME incorporate events as a first-class modeling entity, which is essential to model UIs for multimedia embedded systems. Moreover, LUMME does not employ the task model, which is widely employed in conventional approaches, but incorporates events as navigators. We also provide a modeling tool for LUMME as Eclipse rich-client platform (RCP) using Eclipse Graphical Modeling Framework (GMF). The presented case study with a gallery application in Android targeted for HVGA cell phone shows how LUMME makes the modeling of UIs for multimedia embedded systems concise and allows reusing UI models.

References

1. Mori, G., Paterno, F., Santoro, C.: Design and Development of Multidevice User Interfaces through Multiple Logical Descriptions. IEEE Transactions on Software Engineering 30 (2004)
2. Calvary, G., Coutaz, J., Thevenin, D., Limbourg, Q., Bouil-lon, L., Vanderdonckt, J.: A Unifying Reference Framework for Multi-Target User Interfaces. Interacting with Computers 15, 289–308 (2003)
3. Vanderdonckt, J.: Model-driven engineering of user interfaces: Promises, successes, failures, and challenges. In: Proceedings of Annual Romanian Conference on Human-Computer Interaction, pp. 1–10 (2008)
4. Pinheiro da Silva, P.: User Interface Declarative Models and Development Environments: A Survey. In: Paternó, F. (ed.) DSV-IS 2000. LNCS, vol. 1946, pp. 207–226. Springer, Heidelberg (2001)
5. Pérez-Medina, J.-L., Dupuy-Chessa, S., Front, A.: A Survey of Model Driven Engineering Tools for User Interface Design. In: Winckler, M., Johnson, H. (eds.) TAMODIA 2007. LNCS, vol. 4849, pp. 84–97. Springer, Heidelberg (2007)
6. Coutaz, J.: User interface plasticity: model driven engineering to the limit! In: Proceedings of ACM SIGCHI Symposium on Engineering Interactive Computing Systems (2010)
7. Collignon, B., Vanderdonckt, J., Calvary, G.: Model-driven engineering of multi-target plastic user interfaces. In: Proceedings of International Conference on Autonomic and Autonomous Systems (2008)
8. Kim, S.: Pattern and Event Based Logical UI Modeling for Multi-Device Embedded Applications. In: Lee, G., Howard, D., Ślęzak, D. (eds.) ICHIT 2011. CCIS, vol. 206, pp. 560–567. Springer, Heidelberg (2011)
9. Unified Modeling Language (UML) 2.0. Object Management Group (2007)
10. Lu, X., Wan, J.: User Interface Design Model. In: Proceedings of the ACIS International Conference on Software Engineering, Artificial Intelligence, Networking and Parallel/Distributed Computing (2007)
11. Paternò, F., Santoro, C., Spano, L.D.: Model-Based Design of Multi-Device Interactive Applications Based on Web Services. In: Gross, T., Gulliksen, J., Kotzé, P., Oestreicher, L., Palanque, P., Prates, R.O., Winckler, M. (eds.) INTERACT 2009. LNCS, vol. 5726, pp. 892–905. Springer, Heidelberg (2009)
12. So, P.H.J.C.P.L., Shum, P., Li, X.J., Goyal, D.: Design and Implementation of User Interface for Mobile Devices. IEEE Transactions on Consumer Electronics 50 (2004)
13. Borchers, J.O.: A Pattern Approach to Interaction Design. In: Proceedings of Conference on Designing Interactive Systems: Processes, Practices, Methods, and Techniques (2001)
14. Aquino, N., Vanderdonckt, J., Pastor, O.: Transformation templates: adding flexibility to model-driven engineering of user interfaces. In: Proceedings of ACM Symposium on Applied Computing (2010)
15. Kim, S.: Graphical Modeling Environment for Logical User Interfaces Based on Eclipse GMF. Journal of Information Industrial Engineering 18 (2011)

Efficient Doppler Spread Compensation with Frequency Domain Equalizer and Turbo Code

Haeseong Jeong and Heung-Gyoon Ryu

Department of Electronics and Engineering,
Chungbuk National University
Cheongju, Chungbuk, 361-763, Korea
haeseongz@gmail.com, ecomm@cbu.ac.kr

Abstract. In the satellite communication system, Doppler spread is caused by the movement of the mobile receiver such as high speed aircraft, vessel, and so on. To overcome Doppler spread in the satellite communications, we propose the novel FDE (Frequency Domain Equalizer) and turbo code in order to compensate Doppler spread efficiently in this paper. And we adapt single carrier system in order to save power in satellite system. Also, in order to guarantee channel capacity, we have to reduce interference such as Doppler spread by using FDE. To overcome such shortcomings and secure high SINR (Signal to Interference and Noise Ratio), we propose FDE and turbo code. If we reduce interference and secure high SINR by using FDE and turbo code, the Shannon's channel capacity is guaranteed. Therefore, the purpose of this paper is to improve system performance with low BER (Bit Error Rate) and high SINR. In this paper, we adapt comb type pilot in order to estimate and compensate Doppler spread. As the simulation results, the proposed algorithm has high performance which is satisfied with 2.5dB at 10^{-4} where the number of iterations is 4.

Keywords: Frequency domain equalizer, Turbo code, Doppler spread, Single carrier system.

1 Introduction

In case of the conventional satellite broadcasting, there are many researches such as DVB-S2 (Digital Video Broadcasting-Satellite Second Generation) and DVB-RCS (DVB-Return Channel via Satellite) in Europe [1]. In order to realize seamless wideband broadcasting and telecommunication convergence, the satellite-based broadband mobile and broadcasting market areas also are steadily growing. The civilian and military, public emergency applications require much data rate to be connected to the broadband network at anyplace in anytime. With this atmosphere, satellite communication is also toward broadband and mobile technology [2]. And to overcome power problem in satellite communications system, the single carrier system is adapted.

T.-h. Kim et al. (Eds.): MulGraB 2011, Part II, CCIS 263, pp. 9–18, 2011.

Also, in the study DVB-RCS +M standard, it's mostly studied to overcome channel correlation effect due to mobility with Link layer FEC [3]. And like [4], Decision feedback equalizer (DFE) is considered to be a powerful technique to cope with nonlinear satellite channel distortion in high speed data transmission but it's mainly operated at medium to high SNR.

And in order for a linear block code or a convolutional code to approach the theoretical limit imposed by Shannon's channel capacity in terms of bandwidth and power efficiency, its codeword or constraint length should be increased to such an intolerable degree that the maximum likelihood decoding can become unrealizable. Possible solutions to this dilemma are two classes of powerful error correcting codes, each called turbo codes and LDPC (lower-density parity-check) codes, that can achieve a near-capacity (or near-Shannon-limit) performance with a reasonable complexity of decoder [5].

Also, in the satellite communication system, Doppler spread is caused by the movement of the mobile receiver such as high speed aircraft, vessel, and so on. The Doppler spread is caused by improvement of error probability. Its estimation is extremely important in these systems. Indeed, with the knowledge of this parameter, the velocity of the mobile terminal can be exactly recovered [6], [7] and the optimal adaptation step-size can be properly tuned for optimal adaptive processing in wireless communications [8]. To overcome such shortcomings and secure high SINR, we propose FDE and turbo code. If we reduce interference and secure high SINR by using FDE and turbo code, the Shannon's channel capacity is guaranteed.

Therefore, the purpose of this paper is to improve system performance with low BER and high SINR.

This paper is organized as following. In Section II, we describe the system model of FDE and turbo code. And we describe the detailed FDE and turbo code in Section III. Then according to the analysis and propose this system, the proposed algorithm is simulated and the results are shown in Section IV. Finally, we can draw the following conclusion.

2 System Model

Figure 1 shows a block diagram of overall system for FDE and turbo code. In this paper, we assume channel is the Rician fading channel. Rician fading occurs when one of the paths, typically a line of sight signal, is much stronger than the others. And

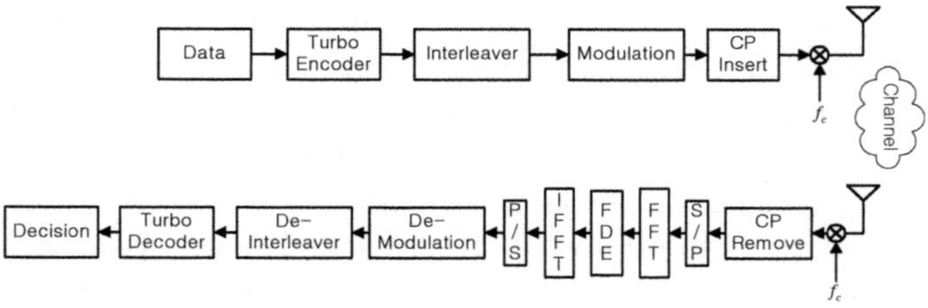

Fig. 1. Block diagram of overall system

we consider single carrier system with turbo code due to the satellite communication. Also, Doppler spread is caused by the movement of the mobile receiver such as high speed aircraft, vessel, and so on. In order to compensate Doppler spread, we adapt FDE and turbo code. In the FDE, the comb type pilot is adapted because it is very useful in order to estimate and equalize Doppler spread.

The binary information bits *d(i)* are encoded using turbo code, resulting in a encode bit stream *m(i)*. And *m(i)* is modulated to *s(i)* which is modulated bit stream without pilot symbol and *x(i)* is modulated bit stream with comb type pilot in order to estimate and compensate Doppler spread.

And *x(i)* is transmitted through the channel and the Doppler spread. In single carrier system, the Doppler spread is caused by phase rotation of the data stream. If there is effect of phase rotation in the data stream, the error probability is increased. Thus, we have to cancel the Doppler spread. In the receiver, we transfer to frequency domain by using FFT (Fast Fourier Transform) in order to adapt FDE. After equalization of Doppler spread, we transfer to time domain again by using IFFT (Inverse FFT). And then we perform turbo decoding process. At final, we do decision data stream.

3 Frequency Domain Equalizer and Turbo Code

In order for a linear block code or a convolutional code to approach the theoretical limit imposed by Shannon's channel capacity in terms of bandwidth and power efficiency, its codeword or constraint length should be increased to such an intolerable degree that the maximum likelihood decoding can become unrealizable. Possible solutions to this dilemma are two classes of powerful error correcting codes, each called turbo codes and LDPC codes that can achieve a near-capacity performance with a reasonable complexity of decoder. The equation of Shannon's channel capacity is as follows.

$$C = BW \cdot \log_2\left(1+\frac{S}{N+I}\right) [bits/\sec], \tag{1}$$

where, BW is bandwidth, S is signal power, N is noise power, and I is interference power. In order to guarantee channel capacity, we have to reduce interference such as Doppler spread by using FDE. And in order to secure high SINR, we propose FDE and turbo code. If we reduce interference by using FDE and secure high SINR by using FDE and turbo code, the Shannon's channel capacity is guaranteed.

A. Turbo encoder in transmitter

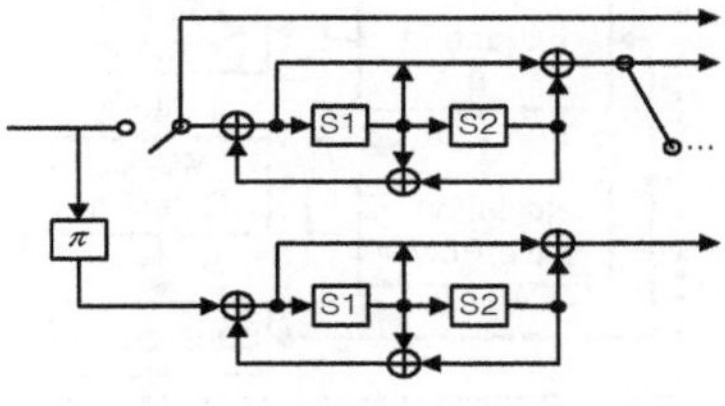

Fig. 2. The structure of turbo encoder

Figure 2 shows a turbo encoder consisting of two RSC (Recursive Systematic Convolutional) encoders and an interleaver where the interleaver permutes the message bits in a random way before input to the second encoder. The interleaver in turbo encoder gives a random property to information sequences and prevents the case in which high-weight codewords are produced from second RSC encoder.

B. FDE with turbo code

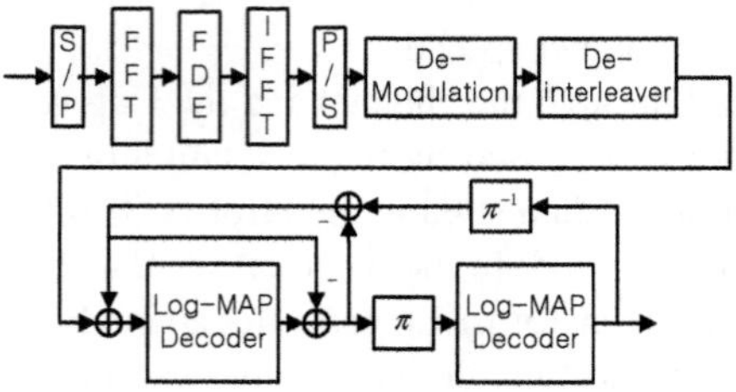

Fig. 3. Block diagram of receiver structure of FDE with turbo code

Figure 3 shows a receiver structure of FDE with turbo code. The received data stream is as follows.

$$y(n) = x(n) * \left\{h(n) \cdot e^{j2\pi f_d n}\right\} + n(n), \tag{2}$$

where, *x(n)* is the transmitted data stream with pilot which is encoded by turbo encoder, *h(n)* is the channel impulse response, *n(n)* is AWGN (Additive White Gaussian Noise), and f_d is the Doppler spread. In this paper, we assume the channel impulse response is LOS channel. After FFT, the received signal is as follows.

$$Y_k = X_k \cdot \left\{H_k \cdot e^{j2\pi f_d n}\right\} + N_k \cdot \tag{3}$$

At (3), in order to analyze the Doppler spread, we are rewritten (4) from (3).

$$\begin{aligned} Y_K &= \sum_{n=0}^{N-1} y(n) \cdot e^{-j\frac{2\pi}{N}kn} = \frac{1}{N}\sum_{n=0}^{N-1}\left[x(n) * \{h(n) \cdot e^{j2\pi f_d n}\} + n(n)\right] \cdot e^{-j\frac{2\pi}{N}kn} \\ &= \frac{1}{N}\sum_{l=0}^{N-1}\sum_{n=0}^{N-1} X_l \cdot H_l \cdot e^{j\frac{2\pi}{N}(l-k+f_d N)n} + N_k \end{aligned} \tag{4}$$

In (4), the Doppler spread is caused by phase rotation at single carrier system. In order to estimate and compensate Doppler spread, we propose FDE with comb type pilot.

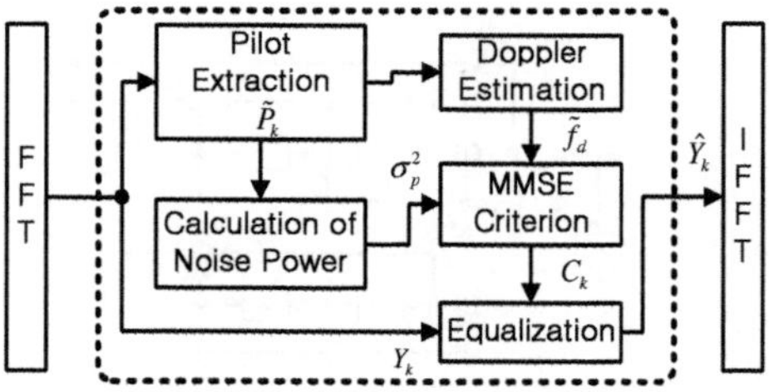

Fig. 4. Block diagram of FDE with comb type pilot

Figure 4 shows FDE with comb type pilot for equalization of Doppler spread. In figure 4, after FFT, we extract received comb type pilot. And we estimate Doppler spread by using comb type pilot. The estimated Doppler spread is as follows.

$$\tilde{f}_d = \frac{\tilde{P}(i)}{P(i)}, \tag{5}$$

where, $P(i)$ is the transmitted comb type pilot, and $\tilde{P}(i)$ is the received pilot. And then, we calculate noise power by using the extracted comb type pilot. The noise power is as follows.

$$\sigma_p^2 = \frac{1}{N_p} \sum \left|\tilde{P}_k\right|^2, \tag{6}$$

where, N_p is the number of comb type pilot in one frame. In order to equalize Doppler spread, we make MMSE (Minimum Mean Square Error) criterion. In order to make MMSE criterion, we need three factors. The first is the estimated Doppler spread, the second is the noise power, and the third is the estimated channel impulse response. Therefore, we can compute MMSE criterion as follows.

$$C_k = \frac{\sum_{k \in s_p} \tilde{f}_d \cdot H_k^*}{\sum_{k \in s_p} \left|\tilde{f}_d \cdot H_k^*\right|^2 + \sigma_p^2}. \tag{7}$$

And the equalized signal from Doppler spread is as follows.

$$\hat{Y}_k = Y_k \cdot C_k. \tag{8}$$

After equalization of Doppler spread such as (8), we transmute (8) into time domain signal by using IFFT process such as $\hat{y}_k$. For turbo decoding process, we adapt Log-MAP (Maximum A posteriori Probability) algorithm in this paper. The MAP algorithm is to maximize the a posteriori probability. And it is to decide by a computation of the likelihood ratio and to minimize the bit error rate. We can expand the previous LLR (Log Likelihood Ratio) equation by Bayes' rule. Thus, the LLR value is as follows.

$$\begin{aligned} L(m_k) &= \log\left(\frac{P(m_k = +1 \mid y)}{P(m_k = -1 \mid y)}\right) \\ &= \log\left(\frac{P(y \mid m_k = +1)}{P(y \mid m_k = -1)}\right) + \log\left(\frac{P(m_k = +1)}{P(m_k = -1)}\right). \end{aligned} \tag{9}$$

In (9), $\log\left(\frac{P(y \mid m_k = +1)}{P(y \mid m_k = -1)}\right)$ is likelihood function, and $\log\left(\frac{P(m_k = +1)}{P(m_k = -1)}\right)$ is a prior probability. And Bayes' rule which is frequently used in turbo decoding is as follows.

$$\begin{aligned} P(A,B) &= P(A \mid B)P(B) = P(B \mid A)P(A) \\ P(A \mid B) &= \frac{P(B \mid A)P(A)}{P(B)} \end{aligned} \quad . \tag{10}$$

In order to do turbo decode process, there are many algorithms such as BCJR, Log-MAP, Max-Log-MAP, SOVA, and so on. In this paper, we adapt Log-MAP algorithm in order to do turbo decode. The probability-domain BCJR (MAP) algorithm is very complicated because there are many multiplications and numerically unstable. In order to solve these problems, we use Log-MAP algorithm. In case of MAP algorithm in log domain, the multiplications are changed by the additions and the exponential terms in branch metrics are disappeared. The forward state metric in log domain is as follows.

$$\begin{aligned}\tilde{\alpha}_k(s) &= \log(\alpha_k(s)) = \log\left(\sum_{s'} \alpha_{k-1}(s')\gamma_k(s',s)\right), \\ &= \log\left(\sum_{s'} \exp\left(\tilde{\alpha}_{k-1}(s') + \tilde{\gamma}_k(s',s)\right)\right)\end{aligned} \tag{11}$$

where, $\alpha_k(s)$ is the forward state metric in probability domain, and $\gamma_k(s',s)$ is the branch metric. In (11), the initial conditions are as follows.

$$\tilde{\alpha}_0(s) = \begin{cases} 0, & s = S_0 \\ -\infty, & s \neq S_0 \end{cases}. \tag{12}$$

And the backward state metric in log domain is as follows.

$$\tilde{\beta}_k(s') = \log(\beta_k(s')) = \log\left(\sum_{s} \exp(\tilde{\beta}_{k+1}(s) + \tilde{\gamma}_k(s',s))\right), \tag{13}$$

where, $\beta_k(s)$ is the backward state metric in probability domain. In (13), the initial conditions are as follows.

$$\tilde{\beta}_k(s) = \begin{cases} 0, & s = S_0 \\ -\infty, & s \neq S_0 \end{cases}. \tag{14}$$

And the branch metric is as follows.

$$\tilde{\gamma}_k(s',s) = \log(\gamma_k(s',s)) = -\log(2\sqrt{2\pi}\sigma) - \frac{\|y_k - c_k\|^2}{2\sigma^2}. \tag{15}$$

And then, we can calculate LLR value.

$$\begin{aligned} L(m_k) &= \log \frac{\sum_{U+} \alpha_{k-1}(s')\gamma_k(s',s)\beta_k(s)}{\sum_{U-} \alpha_{k-1}(s')\gamma_k(s',s)\beta_k(s)} \\ &= \log\left[\sum_{U+} \exp(\tilde{\alpha}_{k-1}(s') + \tilde{\gamma}_k(s',s) + \tilde{\beta}(s)\right] - \log\left[\sum_{U-} \exp(\tilde{\alpha}_{k-1}(s') + \tilde{\gamma}_k(s',s) + \tilde{\beta}(s)\right]. \end{aligned} \tag{16}$$

This is really simple because the multiplications are changed by the additions and the exponential terms in branch metrics are disappeared. In order to do turbo decode process, there are 4 steps. In step 1, we initialize $\tilde{\alpha}_0(s)$ and $\tilde{\beta}_k(s)$. And we get $y_k = \left[y_k^m, y_k^p\right]$, and compute $\tilde{\gamma}_k(s',s)$ and $\tilde{\alpha}_k(s)$ using the forward recursion in step 2. In step 3, we compute $\tilde{\beta}_{k-1}(s')$ using the backward recursion. Finally, we compute $L(m_k)$, and hard decisions by $\widehat{m}_k = sign[L(m_k)]$.

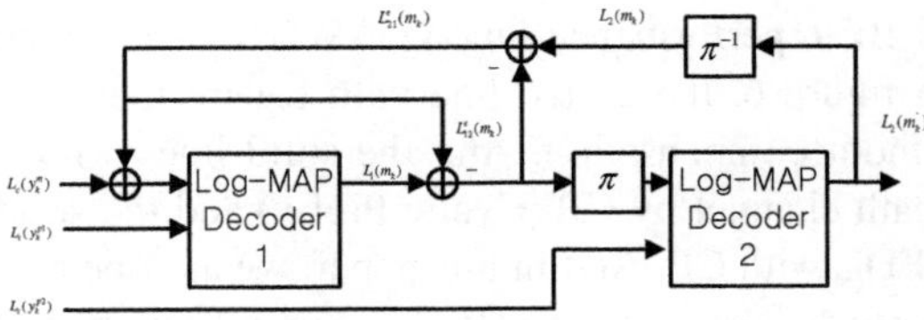

Fig. 5. Block diagram of detailed turbo decoder

Figure 5 shows detailed turbo decoder. In figure 5, the receiver inputs to each decoder are as follows.

$$\begin{aligned} y_1 &= \left[y_1^1, y_2^1, \cdots, y_k^1\right],\ y_k^1 = \left[y_k^m, y_k^{p1}\right] \\ y_2 &= \left[y_1^2, y_2^2, \cdots, y_k^2\right],\ y_k^2 = \left[y_k^{m'}, y_k^{p2}\right] \end{aligned} \quad (17)$$

The Log-MAP decoder 1 and 2 exchange their extrinsic information for fixed iterations.

$$L_{12}^e(m_k) = L_1(m_k) - \frac{2y_k^m}{\sigma^2} - L_{21}^e(m_k), \quad (18)$$

where, the first term of (18) is the produced by the Log-MAP decoder 1, the second term is from channel, and the last term is received from decoder 2. The LLR from turbo decoder output after several iterations is as follows.

$$L(m_k) = \frac{2y_k^m}{\sigma^2} + L^e(m_k) + \max_{U+}{}^{*}\left[\tilde{\alpha}_{k-1}(s') + \frac{p_k y_k^p}{\sigma^2} + \tilde{\beta}_k(s)\right] - \max_{U-}{}^{*}\left[\tilde{\alpha}_{k-1}(s') + \frac{p_k y_k^p}{\sigma^2} + \tilde{\beta}_k(s)\right]. \quad (19)$$

If we set maximum number of iterations, the iterative turbo decoding process performs iterative decoding until maximum number of iterations.

4 Simulation Results

The table 1 is simulation parameters. In the satellite communication system, if there is the Doppler spread, the system performance is worst. Thus, to overcome Doppler spread in the satellite communications, we propose the novel FDE and turbo code in order to compensate Doppler spread efficiently in this paper. At first, in order to verify the performance of FDE, we simulate only FDE without turbo code.

Table 1. Simulation parameters

Modulation	QPSK
Frame size	1,000
# of Frames	10,000
The type of pilot	Comb type pilot
Channel	Rician fading channel
# of iterations	4
Decoding method	Log-MAP algorithm
Doppler spread	92.6Hz, 111Hz

Figure 6 shows BER performance among AWGN case, without FDE cases, and with FDE case. In figure 6, the dotted line with square marker is caused by Rician fading channel without compensation. And the solid lines with circle marker are to compensate multipath channel by CP (Cyclic Prefix) and the solid line with diamond marker is used by FDE with CP. And in this paper, we assume channel estimation and equalization are perfect. The phase rotation factor by Doppler spread is caused by degradation of performance. After using FDE, the BER performance improves significantly. It is almost same to AWGN channel because the characteristic of Doppler spread is static. Thus, the FDE has high performance in order to compensate Doppler spread. Also, as figure 6, the performance of FDE is guaranteed in case of worst Doppler spread such as 92.6Hz or 111Hz.

Figure 7 shows BER performance according to the number of iterations in case of without FDE and with turbo code. In figure 7, we use log-MAP decode process in order to perform turbo decoding process. If the number of iterations is increased, the BER performance is improved. In figure 7, the dotted lines with diamond marker are without FDE and with turbo code. Therefore, in these dotted lines with diamond marker, there remains the Doppler spread and just have the effect of turbo coding.

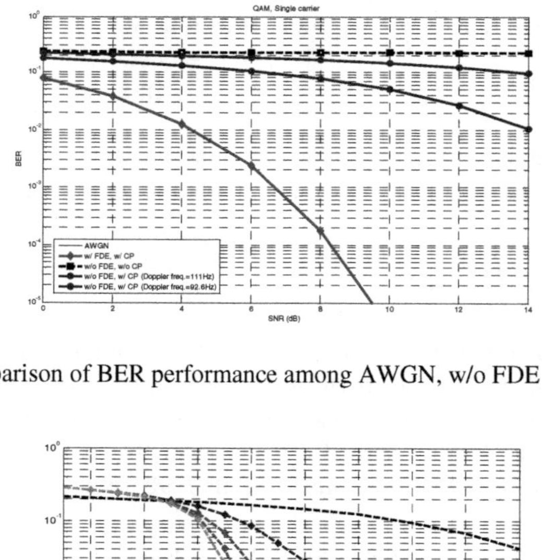

Fig. 6. Comparison of BER performance among AWGN, w/o FDE and with FDE

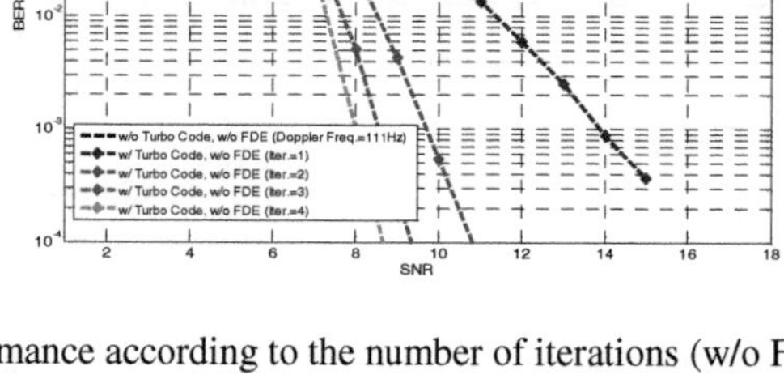

Fig. 7. BER performance according to the number of iterations (w/o FDE, w/ turbo code)

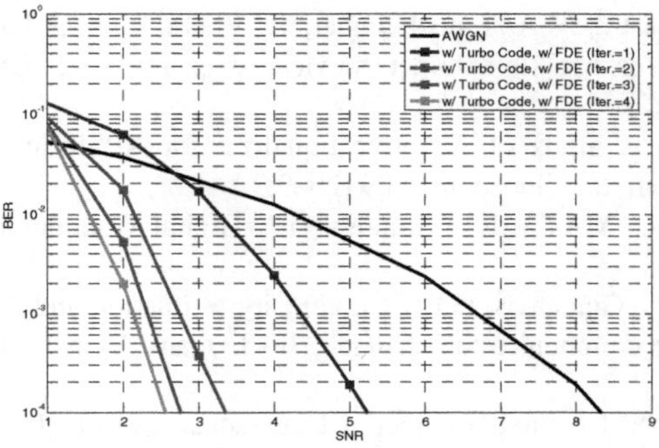

Fig. 8. BER performance of FDE and turbo code

Figure 8 shows BER performance of FDE and turbo code. In figure 8, if we use FDE and turbo code, we can compensate Doppler spread efficiently. Thus, the proposed algorithm has high performance as the result of figure 8. As the simulation results, the proposed algorithm has high performance which is satisfied with 2.5dB at 10^{-4} where the number of iterations is 4.

5 Conclusion

In the satellite communication system, Doppler spread is caused by the movement of the mobile receiver such as high speed aircraft, vessel, and so on. To overcome Doppler spread in the satellite communications, we propose the novel FDE (Frequency Domain Equalizer) and turbo code in order to compensate Doppler spread efficiently in this paper. In order to guarantee channel capacity, we have to reduce interference such as Doppler spread by using FDE. And in order to secure high SINR, we propose FDE with turbo code. If we reduce interference and secure high SINR by using FDE and turbo code, the Shannon's channel capacity is guaranteed. Therefore, the purpose of this paper is to improve system performance with low BER and high SINR. As the simulation results, the proposed algorithm has high performance which is satisfied with 2.5dB at 10^{-4} where the number of iterations is 4.

Acknowledgments. This research was supported by Commission Research Program of Agency for Defense Development(ADD) (Contract No. UD110028ED).

References

1. ETSI EN 302 307 (V1.2.1).: Digital Video Broadcasting (DVB); second generation framing structure, channel coding and modulation system for braodcasting, interactive services, news, gathering and other broadband satellite applications (2009)
2. Kim, P., Han, J., Chang, D.-I., Oh, D.-G.: Efficient channel equalization technique for DVB-S2 standard. In: 2010 5th Advanced Satellite Multimedia Systems Conference (asma) and the 11th Signal Processing for Space Communications Workshop (spsc) (2010)

3. Lei, J., Vázquez-Castro, M.A., Stockhammer, T., Vieira, F.: Link layer FEC for quality-of-service provision for Mobile Internet Services over DVB-S2. IJSCN 28(3-4), 183–207 (2010)
4. Suzuki, Y., et al.: A Study of Adaptive Equalizer for APSK in the Advanced Satellite Broadcasting System. In: Globecom 2009 (2009)
5. Yang, W.Y., et al.: MATLAB / Simulink for Digital Communication, 1st edn. A-Jin Publishing (2009)
6. Tepedelenlioglu, C., Giannakis, G.B.: On velocity estimation and correlation properties of narrowband mobile communication channels. IEEE Trans. Veh. Technol. 50(4), 1039–1052 (2001)
7. Mauritz, O.: A hybrid method for Doppler spread estimation. In: Proc. IEEE Vehicular Technology Conf. (VTC)—Spring, pp. 962–965 (2004)
8. Adaptive space-time processing for wireless CDMA. In: Affes, S., Mermelstein, P., Benesty, J., Huang, A.H. (eds.) Adaptive Signal Processing: Application to Real-World Problems, ch. 10, pp. 283–321. Springer, Berlin (2003)
9. Bengtsson, M., Ottersten, B.: Low-complexity estimators for distributed sources. IEEE Trans. Signal Process. 48(8), 2185–2194 (2000)

Machine Learning-Based Soccer Video Summarization System

Hossam M. Zawbaa[1], Nashwa El-Bendary[2], Aboul Ella Hassanien[1], and Tai-hoon Kim[3]

[1] Cairo University, Faculty of Computers and Information,
Blind Center of Technology, Cairo, Egypt
ABO Research Laboratory, Cairo, Egypt
{hossam.zawba3a,aboitcairo}@gmail.com
[2] Arab Academy for Science, Technology, and Maritime Transport, Cairo, Egypt
ABO Research Laboratory, Cairo, Egypt
nashwa_m@aast.edu
[3] Hannam University, Korea
taihoonn@hannam.ac.kr

Abstract. This paper presents a machine learning (ML) based event detection and summarization system for soccer matches. The proposed system is composed of six phases. Firstly, in the pre-processing phase, the system segments the whole video stream into small video shots. Then, in the shot processing phase, it applies two types of classification to the video shots resulted from the pre-processing phase. Afterwards, in the replay detection phase, the system applies two machine learning algorithms, namely; support vector machine (SVM) and neural network (NN), for emphasizing important segments with logo appearance. Also, in the score board detection phase, the system uses both ML algorithms for detecting the caption region providing information about the score of the game. Subsequently, in the excitement event detection phase, the system uses k-means algorithm and Hough line transform for detecting vertical goal posts and Gabor filter for detecting goal net. Finally, in the logo-based event detection and summarization phase, the system highlights the most important events during the match. Experiments on real soccer videos demonstrate encouraging results. Compared to the performance results obtained using SVM classifier, the proposed system attained good NN-based performance results concerning recall ratio, however it attained poor NN-based performance results concerning precision ratio.

1 Introduction

Sports videos are considered as a good test bed for techniques working on content based video analysis and processing. It involves a variety of problems such as semantic analysis, video retrieval, video summarization and streaming [1].

Most sport games are naturally organized into successive and alternating plays of offence and defence, cumulating at events such as goal or attack. If a sports video can be segmented according to these semantically meaningful events, it then can be used in numerous applications to enhance their values and enrich the user's viewing experiences [2].

T.-h. Kim et al. (Eds.): MulGraB 2011, Part II, CCIS 263, pp. 19–28, 2011.

Soccer is one of the most popular team sports all over the world due to the relative simplicity of its rules and the small amount of required equipment [3]. As watching a soccer match needs a lot of time, many TV fans of sport competitions prefer to watch a summary of football games [4]. According to this, soccer video analysis has recently attracted much research and a wide spectrum of possible applications have been considered. Traditionally soccer videos were analyzed manually but it costs valuable time. Therefore it is necessary to have a tool that does the job automatically.

This paper presents a system for automatic soccer videos summarization using machine learning techniques. The proposed system is composed of six phases; namely, pre-processing phase, shot processing phase, ML-based logo replay detection phase, ML-based score board detection phase, excitement event detection phase, and finally logo-based event detection and summarization phase. The rest of this paper is organized as follows. Section 2 gives an overview of SVM and NN machine learning techniques. Section 3 presents the different phases of the proposed automatic soccer video summarization system. Section 4 shows the obtained experimental results. Finally, Section 5 addresses conclusions and discusses future work.

2 Machine Learning (ML): A Brief Background

2.1 Artificial Neural Network (ANN)

Artificial neural networks (ANN) or simply neural networks (NN) have been developed as generalizations of mathematical models of biological nervous systems. In a simplified mathematical model of the neuron, the effects of the synapses are represented by connection weights that modulate the effect of the associated input signals, and the nonlinear characteristic exhibited by neurons is represented by a transfer function. There are a range of transfer functions developed to process the weighted and biased inputs, among which four basic transfer functions widely adopted for multimedia processing [5].

The neuron impulse is then computed as the weighted sum of the input signals, transformed by the transfer function. The learning capability of an artificial neuron is achieved by adjusting the weights in accordance to the chosen learning algorithm. The behavior of the neural network depends largely on the interaction between the different neurons. The basic architecture consists of three types of neuron layers: input, hidden and output layers.

In feed-forward networks the signal flow is from input to output units strictly in a feed-forward direction. The data processing can extend over multiple units, but no feedback connections are present, that is, connections extending from outputs of units to inputs in the same layer or previous layers. There are several other neural network architectures (Elman network, adaptive resonance theory maps, competitive networks etc.) depending on the properties and requirement of the application [6].

2.2 Support Vector Machine (SVM)

The support vector machine (SVM) algorithm seeks to maximize the margin around a hyperplane that separates a positive class from a negative class [7]. Given a training dataset with n samples $(x_1,y_1),(x_2,y_2),\ldots,(x_n,y_n)$, where x_i is a feature vector in a v-dimensional feature space and with labels $y_i \in -1,1$ belonging to either of two linearly separable classes C_1 and C_2. Geometrically, the SVM modeling algorithm finds an optimal hyperplane with the maximal margin to separate two classes, which requires to solve the optimization problem, as shown in equations (1) and (2).

$$maximize \sum_{i=1}^{n} \alpha_i - \frac{1}{2} \sum_{i,j=1}^{n} \alpha_i \alpha_j y_i y_j . K(x_i, x_j) \tag{1}$$

$$Subject-to: \sum_{i=1}^{n} \alpha_i y_i, 0 \leq \alpha_i \leq C \tag{2}$$

where, α_i is the weight assigned to the training sample x_i. If $\alpha_i > 0$, x_i is called a support vector. C is a regulation parameter used to trade-off the training accuracy and the model complexity so that a superior generalization capability can be achieved. K is a kernel function, which is used to measure the similarity between two samples. Different choices of kernel functions have been proposed and extensively used in the past and the most popular are the gaussian radial basis function (RBF), polynomial of a given degree, and multi layer perceptron. These kernels are in general used, independently of the problem, for both discrete and continuous data.

3 The Proposed Soccer Video Summarization System

The machine learning based soccer video summarization system proposed in this paper is composed of six fundamental building phases; 1) pre-processing phase that segments the whole video stream into small video shots, 2) shot processing phase that applies two types of classification to the video shots resulted from the pre-processing phase, 3) replay detection phase that applies support vector machine (SVM) and neural network (NN) algorithms for emphasizing important segments with logo appearance, 4) score board detection phase that uses SVM algorithm for detecting the caption region providing information about the score of the game, 5) excitement event detection phase that detects both vertical goal posts and goal net using k-means algorithm and Hough line transform for detecting goal posts Gabor filter for detecting goal net, and finally 6) logo-based event detection and summarization phase that highlights the most important events during the match. These six phases are described in detail in this section along with the steps involved and the characteristics feature for each phase.

3.1 Pre-processing Phase

The goal of this phase is to segment the whole video stream into small video shots. Firstly, the dominant color in the video frame is detected, then the shot boundary detection algorithm in [8] is applied in order to output video shots based on dominant color derived features [8,9,10].

3.2 Shot Processing Phase

This phase applies two types of classification; namely, shot-type classification and play/break classification, to the video shots resulted from the pre-processing phase.

For shot-type classification, a set of thresholds have been defined for distinguishing the grass-ratio for the different shot-types [8]. For the proposed system, we applied four threshold ratios, each frame can be classified into one of the previously stated views [10].

On the other hand, for play/break classification, consecutive play shots are considered as a play scene, which usually are ended with a consecutive break shots. Thus, a play-break sequence is a combination of consecutive play and break scenes, and sport games consist of many of this sequences [11,10].

3.3 Replay Detection Phase

Replay is a video editing technique that is often used to emphasize an important segment with a logo appearance for one or several times. In sports video, there is often a highlighted logo that appears at the start and end of a replay segment, which indicates an exciting event within the soccer match [12,10]. Algorithm (1) describes the steps of Logo detection algorithm using support vector machine (SVM) and neural network (NN).

Algorithm 1. Logo Detection Using SVM and NN Classifiers

```
Train the NN classifier with correct logo and false logo samples
Train the SVM classifier with correct logo and false logo samples
for Each frame do
    Adjust image intensity values for increasing the contrast of the input frame
    Select region of interest based on color for returning a binary image
    Calculate frame white ratio = the percentage of white pixels in the whole frame
    if Any frame contains a large contrast object (the white frame ratio be greater than 0.5)
    then
        Get the original colored frame for the classification
        if The logo is real then
            Mark this shot as replay shot
        end if
    end if
end for
```

3.4 Score Board Detection Phase

The score board is a caption region distinguished from the surrounding region, which provides information about the score of the game or the status of the players [13]. The caption often appears at the bottom part of image frame for a short while and then disappears almost after appearing for 5 seconds. When the score board is detected with enough confidence, it can undoubtedly provide the inference of goal event, because after every scored goal the score board is displayed. The lower third of each frame was checked for containing a score board via applying algorithm (1) as well.

3.5 Excitement Event Detection Phase

Most exciting events occur in the goal-mouth area such as goals, shooting, penalties, direct free kicks, etc. Other non-exciting events such as dull passes in the mid-field, defense and offense or some other shots to the audiences or coaches, are not considered as exciting as the former events [14]. Excitement event detection is based on three features; namely, 1) vertical goal posts detection, 2) goal net detection, and 3) audio loudness detection.

3.5.1 Vertical Goal Posts Detection

The two vertical goal posts are distinctively characterized by their vertical strips of white and grow connected pixel gray values of white. Hough transform is used for detecting the two goal posts, as shown in figure 1. Algorithm (2) presents the steps applied to each frame for detecting the vertical goal posts.

Algorithm 2. Vertical Goal Posts Detection

---

for each frame **do**

    Use K-means clustering to convert each frame to binary image using squared Euclidean distances measure

    Given a set of observations $(x_1, x_2, , x_n)$, where each observation is a d-dimensional real vector, k-means clustering aims to partition the n observations into k sets $(k \leq n)$ $S = S_1$, $S_2, , S_k$ so as to minimize the within-cluster sum of squares (WCSS)

$$argsmin \sum_{i=1}^{k} \sum_{x_j \in S_i} \| x_j - \mu_i \|^2 \qquad (3)$$

    where, μ_i is the mean of points in S_{i-1}

    Use Hough transform to detect the two goal posts

$$rho = x * cos(\theta) + y * sin(\theta) \qquad (4)$$

    where, rho is the distance from the origin to the line along a vector perpendicular to the line, and θ is the angle between the x-axis and this vector

    if The overlap between the vertical parallel lines greater than 80% **then**

        mark this frame as goal post frame

    end if

end for

Fig. 1. Hough transform detection for the vertical goal posts

3.5.2 Goal Net Detection

Detection of the two vertical goal posts isn't sufficient for possible exciting play. So, there still a need for an extra step to increase the accuracy of goal-mouth appearances detection. Accordingly, the proposed system checks goal post frames for goal net existence using Gabor filter [15]. The Gabor filter is used due to that the goal net has a unique pattern and repeated many times.

The Gabor filter is basically a Gaussian filter, with variances sx and sy along x and y-axes, respectively. the sx and sy are modulated by a complex sinusoid, with center frequencies U and V along x and y-axes, respectively. The Gabor filer is described by equations (5), (6), and (7).

$$G = \exp\left(\left(\frac{-1}{2}\left(\frac{\acute{x}}{s\acute{x}}\right)^2 + \left(\frac{\acute{y}}{s\acute{y}}\right)^2\right) * \cos 2 * \Pi * f * \acute{x}\right) \tag{5}$$

$$\acute{x} = x * \cos(\theta) + y * \sin(\theta); \tag{6}$$

$$\acute{y} = y * \cos(\theta) - x * \sin(\theta); \tag{7}$$

Where, sx and sy: variances along x and y-axes, respectively, f: frequency of the sinusoidal function, θ: the orientation of Gabor filter, and G: The output filter.

3.5.3 Audio Loudness Detection

Loudness, silence and pitch generated by a commentator and/or crowd are effective measurements for detecting excitement. The volume of each audio frame is calculated using equation (8):

$$Volume = \frac{1}{N} * \sum_{n=1}^{N} |x(n)| \tag{8}$$

Where N is the number of frames in a clip and $x(n)$ is the sample value of the nth frame. To calculate pitch and silence, we applied the sub-harmonic-toharmonic ratio based pitch determination in [16] for its reliability. Louder, less silence, and higher pitch audio frames are identified by using dynamic thresholds presented in [17]. So, we can detect the excitement shots.

3.6 Event Detection and Summarization Phase

The summarized segment may contain only important events, such as: goal shots, attacks, or penalty shots [8]. The proposed system highlights the most important events during the soccer match, such as goals and goal attempts, in order to save the viewer's time and introduce the technology of computer-based summarization into sports field. figure 2 shows the different event type classification.

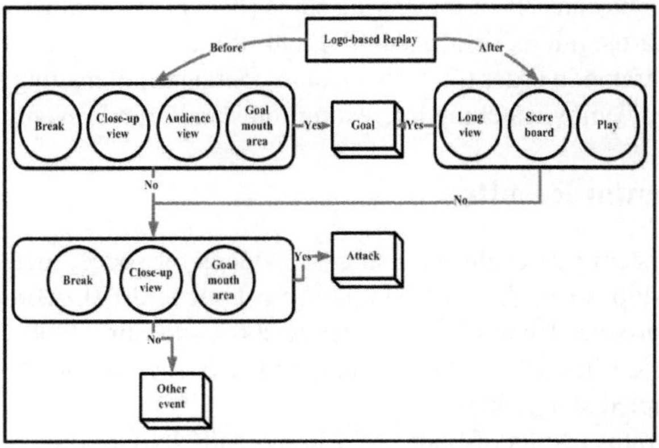

Fig. 2. Event type classification

3.6.1 Goal Event Detection

A goal is scored when the whole soccer ball passes the goal line between the goal posts and under the crossbar. However, it is difficult to verify these conditions automatically and reliably by the state-of-the-art video processing algorithms. The occurrence of a goal event leads to a break in the game [18]. Figure 3 illustrates the sequence of cinematic features after scoring a goal. Finally, the restart of the game is usually captured by a long shot.

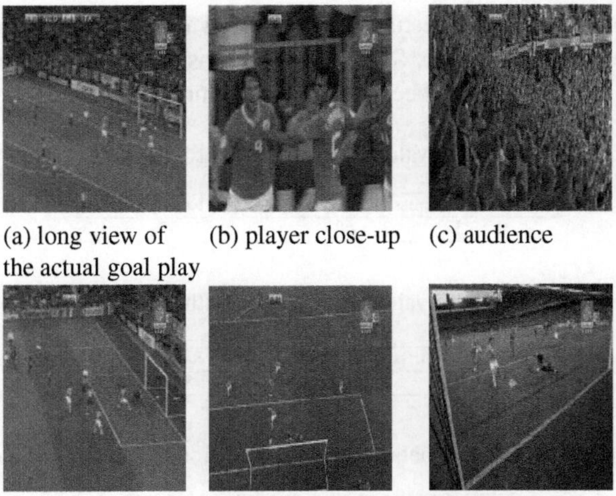

(a) long view of the actual goal play (b) player close-up (c) audience

(d) the first replay (e) the second replay (f) the third replay

Fig. 3. An example of goal broadcast: the temporal order is from (a) to (f)

3.6.2 Attack and Other Event Detection

Attack events may also match a lot of goal event features, although not as consistently as goals. The addition of attack events in the summaries may even be desirable since each of these events consists of interesting shots [8]. There are other interesting events such as: fouls, cards, injure, or offside. The addition of these events in the summaries may even be desirable in order for each event to contain of interesting shots. Therefore, more of users may enjoy watching interesting fouls and offside events.

4 Experimental Results

The proposed system was evaluated using five videos for soccer matches from: World Cup Championship 2010, Africa Championship League 2010, Africa Championship League 2008, European Championship League 2008, and Euro 2008. All soccer videos are in Audio Video Interleave (AVI) format with a frame rate of 30 fps and an audio track that is sampled at 44.1 kHz.

Table 1 illustrates results of both SVM-based and NN-based logo replay detection stage. Compared to the performance results obtained using SVM classifier, the proposed system attained good NN-based performance results concerning recall ratio, however it attained poor NN-based performance results concerning precision ratio.

Table 1. Evaluation of logo based replay using SVM and NN

Factors	SVM	NN
Duration (hh:mm:ss)	1:53:39	1:53:39
Correct	103	98
False	8	43
Miss	2	7
Recall	98.1%	93.3%
Precision	92.8%	69.5 %

Table 2 and table 3 show the results of score board and goal mouth detection, respectively. For score board detection, SVM classifier has been used whereas both Gabor filter and Hough transform have been used for goal mouth detection.

Table 2. Evaluation of score board detection

Duration (hh:mm:ss)	Correct	False	Miss	Recall	Precision
1:53:39	68	5	1	98.5%	93.1 %

Table 3. Evaluation of goal mouth detection

Duration (hh:mm:ss)	Correct	False	Miss	Recall	Precision
1:30:42	247	25	11	95.7%	90.8%

Table 4. Confusion matrix for event detection and summarization

Event Detection	Goal	Attack	Other events
Goal	57	3	0
Attack	6	176	8
Other events	0	18	283
Recall	95%	92.6%	94%
Precision	90.5%	89%	97.3%

Table 4 shows the confusion matrix for event detection and summarization resulted from the proposed system.

5 Conclusions and Future Works

The ML-based system proposed in this paper for broadcast soccer videos summarization was evaluated using videos for soccer matches of five international soccer championships. The proposed system is composed of six phases; namely, pre-processing phase, shot processing phase, replay detection phase, score board detection phase, excitement event detection phase, and logo-based event detection and summarization phase. Compared to the performance results obtained using SVM classifier, the proposed system attained good NN-based performance results concerning recall ratio, however it attained poor NN-based performance results concerning precision ratio. Accordingly, it has been concluded that using the SVM classifier is more appropriate for soccer videos summarization than NN classifier. The proposed system performs very well as its analysis results achieve high accuracy. Experiments show that the system has attained very high precision and reasonable recall ratios. For future research, we can increase the number of soccer videos and championships being examined in order to get more accurate results. Moreover, different machine learning techniques may be applied.

References

1. Chen, C.-Y., Wang, J.-C., Wang, J.-F., Hu, Y.-H.: Event-Based Segmentation of Sports Video Using Motion Entropy. In: Ninth IEEE International Symposium on Multimedia (ISM 2007), pp. 107–111 (2007)
2. Chen, C.-Y., Wang, J.-C., Wang, J.-F., Hu, Y.-H.: Motion Entropy Feature and Its Applications to Event-Based Segmentation of Sports Video. EURASIP Journal on Advances in Signal Processing 2008, Article ID 460913 (2008)
3. D'Orazio, T., Leo, M.: A review of vision-based systems for soccer video analysis. Pattern Recognition 43(8), 2911–2926 (2010)
4. Lotfi, E., Pourreza, H.R.: Event Detection and Automatic Summarization in Soccer Video. In: 4th Iranian Conference on Machine Vision and Image Processing (MVIP 2007), Mashhad, Iran (2007)
5. Yu, B., Zhu, D.H.: Automatic thesaurus construction for spam filtering using revised: back propagation neural network. Journal Expert Systems with Applications 37(1), 24–30 (2010)
6. Bishop, C.M.: Neural networks for pattern recognition. Oxford University Press (1995)
7. Wu, Q., Zhou, D.-X.: Analysis of support vector machine classification. J. Comput. Anal. Appl. 8, 99–119 (2006)
8. Ekin, A.: Sports Video Processing for Description, Summarization and Search. PhD Thesis, University of Rochester, Rochester (2003)
9. Xing-hua, S., Jing-yu, Y.: Inference and retrieval of soccer event. Journal of Communication and Computer 4(3) (2007)
10. Zawbaa, H.M., El-Bendary, N., Hassanien, A.E., Yeo, S.S.: Logo Detection in Broadcast Soccer Videos Using Support Vector Machine. Submitted to: The 2011 Online Conference On Soft Computing in Industerial Applications WWW (WSC16) (2011)
11. Tjondronegoro, D., Chen, Y.P., Pham, B.: The power of play-break for automatic detection and browsing of self-consumable sport video highlights. In: Multimedia Information Retrieval, pp. 267–274 (2004)
12. Ren, R., Jose, J.M.: Football Video Segmentation Based on Video Production Strategy. In: Losada, D.E., Fernández-Luna, J.M. (eds.) ECIR 2005. LNCS, vol. 3408, pp. 433–446. Springer, Heidelberg (2005)

13. Huang, C.-L., Shih, H.-C., Chao, C.-Y.: Semantic analysis of soccer video using dynamic Bayesian network. IEEE Transactions on Multimedia 8(4) (2006)
14. Zhao, Z., Jiang, S., Huang, Q., Ye, Q.: Highlight summarization in soccer video based on goalmouth detection. In: Asia-Pacific Workshop on Visual Information Processing (2006)
15. Wan, K., Yan, X., Yu, X., Xu, C.: Real-time Goal-Mouth Detection in MPEG Soccer Video. In: Proceedings of ACM MM 2003, Berkeley, USA, pp. 311–314 (2003)
16. Sun, X.: Pitch determination and voice quality analysis using subharmonic-to-harmonic ratio. In: The IEEE International Conference on Acoustics, Speech, Signal Processing (ICASSP 2002), Orlando, Florida, USA, vol. 1, pp. 333–336 (2002)
17. Tjondronegoro, D., Chen, Y.P., Pham, B.: Sports video summarization using highlights and play-breaks. In: The fifth ACM SIGMM International Workshop on Multimedia Information Retrieval (ACM MIR 2003), Berkeley, USA, pp. 201–208 (2003)
18. Ekin, A., Tekalp, A.M., Mehrotra, R.: Automatic Soccer Video Analysis and Summarization. IEEE Transactions on Image processing 12(7) (2003)

A Focus on Comparative Analysis: Key Findings of MAC Protocols for Underwater Acoustic Communication According to Network Topology*

Jin-Young Lee[1], Nam-Yeol Yun[1], Sardorbek Muminov[1], Seung-Joo Lee[2], and Soo-Hyun Park[1,**]

[1] Ubiquitous System Lab., Graduate School of BIT, Kookmin University, Seoul, Korea
[2] Information Technical Research Institute, Kookmin University, Seoul, Korea
{jylee9018,anuice,smuminov,aventino,shpark21}@kookmin.ac.kr

Abstract. Underwater acoustic communication can be applicable to many fields, such as oceanic data collection, undersea exploration and development, disaster prevention, underwater environmental monitoring and tactical surveillance. However, it has several challenges to design underwater acoustic sensor networks, for instance, limited bandwidth, multi-path, padding, long propagation delay, high bit error, temporary losses of connectivity and limited battery power. Nowadays many studies are being conducted to overcome abovementioned problems. In this paper, various MAC protocols for underwater acoustic communication are classified by network topology, one is cluster head based MAC protocols and the other one is ad-hoc based MAC protocols. In recent researches, there were not comparative analyses of MAC protocols for underwater acoustic communication according to network topology. So, we summarize and analyze these protocols through comparing each other with some factors. In the future, MAC protocols for underwater acoustic communication will be designed with consideration for each advantage of cluster head and ad-hoc MAC protocols, considering the mobility of nodes to improve underwater acoustic communication, which can be applied to lots of underwater applications.

Keywords: Underwater acoustic communication, MAC protocol, Network topology, Cluster-head, Ad-hoc.

1 Introduction

Underwater acoustic communication can be applicable to many fields, such as oceanic data collection, undersea exploration and development, disaster prevention, underwater environmental monitoring and tactical surveillance [1].

---

* This research was supported by the MKE (The Ministry of Knowledge Economy), Korea, under the ITRC (Information Technology Research Center) support program supervised by the NIPA (National IT Industry Promotion Agency) (NIPA-2011-C1090-1021-0001) and the research program 2011 of Kookmin University in Korea.

** Corresponding author.

T.-h. Kim et al. (Eds.): MulGraB 2011, Part II, CCIS 263, pp. 29–37, 2011.

However, it has several challenges to design underwater acoustic sensor networks, for instance, limited bandwidth, multi-path, padding, long propagation delay, high bit error, temporary losses of connectivity and limited battery power. Nowadays many studies are being conducted to overcome abovementioned problems [1]. In recent researches, there were not comparative analyses of MAC protocols for underwater acoustic communication according to network topology.

In this paper, various MAC (Medium Access Control) protocols for underwater acoustic communication are classified by network topology, one is cluster head based MAC protocols and the other one is ad-hoc based MAC protocols.

The remainder of this paper is organized as follows. Section 2 describes the categorized MAC protocols for underwater acoustic communication according to network topology, including cluster-head based MAC protocols and ad-hoc based MAC protocols respectively. Then, in section 3, we present comparative analysis of these MAC protocols with some factors containing energy consumption, throughput, collision avoidance, advantages and real-time. Finally, we give our conclusions and describe our future works in section 4.

2 MAC Protocols for Underwater Acoustic Communication

In this section, we introduce MAC protocols for underwater environment by categorizing them into two types according to network topology. Cluster-head based MAC protocols are generally used in underwater environment to avoid collision caused by propagation delay of acoustics. And ad-hoc based MAC protocols can be suitable for transmission of real-time data.

We then analyze these MAC protocols with comparing of categorized MAC protocols in section 3.

2.1 MAC Protocols Based on Cluster-Head

In cluster-head based MAC protocols, nodes are distributed at regular intervals and select each cluster-head after making clusters. These selected cluster-heads control their nodes located inside cluster. Figure 1-(a) represents MAC topology based on cluster-head. If the cluster-head has some problem, network performance will be decreased in these MAC protocols.

A protocol proposed in ACMENet (the Acoustic Communication network for Monitoring of Environment in coastal areas Networks) [2] is master-slave network protocol based on TDMA for small underwater acoustic sensor network. Because the lifetime of a slave node is mostly limited by the lifetime of battery, it is important to minimize energy consumption of a slave node in terms of cost efficiency on the whole network. So, the slave-node in ACMENet protocol is designed to be simple, but the master-node has much of the computational complexity and intelligence in ACMENet. If a structure of ACMENet is changed into large underwater sensor networks, it will be large scale network as initial master node is subordinate to upper master node.

MU-Sync [3] is a cluster-based synchronization algorithm for underwater acoustic mobile networks. It avoids frequent re-synchronization by estimating both the clock skew and offset. In the MU-Sync, the clock skew is estimated by performing the linear regression twice over a set of local time information gathered through message exchanges. The first linear regression enables the cluster head to offset the effect of long and varying propagation delay; the second regression in turn obtains the estimated skew and offset. With the help of MAC-level time stamping, it can further reduce the nondeterministic errors which are commonly encountered by those synchronization algorithms that rely on message exchanges.

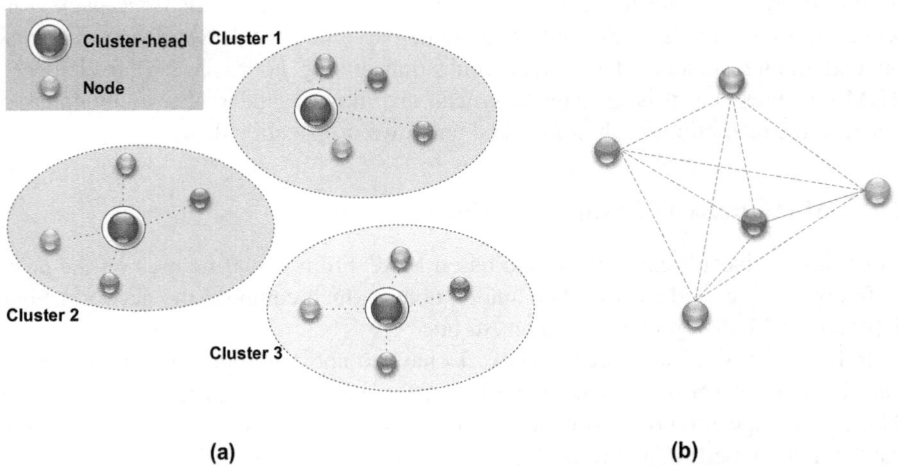

Fig. 1. (a) Cluster-head based and (b) Ad-hoc based MAC topology

P-MAC (Preamble-MAC) [4], which has the network topology like in Figure 1-(a), is TDMA (Time Division Multiple Access) based MAC protocol for underwater sensor network. Each cluster consists of a sink node and sensor nodes. Sink node plays a role of cluster head and sensor node sends periodically collected data to sink node. The sink node also collects and accumulates information of underwater environment. P-MAC is adaptive, dynamic MAC protocol based on the status, variation of underwater channel and propagation delay from a sink node to sensor nodes in the same cluster which are able to be estimated through the consistently accumulated information on underwater channel and environment.

In [5] SBMAC (Smart Blocking MAC) is proposed. This MAC protocol acts adaptively in various underwater environment and it is based on the network topology consisted of a master node and slave nodes. SCB (Smart Calculation Block) included in a mater node decides some policies during network initialization and data transmission. The policies which SCB determines include the decision of TDMA transmission period, data transmission policy (i.e., normal or blocked data), ACK policy (i.e., No-ACK or SMA (Selective-Multiple-ACK) or RWA (Reduced-Whole-ACK) or MBA (Multiple-Block-ACK) or RBA (Reduced-Block-ACK)) and etc. The master broadcasts the beacon, which includes transmission mode, ACK mode, TDMA interval information, gain and guard time, and then all nodes who received the beacon begin data transmission according to their own TDMA schedules. The scheme minimizes transmission of control frames except for data transmission, various transmission methods and ACK methods can be used together.

Cluster-head based MAC protocols are usually designed based on TDMA, as we see at [2], [4], [5]. Therefore, it can have advantages and disadvantages of existing TDMA method. In other words, it minimizes data collision and prevents energy consumption causing retransmission. It can decrease inefficiency of transmission. However, it has some disadvantage, so there is difficulty in attaining real time data, because cluster-head allocates time slot to each node and then nodes can transmit some packet only within allocated time slot. Second, it has some possibility for data collision occurrence on real implementation. Time Synchronization among nodes is a vital element in TDMA method, but it is difficult to synchronize time in underwater communication, due to some restrictions such as long and unknown propagation delays.

2.2 MAC Protocols Based on Ad-Hoc

Cluster-head doesn't exist in Ad-hoc based MAC protocols. It focuses on the design to freely transmit and receive data among nodes which compose the network. Figure 1-(b) shows MAC topology based on Ad-hoc.

In these protocols, all nodes in networks have to not only transmit and receive data, but also operate various functions, such as data analysis, data processing, and so on. Thus, the composition of each node is complex. However, when we want to obtain real data, Ad-hoc based MAC protocols is more appropriate than cluster-head based MAC protocols because the node can transmit immediatly when it has some data to transmit.

In Aloha based scheme, the original Aloha protocol is based on random access of users to the medium and does not try to prevent packet collision. Whenever a user has information to send, it transmits immediately. This naturally leads to a large number of collisions, and hence a number of data packets have to be retransmitted. Therefore, the effective throughput of the Aloha channel is very low, because the probability of packet collisions is high. The Slotted Aloha scheme was developed to deal with the collision problem. In Slotted Aloha, the time is divided into slots, and packet transmission is restricted in these time slots. Thus, the number of collisions is reduced significantly. The throughput with Slotted Aloha is double than basic Aloha.

The limitation of Aloha protocol in underwater environment was analyzed in the papers [6] and [7]. In [6], the paper presents a study on Aloha and Slotted Aloha protocols for UWASNs. The results show that long propagation delay of acoustic signals prohibits the coordinate among nodes, so it does not yield any performance gain. Although, when the nodes send the messages in pre-defined time slot, there is no guarantee that they arrive into time slots. The simple analysis and simulation results show that Slotted Aloha exhibits the same utilization as non-Slotted Aloha. Moreover, in [7], the paper identifies the challenges of modeling contention-based medium access control protocols and presents a model for analyzing Aloha variants for a simple string topology as a first step toward analyzing the performance of contention-based proposals in multi-hop underwater acoustic sensor networks. The limitation factors in the performance of Aloha variants are collisions. Avoiding collisions is the goal of refinements to this protocols class.

In order to deploy the Aloha protocol for UWASNs, adaptive improvements will be added to the original Aloha overcoming the technical issues of this protocol. In [8] study the performance of Aloha-based protocols in underwater networks, and propose two enhanced schemes, namely, Aloha with collision avoidance (Aloha-CA), and Aloha with avoidance notification (Aloha-AN), which are capable of using the long propagation delays to their advantage. Between two protocols, Aloha-CA is simpler and more scalable, as it only needs a small amount of memory, and does not rely on additional control messages. Aloha-AN, on the other hand, requires the use of additional notification (NTF) packets, which serve as advance notification to neighboring nodes, so that they can avoid transmitting packets that could result in collisions. The Aloha-AN needs to collect and store more information, therefore it requires more resources than Aloha. Simulation results have shown that both schemes can boost the throughput by reducing the number of collisions, and, for the case of Aloha-AN, also by reducing the number of unproductive transmissions.

Slotted FAMA [9] is a MAC protocol for underwater acoustic communication, which is a variant to existing FAMA to suitable for underwater environment. Slotted FAMA is to design FAMA combines MACA (Multiple Access Collision Avoidance) method and CS (Carrier Sensing) technique. However, it has some problem such as data collision with long length of RTS/CTS required in FAMA and low transmission rate in underwater environment. Thus, FAMA isn't suitable for underwater environment. To solve this problem, Slotted FAMA for underwater acoustic network is proposed. Each packet (RTS, CTS, DATA or ACK) is transmitted at beginning of one slot. The slot length has to be determined in a manner that ensures absence of data packet collisions.

In [10], it proposed ad-hoc based MAC protocol using a message which has order of priority based on CSMA/CD (Carrier Sense Multiple Access with Collision Detection). DACAP (Distance Aware Collision Avoidance Protocol) [11] is based on minimizing duration of a hand-shake by calculating each receiver's duration, which is different according a distance. Thus, this protocol saves transmission energy by avoiding collisions while maximizing throughput.

In [12], RCMAC (Reservation Channel Acoustic Media Access Protocol) based on RTS/CTS handshaking is a MAC protocol for ad-hoc underwater acoustic sensor network by using channel reservation scheme. It segregates the available bandwidth into a (small bandwidth) control channel and a (majority bandwidth) main channel. If a node has data to send, it needs reservation for main channel time at first by transmitting RTS (Request-to-Send) packets in a control channel. By transmitting short RTS packets on an orthogonal low bandwidth control channel, it can maximize utilization of the majority bandwidth main channel by minimizing the probability of data packet collisions.

In the recent researches for underwater sensor networks, UWAN MAC protocol [13] is an energy-efficient MAC protocol for underwater sensor networks in which nodes are locally synchronized by using SYNC packet. In this paper, authors presented a distributed, scalable, energy-efficient MAC protocol that works despite long, unknown propagation delays of underwater acoustic medium. This protocol can be used for delay-tolerant applications, such as underwater ecological sensor networks among energy-limited nodes. Most of the proposed protocols try to solve synchronization problems and minimize the length of hand-shake procedure for non-synchronized ad hoc UWASNs (UnderWater Acoustic Sensor Networks).

3 Comparison of MAC Protocols

In section 3, we describe comparative analysis of MAC protocols for underwater acoustic communication according to network topology with Table 1 and Table 2. We also present categorized topology for designing MAC protocol for underwater acoustic networks with the existing MAC protocols in the literature. In network topology, deployment of nodes, which is application specific, plays a critical role in the performance of protocol. Therefore, a single protocol cannot be considered as a solution for all the applications in underwater environment. So, we explain our suggestion of the MAC mechanism for underwater acoustic communication by topology fusion in conclusion section.

Table 1 and Table 2 show the comparison of all underwater MAC protocols investigated in this paper respectively.

Table 1. Comparative analysis of cluster-head based MAC protocols for underwater acoustic communication

Network Topology	Protocol	Energy Consumption	Through-put	Collision Avoidance	Advantages	Real-Time
Cluster-head based MAC protocols	ACMENet protocol [2]	Low	Medium	High	· Good scalability	No
	MU-Sync [3]	Low	Medium	High	· Avoiding frequent re-synchronization by estimating both the clock skew and offset	No
	P-MAC [4]	Low	Medium	High	· Adoptive MAC protocol to variation of underwater environment	No
	SBMAC [5]	Low · Saving energy by minimizing transmission of control frames	High	High	· Maintaining an optimized transmission environment	No

Table 2. Comparative analysis of Ad-hoc based MAC protocols for underwater acoustic communication

Network Topology	Protocol	Energy Consumption	Through-put	Collision Avoidance	Advantages	Real-Time
Ad-hoc based MAC protocols	Aloha-based protocol [8]	Medium · Saving by: not transmit packets may cause collision	Low	Medium · Aloha-CA and AN provide the local database table	· Reducing data collision by using overhearing	Yes
	Slotted FAMA [9]	Medium	Low	High · RTS or CTS within transmission range over one slot	· Reducing data collision	No
	DACAP [11]	Medium	Medium	Low · Handshaking with RTS/CTS	· Minimizing duration of RTS/CTS according to each receiver	No
	RCMAC [12]	Low	High	High · Reservation with small RTS packet in a control channel	· Good channel utilization	Yes
	UWAN-MAC [13]	Low	Medium	Medium · Solving synchronization problem	· Propagation delay-tolerant mechanism	Yes

4 Conclusions and Future Works

To update underwater acoustic communication to be applied in various applications, a study of controlling mobile object, such as AUVs (Autonomous Underwater Vehicles) and UUVs (Unmanned Underwater Vehicles), is required prior to beginning of any application. A research of mobility considered MAC protocol based on MANET (Mobile ad-hoc Networks) is also essential for underwater acoustic communication.

So, we suggest fusion architecture of underwater acoustic communication for near future as shown in Figure 2.

The results of fusion architecture presented in Figure 2 to differ greatly from the results compared previously. As an example, all the data packet delivery ratios might be improved by its mobility. Their results are not comparable to ours because of the

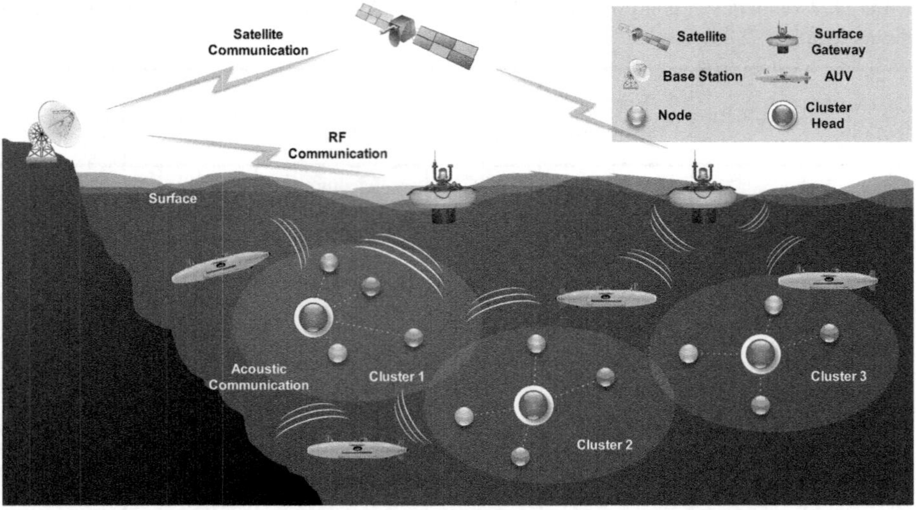

Fig. 2. Fusion architecture for underwater acoustic communication

differences in our simulation environments. Furthermore, our proposed fusion architecture shows the main key features for underwater sensor networks, such as ad-hoc based and cluster-head based networks, and of course the mobility. As we discussed above, mobility has a much greater impact than the other features. As shown in Figure 2, there AUVs and cluster-based nodes are described. There is surface gateway (shown as surface buoy) can gather all necessary information from both kind of networks, and itself communicates with base station through satellite or RF communication. The nodes of each cluster send information to their cluster-heads, and then cluster-heads can have communication with AUVs and surface gateways at same time, as we described it as mobility.

In near future, we will design and implement underwater MAC protocol considered mobility of nodes with advantages of cluster-head based and ad-hoc based MAC protocols for underwater environment.

Acknowledgement. This research was supported by the MKE (The Ministry of Knowledge Economy), Korea, under the ITRC (Information Technology Research Center) support program supervised by the NIPA (National IT Industry Promotion Agency) (NIPA-2011-C1090-1021-0001) and the research program 2011 of Kookmin University in Korea.

References

1. Akyildiz, I.F., Pompili, D., Melodia, T.: Challenges for Efficient Communication in Underwater Acoustic Sensor Network. ACM SIGBED Review 1(1) (July 2004)
2. Acar, G., Adams, A.E.: ACMENet: an underwater acoustic sensor network for real-time environmental monitoring in coastal areas. IEE Proc. Radar, Sonar, and Nav. 153(4), 365–380 (2006)

3. Chirdchoo, N., Soh, W.-S., Chua, K.C.: MU-Sync: a time synchronization protocol for underwater mobile networks. In: Proceedings of the Third ACM International Workshop on UnderWater Networks (WUWNet 2008) (September 2008)
4. Namgung, J.-I., Yun, N.-Y., Park, S.-H., Kim, C.-H., Jeon, J.-H., Park, S.-J.: Adaptive MAC Protocol and Acoustic Modem for Underwater Sensor Networks. In: Proceedings of the Fourth ACM International Workshop on UnderWater Networks (WUWNet 2009) (November 2009)
5. Shin, S.-Y., Namgung, J.-I., Park, S.-H.: SBMAC Smart Blocking MAC Mechanism for Variable UW-ASN (Underwater Acoustic Sensor Network) Environment. In: Sensors 2010, pp. 501–525 (January 2010)
6. Vieira, L.F.M., Kong, J., Lee, U., Gerla, M.: Analysis of Aloha Protocols for Underwater Acoustic Sensor Networks. In: Proceedings of the First ACM International Workshop on UnderWater Networks (WUWNet 2006) (September 2006)
7. Gibson, J.H., Xie, G.G., Xiao, Y., Chen, H.: Analyzing the Performance of Multi-hop Acoustic Sensor Networks. In: Proc. IEEE OCEANS 2007 (June 2007)
8. Chirdchoo, N., Soh, W.-S., Chua, K.C.: Aloha-Based MAC Protocols with Collision Avoidance for Underwater Acoustic Networks. In: 26th IEEE International Conference on Computer Communications (INFOCOM 2007), pp. 2271–2275 (May 2007)
9. Molins, M., Stojanovic, M.: Slotted FAMA: a MAC protocol for underwater acoustic networks. In: Proc. IEEE OCEANS 2006 (May 2007)
10. Smith, S., Park, J.C., Neel, A.: A Peer-to-Peer Communication Protocol for Underwater Acoustic Communication. In: Proc. IEEE OCEANS 1997, vol. 1, pp. 268–272 (October 1997)
11. Peleato, B., Stojanovic, M.: Distance Aware Collision Avoidance Protocol for ad-hoc Underwater Acoustic Sensor Networks. IEEE Communications Letters 11(2) (December 2007)
12. Tracy, L.T., Roy, S.: A Reservation MAC Protocol for ad-hoc Underwater Sensor Networks. In: Proceedings of the Third ACM International Workshop on UnderWater Networks (WUWNet 2008), pp. 95–98 (September 2008)
13. Park, M.K., Rodoplu, V.: UWAN-MAC: An Energy-Efficient MAC Protocol for Underwater Acoustic Wireless Networks. IEEE/MTS Journal of Oceanic Engineering 32(3), 710–720 (2007)

Interference Impact of Mobile WiMAX BS on LTE in TV White Spaces

Yanming Cheng[1,2], Inkyoung Cho[2], and Ilkyoo Lee[3]

[1] Department of Electronic Information, College of Electrical & Information Engineering, Beihua University, China
[2] Department of Information & Communication, College of Engineering, Kongju National University, Budae-dong, Cheonan, Chungnam, 330-717, Korea
[3] Department of Electrical, Electronic & Control, College of Engineering, Kongju National University, Budae-dong, Cheonan, Chungnam, 330-717, Korea
jik2830@kongju.ac.kr

Abstract. Mobile World Interoperability for Microwave Access (WiMAX) and Long Term Evolution (LTE) are assumed to operate on adjacent channels in TV White Spaces(TVWs). Scenario of WiMAX potentially interfering with LTE is analyzed through Spectrum Engineering Advanced Monte Carlo Analysis Tool (SEAMCAT) based on the Monte-Carlo simulation method. As a result, the throughput loss of LTE UL is 5% below when the protection distance between the reference LTE BS(Base station) and the reference Mobile WiMAX BS is 100 km, which can meet the specified transmit power of Mobile WiMAX BS of 43 dBm. Also, when the protection distance between the reference LTE MS and the reference Mobile WiMAX BS is 18 km, which can meet the specified transmit power of Mobile WiMAX BS of 43 dBm.

Keywords: LTE, DTV, WiMAX, Protection Distance, TV White Spaces.

1 Introduction

The Federal Communications Commission's (FCC) desires to make more Very High Frequency (VHF) and Ultra High Frequency (UHF) bandwidth available for wireless communications. Pursuant to this, the FCC adopted rules to allow unlicensed radio transmitters to operate in the broadcast television spectrum at locations where that spectrum is not being used by licensed services. This unused TV spectrum is often termed as TV White Spaces (TVWSs), more TVWSs are freed up by the FCC when the U.S. transits from Analog Television to Digital Television (DTV). TVWSs have several important properties that make them highly desirable for wireless communications as following[1]: Excellent propagation, Ability to penetrate buildings and foliage, Non-line of sight connectivity, Broadband payload capacity. Therefore, TVWSs channels can be used in certain locations by certain devices, such as Long Term Evolution (LTE), Mobile World Interoperability for Microwave Access (WiMAX), Wireless microphone and etc. This paper assumes that LTE and WiMAX are operating on adjacent channels in TVWSs. Also, the specified spectrum emission

T.-h. Kim et al. (Eds.): MulGraB 2011, Part II, CCIS 263, pp. 38–44, 2011.

mask of WiMAX BS(Base station) is taken into consideration. The impact of WiMAX BS potentially interfering with LTE is analyzed by using Spectrum Engineering Advanced Monte Carlo Analysis Tool (SEAMCAT) based on the Monte-Carlo simulation method, which was developed within the frame of European Conference of Postal and Telecommunication administrations (CEPT). The protection distance and the throughput loss and maximum allowable transmit power of Mobile WiMAX BS is figured out through analysis.

2 System Description

2.1 Interference Link

Mobile WiMAX is a rapidly growing broadband wireless access technology based on IEEE 802.16-2004 and IEEE 802.16e-2005 air-interface standards. The WiMAX Forum is developing mobile WiMAX system profiles that define the mandatory and optional features of the IEEE standard that are necessary to build a mobile WiMAX compliant air interface which can be certified by the WiMAX Forum. Main parameters of Mobile WiMAX BS are summarized in Table 1.

Table 1. Some parameters of Mobile WiMAX BS for simulation

Characteristic	Value
Duplex	TDD
Carrier Frequency	589 MHz
Band Width	10 MHz
Thermal Noise	-174 dBm/Hz
I/N	-10 dB
Mobile WiMAX Link Coverage requirement	95% at the coverage edge[2] Log-normal shadowing= 10 dB
Building Penetration Loss	8 dB [3]
Propagation Model	Macro cell propagation model Urban [4]
Coverage Radius	Macro cell propagation model Urban : 1.9939 km
Inter-Side Distance	3.4535 km

Emission limit for Mobile WiMAX BS is illustrated in Table 2.

Table 2. Spectrum emission limit of Mobile WiMAX BS for 10 MHz Bandwidth [5]

Frequency offset from centre (MHz)	Allowed emission level (dBm)	Attenuation in dBc	Measurement bandwidth
5 ~6	−13	-56	100 kHz
6 ~25	−13	-56	1 MHz

2.2 Victim Link

The 3rd Generation Partnership Project (3GPP) Long Term Evolution (LTE) is the latest standard in the mobile network technology tree that produced the GSM/EDGE and UMTS/HSPA network technologies [6][7][8]. It is a project of 3GPP, operating under a name trademarked by one of the associations within the partnership, the European Telecommunications Standards Institute (ETSI).

The main advantages with LTE are high throughput, low latency, plug and play, FDD and TDD in the same platform, an improved end-user experience and a simple architecture resulting in low operating costs. LTE will also support seamless passing to cell towers with older network technology such as GSM, UMTS, and CDMA2000. The next step for LTE evolution is LTE Advanced and is currently being standardized in 3GPP Release 10[9]. LTE has introduced a number of new technologies when compared to the previous cellular systems. They enable LTE to be able to operate more efficiently with respect to the use of spectrum and also to provide the much higher data rates that are being required. Main parameters of LTE are summarized in Table 3.

Table 3. Characteristics of LTE

Characteristic	Value
Duplex	FDD
Carrier Frequency(DL)	595 MHz(Channel 35,36)
Carrier Frequency(UL)	579 MHz(Channel 32,33)
Band Width	10 MHz
Thermal Noise	-174 dBm/Hz
I/N	-10 dB
LTE Link Coverage requirement	Log-normal shadowing =10 dB[10]
Building Penetration Loss	8 dB[11]
Propagation Model	Macro cell propagation model Urban [12]
Coverage Radius	2.8668km
Inter-Side Distance	4.9654km
Sectorization	Tri- sector antennas
Minimum Coupling Loss	70 dB
Number of Available Resource Blocks (M)	24
Number of Resource Block per UE (N)	1
Number of Active UEs per Cell (K)	24 (K=M/N)
Minimum subcarrier usage per Base Station	assumed full loaded system 100%
Bandwidth of Resource Block	375 KHz
Hand Over (HO) Margin	3 dB

3 Simulation Results and Analysis

3.1 Interference Scenario

Figure. 1 shows the scenario of Mobile WiMAX potentially interfering with LTE.

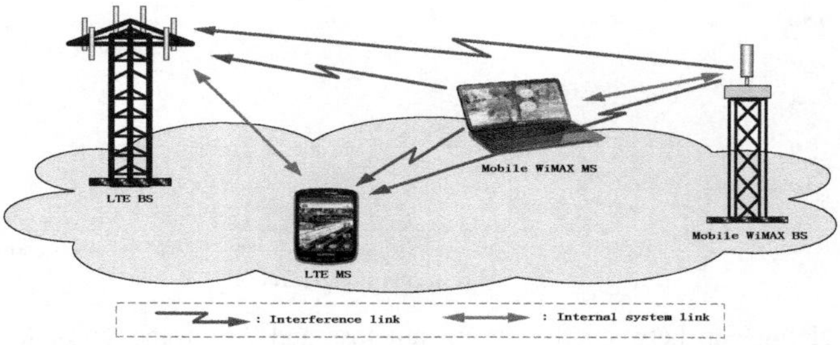

Fig. 1. The scenario of Mobile WiMAX interfering with LTE

If throughput loss of LTE is required to be keep 5% below, the protection distance between two systems and the maximum allowable transmit power of Mobile WiMAX BS is analyzed subsequently.

3.2 The Case of Mobile WiMAX BS Interfering with LTE BS

In the case of WiMAX BS interfering with LTE BS, main setups for simulation in SEAMCAT are summarized. Therefore, the evaluation of the relationship between the maximum allowable transmit power of Mobile WiMAX BS and the protection distance will be conducted in SEAMCAT. Simulation scenario of Mobile WiMAX BS interfering with LTE BS in SEAMCAT is shown in Figure. 2 when snapshot is 100.

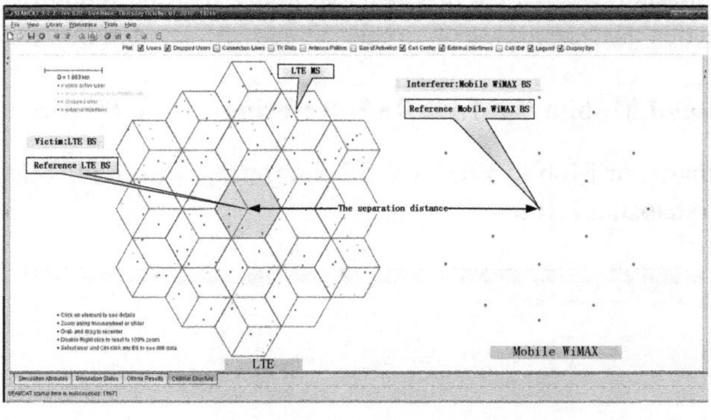

Fig. 2. The relationship between the throughput loss and the protection distance in case of Mobile WiMAX BS interfering with LTE BS

The throughput loss of LTE UL is evaluated and illustrated in Figure. 3 based on the different protection distance the reference Mobile WiMAX BS and the reference LTE BS.

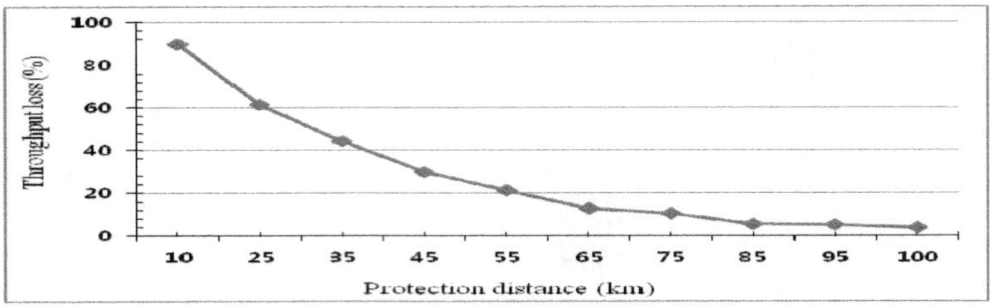

Fig. 3. The relationship between the throughput loss and the protection distance in case of Mobile WiMAX BS interfering with LTE BS

Figure. 3 shows that the throughput loss of LTE UL is 5% below when the protection distance between the reference LTE BS and the reference Mobile WiMAX BS is 100 km, which can meet the specified transmit power of Mobile WiMAX BS of 43 dBm.

According to the different protection distance between the reference LTE BS and he reference Mobile WiMAX BS, the maximum allowable transmit power of Mobile WiMAX BS can be determined in Figure. 4.

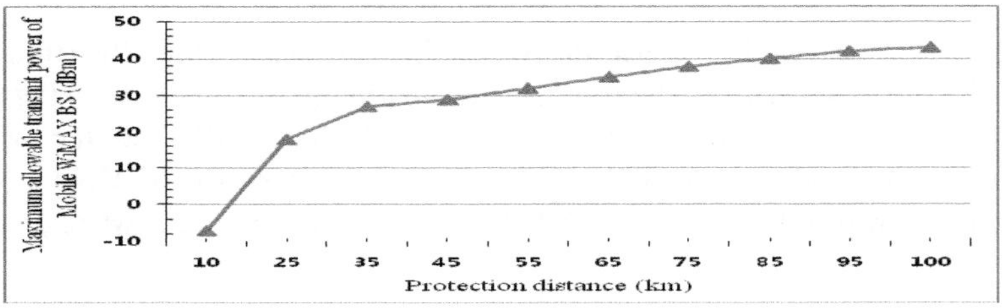

Fig. 4. The relationship between the maximum allowable transmit power of Mobile WiMAX BS and the protection distance in case of Mobile WiMAX BS interfering with LTE BS

3.3 The Case of Mobile WiMAX BS Interfering with LTE MS

Simulation scenario of Mobile WiMAX BS interfering with LTE MS is illustrated in Figure. 5 when snapshot is100.

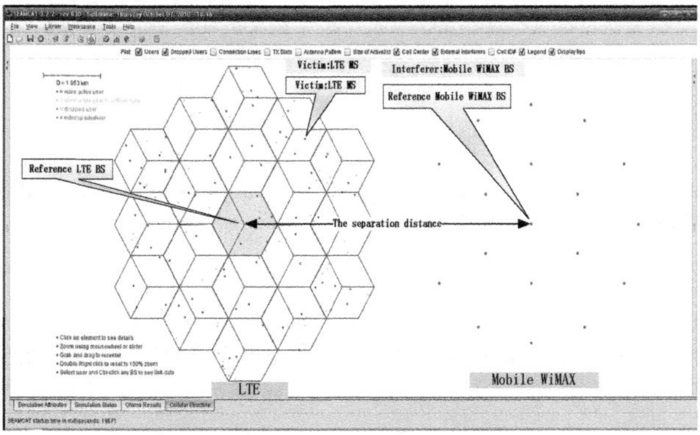

Fig. 5. Scenario of Mobile WiMAX BS interfering with LTE MS in SEAMCAT

Figure 5 shows that the throughput loss of LTE DL is 5% below when the protection distance between the reference LTE MS and the reference Mobile WiMAX BS is 18 km, which can meet the specified transmit power of Mobile WiMAX BS of 43 dBm.

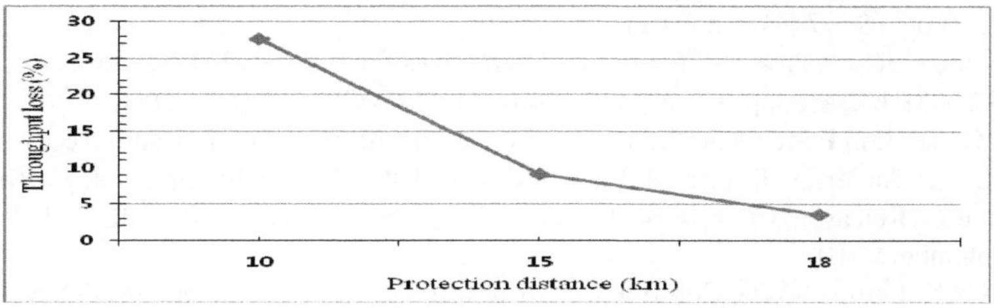

Fig. 6. The relationship between the throughput loss and the protection

According to the different protection distance between the reference LTE MS and the reference Mobile WiMAX BS, the maximum allowable transmit power of Mobile WiMAX BS can be determined in Figure. 7.

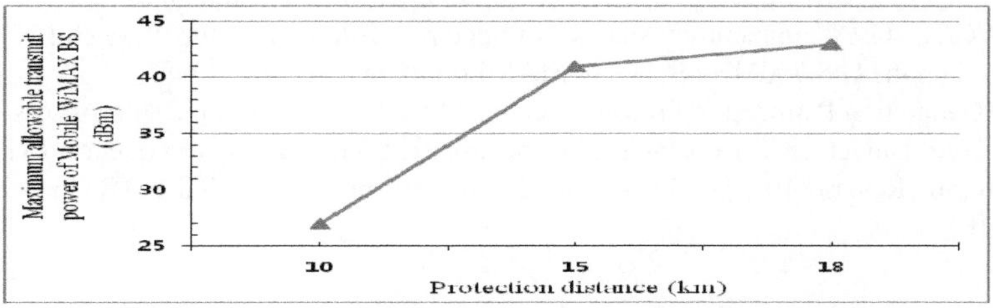

Fig. 7. The relationship between the maximum allowable transmit power of Mobile WiMAX BS and the protection distance in case of Mobile WiMAX BS interfering with LTE MS

4 Conclusions

The scenario of Mobile WiMAX BS potentially interfering with LTE is assumed in TVWSs. If throughput loss of LTE is required to be keep 5% below, the protection distance between two systems and the maximum allowable transmit power of Mobile WiMAX BS is analyzed by using SEAMCAT.

As a result of study, the throughput loss of LTE UL is 5% below when the protection distance between the reference LTE BS and the reference Mobile WiMAX BS is 100 km, which can meet the specified transmit power of Mobile WiMAX BS of 43 dBm. Also, when the protection distance between the reference LTE MS and the reference Mobile WiMAX BS is 18 km, which can meet the specified transmit power of Mobile WiMAX BS of 43 dBm.

The results can be as a guideline and reference in making plan for the coexistence of LTE and Mobile WiMAX in TVWSs.

References

1. Ofcom, Digital Dividend Review: 550-630MHz and 790-854MHz, Consultation on detailed award design (2008)
2. Digital Video Broadcasting (DVB); DVB-H Implementation Guidelines. ETSI TR 102 377 V1.3.1, pp. 92–97 (March 2009)
3. A comparative Analysis of Spectrum Alternatives for WiMAXTM Networks Based on the U.S.700MHz Band, pp. 19, WiMAX Forum, by MWG/AWG (June 2008)
4. 3rd Generation Partnership Project; Technical Specification Group Radio Access Network; Evolved Universal Terrestrial Radio Access (E-UTRA);Radio Frequency (RF) system scenarios(Release 10), pp. 14–15, pp. 23–39, pp. 76–77, 3GPP TR 36.942 V10.1.0 (September 2010)
5. WiMAX Forum TWG Contribution to development of Candidate IMT-Advanced RIT based on IEEE 802.16
6. WGSE - SEAMCAT Technical Group, OFDMA algorithm description (2010)
7. 3GPP LTE Encyclopedia, An Introduction to LTE (2010)
8. Motorola, Long Term Evolution (LTE): A Technical Overview (2010)
9. 3GPP LTE Encyclopedia, LTE – An End-to-End Description of Network Architecture and Elements (2009)
10. Digital Video Broadcasting (DVB), DVB-H Implementation Guidelines (2009)
11. MWG/AWG, A comparative Analysis of Spectrum Alternatives for WiMAXTM Networks Based on the U.S.700MHz Band, WiMAX Forum, pp. 19 (June 2008)
12. 3rd Generation Partnership Project, Technical Specification Group Radio Access Network; Evolved Universal Terrestrial Radio Access (E-UTRA);Radio Frequency (RF) system scenarios(Release 10), pp. 14–15, pp. 23, pp. 39, pp. 76–77, 3GPP TR 36.942 V10.1.0 (2010)

Generating Optimal Fuzzy If-Then Rules Using the Partition of Fuzzy Input Space

In-Kyu Park[1], Gyoo-Seok Choi[2,*], and Jong-Jin Park[2]

[1] Dept. of Computer Science, Joongbu University,
101 Daehak-Ro, Chubu-Myeon, Kumsan-Gun, Chungnam, 312-702, South Korea
ikpark@joongbu.ac.kr

[2] Dept. of Internet and Computer Science, Chungwoon University
San 29, Namjang-ri, Hongseong, Chungnam, 350-701, South Korea
{jjpark,lionel}@chungwoon.ac.kr

Abstract. This paper proposes an extended fuzzy entropy-based-method for selecting an optimal number of fuzzy rules to construct a compact fuzzy classification system with high classification power. An optimal number of rules are generated through the optimal partition of input space via the extended fuzzy entropy to define an index of feature evaluation in pattern recognition problems decreases as the reliability of a feature in characterizing and discriminating different classes increases. A set of fuzzy if-then rules is coded into a string and treated as an individual in genetic algorithms. The fitness of each individual is specified by the two objectives. The performance of the proposed method for training data and test data is examined by computer simulations on the Mackey-Glass chaotic time series prediction.

Keywords: fuzzy entropy, fuzzy input partition, genetic algorithm, time series.

1 Introduction

Fuzzy logic is quite useful concept for reducing information loss in dealing with imprecision and uncertainty situations. In most fuzzy control systems fuzzy if-then rules were typically derived from operator's experience and/or human expert's knowledge of the system. So far, several approaches such as neural networks[1,2,3], complex methods[4,5,6], gradient descent based method[7,8,9] and genetic algorithms[10] have been proposed for automatically generating fuzzy if-then rules from numerical data.

Among them fuzzy partitions of input spaces were determined in Nomura et al[16]. That is, both the number of fuzzy sets and the membership function of each fuzzy sets were determined. In Thrift[11], an appropriate fuzzy set in the consequent part of each fuzzy if-then rule was selected. These approaches applied genetic algorithms to fuzzy control problems by coding a fuzzy rule table(i.e., a set of fuzzy if-then rules) as an individual. Ishibuchi et al[12] proposed a generation method of fuzzy if-then rules

* Corresponding author.

T.-h. Kim et al. (Eds.): MulGraB 2011, Part II, CCIS 263, pp. 45–53, 2011.

from numerical data for classification problems. Generation of fuzzy if-then rules from numerical data consists of fuzzy partition of a pattern space into fuzzy subspaces and determination of a fuzzy if-then rule for each fuzzy subspace. the fuzzy partition by a simple fuzzy grid was employed. The performance of a fuzzy classification system based on fuzzy if-then rules depends on the choice of a fuzzy partition. If a fuzzy partition is too coarse, the performance may be low(i.e., many patterns may be misclassified). If a fuzzy partition is too fine, many fuzzy if-then rules cannot be generated because of the lack of training patterns in the corresponding fuzzy subspaces. Therefore the choice of a fuzzy partition is very important.

To cope with this difficulty, the concept of the information entropy introduced by Shannon was proposed where it is a measure which represents the value of information in numerical value. Generally when the result is obvious before receiving related information, the value of information is low, on the contrary, the more ambiguous the result is , the higher the value of information becomes.

In this paper, it develops the simplified algorithm which has the good general performance without a large increase of the calculation which used to a learning procedure. It used an extended fuzzy entropy and Shannon function in order to get the optimal control rule by the effective partition of input space, and the algorithm which will be able to create a fuzzy control rule. Also the proposed network implements the rule base and reasoning of fuzzy controller with genetic algorithms.

2 A Proposed Partition Algorithm of Fuzzy Input Space

2.1 Fuzzy Entropy in a Time Series

A time series *X* with size *N* having L values ranging from L_{min} to L_{max} can be defined as an array of fuzzy singletons[13]. Each has a membership function value denoting its degree of membership relative to some values, $\ell(\ell = 1,2,\dots,L)$. Therefore, in fuzzy set notation, we can write

$$X = \{\mu_X(x_t),\ t = 1,2,\dots,N\} \tag{1}$$

where $\mu_X(x_t)$ denotes the grade of some value property possessed by the *n*th number. The degree of ambiguity in a series *X* can be measured by the entropy of a fuzzy set *X*:

$$H(X) = \frac{1}{Nln2}\sum_{i=1}^{N} S(\mu_X(x_t)) \tag{2}$$

with Shannon's function

$$S(\mu_X(x_t)) = -\mu_X(x_t)log_2\mu_X(x_t) - (1-\mu_X(x_t))\,log_2(1-\mu_X(x_t)) \tag{3}$$

H(μ) gives a measure of the average fuzziness of a fuzzy set and can be interpreted as the average amount of information arising from fuzziness in Fig. 1,. $H(X)(0 \le H(X) \le 1)$ measures the fuzziness in *X*. Shannon function $S_n(\cdot)$ increases monotonically in [0, 0.5] and decreases monotonically in [0.5 1] with a

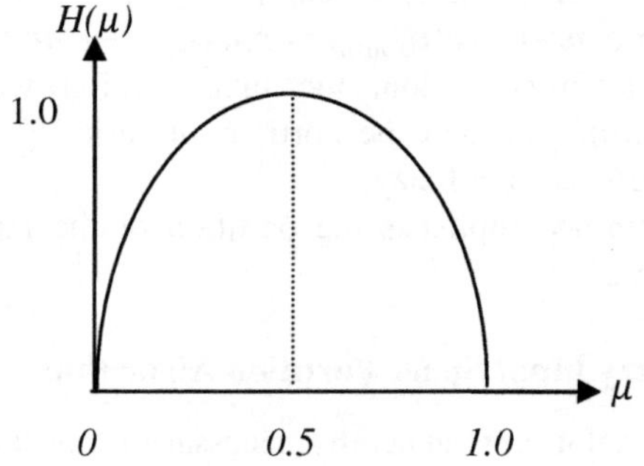

Fig. 1. Fuzzy entropy $H(\mu)$

maximum at $\mu_X(x_t))$= 0.5. Entropy under the probability measurement is often used to indicate the uncertainty of probabilistic systems. When we think that the pattern indeterminacy in a series is caused by its inherent fuzziness, we should use membership function $\mu_X(x_t)$ to measure the fuzziness of the series X. The extended S-function is applied to define the membership function $\mu_X(x_t)$:

$$\mu_X(x) = S(x, min_{band} = L_{min} + band, center, max_{band} = L_{max} + band) \quad (4)$$

$$band = \frac{\sum_{t=0}^{n} x(t) \sum_{t=0}^{n} Histogram_{interval}[x(t)]}{\sum_{t=0}^{n} x(t) \sum_{t=0}^{n} Histogram_{interval}[t]} \quad (5)$$

$$\mu_X(x) = \begin{cases} 0, & x(t) \le min_{band} \\ 2.0(x(t) - min_{band})/max_{band} - x(t))^2, & min_{band} \le x(t) \le center \\ 1 - 2.0(center - x(t))/x(t) - max_{band})^2, & center \le x(t) \le max_{band} \\ 1.0, & max_{band} \le x(t) \end{cases} \quad (6)$$

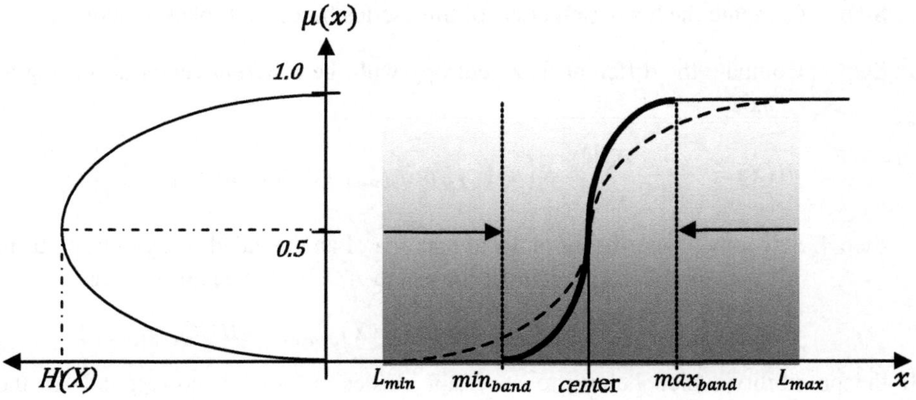

Fig. 2. Fuzzy entropy using variable length

In figure 2, the cross-over point is center($(min_{band} + max_{band})/2$) and the bandwith is $\delta center = center - min_{band} = max_{band} - center$. The interval $[min_{band}, max_{band}]$ is a fuzzy region, the fuzzy region width is defined as $2\,\delta center = max_{band} - min_{band}$, and the portions of series X in $[L_{min}, min_{band}]$ and $[L_{max}, max_{band}]$ are crisp or nonfuzzy.

The following algorithm accomplishes the partition of the input space which is allocated to an each variable.

2.2 The Proposed Fuzzy Input Space Partition Algorithm

Only one local maximum solution is generally necessary in most existing algorithms for implementing maximum entropy principle. In an attempt to partition the input space in time series prediction problem. Finding all of local maxima including the global will be necessary for the classification requirement. To determine the membership of the different values of the series we use the Stokes's theorem which constructs each different values of time series using arbitrary interval range. Then the fuzzy entropy will be as following:

$$H(X) = \frac{1}{N \ln 2} \sum_{i=1}^{N} S(\mu_X(x_t, a, b, c))h(x_t) \tag{7}$$

where $h(x_t)$ denotes the number of occurrences of the series's value x_t Given the parameter $max_{band} - min_{band}$, the algorithm for time series can be stated as follows:

Step 1. Construct the membership which measures the fuzziness of time series according to the width the variable length was applied to the right and left of Shannon function respectively.

$$for(\,i\; = \; L_{min}\; ;\; i\; \le \; L_{max}\; ;\; i++)$$
$$for(\,i\; = \; L_{min}\; ;\; i\; \le \; L_{max}\; ;\; i++)$$
$$\mu_X(x_t, min_{band}, center, max_{band}) = S(\mu_X(x_t, min_{band}, center, max_{band}))$$

Step 2. Compute the histogram h(x_t) of time series based on Stokes's theorem.

Step 3. Compute the different fuzzy entropy with the different center according to x axis.

$$H(X) = \frac{1}{N \ln 2} \sum_{i=1}^{N} S\left(\mu_X(x_{t_t}, min_{band}, center, max_{band})\right) h(x_t)$$

Step 4. Select the center based on local maxima of an extended fuzzy entropy from $[L_{min} + band,\ L_{max} - band]$, for which *H(X)* of the center satisfies :

$$(H(X)_{center} > H(X)_{center+1})\ and\ (H(X)_{center} > H(X)_{center-1})$$

If the possibility which belong to a certain cluster is large, it corresponds to the boundary of cluster in the case of clustering of input-output data, and if the entropy value will be small, it corresponds to the center. And the center value of the obtained clusters corresponds to the center(*C*) of gaussian membership functional. It composes a membership function for each cluster using the boundary value of each cluster.

3 Application to Time-Series Prediction

The fuzzy neural network input consists of 4 input with x_1, x_2 ,x_3 and x_4 in input layer in fig. 3. mf layer describes the membership functions which correspond to the coarse database by the partition of input space and according to each variable the membership function is a fuzzy set which are divided by a fuzzy entropy[14][15][16].

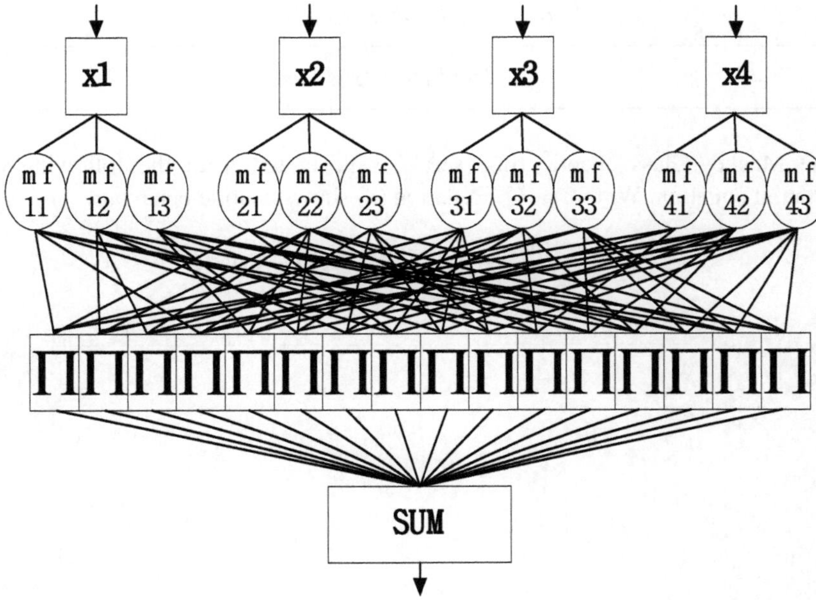

Fig. 3. The fuzzy neural network system

The parameters(center, width of $\mu(x)$ and β for defuzzification) are adapted by the conventional genetic algorithm.

```
Genetic Algorithm() {
        t <- 0;
        Initialize(P(t));
        Evaluate(P(t));
        while(not Finished()){
        t <- t+1;
        Select P(t) from P(t-1);
        Recombine P(t);
        Mutate P(t);
        Evaluate(P(t));
        }
        solution <- BestOf(P(t));
}
```

Table 1. The configuration of chromosome

x(t-18)		*x(t-12)*		*x(t-6)*		*x(t)*		*X(t+6)*
center	*width*	*center*	*width*	*center*	*width*	*center*	*width*	*consequence*
antecedent								
16bits	*16bit*	*16bits*	*16bits*	*16bits*	*16bits*	*16bits*	*16bits*	*16bits*
*16bits * 8 + 16bits = 128bits*								
*144bits * 16 = 2304 bits*								

The Mackey-Glass chaotic time series is generated from the following delay differential equation. When $\tau > 17$, Equation (8) shows chaotic behavour.

$$x(t) = \left(\frac{0.2x(t-\tau)}{1} + x^{10}(t-\tau)\right) - 0.1x(t) \tag{8}$$

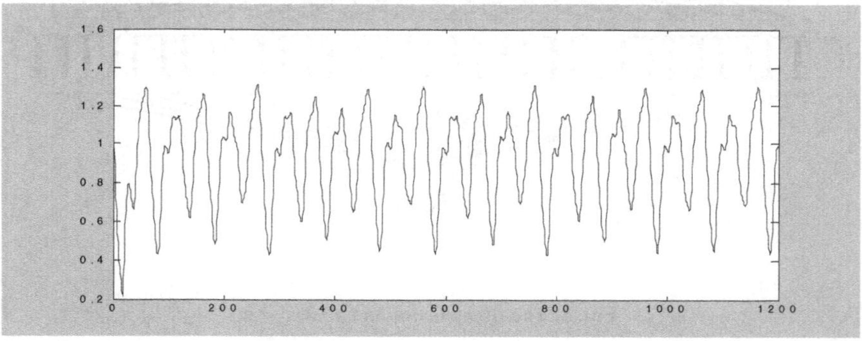

Fig. 4. 1,200 patterns of the Mackey-Glass chaotic time series

Fig. 4 is to show the data which occurs 1200 using the 4th Runge-Kuta law by equation (8) with the Mackey-Glass data set. Table 2 is the partition results of 4 input variables(*x(t), x(t-6), x(t-12) and x(t-18))* using the extended fuzzy entropy..

Table 2. Partition results of the input space

x(t-18)	0.135773	0.181558	0.230613	0.279668	0.312371	0.392457
x(t-12)	0.143828	0.178045	0.275810	0.422458	0.432234	0.529999
x(t-6)	0.143828	0.187822	0.275810	0.422458	0.432234	0.529999
x(t)	0.175664	0.280528	0.418759	0.433059	0.533157	0.609422

It is $x(t) = 0$ at $t<0$ interval, and the initial value is 1.2. 600 training data(from500 at 1,200 data which occurs at figure 6 used in learning, and remainder 600 used in the prediction. The input and output format of a learning pattern is *x(t-18), x(t-12), x(t-6), x(t)* and *x(t+6)* with each 6 intervals respectively.

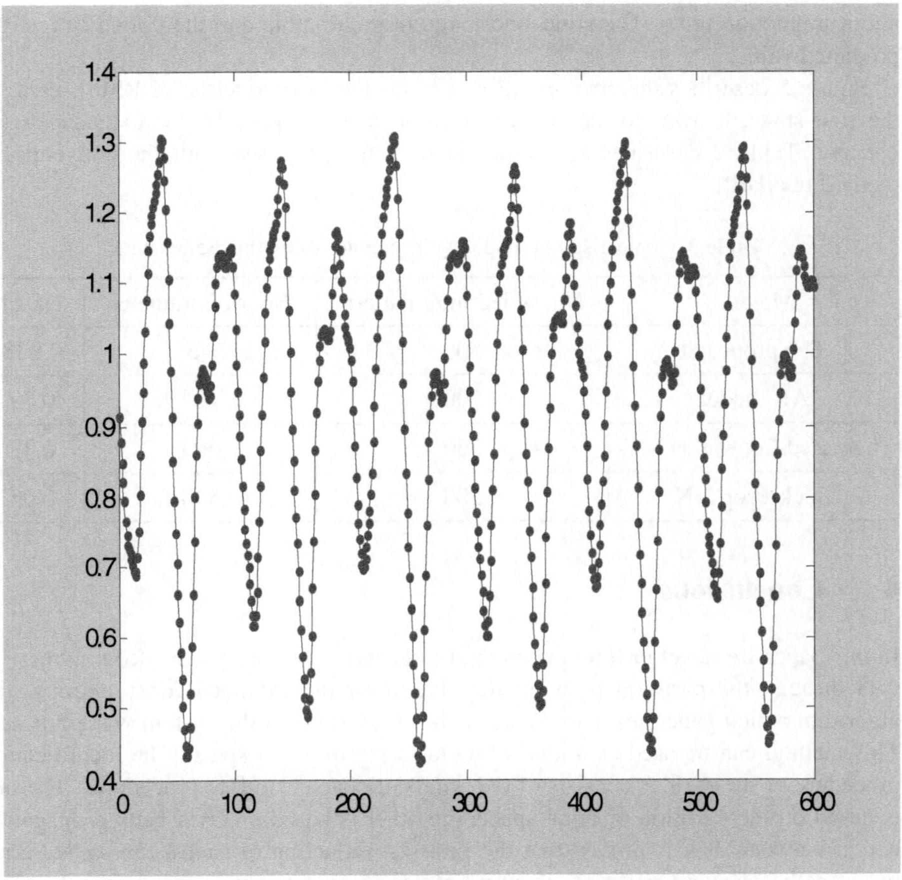

Fig. 5. Prediction results

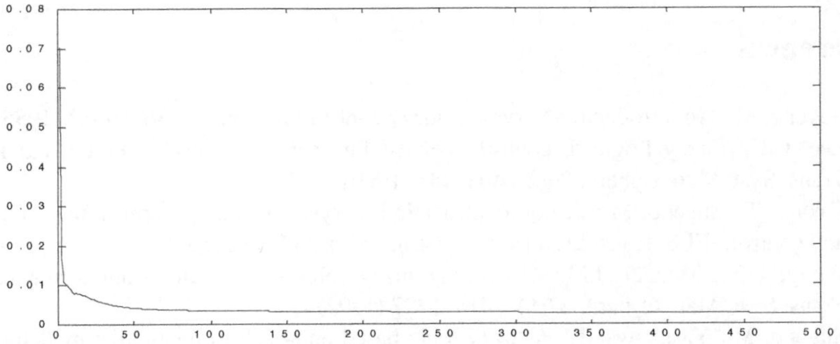

Fig. 6. RMSE of training

The parameters of premise and consequence is 30 and 16 respectively. The system has the total 46 parameters. Fig. 4 and Fig. 5 show a prediction result of a time series and a prediction error. The solid line is the original value and the dotted line is the predicted value.

Figure 5 describes the error curve which has the fast reduction of RMSE error in the first stage. It owes to the coarse partition of input space by the extended fuzzy entropy. Table 2 describes the comparison of the proposed with the conventional method in NDEI.

Table 3. Comparison of modeling techniques using time series data

Method	No. of learning Pattern	No. of Parameter	NDEI
The proposed	500	46	0.038
AR model	500	104	0.39
Cascaded-Correlation NN	500	693	0.32
Back-Prop NN	500	540	0.05

4 Conclusions

In this paper we developed a new method to generate the fuzzy rules from numerical data through the partition of input data based on the extended fuzzy entropy. the algorithm which generates automatically the fuzzy rules of the system was proposed. This method can be used as a kind of a clustering on input space. The identification procedure of fuzzy rules consists of two kinds of coarse and fine procedures. The one is based on the partition of input space, the other is based on error-back propagation neural network. It was proved that the first fast reduction of root mean square error owes to the efficient partition of input spaces in an attempt to overcome the slow convergence of neural network.

References

1. Sugeno, M.: An introductory survey of fuzzy control. Inform. Sci. 36, 59–83 (1985)
2. Lee, C.C.: Fuzzy Logic in control systems: Fuzzy logic controller-Part I and II. IEEE Trans. Syst. Man. Cybern. 20(2), 404–435 (1990)
3. Takagi, T., Sugeno, M.: Fuzzy identification of systems and its applications to modeling and control. IEEE Trans. Syst. Man. Cybern. 15(1), 116–132 (1985)
4. Wang, L.X., Mendel, J.M.: Generating fuzzy rules by learning from examples. IEEE Trans. Syst. Man. Cybern. 22(6), 1414–1427 (1992)
5. Sugeno, M., Yasukawa, T.: A fuzzy logic based approach to qualitative modeling. IEEE Trans. Fuzzy Systems 1(1), 7–31 (1993)
6. Ichibuchi, H., Watanabe, T.: Learning control by fuzzy models using a simplified fuzzy reasoning. J, Japan Soc. Fuzzy Theory Syst. 2(3), 429–437 (1990)
7. Lin, C.T., Lee, C.S.G.: Neural network based fuzzy logic control and decision system. IEEE Trans. / Comput. 40(12), 1320–1336 (1991)

8. Jang, J.S.R.: Self-learning fuzzy controllers based on temporal back propagation. IEEE Trans. Neural Networks 3(5), 714–723 (1992)
9. Brtrenji, H.R., Khedkar, P.: Learning and tuning fuzzy logic controllers through reinforcements. IEEE Trans. Neural Networks 3(5), 724–740 (1992)
10. Horikawa, S., Furuhashi, T., Uchikawa, Y.: On fuzzy modeling using fuzzy enural networks with the back-propagation algorithm. IEEE Trans. Neural Networks 3(5), 801–806 (1992)
11. Nomura, H., Hayashi, I., Wakami, N.: A self-tuning method of fuzzy reasoning by genetic algorithm. In: Proc. 1992, Int. Fuzzy Syst. Int. Contr. Conf., Louisville, March 16-18, pp. 236–245 (1992)
12. Ishibuchi, H., Nozaki, K., Tanaka, H.: Distributed representation of fuzzy rules and its application to pattern classification. Fuzzy Sets and Syst. 52, 21–32 (1992)
13. Pal, S.K., Chakraborty, B.: Fuzzy set theoretic measure for automatic feature evaluation. IEEE Tran. on SMC, 754–759 (September / October 1986)
14. Wang, L.-X., Mendal, J.M.: Generating fuzzy rules by learning from examples. IEEE Trans. SMC 22(6), 1414–1427 (1992)
15. Ichihashi, H.: Iterative fuzzy modeling and a hierarchical network. In: Proc. of the 4th IFSA Congress, Eng., Brussels, pp. 49–52 (1991)
16. Araki, D., Nomura, H., Hayashi, I., Wakami, N.: A self generating method of fuzzy inference rules. In: Terano, T., et al. (eds.) Fuzzy Engineering Toward Human Friendly Systems, pp. 1047–1058 (1991)

A Design of Embedded Integration Prototyping System Based on AR

Sin Kwan Kang[1], Jung Eun Kim[2], Hyun Lee[2],
Dong Ha Lee[2], and Jeong Bae Lee[3]

[1] Dept. of Visual Media, Korea Polytechnic IV College, Asan, 336-781, South Korea
[2] Division of Robotics System, DGIST, Daegu, 711-873, South Korea
[3] Dept. of Computer Engineering, Sunmoon University, Asan, 336-708, South Korea
kandsk@kopo.ac.kr, {jekim,hlee,dhlee}@dgist.ac.kr, jblee@sunmoon.ac.kr

Abstract. Because of increasing usage of smart phones in recent years, the application field of convergence industry between IT technology using smart phone-based mobile communication networks and other industry branches is expanding. In addition, R&D technologies in other fields are applied to smart phone applications effectively in order to develop products and support daily life more convenient. However, it is very hard to control these products and there is no efficient solution for this problem when many people are sent to specific area for big events, such as Biennale, Film Festival, EXPO, and so on. In order to solve this problem, this paper describes a network-based ticket reservation system and its organization using smart phone augmented reality and mobile communication networks. In particular, we propose a method of designing and developing prototyping system based on smart phone application design technologies, prior to developing real smart phone application.

Keywords: Smart Phone Appl., Augmented Reality, Embedded Integrated Prototyping, GPS.

1 Introduction

The application field of convergence industry between IT technology using smart phone-based mobile communication networks and other industry branches is expanding, because of increasing usage of smart-phones recently [1]. For instance, various kinds of service can be provided by using GPS and Gyro sensors built in a smart-phone with WiFi-based smart-phone service technique in order to develop an application program that works in only specific area [2], [3]. These smart-phones provide various convenient products and services as an intelligent device that functions of internet communication and searching are added by increasing usage of mobile network [3]. However, the convergence industry based on smart phone-based mobile communication networks needs more research and technical efforts, because of novel products involving additional functions are frequently developed and produced then the designing and developing techniques of smart-phone system become more complicate for adapting new technologies into

T.-h. Kim et al. (Eds.): MulGraB 2011, Part II, CCIS 263, pp. 54–61, 2011.

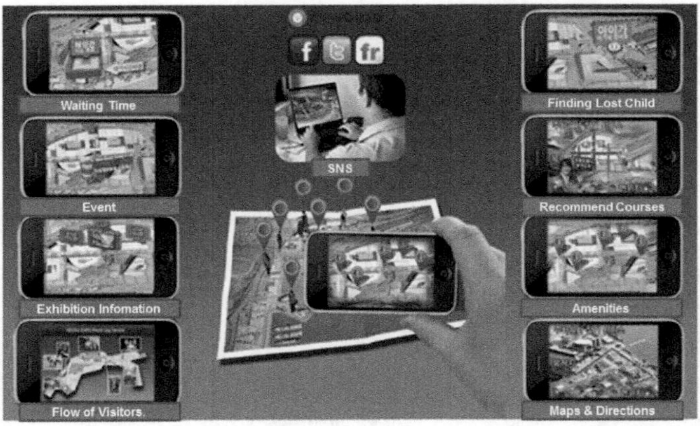

Fig. 1. An example of Smart-Phone Applications based on Augmented Reality

Fig. 2. An example of Smart-Phone Applications applied to YEOSU EXPO

the mobile-communication network. Particularly, it is very hard to control these products and there is no efficient solution for the problem when many people are sent to specific area for big events, such as Biennale, Film Festival, EXPO, and so on. Thus, R&D technologies in other fields are applied to smart-phone applications effectively so as to develop products and support daily life more convenient using smart-phone system. For example, a network based ticket booking system and it's method of operation based on smart-phone with augmented reality and technology based on established mobile network [4], [5], [6] can be applied to the products so as to support convenient daily life of the customer. In particular, in this paper, we propose a method of designing and developing prototyping system based on smart-phone application design technologies as shown in Figure 1, prior to developing real smart-phone application. Furthermore, we apply our method into the YEOSU EXPO as shown in Figure 2.

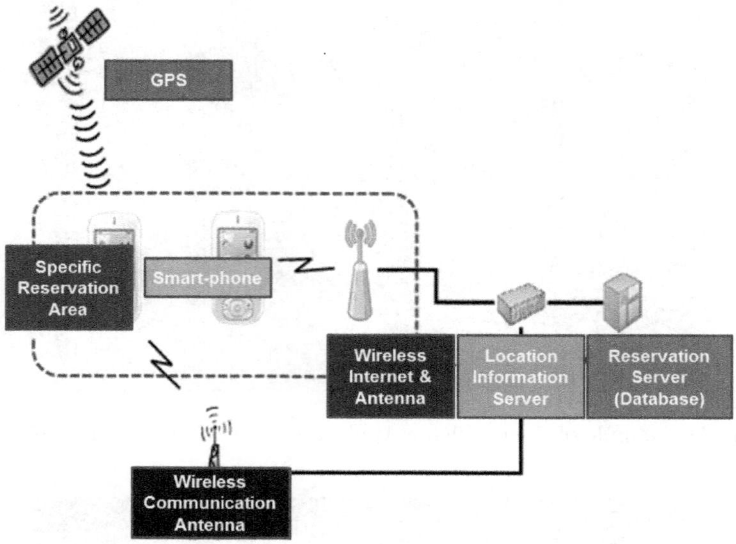

Fig. 3. GPS-based Reservation System Structure

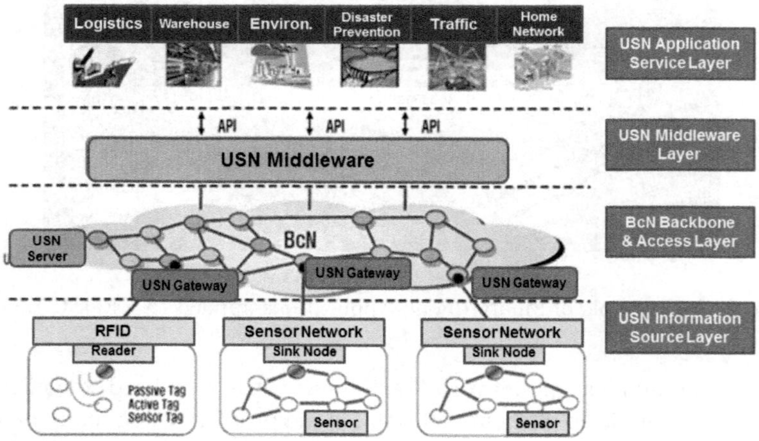

Fig. 4. The defined Structure of Ubiquitous Sensor Network (USN)

The rest of the paper is organized as follows. For network based operating reservation system, a GPS based reservation system is explained in section II. We introduce a method of smart-phone application designing and developing which suitable for USN structure in section III. We propose a design of embedded integration prototyping system based on augmented reality by analyzing and designing the synchronized techniques between smart-phone application and server system for real-time reservation in section IV. Finally, we conclude the paper in section V.

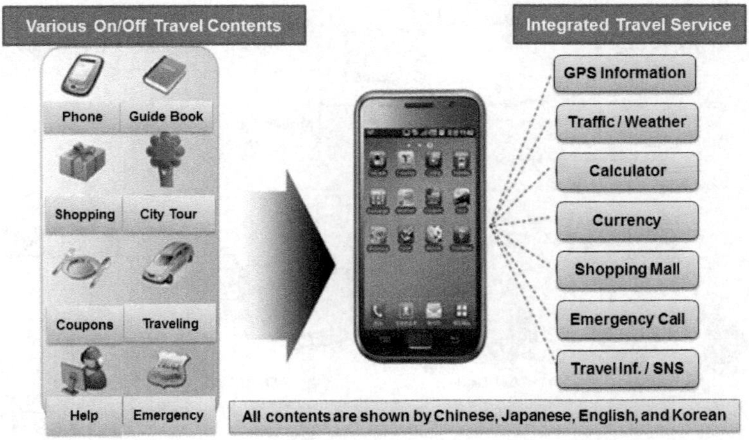

Fig. 5. An example of the Convergence of U2M with Travel Information

2 Structure of GPS Based Reservation System

For ticketing reservation system operated by a smart-phone, a network based reservation system which is installed more than one exhibition is designed into specific reserved area in order to make a database of the ticketing management depending on the location of the exhibition as shown in Figure 3. In addition, an operation server connected through a ticketing machine and network and a smart-phone that processes ticket reservation connected through an operation server transmit information of current user's location to operation server and then, operation server makes decision an approval of this reservation according to whether user's location is belong to reservation areas or not. This procedure induces making the flow of audience or visitor traffic efficiently, thereby audience or visitor traffic can be minimized.

3 A Method of Smart-Phone Application Designing and Developing

At first, we link a smart-phone with U-ticket system based on Ubiquitous Sensor Network (USN) structure in order to analyze the method of a smart-phone application designing and developing that is necessary for a network based reservation system. It means that we define the concepts of Ubiquitous to Mobile (U2M) functions so as to support audiences or visitors convenience in exhibition as shown in Figure 4. For instance, we induce the idea correction for usage of related technique from two layers such as USN application service and the network structure information source on Figure 4 by separating techniques and by defining concepts of the smart-phone application designing and developing. Particularly, we consider problems caused by the link of a smart-phone and the U-ticket system.

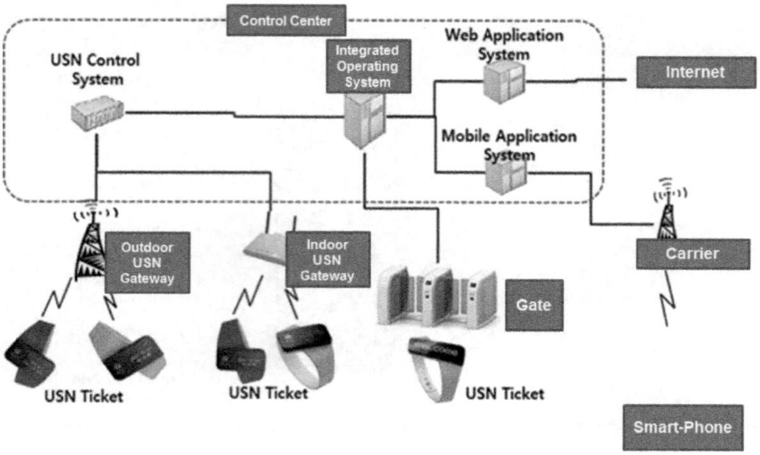

Fig. 6. Integrated System Configurations

As an example of the convergence of U2M with travel information on Figure 5, the direction of system designing is suggested to apply on a smart-phone through designing smart-phone application systems. Then, we apply related techniques into the system in order to optimize them on Android phone and I-phone concurrently. Moreover, we add various applications about travel information that can increase visitors convenience based on the method of application system simulation into the smart-phone application designing and developing procedure.

4 Proposed Design of Embedded Integration Prototyping System based on Augmented Reality

In order to make a design of embedded integration prototyping system based on augmented reality, we first analyze and design linking techniques between applications of a smart-phone and server system. In particular, we analyze the environment that supports linking technologies between the two. In addition, we implement integrated designing system based on the established developing environment then apply the real time reservation technique into the linking system of the two such as smart-phone applications and server system.

As shown in Figure 6, we construct an integrated system configuration for smart application in exhibition area. If a visitor or an audience who uses a GPS built in smart-phone is arrived at a certain specific zone in front of exhibition, the linking technique between U-ticket and the smart-phone application can be utilized. Then, a real time reservation procedure and visitors' or audiences' movement management is usefully performed based on the process of the integrated system configuration as shown in Figure 7.

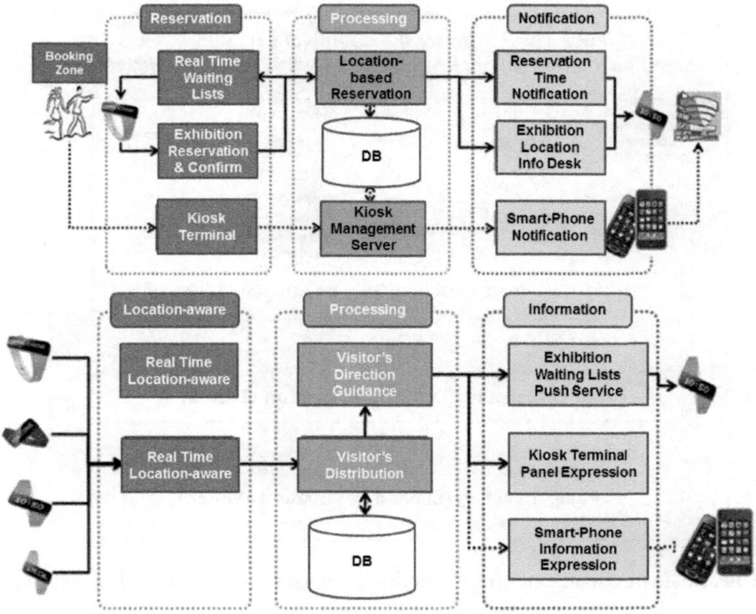

Fig. 7. Location-based Realtime Reservation and Visitor's Movement Management

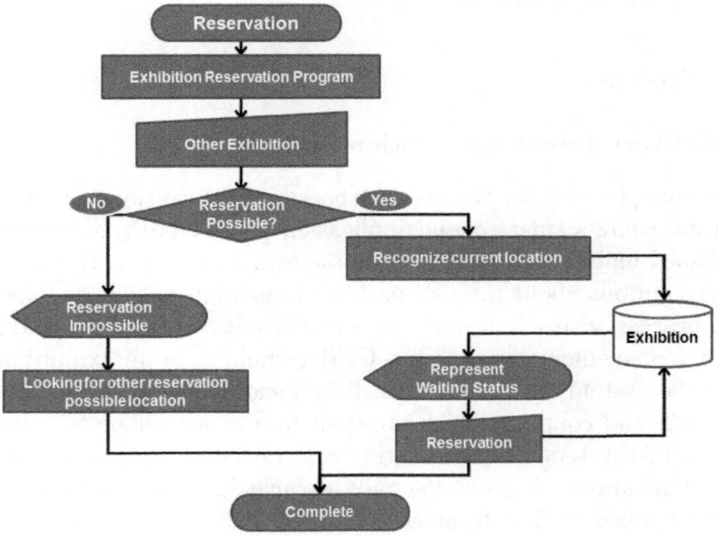

Fig. 8. Reservation Flow-Chart

In particular, a reservation procedure can be processed through the reservation system which is consist of printing waiting time system, telecommunication system, and GPS built in smart-phone and application programs. We define a reservation flow-chart as shown in Figure 8. This technique is expected to

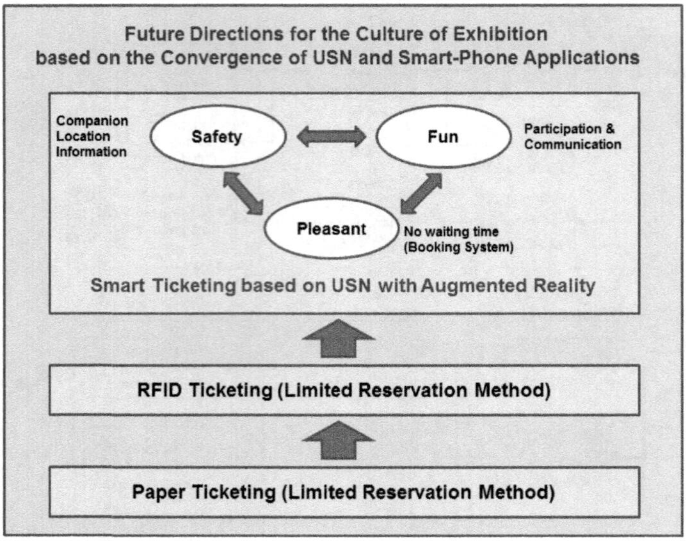

Fig. 9. Expectation of the Embedded Integration Prototyping System

give lots help to commercialize network based reservation system and operating method using a smart-phone and USN.

5 Conclusion

5.1 A Network Based Reservation System

The prototyping is made for the network based reservation system and the operating method using a smart phone application based on augmented reality and the established mobile telecommunication network technique. In this paper, we show some solutions about the real problem in exhibition such as a location information process, visitor's or audience's movement management, and real time reservation management by applying U2M technique to an exhibition service. Moreover, the system that can be used for location based service is designed based on GPS and compass which are built in a smart-phone by adapting the integrated whole system into the existing reservation method of the limited specific zone. This approach gives not only a convenience reservation system but also, can be applied to time to market efficiently.

5.2 Expected Effect

Through providing the location recognition service (e.g., LBS) [7], [8] based on the differentiated USN based U-ticket, the expected effect can be expected as shown in Figure 9. For instance, the visitor's or audience's satisfaction and safety is maximized and the waiting time can be reduced because of real time reservation system. In addition, the operation of the reservation system efficiency can be increased because of establishing the best operating back up service and system. Moreover, some limited problems caused by a paper ticket or a simple RFID ticket can be solved through established various services. Then, we can expect increasing fast processing tasks and visitor's or audience's reliability for the reservation system. Therefore, the prototyping for the network based reservation system and the method of operating can be had the expected effect about making and expanding USN business model using developed service and device.

Acknowledgments. This work was supported by the DGIST R&D Program of the Ministry of Education, Science and Technology of Korea (11-BD-01), the R&D program of the YEOSU EXPO center, the ITRC R&D program of the Sunmoon University, and the the MKE(The Ministry of Knowledge Economy) Korea under the ITRC(Information Technology Research Center) support program supervised by the NIPA(National IT Industry Promotion Agency)(NIPA-2011-C1090-1131-0004).

References

1. Gartner Group, Worldwide Mobile Device Sales to End Users Reached 1.6 Billion Units in 2010; Smartphone Sales Grew 72 Percent in 2010, `www.gartner.com/it/page.jsp?id=1540314` (February 2011)
2. Kubber, A.: Location based Services. Wiley and Sons (2005)
3. Vaughan-Nichols, S.J.: Will Mobile Computing's Future Be Location? IEEE Computer (2009)
4. Lee, J.H., Jin, A.Y., Park, Y.H.: Next-generation smartphones Technology Trend Analysis. In: KIPS Conference, vol. 18(1) (2011)
5. Azuma, R.: A Survey of Augmented Reality Presence: Teleoperators and Virtual Environments, pp. 355–385 (August 1997)
6. Harrison, A., Ollila, M.: UMAR: Ubiquitous Mobile Augmented Reality. In: The Proc. of the 3rd Intl. Conf. on Mobile and Ubiquitous Multimedia, New York, USA, pp. 41–45 (2004)
7. Jung, G.M., Choi, A.S.: Smart-Phone based LBS Technology Trend Analysis. TTA Journal 33 (2010)
8. Hooi, T.C.: An Integrated GIS Database Server for Malaysian Mapping, Cadastral and Location-Based Systems (LBS). In: WRI World Congress on Computer Science and Information Engineering, Los Angels, USA, pp. 162–167 (2009)

Optimization Conditions of OCSVM for Erroneous GPS Data Filtering

Woojoong Kim and Ha Yoon Song*

Department of Computer Engineering, Hongik University, Seoul, Korea
veritaswjkim@gmail.com, hayoon@hongik.ac.kr

Abstract. The topics on human mobility model have long been researched by various academic and industrial fields. It has been proven that human mobility has specific patterns and can be predicted up to the probability of 93%, since the mobility of a person cannot be random while peoples have their own frequent visiting places such as home, office, haunt restaurants, and so on. The positioning data of a human can be obtained by GPS or similar positioning system, however, it contains inherited environmental errors. In this paper we will present filtering method of erroneous GPS data of human mobility. With the use of One Class Support Vector Machine (OCSVM), we adapted Radial Basis Function (RBF) as kernel function. Experimental values of the critical parameter γ for RBF has been found for optimal filtering.

Keywords: Human Mobility, Global Positioning System, One Class Support Vector Machine, Radial Basis Function, Parameter Optimization.

1 Introduction

The resent advances of mobile devices enable various location based services over human mobility, especially the introduction of smart phone with GPS or other positioning equipment. However these positioning data have error according to its operational environment. In such cases, many of applications require filtering of such erroneous positioning data. As we experienced by our experiments, more than 4% of positioning data were erroneous by use of smart phones. This simple experiment was done by use of smart phone app over Samsung Galaxy Tab and it internally uses the position of 3G base station. Another aspect of location based research is regarding the human mobility model. Several interesting results were drawn from psychologist. The results contain route selection of a person [1], transportation method selection [2][3][4], which denotes psychological factors are major factor of human mobility as well as functionality factors of human mobility [6]. Also habits of humans are major factors such as commuting habits

* This research was supported by Basic Science Research Program through the National Research Foundation of Korea(NRF) funded by the Ministry of Education, Science and Technology(No. 2011-0025875).

T.-h. Kim et al. (Eds.): MulGraB 2011, Part II, CCIS 263, pp. 62–70, 2011.

concerned with transportation methods [7]. Another research field of complex system physics showed that up to 93% of human mobility can be predicted since peoples avoid the random selection of next destination instead selects their place frequented and their route frequented [5]. On the result of past research results, it is now possible to obtain positioning data of a human mobility pattern with GPS or other positioning systems as shown in figures 1 and 2. The sets of positioning data will be a basis for human mobility model construction. In this paper, we will propose a filtering technique which filters erroneous positioning data with the use of OCSVM [8]. The RBF of OCSVM has a specific parameter called γ and it affects a trade-off between class size and density. The key point of using OCSVM is to figure out the appropriate range of γ. With the various sets of positioning data, we conducted experiments for optimal parameter value of RBF and then presented our experimental results. In section 2 we summarizes the OCSVM, and the following section 3 shows our technique for filtering, basic experiments for calibration. Section 4 shows our experimental results and the results will be discussed in section 5. We will finalize this paper in section 6.

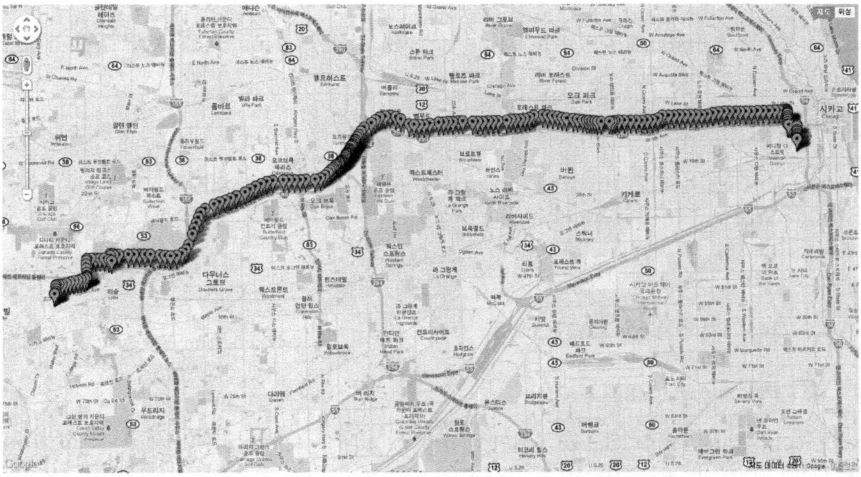

Fig. 1. A Trail of GPS Positioning Data Set over Illinois, USA

2 One Class Support Vector Machine

We will discuss of OCSVM and its kernel function, RBF. OCSVM was proposed in 2001 and it filters input data into two categories: class members and others. For a set of data with the cardinality of N,

$$X_1, X_2, \ldots, X_n \in \aleph, n \in N$$

denotes members of the data set. These data elements will be placed into *Feature Space* in higher dimension than the dimension of data elements. Thus we can lead an optimality problem which minimizes the size of *Hyper Sphere* with data

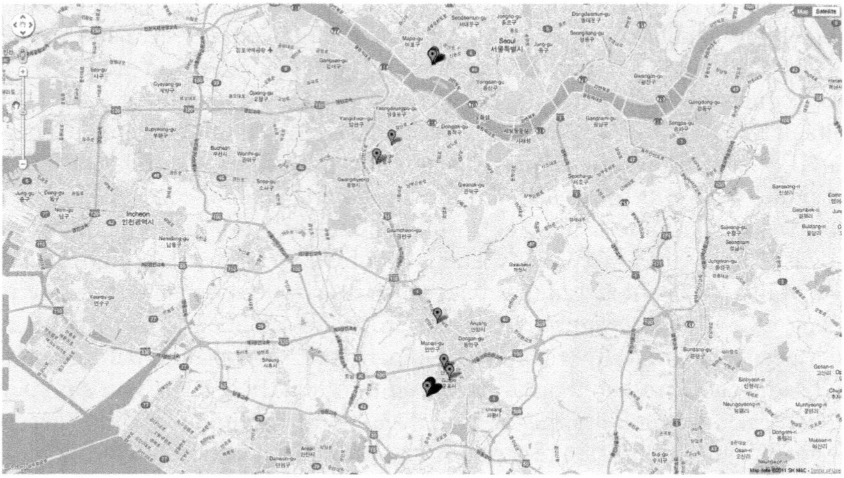

Fig. 2. A Trail of 3GBS Positioning Data Set over Seoul, Korea

elements. We must use a kernel function in order to increase the dimension as Radial Basis Function shown in equation 1.

$$\Phi(u, v) = e^{(-\gamma \times |u-v|)} \tag{1}$$

where u and v are coordinates of data elements on the space and $|u - v|$ stands for their Norm value. Here comes the parameter value of RBF, γ, which is user controllable for their specific use.

3 Experimental Process

3.1 Filtering Algorithm

We basically use sets of GPS data, representing a mobility trail of a human. The GPS data is usually in a form of $< latitude, longitude, time, id >$ where id is identification of a set. An example of GPS data sets can be found in [11], and we use these sets for our filtering experiments. Another positioning data set based on 3G base station information also has the same form in positioning data. This positioning data set obtained by the authors will be also used for primary filtering experiments.

With the every two consecutive pair $< latitude_2, longitude_2, time_2, id >$ and $< latitude_1, longitude_1, time_1, id >$ in data set, we can calculate the difference of latitude and longitude as shown in equations 2 and 3.

$$\Delta Latitude = \frac{Latitude_2 - Latitude_1}{t_2 - t_1} \tag{2}$$

$$\Delta Longitude = \frac{Longitude_2 - Longitude_1}{t_2 - t_1} \tag{3}$$

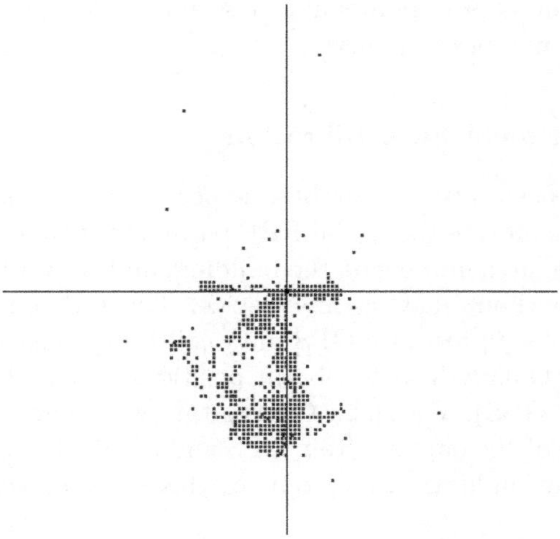

Fig. 3. A Typical Representation of Data Set

Then we can get a coordinate tuple of

$$(\Delta Latitude, \Delta Longitude) \tag{4}$$

which is a very small value and normalized by multiplying constant 300,000. Those set of tuples, named as *points*, can be drawn as in figure 3.

Set of data from figure 3 will be used as input for OCSVM with various RBF parameters. We call the resulting values as *pixels* which compose set of total class. Also, number of points in a class, number of total points, and number of stable points are notable parts of results. The stable points of human mobility are tuples with value of $< 0, 0 >$, while other tuples will be regarded as mobile points. The filtering process are divided into three categories like the followings:

- Filtering only with stable points: the RBF parameter with stable points will be bases for other case.
- Filtering only with mobile points: the number of mobile points are dominating and will greatly affect the RBF parameter value.
- Filtering with both stable and mobile points: the ultimate experiments.

Several resulting values can be drawn from the result of filtering process, such as size, density of cluster, hit rate of points. Density can be drawn from

$$Density = \frac{n(P_{Class})}{n(ClassSize)} \tag{5}$$

where $n(P_{Class})$ is number of points in a class and $n(ClassSize)$ is number of pixels in a class.

And the hit rate of class can be defined as

$$HitRate = \frac{n(P_{Class})}{n(P_{Total})} \tag{6}$$

where $n(P_{Class})$ is number of points in a class and $n(P_{Total})$ is number of points as inputs, i.e. total number of points.

3.2 Basic Experiment for Calibration

We experienced a basic test as our base experiment to check the positioning data accuracy and calibrate the initial RBF parameter value. We fix positioning devices both outside area and inside the building, and collected positioning data for several hours without moving any device. The first positioning device is Garmin GPSMAP62s [9] for pure GPS data collecting. The second positioning device is Samsung Galaxy Tab to obtain positioning data from its connected 3G base stations (3GBS). We guess Galaxy tab will show more error in both situation, and both of the data set from GPS and 3GBS shows positioning error, especially inside the building. The result of this basic experiment is listed in table 1.

The variance in position data is regarded as errors and distance of error can be calculated form the position data. As we guessed, 3GBS shows larger error rate, larger error in distance, larger maximum error distance, and bigger standard deviation in error distance. Due to the producer's policy of Garmin GPSMAP62s, which estimates the user's location upon past velocity while it lost the GPS signal, it shows drastic error value inside the building. Thus we think the GPS inside a building cannot be a meaningful data. GPS data from outside area is very accurate enough to precise localization and even the maximum error distance is in a reasonable range of 52 meters. We concluded that the following experiments with real human mobility data will be based on the positioning data sets of GPS and 3GBS from outside area. The value range of RBF parameter (γ) shown in table 1 will be considered as a core parameter value for further experiments.

Table 1. Result of Base Experiments

Building	*3G Base Station GPS*		*GPS*	
Inside	n(Data Point)	893	n(Data Point)	2186
	n(Error Point)	434	n(Error Point)	939
	Error Rate	48.6%	Error Rate	43.0%
	E[Error Dist]	52.5530m	E[Error Dist]	43.5506m
	Max(Error Dist)	156.7578m	Max(Error Dist)	10769.72m
	$\sigma_{ErrorDist}$	32.6859m	$\sigma_{ErrorDist}$	370.6034m
	Range of γ	$5 \times 10^{-3} \sim 5 \times 10^{-6}$	Range of γ	$5 \times 10^{-3} \sim 5 \times 10^{-5}$
Outside	n(Data Point)	331	n(Data Point)	1690
	n(Error Point)	122	n(Error Point)	208
	Error Rate	36.9%	Error Rate	12.3%
	E[Error Dist]	52.6618m	E[Error Dist]	4.4498m
	Max(Error Dist)	206.3526m	Max(Error Dist)	51.7789m
	$\sigma_{ErrorDist}$	23.5953m	$\sigma_{ErrorDist}$	7.1696m
	Range of γ	$5 \times 10^{-3} \sim 5 \times 10^{-5}$	Range of γ	$5 \times 10^{-3} \sim 5 \times 10^{-5}$

4 Experimental Results

We use three sets of data set for our experiments.

- GPS-Illinois: GPS data over Illinois, USA collected in (2006.MAY.30∼2006.MAY.31) as shown in [11].
- 3GBS: 3G base station positioning data over Metropolitan Seoul Area, Korea voluntarily collected in (2011.JUN.03∼2011.JUN.06) by one author of this paper.
- GPS-Seoul: GPS data over Metropolitan Seoul Area, Korea voluntarily collected in (2011.JUL.18∼2011.JUL.26) by a researcher.

Figures 4, 6, 8 shows the result for GPS-Illinois data set. The data legends of (S) denotes result for stable points only, (M) denotes results for mobile points only and (M+S) denotes for total points. As well figures 5, 7, 9 shows similar results for the 3GBS data set. Due to the page limit, the result of GPS-Seoul data set cannot be figured here however the results are significantly the same to those of GPS-Illinois.

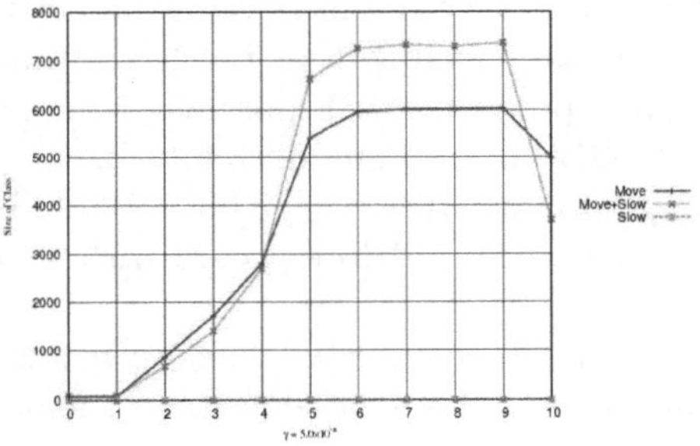

Fig. 4. Size of Class over GPS data

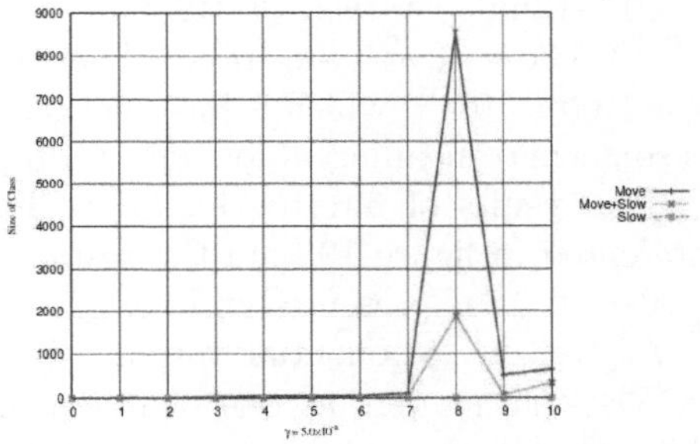

Fig. 5. Size of Class over 3GBS data

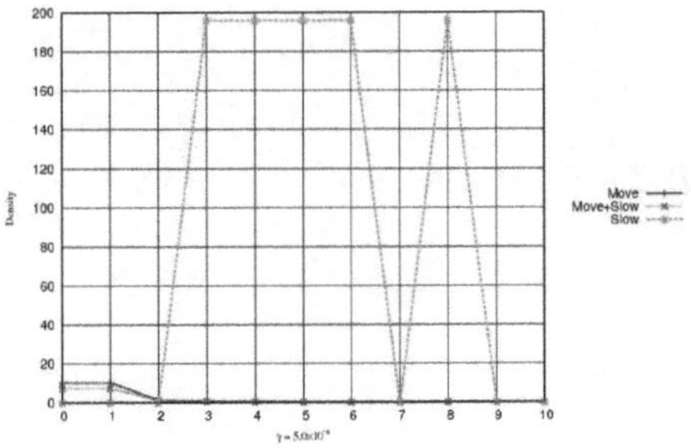

Fig. 6. Density of Class over GPS data

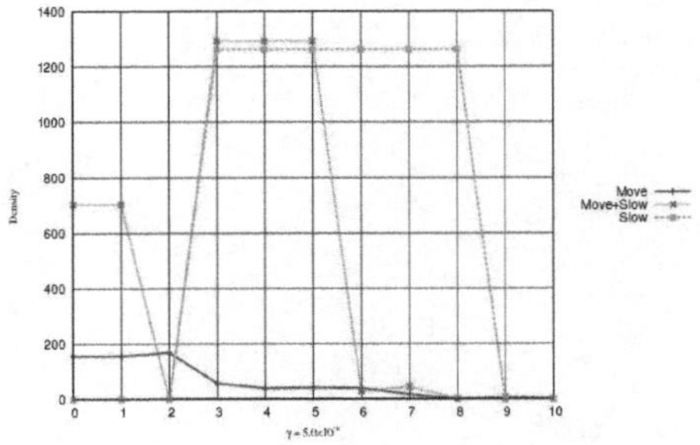

Fig. 7. Density of Class over 3GBS data

5 Analysis of Results

As the numerical results shows in section 3, we found the value of γ parameter in $(0, 5.00 \times 10^{-01}]$ is meaningless because of the nature of RBF as shown in

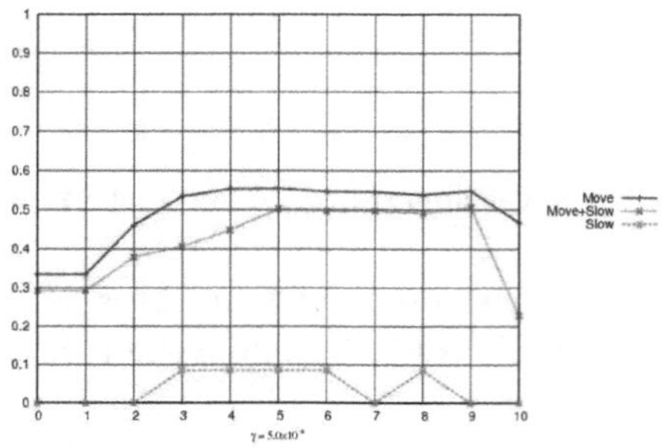

Fig. 8. Hit Rate of Class over GPS data

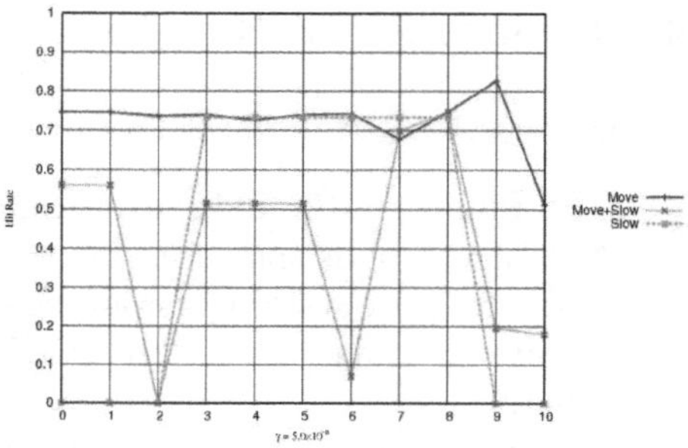

Fig. 9. Hit Rate of Class over 3GBS data

equation 1. The parameter value in $[5.00 \times 10^{-05}, 5.00 \times 10^{-09}]$ are stable in 30th May set of GPS-Illinois data sets with both Mobile data and Mobile+Stable data. The same results can be applied to the data set on 31st of May. While the Stable data from GPS-Illinois set shows RBF parameter value in $[5.00 \times 10^{-03}, 5.00 \times 10^{-06}]$. The range of γ for GPS-Seoul data set is very similar to that of GPS-Illinois. As well, 3GBS data set shows that the parameter value in $[5.00 \times 10^{-03}, 5.00 \times 10^{-05}]$ are stable. Therefore, we can conclude that the RBF value $\gamma = 5.00 \times 10^{-05}$, which is intersection of all appropriate RBF parameter range, is somewhat meaningful for both GPS and 3GBS positioning data filtering.

The results of filtering for GPS-Illinois data set with $\gamma = 5.00 \times 10^{-05}$ is presented in figure 10, and the results of filtering for 3GBS data set with $\gamma = 5.00 \times 10^{-05}$ is presented in figure 11.

As well as exponential variance in γ values, we conducted linear variance in RBF parameters as one of minor experiments. We experienced very small difference in this linear case, and only trade-offs between class size and class

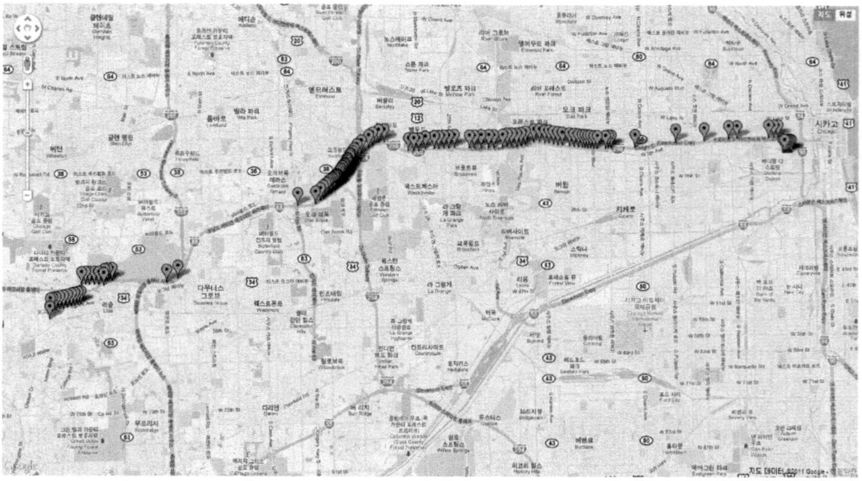

Fig. 10. Mapping of Filtered Positioning Data from GPS-Illinois Positioning Data Set

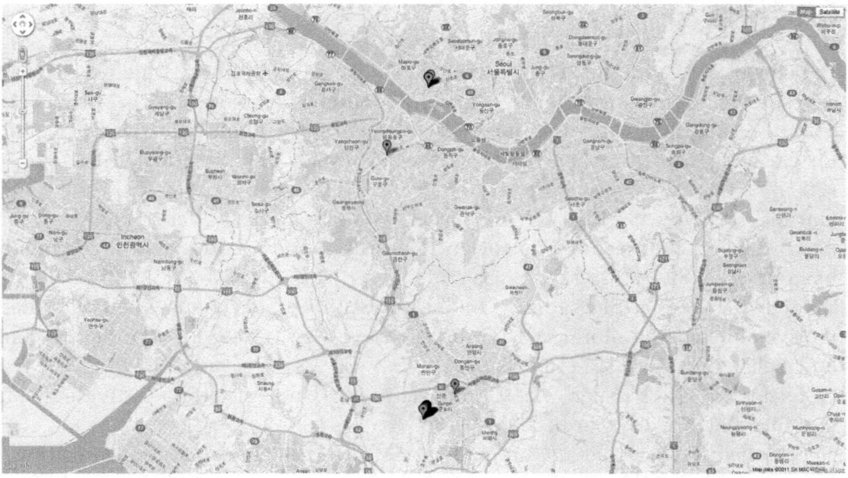

Fig. 11. Mapping of Filtered Positioning Data from 3GBS Data Set

density can be found. Thus we will not show detailed result of minor experiment in this paper. We also experienced stability in class size and number of class members with RBF parameters over than $\gamma = 5.00 \times 10^{+01}$, where the class size is 120 and 1176 data in the class.

6 Conclusion and Future Research

For the filtering purpose of erroneous positioning data, we used OCSVM and found some adequate results. We conducted basic experiment both in 3GBS and GPS positioning data, and found 3GBS data shows more error in position.

Comparing figure 1 and figure 10, filtering-out of positioning data can be visualized. One of the problems is that our filtering algorithm filters out correct position data. Our next research topic is to overcome those over-filtered data. Two simple directions can be suggested. The first one is a simple interpolation, which just inserts missing data by mathematical interpolation over time. The second one is more complicated version of iterative OCSVM filtering. The filtered data set can be re-filtered by OCSVM iteratively so that more data would be filtered-in. Otherwise, simple clustering algorithm will be used based on the data set only in the class, and the clustered can be extended in such a way to include possibly-correct positioning data.

We hope our research can be a clue to human mobility modeling. For example, we are now doing a research on human mobility modeling based on real positioning data with use of clustering technique. A student's real mobility data is under processing to figure out the daily mobility pattern of the student [12].

References

1. Bailenson, J.N., Shum, M.S., Uttal, D.H.: Road climbing: Principles governing asymmetric route choice on maps. Environmental Psychology 18(3), 251–264 (1998)
2. Steg, L.: Car use: Lust and must. Instrumental, symbolic and affective motives for car use. Transportation Research Part A: Policy and Practice 39(2-3), 147–162 (2005)
3. Garling, T., Fujii, S., Boe, O.: Empirical tests of a model of determinants of script-based driving choice. Transportation Research Part F: Traffic Psychology and Behaviour 4(2), 89–102 (2001)
4. Steg, L., Vlek, C., Slotegraaf, G.: Instrumental-reasoned and symbolic affective motives for using a motor car. Transportation research part F: Traffic psychology and behaviour 4(3), 151–169 (2001)
5. Gonzalez, M.C., Hidalgo, A., Barabasi, A.-L.: Understanding individual human mobility patterns: Nature (2008)
6. Verplanken, B., Aarts, K., Knippenberg, A.V.: Habit, information acquisition, and the process of making travel mode choice. European Journal of Social Psychology 27(5), 539–560 (1997)
7. Fujii, S., Garling, T.: Development of script-based travel mode choice after forced change. Transportation Research Part F: Traffic Psychology and Behaviour 6(2), 117–124 (2003)
8. Schlkopf, B., Platt, J., Shawe-Taylor, J., Smola, A.J., Williamson, R.C.: Estimating the support of a high-dimensional distribution. Neural Computation 13, 1443–1471 (2001)
9. Garmin GPSMAP62s, `https://buy.garmin.com/shop/shop.do?pID=63801`
10. Kim, W., Song, H.Y.: A Study on Novelty Detection of GPS Data Using Human Mobility and OCSVM(One-class SVM). In: Proceedings of the Korea Information Processing Society Conference, pp. 1060–1063 (2011)
11. GPS Real Trajectory, University of Illinois at Chicago, `http://www.cs.uic.edu/~boxu/mp2p/gps_data.html`
12. Kim, H., Song, H.Y.: Daily Life Mobility of A Student: From Position Data to Human Mobility Model through Expectation Maximization Clustering. Will be Presented in the Proceedings of MULGRAB (2011)

An Enhanced Dynamic Signature Verification System for the Latest Smart-Phones*

Jin-whan Kim

Dept. of Computer Engineering, Youngsan University
San 150 Junam-dong, Yangsan, Gyungnam, 626-790 Korea
kjw@ysu.ac.kr

Abstract. We propose an algorithm for dynamic signature verification using the latest Smart-phones such as iPhone, android phone and MS windows phone. Also, we suggest simple signature patterns, the performance of a dynamic signature verification system, which determine the authentication of signatures by comparing and analyzing various dynamic data such as shape of the signature, writing speed, slant of shape, and the order and number of strokes for personal signatures for the smart-phones. In ubiquitous society, the smart-phone will be very important portable device for the mankind.

Keywords: Dynamic Signature, Verification, Biometric Authentication, Smart-phone, security, ubiquitous.

1 Introduction

Authentication security becomes a more important problem with the increasing use of the computer network, wired/wireless Internet and Smart-phones. The biometrics technology using physical and behavioral characteristics of a person is an important issue for user authentication nowadays. Many different types of human biometrics technologies such as fingerprint, face, iris, vein, DNA, brain wave, palm, voice, dynamic signature, etc. have been studied widely but remain unsuccessful because they do not meet social demands. Recently, however, many of these technologies have been actively revived and researchers have developed new products in various commercial fields. The dynamic signature verification technology is intended to verify the identity of the signer by calculating his writing manner, speed, angle, and the number of strokes, order, the down/up movement of the pen when the signer inputs his signature with an electronic pen for his authentication [1,2.3]. Then the signature verification system collects the various feature information mentioned above and compares it with an original and simultaneously analyzes it to decide whether the signature is a forgery or not. The prospect of signature verification technology is promising and its use will be wide spread in terms of economy, security, practicality, stability and convenience for the various Smart-phones.

* This thesis was supported by the research funding of Youngsan University.

T.-h. Kim et al. (Eds.): MulGraB 2011, Part II, CCIS 263, pp. 71–77, 2011.

Expanded use of computer for business in most areas makes computer related crimes unavoidable. To reduce such crimes, we have researched handwriting signature security for the wireless Internet and Smart-phone market.

Fig. 1. Smart-phones

In this paper, we describe how this signature security system works when the signer signs his signature with the touch pen of Smart-phones in Fig. 1. Using not only signature shape but also the various information from signer's writing speed, angles, strokes, etc., this system decides whether the signature is a forgery or not.

This technology can be applied to various security fields for electronic transactions, Internet banking systems, home trading systems, computer files, servers and networks against computer crimes as well as a security of access and contents in Smart-phone.

2 Dynamic Signature Verification System

Dynamic signature is to sign your electronic signature by using an input device such as an electronic pen or a digitizer. The system obtains the dynamic information of the signature such as writing order, time consumption and pressure on the pen when the signer signs [4,5]. This case we call dynamic (on-line) signature verification. Fig. 2 shows the diagram of a typical dynamic signature verification system (DSVS). DSVS, like all other biometric verification systems, involves two processing modes: registering and verifying. In the registering mode include three phases: training, testing and saving. In the training, the user provides signature samples that are used to construct a template (or prototype feature vector) representing some distinctive characteristic of his signature. In the testing, the user provides a new signature to judge authenticity of the presented sample and choose his own threshold security level for him. The performance of a verification system is generally evaluated with Type I and Type II error rates. The Type I error rates, or False Rejection Rate (FAR), measures the number of genuine signatures classified as forgeries as a function of the classification threshold. The Type II error rate, or False Acceptance Rate (FAR), evaluates the number of false signatures classified as real ones as a function of the classification threshold. The equal error rate (EER), that is the error rate at which the percentage of false accepts equals the percentage of false rejects, provides an estimate of the statistical performance of the algorithm, i.e., it provides an estimate of its generalization error.

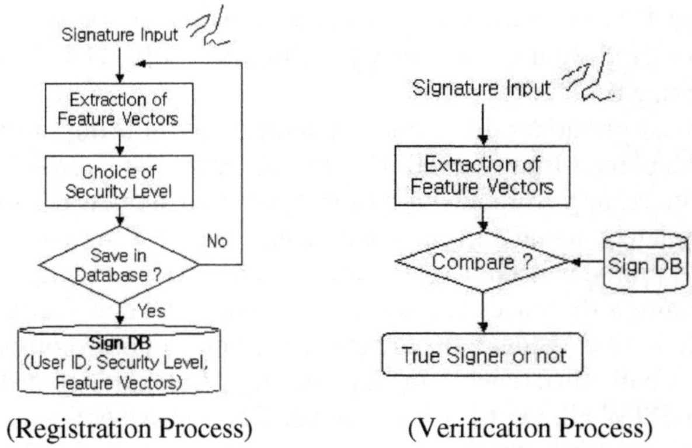

Fig. 2. Dynamic Signature Verification System

To describe the on-line system we can classify it into several processes. To compare a true signature with a forgery, the variation range of each signature has to be reduced and the feature points are subtracted. To verify an authentic signature the feature information must be registered. To calculate the degree of similarity, a comparing process will be used. To verify a true signature, a decision process will be needed.

3 Proposed Feature Extraction and Comparison

We introduce useful feature points in our on-line signature verification system. Finding out the best method to calculate the degree of similarity is very important. The previous approach for that is to select and arrange distinctive points [6]. For the best signature verification, it is important to reduce the range of variation of the true signature and to extend distinctiveness between the true and forgeries. Assigning the adequate weight for each feature is another important point [7,8].

Our system primarily uses directions and absolute distances (Fig. 3) between two points for the pen down/up strokes.

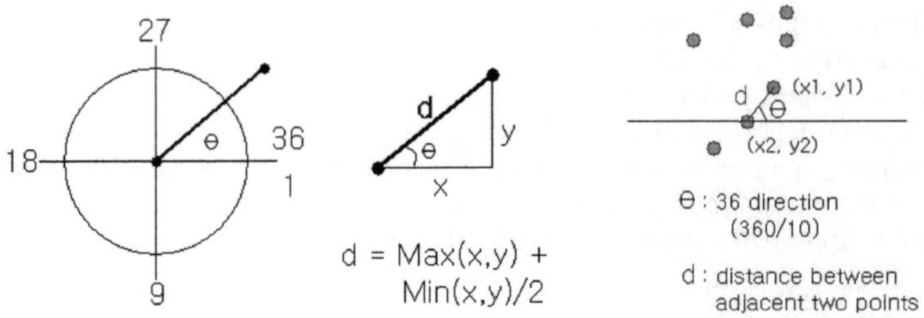

Fig. 3. Signature features of direction and distance

The feature vectors of pen down movement have values of 1 to 36 directions. And the feature vectors of pen up movement have values of 91 to 126 directions. But, distances have absolute length of value between two points as Fig. 4. All distances are defined less than 128. So, these directions and distances can be stored in byte strings of small memory. And we use 'd=Max(x,y)+Min(x,y)' instead of 'd=SQRT(x^2+y^2)' to speed up processing time.

One of the most important difficulties in authentication using on-line signatures is the choice of the comparison method. On-line signatures are given by a sequence of points sorted with respect to acquisition time. Since two signatures of the same person cannot be completely identical, we must make use of a measure that takes into account this variability. Indeed, two signatures cannot have exactly the same timing, besides these timing differences are not linear. Dynamic Time Warping (DTW) is an interesting tool; it is a method that realizes a point-to-point correspondence. It is insensitive to small differences in the timing. Calculation distances between signatures with DTW allows to achieve a verification system more flexible, more efficient and more adaptive than the systems based on neural networks or Hidden Markov Models, as the training phase can be incremental. This aspect is very important when we envisage elaborate authentication method that takes into account the evolution of the signature along the years. Below expression and pseudo codes are our modified DTW and algorithm.

[Pseudo codes of modified DP matching algorithm]

```
#define INIT_SUMM 100000 /* arbitrary large number∞ */
#define MAX_CPNT 500/* max number of feature vectors */
BYTE iv[MAX_CPNT], rv[MAX_CPNT]; /* feature vectors of two signatures */
int ifp, rfp; /* number of feature vectors for two signatures */
int dp_sum1[MAX_CPNT], dp_sum2[MAX_CPNT];
int *sum1, *sum2; /* temporary arrays to store the DTW Matching results */
int DP_result;
for(int i=1; i<rfp; i++)
{
 int minimum;
 minimum = INIT_SUMM;
  if ( i%2 != 0 ) { sum1 = dp_sum1; sum2= dp_sum2; }
  else { sum1 = dp_sum2; sum2 = dp_sum1; }
  for(int j=1; j<ifp; j++)
  {
     WORD diff, hori, vert, center;
     diff=cost(iv[pos_y], rv[pos_x]);
     hori=sum1[pos_y] + diff + (W1);
     vert=sum2[pos_y-1] + diff + (W2);
     center=sum1[pos_y-1] + diff+ (W2);
     sum2[pos_y] = min(hori, center, vert); /* choose minimum value of three values */
     DP_result = sum2[pos_y-1] /(i+j);
     if(minimum > DP_result) minimum = DP_result;
  }
 sum1[0]=INIT_SUMM;
 sum2[0]=INIT_SUMM;
}
minimum ➔  final G(n,m)
```

W1 is a weight value adopted in case horizontal path or vertical path, and w2 is a weight value adopted in case orthogonal path. To calculate the DTW distance G(A,B) for the two sequences A = (a[1], a[2], ..., a[n]) and B = (b[1], b[2], ..., b[m]), we can first construct an n-by-m matrix, then, we find a path in the matrix which starts from cell (1, 1) to cell (n,m) so that the average cumulative cost along the path is minimized.

4 Proposed Simple Signature Patterns for the Smart-Phones

Most of smart-phones have touch panel as input device to input some instructions of user. Touch panels are largely divided into capacitive touch and pressure touch. Nowadays, capacitive touch panels using finger are widely used because of various merits such as convenience and fast reaction. But finger action is not elaborate. So, we could recommend simple signature patterns.

As shown in Fig. 4, proposed comparison algorithm precisely calculates minute changes between two patterns according to the simplicity as well as complexity of the signature's patterns.

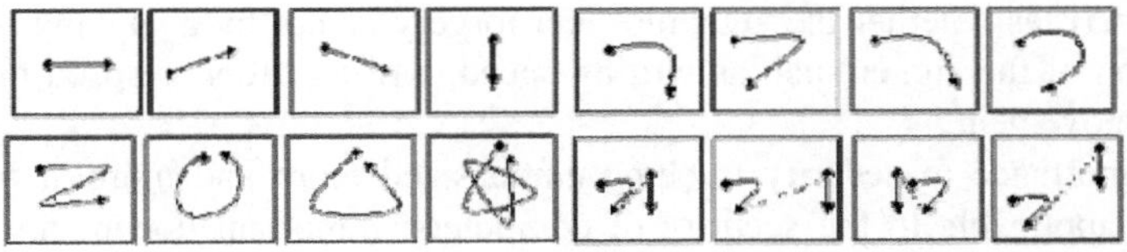

Fig. 4. Simple signature patterns

5 System Performance

The characteristics of our system are as follows:

(1) Error rate is low and the function is robust for weather, temperature, physical conditions and outside noises.
(2) Dynamic Time Warping (DTW), a well-known and excellent pattern-matching algorithm has been modified and applied to this system.
(3) Database for the signature is very small. It needs only 250bytes of memory to register the feature information of a signer.
(4) Processing time must be fast for the verification. In the general DTW system, it is good to check similarities between patterns, but its defect is an increase in processing time because of the computational complexity of the data to be processed. In our system, however, we compress the data and the structure is well designed so that verification is processed within 0.01 second.
(5) Security must be excellent. On the recommendation of the feedback system, the signer can choose from security levels of seven levels according to the ability of the signer.
(6) The size of the signature engine is small. The size of our engine is 6KB for WinCE and JAVA so our system can be used in small, handy devices like smart-phones.

(7) Like changing PIN numbers and passwords, the signer can change his signature if he wants.
(8) Using dynamic information makes hacking nearly impossible.
(9) Accuracy rate (acceptance rate for true signers and rejection rate for forgeries) is very high
(10)The signature security system using a smart-phone is economical and simple because you can install signature verification software without purchasing any signature input devices.
(11)The signer's training and efforts are needed for the higher security levels of the signature system.

6 Conclusion

The on-line (dynamic) signature verification system tells true signatures from forged ones. While the signer input his signature with an input device such as an electronic pen, our system analyzes and extracts feature information from the dynamic signature data and verifies whether the signature is a forgery or not by analyzing the dynamic information of the signer such as writing speed, writing order, elapsed time and pen up/down movement.

The importance of security is being emphasized more and more at present. Our system is applicable to the security of computers, important documents, the access restriction of network servers, on-line shopping, credit cards, military secrets, national administrative security, internet banking, cyber trading, admittance to buildings, personal approval and so on. This dynamic signature verification technology for the security of smart-phones has been recognized as a highly valued, useful and efficient technology for ubiquitous world.

References

1. Kim, J.W., Kim, G.B., Cho, J.H.: A Study on an Advanced Evaluation Method for Dynamic Signature Verification System. International Journal of Maritime Information and Communication Sciences, 140–144 (2010)
2. Kim, J.W., Cho, H.G., Cha, E.-Y.: A Study on Enhanced Dynamic Signature Verification for the Embedded System. In: De Gregorio, M., Di Maio, V., Frucci, M., Musio, C. (eds.) BVAI 2005. LNCS, vol. 3704, pp. 436–446. Springer, Heidelberg (2005)
3. Kim, J.W., Cho, H.G., Cha, E.Y.: A Study on the Dynamic Signature Verification System. International Journal of Fuzzy Logic and Intelligent System 4(3), 271–276 (2004)
4. Lei, H., Govindaraju, V.: A Study on the Consistency of Features for on-line Signature Verification. In: Fred, A., Caelli, T.M., Duin, R.P.W., Campilho, A.C., de Ridder, D. (eds.) SSPR&SPR 2004. LNCS, vol. 3138, pp. 444–451. Springer, Heidelberg (2004)
5. Wirotius, M., Ramel, J.-Y., Vincent, N.: Selection of Points for On-Line Signature Comparison. In: Ninth International Workshop on Frontiers in Handwriting Recognition (IWFHR 2004), pp. 503–508 (October 2004)

6. Lei, H., Palla, S., Govindaraju, V.: ER^2: An Intuitive Similarity Measure for On-Line Signature Verification. In: Ninth International Workshop on Frontiers in Handwriting Recognition (IWFHR 2004), pp. 191–195 (October 2004)
7. Schimke, S., Vielhauer, C., Dittmann, J.: Using Adapted Levenshtein Distance for On-Line Signature Authentication. In: 17th International Conference on Pattern Recognition (ICPR 2004), vol. 2, pp. 931–934 (August 2004)
8. Rioja, F.R., Miyatake, M.N., Meana, H.P., Toscano, K.: Dynamics features Extraction for On-Line Signature verification. In: 14th International Conference on Electronics, Communications and Computers, p. 156 (February 2004)

Illumination Invariant Motion Estimation and Segmentation

Yeonho Kim[1] and Sooyeong Yi[2,*]

[1] Samsung Advanced Institute of Technology, Korea
ynho.kim@gmail.com
[2] Seoul National University of Science and Technology, Korea
suylee@seoultech.ac.kr

Abstract. Extracting moving objects from their background or partitioning them have been one of the most prerequisite tasks for various computer vision applications such as surveillance, tracking, human machine interface, etc. Though many previous approaches have been working in a certain level, still they are not robust under various unexpected situation such as large illumination change. In this paper, we propose a motion segmentation method based on our robust illumination invariant optical flow estimation. We present the superiority of our motion estimation method with synthesized images and improved segmentation results with real images.

Keywords: Motion estimation, Optical flow, Segmentation, Illumination invariant.

1 Introduction

Motion based image segmentation algorithms seek to partition an image into regions on the basis of the properties of the motions experienced by the pixels. That a motion property can serve as a rich basis for grouping pixels together is intuitively obvious and has been known so in the research community for a long time [1]. It has also been known for a long time that adding motion as a criterion for segmentation can alleviate some of the shortcomings of the more traditional algorithms that try to segment an image on the basis of static attributes such as intensity, edge, color, texture, etc. However, unfortunately, estimating motion parameters from a sequence of images is still not easy though lots of research have been done in this area [2]. This makes motion-based segmentation of images double difficult.

The simplest approach of segmenting moving objects in an image sequence is by taking differences of consecutive images in a video sequence [3]. Though such differencing provides information about the locations of moving pixels and the gross motions associated with a region, it does not estimate motions precisely enough so that other motion estimation technique such as optical flow method could be

* Corresponding author.

T.-h. Kim et al. (Eds.): MulGraB 2011, Part II, CCIS 263, pp. 78–87, 2011.

computed. Additionally, the technique is susceptible to false alarms caused by sensitivity drifts, sudden illumination changes, etc. Nonetheless, because of its simplicity and speed, this technique is suitable for many practical applications where only a rough sense of the motions is needed; one such application is the surveillance from a fixed camera monitoring an ATM.

For more precise motion based segmentation, in most cases one must resort to multiple motion estimation. Obviously, if a multiple-motions estimator is doing a good job, it would be easy to group the pixels together on the basis of the different motions corresponding to the different objects. Mitiche [4] has classified the more advanced techniques (that is, techniques more advanced than the differencing method and possibly using multiple motion estimation) for motion based segmentation into two groups: border placement scheme and region extraction scheme. While a border placement scheme looks for motion boundaries between regions that have different motion properties, a region extraction scheme looks for regions that maximize some motion related homogeneity criterion. Though this classification is useful to understand basic concepts to classify different motion segmentation methods, it does not include recent approaches such as methods that estimate motion and carry out segmentation simultaneously.

Different classifications that include these more recent methods and that also focus on optical flow based methods that we are particularly interested in have been proposed by several authors recently [5][6][7]. Although these authors may use different labels for the different categories of approaches, we believe that the suggested categories fall into the three: simultaneous approaches, top-down approaches, and bottom-up approaches. The top-down approaches commonly start from the optical flow that is estimated globally from a sequence of images. Then the optical flow field is partitioned into several regions that have similar motion properties in each region using a segmentation method [8][9][10]. While in the top-down approaches, the optical flows once estimated are not updated, in the simultaneous approaches the optical flows are updated in an iterative framework and simultaneously the image is segmented based on the uniformity of optical flows. The optical flow calculations and motion-based segmentations carried out using the EM (Expectation Maximization) framework can be considered to belong to the simultaneous approaches category [11][12][13].

One of the major problems of the top-down and simultaneous approaches is the detection of incorrect motion boundaries when multiple motions are present. In order to overcome this problem, bottom-up approaches use potential motion boundaries that in most cases correspond to the boundaries of the regions output by static image segmentation [5][6][14]. Our discussion on above points is related to the extensive body of research that has already been reported in motion based segmentation. Nevertheless, many fundamental problems remain unsolved. One of the most important problems is the difficulty in motion estimation under large illumination change and at motion discontinuity.

All of these motion segmentation method based on optical flow estimation methods that rely on the constant brightness assumption and motion smoothness constraint that can be easily violated. Consequently, the segmentation results will be severely contaminated under the situation mentioned above. In this paper, we present an improved motion segmentation method based on optical flow estimation technique that is robust against illumination change and a general clustering algorithm. In Secs. 2 and 3, we present the optical flow estimation technique and the motion segmentation respectively. In Sec. 4, we will show the experimental results of the proposed method in comparison with other methods.

2 Optical Flow Estimation

In this paper, we propose a robust optical flow estimation method that reformulates the brightness constancy constraint of Gennert and Negahdaripour [15][16] within the robust statistical framework of Black and Anandan [17]. By this new approach, we can alleviate the problem of the illumination change and the motion discontinuity at the same time. The classical brightness constancy constraint, $I(x+\delta x, y+\delta y, t+\delta t) = I(x, y, t)$ [18], is replaced by the following more general form

$$I(x+\delta x, y+\delta y, t+\delta t) = M(x, y, t)I(x, y, t) + C(x, y, t) \tag{1}$$

in which $I(x, y, t)$ is the intensity of a pixel at (x, y) in an image and time t, and $M(x, y, t)$ and $C(x, y, t)$ are multiplicative and additive radiometric parameters. We can let $M = 1+\delta M$ and $C = \delta C$ since M and C are expected to change only a little from 1 and 0 respectively. Furthermore, approximating the left side of (1) using Taylor expansion up to the first order and dividing both side by δt yields

$$I_x u + I_y v + I_t - I_m - c = 0 \tag{2}$$

where $I_x = \lim_{\delta x \to 0} \frac{\delta I}{\delta x}$, $I_y = \lim_{\delta y \to 0} \frac{\delta I}{\delta y}$, $I_t = \lim_{\delta t \to 0} \frac{\delta I}{\delta t}$, $u = \lim_{\delta t \to 0} \frac{\delta x}{\delta t}$, $v = \lim_{\delta t \to 0} \frac{\delta y}{\delta t}$, $I_m = \lim_{\delta t \to 0} \frac{\delta M}{\delta t}$ and $c = \lim_{\delta t \to 0} \frac{\delta C}{\delta t}$. We estimate optical flow by minimizing the same objective function that is used in the method of Gennert and Negahdaripour [15] but employ the discretized smoothness constraint and the robust M-estimators that are used by Black and Anandan [17] as follows:

$$(u, v)^T = \arg min \iint \left(E_b + \lambda_s E_s + \lambda_m E_m + \lambda_c E_c\right) dxdy \tag{3}$$

where λ_s, λ_m and λ_c are relative weighting parameters and

$$\begin{aligned} E_b &= \rho_b\left(I_x u + I_y v + I_t - I_m - c, \sigma_b\right) \\ E_s &= \sum_{n \in N}\left[\rho_s\left(u - u_n, \sigma_s\right) + \rho_s\left(v - v_n, \sigma_s\right)\right] \\ E_m &= \sum_{n \in N} \rho_m\left(m - m_n, \sigma_m\right) \\ E_c &= \sum_{n \in N} \rho_c\left(c - c_n, \sigma_c\right) \end{aligned} \tag{4}$$

in which $\rho(\cdot)$ is a robust M-estimator and σ_s are scale parameters for each estimator. u_n, v_n, m_n and c_n are horizontal velocity, vertical velocity, time derivatives of multiplicative and additive radiometric parameters of pixels belonging to a neighborhood N, respectively. The Lorentzian function is chosen as the estimator $\rho(\cdot)$ and the objective function is minimized using the Graduated Non-Convexity Continuation (GNC) method and a gradient based Successive Over Relation (SOR) method as presented in [17]. The recursive equations that are used in the SOR phase are given by:

$$
\begin{aligned}
u^{(n+1)} &= u^{(n)} - \omega \frac{1}{T(u^{(n)})} \frac{\partial E}{\partial u}\bigg|_{u=u^{(n)}} \\
v^{(n+1)} &= v^{(n)} - \omega \frac{1}{T(v^{(n)})} \frac{\partial E}{\partial v}\bigg|_{v=v^{(n)}} \\
m^{(n+1)} &= m^{(n)} - \omega \frac{1}{T(m^{(n)})} \frac{\partial E}{\partial m}\bigg|_{m=m^{(n)}} \\
c^{(n+1)} &= c^{(n)} - \omega \frac{1}{T(c^{(n)})} \frac{\partial E}{\partial c}\bigg|_{c=c^{(n)}}
\end{aligned}
\tag{5}
$$

where $0 < \omega < 2$ is a relaxation parameter that controls the speed of convergence, and the derivatives of E with respect to each variables and their upper bound T are as follows:

$$
\begin{aligned}
\frac{\partial E}{\partial u} &= \iint \left\{ I_x \varphi_b \left(I_x u + I_y v + I_t - I_m - c \right) + \lambda_s \sum_{n\in N} \varphi_s \left(u - u_n \right) \right\} dxdy \\
\frac{\partial E}{\partial v} &= \iint \left\{ I_y \varphi_b \left(I_x u + I_y v + I_t - I_m - c \right) + \lambda_s \sum_{n\in N} \varphi_s \left(v - v_n \right) \right\} dxdy \\
\frac{\partial E}{\partial m} &= \iint \left\{ -I \varphi_b \left(I_x u + I_y v + I_t - I_m - c \right) + \lambda_m \sum_{n\in N} \varphi_m \left(m - m_n \right) \right\} dxdy \\
\frac{\partial E}{\partial c} &= \iint \left\{ -\varphi_b \left(I_x u + I_y v + I_t - I_m - c \right) + \lambda_c \sum_{n\in N} \varphi_c \left(c - c_n \right) \right\} dxdy
\end{aligned}
\tag{6}
$$

$$
T(u) = \frac{I_x^2}{\sigma_b^2} + \frac{4\lambda_s}{\sigma_s^2}, \quad T(v) = \frac{I_y^2}{\sigma_b^2} + \frac{4\lambda_s}{\sigma_s^2}, \quad T(m) = \frac{I^2}{\sigma_b^2} + \frac{4\lambda_m}{\sigma_m^2}, \quad T(c) = \frac{1}{\sigma_b^2} + \frac{4\lambda_c}{\sigma_c^2} \tag{7}
$$

3 Motion Segmentation

Among the motion segmentation methods that are classified in Sec. 1, we choose the top-down method because it is simple but enough to show the effectiveness of our optical flow method. For the clustering step needed in this kind of an approach, we will group pixels together on the basis of similarity of motion direction. An alternative approach would consist of grouping pixels in velocity $(u-v)$ space directly. We believe that clustering directly with respect to motion direction yields superior results on account of the immunity gained vis-a-vis the magnitude of the optical flow vector. With regard to the specifics of how clustering is accomplished with respect to motion direction, we have experimented with three different method such as the valley seeking method [19], the region growing method and the split-and-merge method. However, we will show only the result using split-merge algorithm in this paper because there is not much difference between their results.

The split-and-merge algorithm works in a way that is the opposite of the region-growing method. The initial region, which at the beginning is the entire image, is divided into quad regions if the average of the differences of the motion directions of all pixels is larger than a certain value. This process is repeated for each one of the quad regions until no more splits occur. After finishing this splitting process, the neighboring regions are merged if the average of the differences of their motion directions is smaller than a certain value.

4 Experimental Results

To show effectively the robustness of our optical flow estimation method at varying illumination and motion discontinuity, we use synthesized images shown in Fig. 1 (a). The robustness can also be verified with real images in Fig. 2. In Fig. 1 (a), shown on

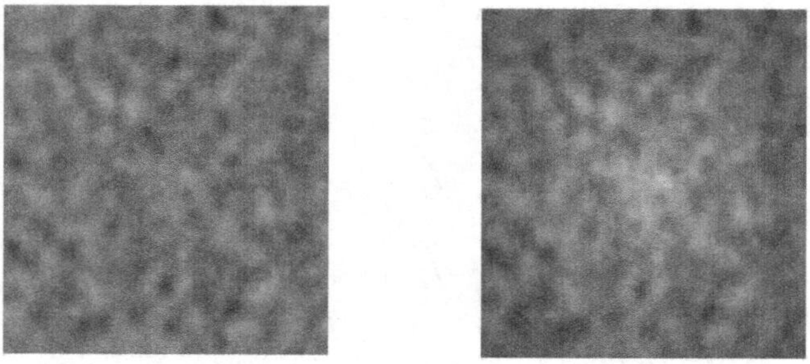

(a) Test image frames: the right image is synthesized by displacing the right half of the left image by one pixel to the left

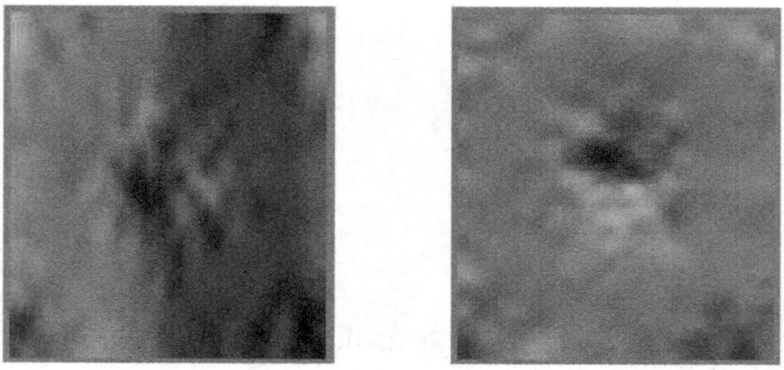

(b) Results (u and v) of the method in [8]

Fig. 1. Optical flow results with motion discontinuity and illumination change

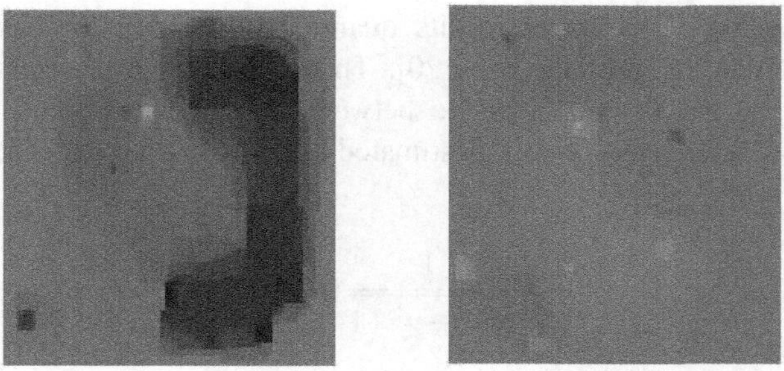

(c) Results (u and v) of the method in [4]

(d) Results(u and v) of the method in [6]

(e) Results(u and v) of our proposed method

Fig. 1. *(continued)*

the left is a random dot pattern, and shown on the right is the same pattern in which the right half of the image is displaced by one pixel to the left. To simulate illumination change, the intensity of the pixels in the right image is multiplied by a factor that varies linearly from the center of the image to the corner of the image radially (1.25 at the center and 0.75 at the corner). We ignore the offset term in the illumination model because it is very small in most practical cases [15]. The estimated optical flow results using the three previously published methods are shown in Figs. 1 (b), (c), and (d). On the other hand, the results obtained by our method are shown in Fig. 1 (e). The white, gray and black in the images for u and v terms denote 1.5, 0.0, and -1.5 pixels/frames. We can clearly see that the result obtained by our new method is the most accurate one with the sharpest motion boundary. Also, our result is affected the least by illumination changes.

We can evaluate the above results quantitatively using the optical flow error measurement method presented in [20]. There the authors calculate the errors in optical flow by measuring the angle between the 3D normalized versions of the correct optical flow vector and the estimated optical flow vector. The normalized 3d vector is define as

$$\vec{v} = \frac{1}{\sqrt{u^2 + v^2 + 1}}(u, v, 1)^T \tag{8}$$

and the angular error is calculated as $E = \arccos(\vec{v}_c \cdot \vec{v}_e)$, where the normalized 3D vector $\vec{v}_c$ corresponds to the correct velocity and $\vec{v}_e$ to the estimated velocity. For the results we have shown in this section, the mean and the standard deviation of the angular error for the estimated optical flow of Fig. 1 (b) are 14.94^o and 10.55^o; for those of Fig. 1 (c) 13.64^o and 13.81^o; for those of Fig. 1 (d) 4.47^o and 4.62^o; and for those of Fig. 1(e) 1.15^o and 4.71^o, respectively.

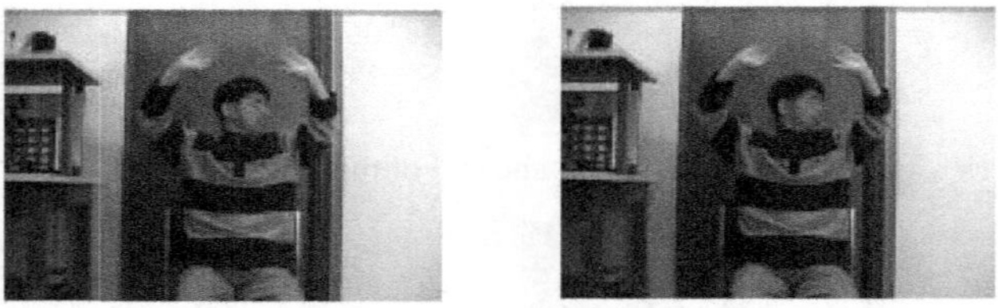

(a) Human Motion

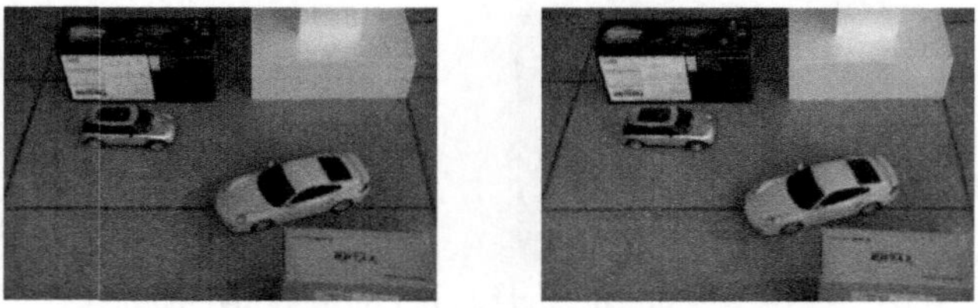

(b) Moving Cars

Fig. 2. Test image frames: Real

We employed our new optical flow estimation method to the motion based segmentation with a top-down approach as explained in Sec. 3. We verified the superiority of our method by experiments with two real image sequences. Fig. 2 shows two image frames from the two real image sequences each other. Fig.2 (a) shows the image sequence for human motion and (b) for moving cars under illumination changes in both cases. Fig. 3 and 4 show the optical flow results using three previously published methods and our new method for two image sequences each other. The order of the results in Fig. 3 and 4 follow the order shown in Fig. 1. With these results we can see clearly the motion estimated by our method is closest to the correct motion of moving subject with least effect from illumination change.

(a) Result of the method in [18]

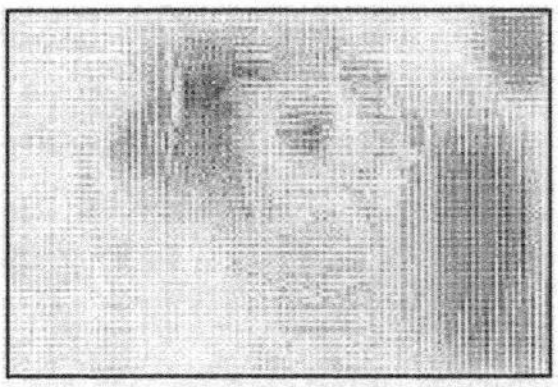
(b) Result of the method in [17]

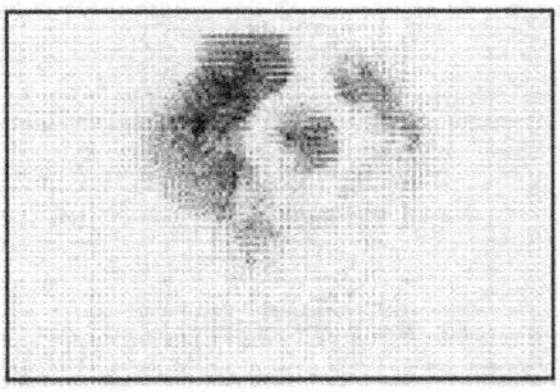
(c) Result of the method in [15]

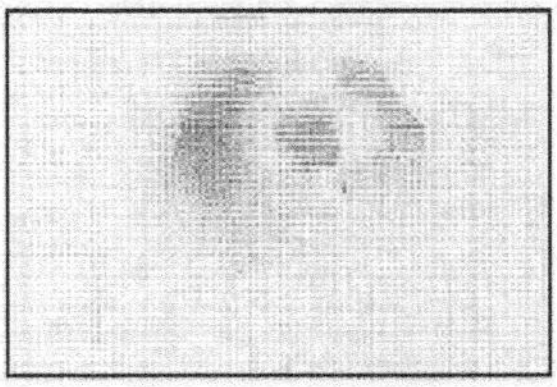
(d) Result of our proposed method

Fig. 3. Optical flow results for Human Motion sequence

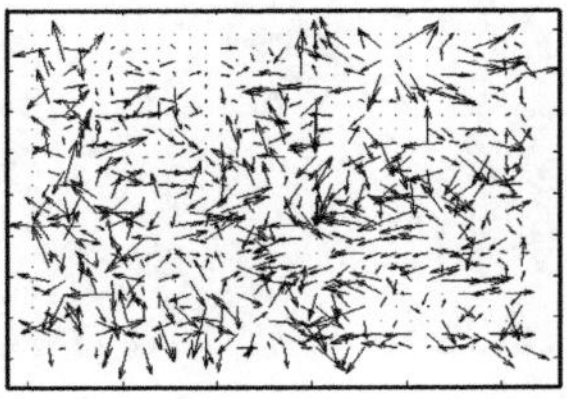
(a) Result of the method in [18]

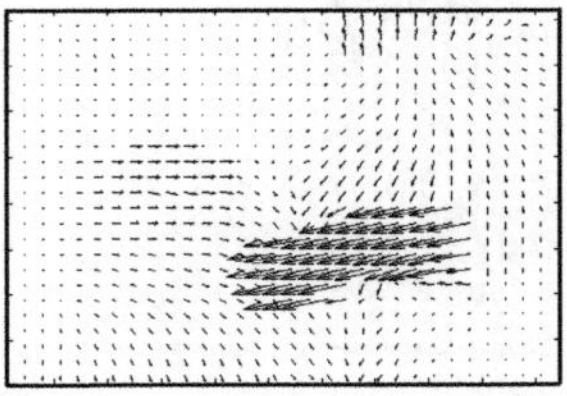
(b) Result of the method in [17]

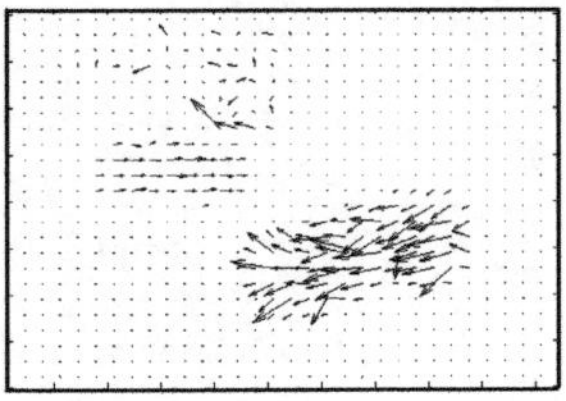
(c) Result of the method in [15]

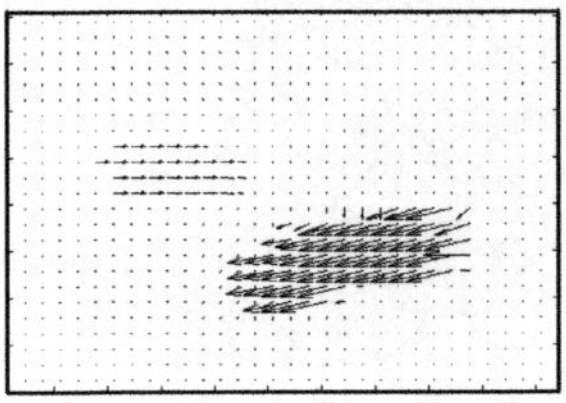
(d) Result of our proposed method

Fig. 4. Optical flow results for Moving Cars sequence

Fig. 5 and 6 show the segmentation results from the optical flow results for two image sequences each other. As we can see in these results, the motion segmentation based on our robust illumination invariant motion estimation method is more reliable to be used in higher processing of computer vision application.

(a) Result of the method in [18]

(b) Result of the method in [17]

(c) Result of the method in [15]

(d) Result of our proposed method

Fig. 5. Motion Segmentation Results for Human Motion sequence

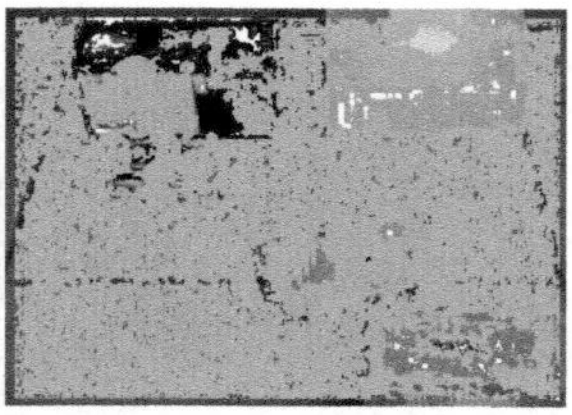

(a) Result of the method in [18]

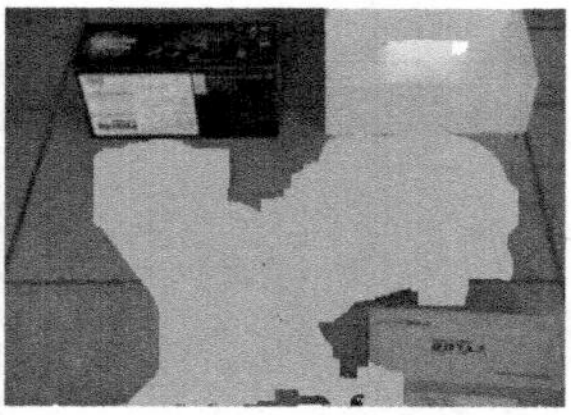

(b) Result of the method in [17]

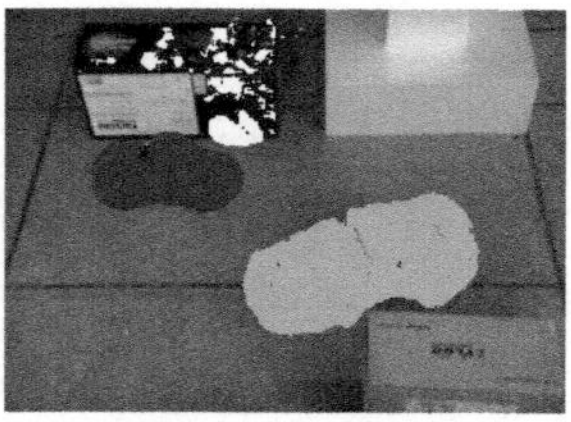

(c) Result of the method in [15]

(d) Result of our proposed method

Fig. 6. Motion Segmentation Results for Moving Cars sequence

5 Conclusions

We presented in this paper a new optical flow estimation method that is robust at large illumination change and motion discontinuity by combining two previous methods in a single computation frame. The comparison with other previous methods was shown and the superiority was verified using a synthesized images and real images. We also presented a top-down motion segmentation approach using the split-and-merge algorithm based on optical flow estimated by our method that is more reliable than based on other optical flow estimation methods.

References

1. Potter, J.L.: Scene segmentation using motion information. Computer Vision Graphics Image Process. 6, 558–581 (1977)
2. Aggarwal, J.K., Nandhakumar, N.: On the computation of motion from sequences of images-A review. Proc. of the IEEE 76(8), 917–935 (1988)
3. Jain, R., Martin, W.N., Aggarwal, J.K.: Segmentation through the detection of changes due to motion. Computer Vision Graphics Image Process 11, 13–34 (1979)
4. Mitiche, A.: Computational Analysis of Visual Motion: ch.8 Detection, computation, and Segmentation of Visual Motion. Plenum Press (1994)
5. Dufaux, F., Moscheni, F., Lippman, A.: Spatio-temporal segmentation based on motion and static segmentation. In: Proc. of International Conference on Image Processing, Washington DC, vol. 1, pp. 306–309 (1995)
6. Gelgon, M., Bouthemy, P.: A region-level graph labeling approach to motion-based segmentation. In: Proc. of IEEE International Conference on Computer Vision and Pattern Recognition (CVPR), pp. 514–519 (1997)
7. Moscheni, F., Bhattacharjee, S., Kunt, M.: Spatiotemporal segmentation based on region merging. IEEE Trans. on Pattern Analysis and Machine Intelligence. 20(9), 897–915 (1998)
8. Schunck, B.: Image flow segmentation and estimation by constraint line clustering. IEEE Trans. on Pattern Analysis and Machine Intelligence 11(10), 1010–1027 (1989)
9. Wang, J.Y.A., Adelson, E.H.: Representing moving images with layers. IEEE Trans. on Image Processing 3(5), 625–638 (1994)
10. Weber, A., Malik, J.: Rigid body segmentation and shape description form optical flow under weak perspective. IEEE Trans. on Pattern Analysis and Machine Intelligence 19(2), 139–143 (1997)
11. Ayer, S., Sawhney, H.S.: Layered representation of motion video using robust maximum-likelihood estimation of mixture models and MDL encoding. In: Proc. of International Conference on Computer Vision (ICCV), pp. 777–784 (June 1995)
12. Vasconcelos, N., Lippman, A.: Empirical bayesian motion segmentation. IEEE Trans. on Pattern Analysis and Machine Intelligence. 23(2), 217–221 (2001)
13. Weiss, Y.: Smoothness in layers: Motion segmentation using nonparametric mixture estimation. In: Proc. of IEEE International Conference on Computer Vision and Pattern Recognition (CVPR), pp. 520–526 (1997)
14. Thompson, W.B.: Combining motion and contrast for segmentation. IEEE Trans. on Pattern Analysis and Machine Intelligence 2(6), 543–549 (1980)
15. Gennert, M.A., Negahdaripour, S.: Relaxing the brightness constancy assumption in computing optical flow. MIT A.I. Lab. Memo No.975 (1987)
16. Negahdaripour, S.: Revised definition of optical flow: Integration of radiometric and geometric cues for dynamic scene analysis. IEEE Trans. on Pattern Analysis and Machine Intelligence 20(9), 961–979 (1998)
17. Black, M.J., Anandan, P.: A framework for the robust estimation of optical flow. In: Proc. of Int'l Conference on Computer Vision (ICCV), Berlin, Germany, pp. 231–236 (May 1993)
18. Horn, K.P.: Robot Vision, 3rd edn. MIT Press, Cambridge MA (1987)
19. Koontz, W.L.Z., Fukunaga, K.: A nonparametric valley seeking technique for cluster analysis. IEEE Trans. on Computers, C 21, 171–178 (1972)
20. Barron, J.L., Fleet, D.J., Beauchemin, S.S.: Performance of optical flow techniques. Int'l Journal of Computer Vision 12(1), 43–77 (1994)

Daily Life Mobility of a Student: From Position Data to Human Mobility Model through Expectation Maximization Clustering

Hyunuk Kim and Ha Yoon Song*

Department of Computer Engineering, Hongik University, Seoul, Korea
gizingun@gmail.com, hayoon@hongik.ac.kr

Abstract. There has been large number of research results to describe human mobility for various purposes. It has been researched that a person's mobility pattern can be predicted with the probability up to 93%, even though various factors and parameters can affect the human mobility pattern. In this research we tried to build a bridge between positioning data and human mobility pattern. Human mobility trails of a person can be presented in forms of positioning data sets. Positioning data from GPS or WPS and so on are somewhat accurate and usually in a tuple form of <time, latitude, longitude> while these form of data is barely interpreted by human perception. Humans can precept location information as street names, building names or shapes, etc. The error prone accuracy of positioning data leads a problem of clustering in order to figure out the point of frequent places for human mobility. These places and human mobility trails can be identified by clustering techniques, and we used Expectation Maximization clustering technique with the use of probability models derived from Levy Walk researches. We believe our research can be a starting point to model a human mobility pattern for further use.

Keywords: Human Mobility, Expectation Maximization, Clustering, Global Positioning System.

1 Introduction

There have been a requirement of more realistic human mobility patterns from various field of research and industry since the human mobility model can make precise research result or more value added products, especially for computer science and electronic engineering including many other area of study. For example, the spread pattern of epidemic deceases or the spread pattern of virus over the Internet must be affected by human mobility pattern and thus related researched were conducted [1,2,3]. As well, for the purpose of juvenile care, frequent visiting locations of young peoples are investigated in order to figure out

* This research was supported by Basic Science Research Program through the National Research Foundation of Korea(NRF) funded by the Ministry of Education, Science and Technology(No. 2011-0025875).

T.-h. Kim et al. (Eds.): MulGraB 2011, Part II, CCIS 263, pp. 88–97, 2011.

the effect of the locations, and of course this research is based on the mobility data collected by portable Global Positioning System (GPS) devices carried by young people [4,5]. The biggest requirements of human mobility models are from the field of MANET(Mobile Ad-hoc Network) for the performance prediction and simulation purpose [6,7]. Thus there have been the strong requirements of realistic human mobility model by various fields of researchers. One of the resent research result in a field of complex system physics shows that up to 93% of human mobility patterns can be predicted [13]. With the wide use of mobile devices with positioning system such as Smart Phones or Navigation System, we can collect more information for human mobility pattern in very high precision. Usually such devices have embedded functionalities of GPS or WPS (Wifi-based Positioning System). Another simpler method of positioning is that to get a base station location when a mobile phone is connected to its neighboring base station. This new environment leads to a next stage of human mobility research. For example, with GPS or WPS devices pre-scheduled to collect location information of a carrier, such information can be stored and manipulated to figure the human mobility pattern of the person.

Researches on human mobility can be roughly divided into two parts: a personal model and a group model. Personal model is affected by personal parameters such as gender, age, job, and so one and of course affected by psychological parameters of the person. For instance a person's habit or trend to select the route was studied [8] and resulted that a straight, taut roads are preferred. Also a social orbit based research conducted which figured out haunts based on a person's social network [9]. Group Mobility model can surely found in a military group. In such groups, a leader can greatly affect the group's mobility pattern [10].

In this paper, we studied to figure out a student's daily life mobility as a basis of complicated human mobility model construction. A student's daily life mobility pattern collected by the student himself carrying a commercial portable GPS device [15]. The GPS data collected by the GPS device has been stored for more than 20 days. The location data contains <time, latitude, longitude> tuple as well as some non-essential information. However, we cannot use this raw, numerical form for the following reasons:

- The numeric data are not intuitive and cannot be perceived by human. They must be interpreted into human friendly form.
- Due to the nature of GPS system, the data contains inherent error in position. Even though a GPS device stops for a while, a movement in collected data can be found because of the inherent error and as well because of the locational environment. The error from locational environment are more serious, i.e., a large amount of locational error as well as consecutive errors can be collected due to low GPS signals blocked or distorted by buildings or obstacles, especially when the device is inside a building.
- Therefore, a single point of location data cannot represent a person's location. A set of data must be identified with a considerable cardinality and for considerable time duration.

We must identify a set of data with *considerable numbers* and with *considerable time duration*. For this purpose, we use clustering techniques. And finally the clustered data are presented as location information such as building names, street names, city names, universities, and so on. Practically, the collected GPS data are clustered. We Proposed clustering technique based on Expectation Maximization (EM) algorithm [11] for personal mobility configuration and we proposed proper clustering policy based on recent research such as Levy Walk [13,14]. For this purpose, EM clustering algorithm is reviewed in section 2 and our policy of EM clustering calibration is described in section 3. In section 4, we discuss our experiment based on collected GPS data, and in section 5 we explain and analyze the results of our experiments. Finally, section 6 will conclude this paper.

2 Clustering with Expectation Maximization

We will shortly discuss EM based clustering algorithm in this section. Expectation Maximization algorithm was first introduced by Hartley et. al in 1958 [11] and developed by Dempster et. al in 1977 [12]. EM algorithm generates the first model and iterative refinement of the data set will lead to maximum likelihood, as known as optimal model. The probabilities of object's belonging to a mixture model can be iteratively calibrated to optimal model and the adequateness of model can be determined by log-likelihood functions. In other words, EM algorithm is an algorithm for probability based clustering. With parameter Θ, random variable X with observation results, and random variable Z which cannot be observed, the probability distribution of (X,Z) can be written as $L(\theta;X,Z) = p(X,Z|\theta)$. Thus it must be maximized with likelihood function:

$$L(\theta; X) = p(X|\theta) = \sum_{Z} p(X, Z|\theta) \tag{1}$$

And the stepwise approach of EM algorithm requires parameter $\theta^{(t)}$ and searchers next-step parameter $\theta^{(t+1)}$. These steps are also classified into Expectation (E) step and Maximization (M) steps. In the expectation stage, the algorithm defines expectation Q of likelihood function given $\theta^{(t)}$.

$$Q(\theta|\theta^{(t)}) = E_{Z|X,\theta^{(t)}}[\log L(\theta; X, Z)] = \sum_{Z} p(Z|X, \theta^{(t)}) logL(\theta; X, Z) \tag{2}$$

In the maximization stage, the algorithm calculates $\theta^{(t+1)}$ maximizing Q.

$$\theta^{(t+1)} = arg_{\theta} max Q(\theta|\theta^{(t)}) \tag{3}$$

In the practical usage, we initialize $\theta^{(0)}$ with any other proper values (or vectors) and iteratively calculate $\theta^{(t)}$ to a desirable range of approximation level.

3 Policy for our Expectation Maximization Clustering

User must define the proper policy for EM clustering. We will use human mobility data collected from GPS devices and thus need to determine the probability model for EM clustering. Another approaches usually introduce Normal distribution (as known as Gaussian distribution) while the normal distribution is inadequate for our purpose. Based on our experiment with the normal distribution, we had very inaccurate clustering results since the human mobility model shows a probability distribution of heavy tailed distribution or so called Levy Walk. As well, our observation results in the fact that human mobility pattern is usually concentrated in the region of one or two kilometer (residence area) for certain time durations (residence period of human mobility). Then the transition between resident areas shows power law distribution (transition period of human mobility). Thus we will introduce power-law distribution which is similar to exponential distribution [13]. We call the distribution as transformed exponential distribution, which parameter is distance of human mobility from the center point of residence areas. The following equation shows our probability distribution:

$$P(x) = e^{-\lambda x} \tag{4}$$

Where λ is a controllable parameter denoting the maximum distance of a cluster and we usually fix it in a constant value, and x is distance between the current position of human and the center of a cluster.

In addition, we must consider velocity of human mobility. In a residence period of human mobility, a stay state can be identified with the velocity less than 10Km/hour. We can calculate the velocity of mobile human as a certain time with GPS data, and the speed threshold of 10Km/hour is from the maximum walking speed of human being. Also, GPS data with the speed more than 10Km/hour is regarded in transition period and the human is in move state.

With this classification of move state and stay state, we must consider other parameter of the area size of cluster, i.e. cluster diameter. We define cluster diameter up to few kilometers considering the usual walking distance of humans and the maximum size of building complex. With larger cluster diameter, we can figure out rough mobility pattern of human while we can obtain more precise human mobility pattern with smaller cluster diameter. However with smaller cluster diameter we also experienced the explosion of computational amount. As a result we choose cluster diameter as 2 kilometer or 3 kilometer based on our initial stage experiments. With these consideration of basic parameters, out clustering for human mobility works like the followings.

- Initialize clusters with GPS points inside a cluster.
- Calculate the number of points in clusters.
- Determine the center of clusters with probability distributions shown in equation 4.
- Calibrate the probability of a point belonging to a cluster with velocity of the point.
- Iterate EM clustering algorithm.

Table 1. Numerical Result of Positioning Data Error

Location	# of Data	Average	Std. Dev.	Maximum	Error Ratio
GPS-Outside	1691	4.4498	7.1695	51.7788	12.30%
GPS-Inside	2187	N/A	N/A	10769.72	N/A
3GBS-Outside	332	52.6618	23.5953	206.3526	36.75%
3GBS-Inside	894	52.5530	32.6859	156.7578	48.66%

We must calibrate the probability of a point's belonging to a cluster with velocity of the point since the higher velocity implies a mobile state of the point and thus implies the point has low chance to be a member of a cluster. With high velocity, the calibration process drastically decreases the probability of a point being a member of a cluster.

4 Experimental Processes

4.1 Basic Experiment

We used location data for a student's daily life from the positioning systems. Among the positioning systems, we noticed two general positioning systems under actual service: Global Positioning System and 3G base station positioning system. However we first figure out the usefulness of positioning data, i.e. we must check whether the data collected from positioning systems are accurate enough to represent real position with tolerable errors. Usual positioning technique with 3G base station (3GBS) locations are prone to have error in position (frequent change of base station) due to the weakness of RSS (Radio Signal Strength) system and are suspected its usefulness for our research. And current GPS systems have a clear problem: the GPS signal must be diminished or distorted inside a building. Thus we conducted very basic experiment. For fixed locations both GPS and 3GBS location data were collected for several hours, and the locations are of course an outside area and inside a building as well. For the GPS data collection we used Garmin GPS device [15], and for the 3GBS data collection we used commercial Galaxy Tab with 3G positioning features, which points the nearest base station connected to Galaxy Tab.

Table 1 shows the results of our basic experiment. According to GPS or 3GBS, and the combination of inside a building or outside area were presented. The *# of data* means the number of total data obtained for each experimental situation. For example, we obtained 2187 position data with GPS and outside area situation. For the detection of position change between two consecutive positioning data, we regard the data as error since we fix the positioning device at the experimental location, and the distance between two consecutive data is error distance. The error distance in the unit of meters. The column Average shows the average value in error distance, and the standard deviation of error distance as well. And Maximum shows the maximum distance error. Final column of Error Ratio shows the ratio of error in each sub-experiment. One of the

Fig. 1. A Typical Trail of Student's Mobility Pattern

sub-experiments, *G*PS-Inside, shows an interesting result. We found the indoor result is meaningless with Garmin GPS device since the device automatically assumes the device's position with past velocity data once it cannot obtain GPS signal. In other words, the device lost GPS signals inside a building and it only assumes current positions. This "user friendly assumption" feature of the device manufacturer's policy leads to drastic errors in position data, thus we discarded the experimental result since they are not realistic. We found 3GBS works even inside a building while it shows far bigger position error in general comparing to GPS data. In addition more than 36% 3GBS data are erroneous. GPS data shows 12.30% of error while the distance in error position is 52 meters maximum, which is in a range of usual building. As a result we will use GPS device for further positioning data collection for this research.

4.2 Clustering for Mobility Identification

From the collected data set of student's daily mobility, as shown in figure 1 we set clustering experiment. We used portable GPS device and visualized the result with MapSource and Google Earth. The data had been collected over one month period, and visually verified by the volunteer collector with use of Google map. The area of data collection is actual metropolitan area of Seoul, Korea including student's home at Inchon, student's university at Seoul, including his actual mobility trail at Bucheon and Gimpo. In figure 1, GPS data collection per minute was shown using Google Earth. As expected, a lot of positioning spots

Table 2. Numerical Result of EM Clustering

Attributes	Cluster #1	Cluster #2
Center Position	37.55063433212, 126.924338173	37.53103155017, 126.738378099
Std.Dev. of Positions	0.001421985754, 0.0018165770	0.004433808732, 0.0106206104
Init. Max. Distance	1.2895475083Km	1.6346787354Km
Mean Radius	0.4230522023Km	0.8602108048Km
Std.Dev. of Radius	0.1510241812Km	0.2611918062Km
Mean Velocity	1.7603687520Km/h	1.7167060110Km/h
Stay Time	192h 41min 51sec	174h 32min 49sec
Stay Time Ratio	0.48401121	0.43842124
# of GPS data	36068	36291
	Cluster #3	**Cluster #4**
Center Position	37.50888469813, 126.745592885	37.56163253234, 126.984433796
Std.Dev. of Positions	0.002622770045, 0.0049952464	0.001092322042, 0.0016551943
Init. Max. Distance	1.0622189806Km	0.7402234633Km
Mean Radius	0.7908515486Km	0.8602108048Km
Std.Dev. of Radius	0.2709407549Km	0.1155222349Km
Mean Velocity	4.4234336044Km/h	3.7164649020Km/h
Stay Time	1h 23min 59sec	2h 39min 38sec
Stay Time Ratio	0.00351578	0.00668270
# of GPS data	776	369
	Cluster #5	**Cluster #6**
Center Position	37.61160856301, 126.725829209	37.50117796238, 127.024098038
Std.Dev. of Positions	0.001998271866, 0.0011028002	0.002822730855, 0.0036000113
Init. Max. Distance	0.9545632012Km	0.9845817834Km
Mean Radius	0.4143471803Km	1.9565636861Km
Std.Dev. of Distance	0.1675891550Km	0.2085686049Km
Mean Velocity	3.5441394683Km/h	6.4222173338Km/h
Stay Time	1h 33min 39sec	2h 25min 49sec
Stay Time Ratio	0.00392045	0.00610429
# of GPS data	674	474

are concentrate on two areas: home and office. With EM based clustering techniques, this GPS data set was clustered and several major clusters are identified. The following section 5 will show the detailed results of these experiments and discussions.

5 Experimental Results and Analysis

Table 2 shows the numerical result of clustered position data set. Six clusters were identified and verified by the positioning data collector. The table contains cluster information including the center position of each cluster, standard deviation of positions of cluster members in each cluster, maximum cluster radius in the initialization phase, average radius of each cluster, standard deviation of radius, average speed of cluster members in each cluster, time spend in each cluster, ratio of stay time inside each cluster, number of position data in each cluster. The biggest clusters are spotted around home at Incheon and office area around Mapo, Seoul as expected, while other minute clusters are for downtown area of Bucheon, a gourmet restaurant at Gimpo, an unusual visit to the center of Seoul, and a dental clinic visit to southern part of Seoul usually known as Gangman. Figure 2 shows the clusters located on the real map as a visualization of results in table 2. For example, in human perception, cluster one denotes Hongik University where the first author is now belonged. This intuitive result will be more human friendly once we can automatically map between numerical location data to institute names.

In this clustering experiment, we successfully extract critical areas of human mobility model for a given data set.

Fig. 2. Clustering Results of a Student's Mobility on Real Map

6 Conclusion and Future Research

A student's daily human mobility patterns were identified. From GPS trajectory data, the major locations for the student's life were identified by EM clustering technique. Even though our simple results have much room to be applied for more complicated patterns, we successfully deduced a human mobility model. For the very next stage, we can generate the mobility model in a form of Markov Chain as shown in figure 3.

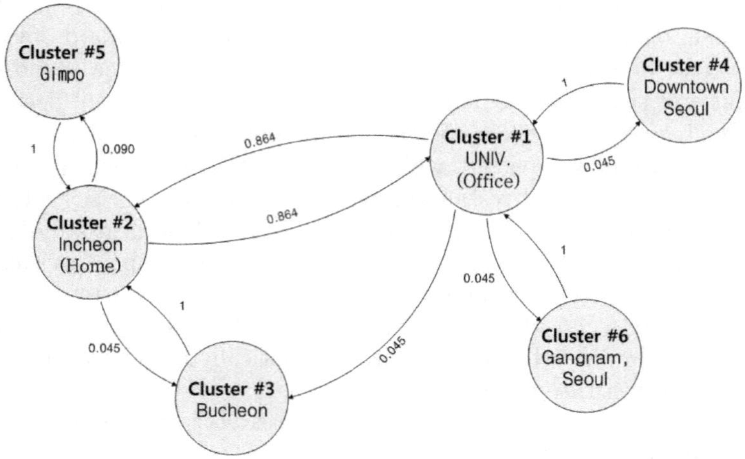

Fig. 3. A Pseudo Markov Chain from the Clustering Results

Our future research will be focused on several directions. First, of course, we need to collect more GPS trajectory for precise modeling. For this purpose, we developed smart phone apps and participating researchers are now carrying their smart phones in order to collect their GPS location data for days. We guess the more data will show more complicated mobility patterns of human mobility according to various situations. As well, more data can add more confidentiality on our research result. Second, we need to develop more efficient clustering technique. For our relatively simple mobility data, we experienced large computational time for EM clustering. It can be easily predicted that we will experience more and more amount of computational time as we add more mobility data for clustering. From this aspect we need to improve the efficiency of clustering calculations.

Finally, we need to add preprocessing stage and postprocessing state on the clustering stage. The preprocessing stage will filter out erroneous location data. We experienced the erroneous data harms the correctness of clustering, and this tend to be serious once we use less accurate positioning system such as WIFI or 3G based positioning system. For filtering purpose, we are now developing techniques using One Class Support Vector Machine, and now experiencing sufficient result [16]. The filtering stage will be combined with clustering stage and then we can figure our more correct human mobility model. The postprocessing stage is for human intuition and perception. The names of locations must be human friendly ones, such as building names, street names, famous statues or milestones. Our approach is to plot clustered data on the map for easier human recognition of clustering result, since clustering results are in a form of <latitude, longitude> tuple. However, for more intuitive representation of human mobility results, we need to introduce automatic mapping technique from numerical results to human friendly results.

References

1. Colizza, V., Vespignani, A.: Epidemic modeling in metapopulation systems with heterogeneous coupling pattern: Theory and simulations. Journal of Theoretical Biology 251(3), 450–467 (2008)
2. Ni, S., Weng, W.: Impact of travel patterns on epidemic dynamics in heterogeneous spatial metapopulation networks. Physical Review E 79(1) (2009)
3. Wang, P., Gonzalez, M.C., Hidalgo, C.A., Barabasi, A.L.: Understanding the spreading patterns of mobile phone viruses. Science 22 324(5930), 171–1076 (2009)
4. Wiehe, S.E., Hoch, S.C., Liu, G.C., Carroll, A.E.: Adolescent travel patterns: pilot data indicating distance from home varies by time of day and day of week. Journal of Adolescent Health 42(4), 418–420 (2008)
5. Sarah, W., Aaron, C., Gilbert, L., Kelly, H., Shawn, H., Jeffery, W., Dennis, F.J.: Using GPS-enabled cell phones to track the travel patterns of adolescents. International Journal of Health Geographics 7(1) (2008)
6. Bai, F., Sadagopam, N., Helmy, A.: Important: A framework to systematically analyze the Impact of Mobility on Performance of Routing Protocol for Ad hoc Networks. In: Twenty-second Annual Joint Conference of The IEEE Computer And Communications Societies, vol. 2, pp. 825–835 (2003)
7. Zhou, B., Xu, K., Gerla, M.: Group and swarm mobility models for ad hoc network scenarios using virtual tracks. In: IEEE Military Communications Conference, vol. 1, pp. 289–294 (2004)
8. Bailenson, J.N., Shum, M.S., Uttal, D.H.: Road climbing: Principles governing asymmetric route choice on maps. Environmental Psychology 18(3), 251–264 (1998)
9. Ghosh, J.: Sociological orbit aware location approximation and routing (SOLAR) in MANET. Ad Hoc Networks 5(2), 189–209 (2007)
10. Williams, S.A.: A group force mobility model. In: 9th Communications and Networking Simulation Symposium (2006)
11. Hartley, H.O.: Maximum Likelihood Estimation from Incomplete Data. Biometrics 14(2), 174–194 (1958)
12. Dempster, A.P., Laird, N.M., Rubin, D.B.: Maximum Likelihood from Incomplete Data via the EM Algorithm. Journal of the Royal Statistical Society. Series B (Methodological) 39(1), 1–38 (1977)
13. Song, C., Zehui, Q., Nicholas, B., Albert-Laszio, B.: Limits of Predictability in Human Mobility. Science 19 327(5968), 1018–1021 (2010)
14. Gonzalez, M.C., Hidalgo, A., Barabasi, A.-L.: Understanding individual human mobility patterns. Nature (2008)
15. Garmin GPSMAP62s, `https://buy.garmin.com/shop/shop.do?pID=63801`
16. Kim, W., Song, H.Y.: Optimization Conditions of OCSVM for Erroneous GPS Data Filtering. Will be Presented in MULGRAB 2011 IPS (2011)

A Fast Summarization Method for Smartphone Photos Using Human-Perception Based Color Model

Kwanghwi Kim, Sung-Hwan Kim, and Hwan-Gue Cho

Dept. of Computer Science and Engineering,
Pusan National University, Busan, Korea
{kwanghwi,sunghwan,hgcho}@pusan.ac.kr
http://pearl.cs.pusan.ac.kr/

Abstract. With an increasing number of smartphone user, people can easily take a hundreds of daily photos with their smartphone. However the growth of taken photos cause problems that the user are hard to browse, search and manage them. In this paper, we describe our spatial clustering method to enhance photo management in smartphone with considering perceptual color distribution. We address how to group nearly identical photos(NIP) taking duplicate photos in order to get a better quality photo. To measure perceptual differences between two photos, we conduct the CIELAB color metric and the optimal matching by dominant colors and specific colors. Also, we try to investigate the key features of NIP such as the similarity threshold and the number of dominant colors and specific colors. The result of experiments shows that our method enable to classify NIP groups similar to manual operation result and the average accuracy is 0.95.

Keywords: photo clustering, CIELAB, color-base clustering, nearly identical photos.

1 Introduction

Recently, the smartphone make a change mobile technology trends with many functions such as camera, gps, gyroscope and accelerometer. Especially it's camera enable people to be able to take daily photos easily, and they get more photos that need to be managed. Browsing and managing photos are much harder in the smartphone environment due to limited screen size. Therefore, clustering and summarizing hundreds of photos automatically are needed.

We observed user's using patterns closely and found that they take many duplicate photos. Smartphone camera users tend to take more duplicate photos than typical camera users because it is easy to be shaken and it doesn't provide any manual funtion to adjust it's quality. Thus, people try to overcome these limitation by taking duplicate scenes. We define these photos as nearly identical photos(NIP) and believe that grouping NIPs automatically can make browsing

T.-h. Kim et al. (Eds.): MulGraB 2011, Part II, CCIS 263, pp. 98–105, 2011.

hundreds of photos better. Figure 1 shows an example of NIP. Photos in each red box shows very similar scene and we consider these photos as NIP group. If we can find and overlap these photo, space efficiency will be increased.

Fig. 1. An example of the nearly identical photos(NIP) group

In this paper, we propose a method summarizing NIPs automatically with considering perceptual color distribution. Each photo is characterized by 25 color histogram to increase comparing speed and memory efficiency. The color quantization we conduct CIELAB color space to measure perceptual color differences between two photos.

2 Related Work

There are numerous research to classify photos automatically for viewing and managing collection easily. Table 1 shows several related works to manage photos and images. Graham[8] detected a temporal feature for clustering. Cooper[3] proposed an clustering method by photo taken time. Platt[7] introduced PhotoTOC clustered by creation time and the color of the photographs and using an overview+detail design. Ryu[4] proposed web-based photo management system with temporal clustring and quality evaluation. He introduced a layout system, Photoland[6], considering temporal-spatial information. Mota[10] developed Agrafo using several grouping criteria such as, presence of faces, indoor/outdoor, urban/nature scenes and low-level features. Since it's architecture is modular, adding new criteria is very easy. Jang[9] introduced a clustering method for concurrent photos obtained from multiple cameras. Blazica[11] proposed a measure of the user's affinity for picture: time spent viewing a picture. Prasad[1] proposed region-based image retrieval using 25 perceptual colors. We employ this 25 perceptual colors for the clustering. There is Color-based clustering method coupled with pyramid matching[5]. Though this approach showed good result, it is not suitable to smartphone's computing power. Therefore, we need to develop a lightweight algorithm for photo management in smartphone environment.

Table 1. Several methods/tools to manage photos

Method	Clustering Criteria	Feature Description
Graham et al.[8]	Time	Hierarchical photo structure
Cooper et al.[3]	Time and content	Using logistic funtion with taken time intervals
Jang [9]	Time and content	Clustering for concurrent photos obtained from multiple cameras
PhotoTOC [7]	Time and color histogram	Table of Contetns interface
PhotoLand [6]	Time and color histogram	Hierarchical clustering base on a grid
Agrafo[10]	Time and semantic information	Using semantic information such as face, indoor/outdoor and nature
ShoeBox[11]	User Affinities	Defining a measure of the user's affinity for a picture

The CIELAB system is an important international standard for measuring color difference[2]. As uniform changes of components in the CIELAB color aim to uniform changes in perceived color, the relative perceptual differences between two colors in L*a*b* can be approximated by the Euclidean distance between them[12]. Thus, we employ the CIELAB color metric to get more accurate result considering human visual sensitivity.

3 Color-Based Clustering

A color information is essential key to classify NIP groups since two nearly identical photos shows similar color distribution. Figure 2 shows our proposed method overview. We can find that P_1 and P_2 are very similar photo and they show similar color distribution while P_3 has different color distribution. For enabling to compare two photos, each photo is characterized by 25-color vector by following 3 steps. First, we convert each photo's color space from RGB to CIELAB in order to calculate human perceptual color differences. Second, we perform color quantization with 25 perceptual colors due to memory limitation and computing power of smartphone. Third, we construct 25-color histogram bins by counting each pixel's quantized color.

For color comparision, we defined the similarity as

$$S(P_i, P_j) = w_d \cdot S_d(P_i, P_j) + w_s \cdot S_s(P_i, P_j). \quad (1)$$

where $S_d(P_i, P_j)$ means similarity with dominant colors and $S_s(P_i, P_j)$ means similarity with specific colors. Dominant colors that make simliar atmosphere of photos are selected by top n_d colors from the color histogram in descending order. Specific color that express small interested region are selected by n_s colors over threshold θ_s from the color histogram in descending order. $S_d(P_i, P_j)$ are calculated by optimal assignment between two photos' dominant colors and $S_s(P_i, P_j)$ between two photos' specific colors. We made weight of dominant color

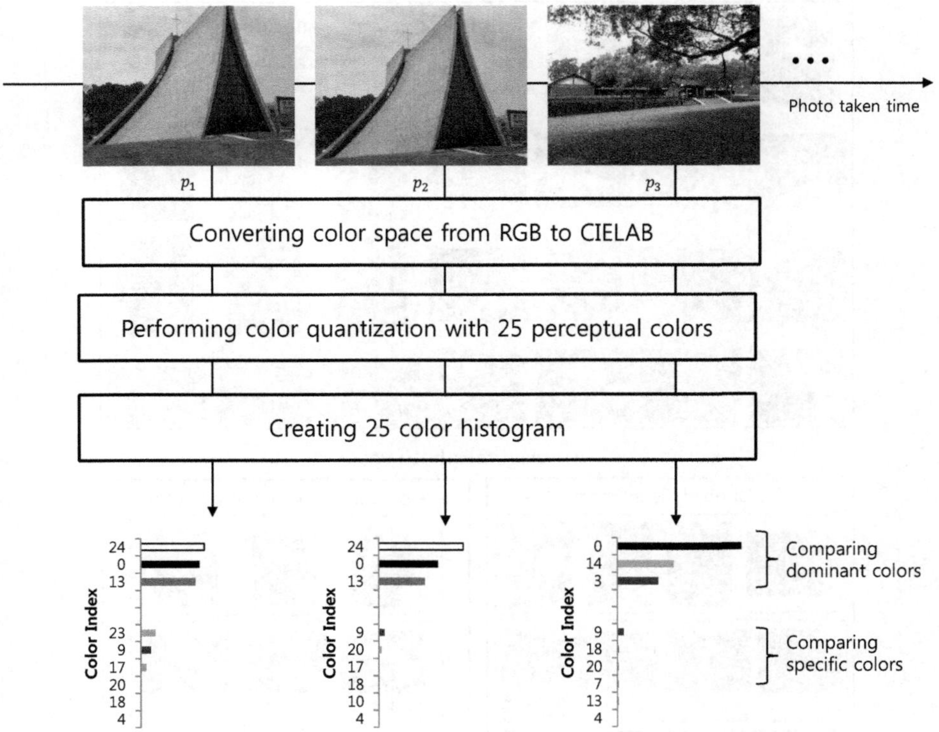

Fig. 2. Overview of proposed clustering method

similarity w_d and weight of speicific color similarity w_s that adjust effection of each value.

4 Experiment

4.1 Testing Photo Set Description

We asked participants to group nearly identical photos by hand. The input photo sets are described in Table 2. Each photo set consists of various number of photos from different place and a number of clusters is a result true sets considered as nearly identical photos by participants. We can predict the density from the period of photo sets, for example, D photo set has less clusters, bigger NIPs, than C despite more photos since many duplicate photos were taken in short time. Figure 3 (a) shows an example of photo set and (b) shows the true set made by hand. Participants grouped the set: two 4-pair NIPs, three 3-pair NIPs, three 2-pair NIPs and five singletone photos. 8 NIP groups and 5 singletone photos were classified as a result, and 53% of photos summarized. We considered clustered photo set (b) by hand as true set and compared our method result.

(a) Original photo set

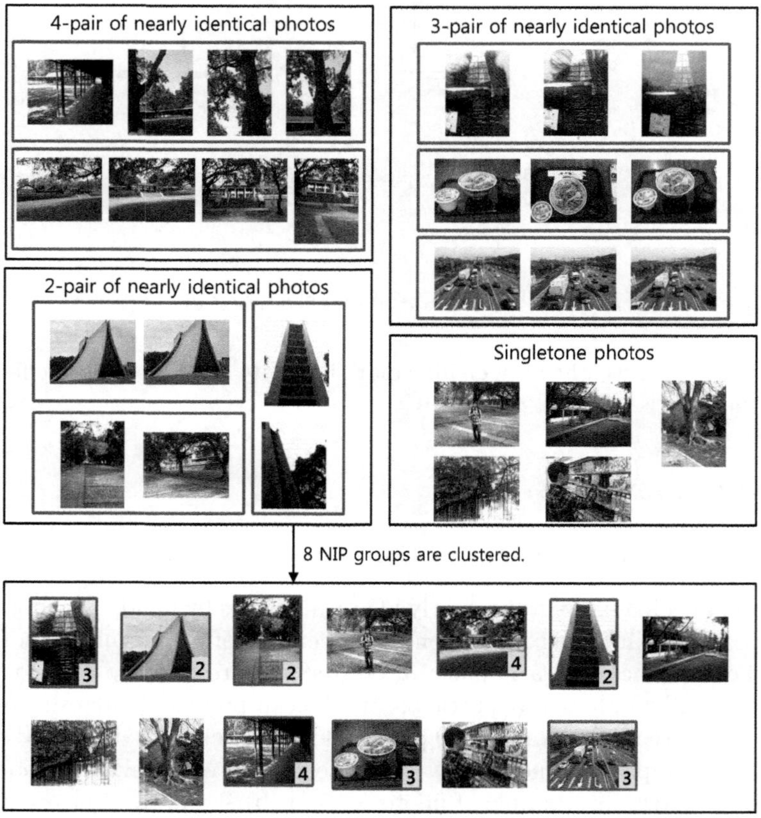

(b) True photo set clustered by maunal operation

Fig. 3. Original photo set (a) and clustered photo set (b). This photo set is classified to 4 kinds cluster: 4-pair, 3-pair, 2-pair and singletone. When we consider NIP groups, 53% of photos can be summarized as a result.

Table 2. Input Photo sets. The 'Clusters' means true sets considered as nearly identical photos.

Photo Set	No. of photos	No. of Clusters	Period(hour)	Place
A	25	13	27	Taichung, Taiwan
B	50	24	2	Taoyuan, Taiwan
C	100	69	51	Malaysia
D	150	55	5	Kyoungju, Korea
E	200	113	45	Taichung, Taiwan
F	250	191	103	Prague, Czech
G	300	183	101	Cyprus

4.2 Sensitivity and Specificity Analyzing

We measured sensitivity and specificity between our clustering result with the true set in order to find optimal value for our criteria: a number of dominant colors, a number of specific colors, weights of the factors and similarity threshold. Figure 4 shows the sensitivity-specificity curve. From the experiment, we could gain each set's optimal value as 0.820 and 0.840. We predicted the optimal threshold value of similarity experimentally, and 0.820 in $d_n = 4$, $d_s = 3$ and $\theta_s = 20$ were selected for optimal to cluster NIPs.

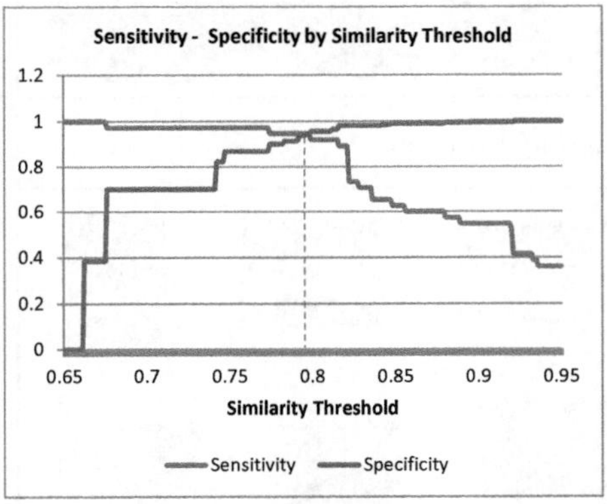

(a) Photo Set A

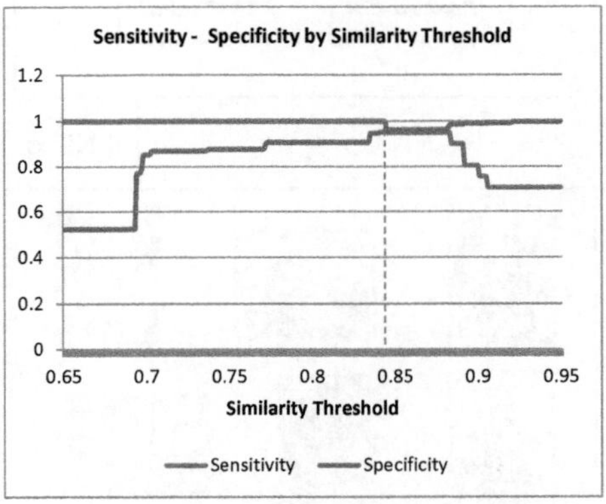

(b) Photo Set B

Fig. 4. Graphs of the relation between sensitivity and specificity and similarity threshold. (a) and (b) consists of 25 photos and each optimal threshold value is 0.820 and 0.840. (c) consists of 50 photos and the optimal threshold is 0.818. (d) consists of 60 photos and the optimal threshold is 0.810.

4.3 Result

In order to evaluate our method, we adopted our clustering method with optimal value and compared the result to true set. Figure 5 shows the result of our method. Photos were grouped 4-kind of sets: two 4-pair NIPs, four 3-pair NIPs, two 2-pair NIPs and four singletone photos. 8 NIP groups were classified and the set was summarized into 12 groups. With the optimal similairy 0.82, the result is similar to manual operated photo set figure 3 (b). The accuracy of our method is 0.95 on average.

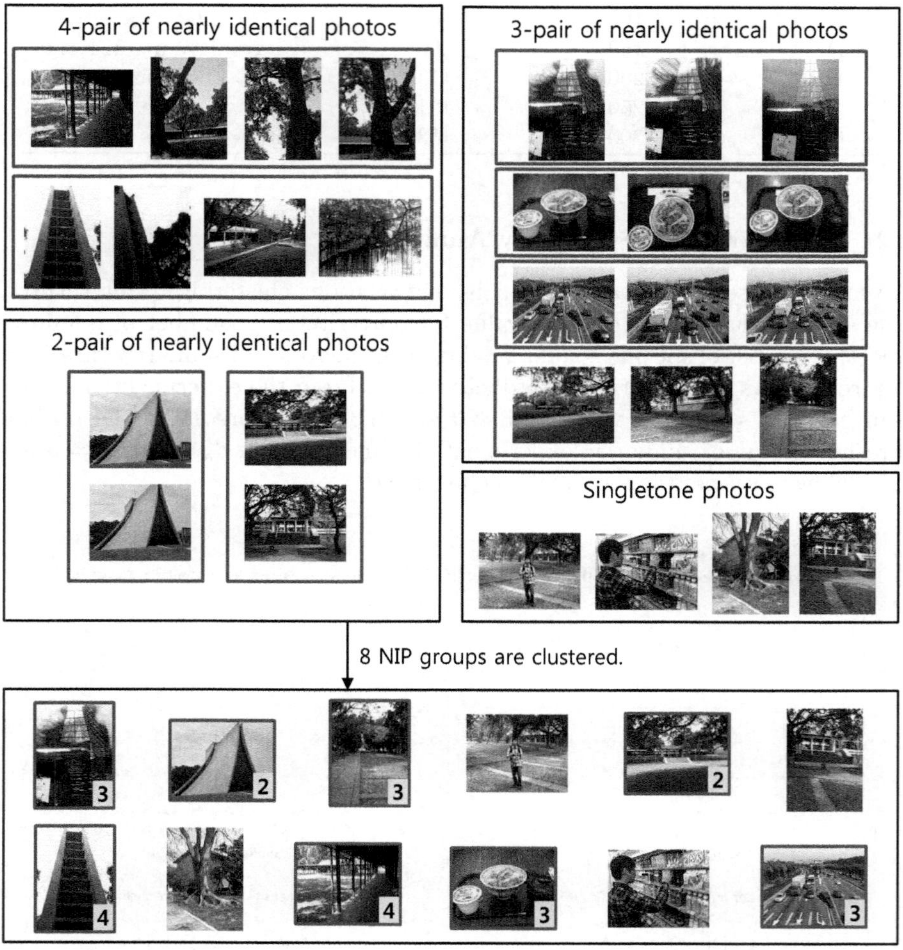

Fig. 5. Overview of proposed clustering method

5 Conclusion

In this paper, we proposed a lightweight summarizing method for smartphone by using human-recognition color. We created 25 perceptual color vector and comparing two photos with domaniant and specific color vector to classify nearly identical photos automatically. Our experimental results enabled our method to classify NIPs as manual operation result. When similarity threshold is 0.820 under $d_n = 4$, $d_s = 3$ and $\theta_s = 20$, the accuracy was 0.95 on average.

For future work, we need to increase color quantization speed and develop visualization method for smartphone to show NIP groups effectively. We will adopt feature-based clustering also since some duplicated scene did not classified well due to auto white balace and different composition. Adding feature detect method such as SIFT and SURF can be a solution.

Acknowledgment. This work was supported by the IT R&D program of MKE/MCST/KEIT (KI001820, Development of Computational Photography Technologies for Image and Video Contents).

References

1. Prasad, B.G., Biswas, K.K., Gupta, S.K.: Region-based image retrieval using integrated color, shape, and location index. J. Comput. Vis. Image Underst. 94(1-3), 193–233 (2004)
2. Zhang, X., Wandell, B.A.: A spatial extension of CIELAB for digital color-image reproduction. J. SID 5(1), 61–63 (1997)
3. Cooper, M., Foote, J., Girgensohn, A., Wilcox, L.: Temporal event clustering for digital photo collections. J. ACM Trans. Multimedia Comput. Commun. Appl. 1(3), 269–288 (2005)
4. Ryu, D., Kim, K., Park, S., Cho, H.: A web-based photo management system for large photo collections with user-customizable quality assessment. In: Proc. of the ACM SAC, pp. 1229–1236 (2011)
5. Ryu, D.-S., Kim, K., Cho, H.-G.: An Intelligent Clustering Method for Highly Similar Digital Photos Using Pyramid Matching with Human Perceptual 25 Color Histogram. In: Kim, T.-h., Adeli, H., Robles, R.J., Balitanas, M. (eds.) ISA 2011. CCIS, vol. 200, pp. 359–366. Springer, Heidelberg (2011)
6. Ryu, D., Chung, W., Cho, H.: PHOTOLAND: a new image layout system using spatio-temporal information in digital photos. In: Proc. of the ACM SAC, pp. 1884–1891 (2010)
7. Platt, J.C., Czerwinski, M., Field, B.A.: PhotoTOC: automatic clustering for browsing personal photographs. In: Proc. of the ICICS-PCM, pp. 6-10 (2003)
8. Graham, A., Garcia-Molina, H., Paepcke, A., Winograd, T.: Time as essence for photo browsing through personal digital libraries. In: Proc. of the 2nd ACM/IEEE-CS Joint Conference on Digital Libraries, pp. 326–335 (2002)
9. Jang, C., Cho, H.: A clustering method for concurrent photos obtained from multiple cameras using max-flow network model. J. Multimedia Systems, 1–23 (2011)
10. Mota, J., Fonseca, M.J., Gonçalves, D., Jorge, J.A.: Agrafo: a visual interface for grouping and browsing digital photos. In: Proc. of the AVI, pp. 494–495 (2008)
11. Blazica, B., Vladusic, D., Mladenic, D.: ShoeBox: A Natural Way of Organizing Pictures According to User's Affinities. In: Proc. of the HCII, pp. 519–524 (2011)
12. Lab color space, `http://en.wikipedia.org/wiki/Lab_color_space`

Context-Driven Mobile Social Network Discovery System

Jiamei Tang[1] and Sangwook Kim[2]

[1] School of Electrical Engineering and Computer Science, Kyungpook National University, Korea
[2] School of Computer Science and Engineering, Kyungpook National University, Korea
{jmtang,kimsw}@knu.ac.kr

Abstract. Nowadays social network systems become essential ingredients in daily life. Meanwhile, with the booming of smart mobile terminals, mobile social network catches the attention of world. However, most widely used mobile social network systems are focused on perceiving neighbors with common interests, which is just a cross-section of social network. This paper proposes Context-driven Mobile Social Network Discovery System, a system that enables users to have an overall view of nearby social network resources and provides a platform for discovering and recommending nearby social network, taking an active part in social activities and establishing more useful relationships in social communities.

Keywords: Context Information, Theme Awareness Procedure, Smart Mobile Devices, Mobile Social Network.

1 Introduction

Social network system on PCs such as Facebook and MySpace improve social connection by enabling more interactive ways on-line and start a new trend of virtual social communities. However, people living in realistic social communities miss many opportunities to establish interpersonal relationships. Additional, they are not conscious of nearby social activities and relationship, which they would like to attend or acquaint.

Mobile social network discovery systems can make use of mobile devices' portable features, well-developed wireless networks, and real-time location-aware technology to help users get more chances to perceive surrounding realistic social resources.

This paper presents the Context-driven Mobile Social Network Discovery System, a mobile social network discovery system to provide more potential information about nearby social activities, and help users get more involved in social events and be in touch with more like-minded people. To be more specific, this system supports to dynamically detect social networks near users, intelligently recommend appropriate social events to users according to context information at that time, and conveniently interactive communication among users who are in the same social event.

This paper outlines that how this system supports mobile devices with social network discovery and makes in particular the following contributions:

T.-h. Kim et al. (Eds.): MulGraB 2011, Part II, CCIS 263, pp. 106–115, 2011.

- This paper presents a dynamic social network discovery system based on context information, which can remind users of social resources nearby them, and help them get better involved in a social event at certain time and place.
- The proposed system solves the problem of information overload in web-based social network system by setting time limit and area coverage.
- Convenient interactions in this system provide better platforms to help users better align social activities in social life and get more opportunities to establish new social relationships.

The reminder of this paper is organized as follows: the second section contains brief review of related works. The third section shows a basic description of Context-driven Mobile Social Network Discovery System. After that, the forth section goes deeply into the model of this proposed system. Then the next section presents the implementation of this system. Finally, some conclusions are drawn and future works are presented.

2 Related Work

A mobile social network is a virtual community for individuals to connect with one others using mobile devices, such as mobile phones and PDAs [1], Nowadays there are many mobile social network systems are applied. A general architecture [9] for building mobile social network services is proposed by Chang Yao-Jen et.al. It consisted of four main components: the client devices, the wireless access network, the Internet and its host, and the server side.

Context-aware computing [7] is a mobile computing paradigm in which application can discover and take advantage of contextual information (such as user location, time of day, nearby people and devices and user activity). Schilit defined context-aware computing as proximate-selection, automatic contextual reconfiguration, contextual information and commands and Context-trigger actions [8].

Also location is strong and valuable information for building and retaining social interaction [4]. Kuo-Fong Kao et.al [5] proposed an indoor location-based service using access points as signal strength data collectors. In their paper, they proposed a non-client reading model for indoor location determination using access points as signal strength data collectors. STEAM [6] is a location-aware mobile application on event-based middleware, which is particularly well suited to deployment in ad hoc network environment.

3 Overview of System

This section presents an overview of Context-driven Mobile Social Network Discovery System.

3.1 System Description

Context-driven Mobile Social Network Discovery System is a good tool to help user take an active part in realistic social activities. It supports to perceive surrounding social environment, and recommend an optimum social activity to users based on much contextual information. Besides, users can easily make dialogues with one or groups of people after joining a social activity, which creates more opportunities to discover surrounding potential social relationship resources. Nevertheless, when the user gets away from this social activity's area coverage, system would stop the supply of this activity's services to user. Also social networks in this system have own effective time to guarantee the time-sensitive of activities, and all related information will be discontinued once timeout. It should be noted that the time-sensitive and region-sensitivity of this system solve the problem of information overload in usual web-based social network systems.

Specifically speaking, various social activities should be registered by service providers in advance in this system. From users' point of view, there might be several activities around them. Then mobile devices at hand can automatically detect on-going activities near them, and intelligently find out an optimum one for them to attend. After they agree to join in a activity, they can browse a list of other participants and their public basic personal information and also other released information. They can pick out one or groups of persons who interest them, and make interactive conversations with the consent(s) of opposite side(s). If users desire to establish lasting relationships with others, they can follow opposite side(s) or exchange Context-aware Business Cards with opposite side(s). For example:

There is a Computer Computing Conference in 2th Floor of Maple Hotel, and there are 3 sessions in 18th June 2011. Computer Computing Association is a sponsor of this conference, and registers these 3 sessions in advance.

John is a master student whose major is clouding computing. This system recommends the session 1(Clouding Computing Lecture) after him appearing in this conference, then he agrees to attend this session. He finds a PHD whose major is also clouding computing when he browses the attendee list. After getting the PHD's approval, they exchange views on issues of clouding computing and then exchange Context-aware Business Cards. After this conference, John still keeps in touch with this PHD.

3.2 System Architecture

The Context-driven Mobile Social Network Discovery System is based on C/S structure. Server is a remote host and in charge of data analyzing, matching and feedback, besides it has the ability of data storage and data query. Client is realized by a mobile terminal which is equipped with the abilities of data collection and submission.

Figure 2 shows the architecture of Context-driven Mobile Social Network Discovery System.

Server. It is made up by six parts: Connector, Theme Manager, Interaction Manager, Context-aware Business Card Manager, and Theme Database and User Database. Server is equipped with the ability of multithread work that meets the requirement of handling coinstantaneous requests from several clients.

Connector is in charge of communicating with Clients, and delivering received data to upper layers. Theme Manager deals with contextual data which includes tracing surrounding available Theme(s), handling activity register, and managing Actor list in Themes. Interaction Manager manages interactive actions in Themes. Context-aware Business Card Manager is used to provide services when users exchanging their cards. And Theme Database and User Database store the data of Theme and user information respectively.

Server in this system provides various services to users, and manages all the Themes and Actors. It is a vital part of this Context-driven Mobile Social Network Discovery System.

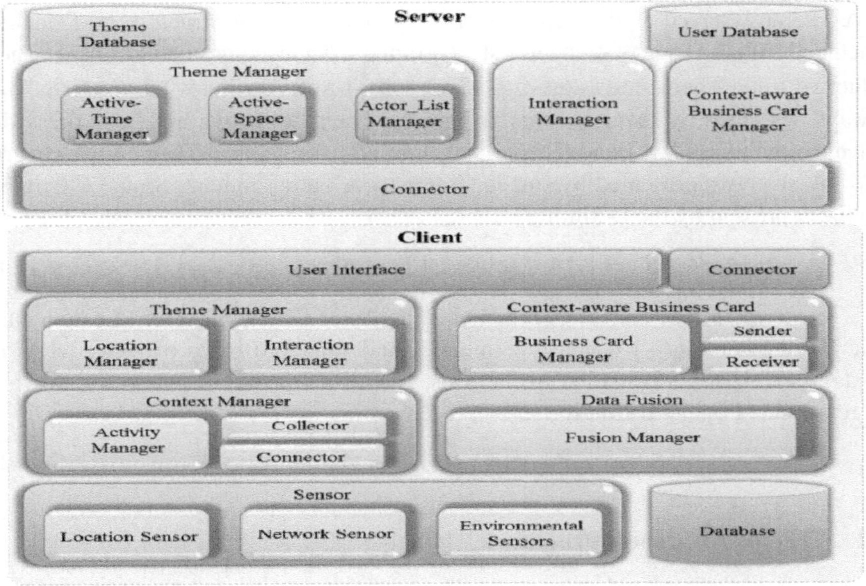

Fig. 1. Context-driven Mobile Social Network Discovery System Architecture

Client. It is realized by users' mobile handheld devices. Client architecture contains eight parts: Sensor, Context Manager, Data Fusion, Theme Manager, Context-aware Business Card, Connector, User Interface and Database.

Sensor Part contains different sensors that can collect network information, location information and other environmental information. All the sensor information and other contextual information in devices are delivered to Context Manage to be preprocessed. Then the results are sent to Data Fusion. After information fusing, this processed contextual information is submitted to Server through Connector. Theme Manager manages Theme information in client devices, and when exchanging Context-aware Business Cards, Context-aware Business Card Part provides services for users to complete exchange actions.

Client in this system is an intermediary between Server and users, which delivers the users' instructions to Server, and displays feedbacks from Server.

4 Design of System Model

4.1 System Components Definition

In the Context-driven Mobile Social Network Discovery System, there are two components: a registered activity is called a Theme; and users who take part in this system are Actors. A Theme namely is the common environment for users who participate in a same social activity. And Actors are the participants in social activities.

A Theme is saved as the structure of $\mathcal{T}$ in this system. A structure of $\mathcal{T}$ includes Theme ID ($\mathcal{T}_{ID}$), Theme attendee list ($\mathcal{T}_{AL}$), and Theme main content ($\mathcal{T}_{MC}$), Theme effective time, Theme area coverage ($\mathcal{T}_{AC}$) and Theme Attributes ($\mathcal{T}_{AT}$). And $\mathcal{T}_{MC}$ is always described by several words or phrases. Theme effective time is expressed by Theme start time ($\mathcal{T}_{Et-}$) and Theme end time ($\mathcal{T}_{Et+}$) together. Theme area coverage ($\mathcal{T}_{AC}$) is always represented by surrounding network environment. So the $\mathcal{T}$ structure can be expressed by the Definition 1:

$$\mathcal{T} = \{\mathcal{T}_{ID}, \mathcal{T}_{AL}, \mathcal{T}_{MC}, (\mathcal{T}_{Et-}, \mathcal{T}_{Et+}), \mathcal{T}_{AC}, \mathcal{T}_{AT}\} \qquad \text{Def(1)}$$

A is an expression of an Actor. It contains the Actor ID (A_{ID}), Actor Location (A_{LO}), The ID of Theme ($\mathcal{T}_{ID}$) which is joining in, and some attributes of Actor (A_{AT}) that contains the basic information of interests, calendar schedulers and so on. So A can be represented by the Definition 2:

$$A = \{A_{ID}, A_{LO}, \mathcal{T}_{ID}, A_{AT}\} \qquad \text{Def(2)}$$

4.2 Theme Awareness Procedure

In this part, social network discovery mechanism in this proposed system will be emphasized. And this mechanism is realized by the procedure of Theme Awareness.

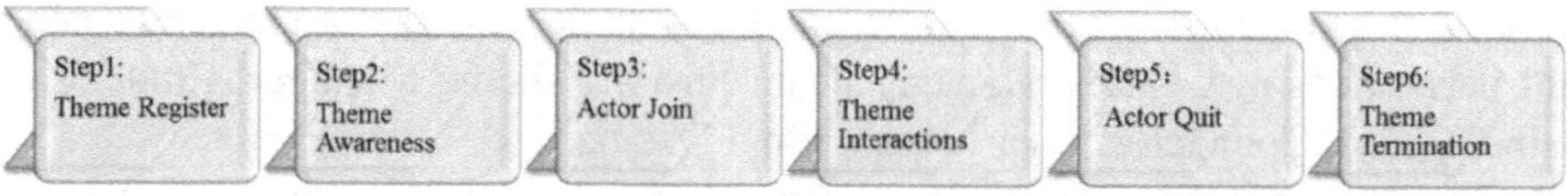

Fig. 2. The Whole Life Cycle of a Theme

Above picture (Figure 2) is a view of a Theme Activity's whole life cycle including Theme Register, Theme Awareness, Actor Join, Theme Interactions, Actor Quit and Theme Termination. And Theme Awareness procedure is a vital step in this proposed system, which is a process to detect surrounding on-going Themes, and recommend an optimum Theme to Actor with the help of contextual information.

Theme Awareness procedure is based on contextual information to infer user's desired Theme. In this system, the context information contains two major parts: environmental context information and personal context information. Environmental context information includes natural information and pre-existing information in mobile device. Besides this environmental context information, people always change their minds after knowing more new information about nearby on-going Themes at the scene. So this proposed system takes these into consideration and add the personal context information items to better infer personal Theme choices for various users.

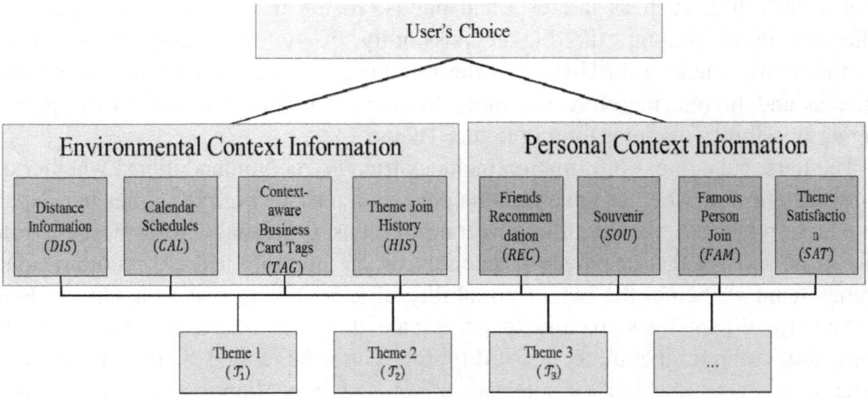

Fig. 3. Context Information in Theme Awareness

The detailed context information items were shown in Figure 3. Based on these eight factors, this Context-driven Mobile Social Network Discovery System proposed a way to quantize context information. And persons have individual differences, so just simple quantizing is hardly to achieve maximum satisfaction of everyone. Therefore, this proposed system applied a weighted quantization of Context information, which gives different weight values to different factors by learning user's history. Lastly, every Theme's sum of weighted quantization of context information becomes the reference to rank nearby Themes, and the Theme that has the biggest sum will be recommended to the Actor. This process is called Theme Aware procedure and processed as the following Equation 1.

Suppose there are m Themes nearby this user, and Q_{ij} denotes Theme j's quantitated value of i_{th} context information. And W_i presents the weight of i_{th} context information.

$$Sum_j = \sum_{i=1}^{8} Q_{ij} * W_i$$

$$Sum_{max} = MAX\{Sum_1, Sum_2, Sum_3 \ldots Sum_j\}$$

$$0 \leq Q_{ij}, W_i \leq 1;\ i = 1,2,3 \ldots 8;\ j = 1,2,3 \ldots m \quad (1)$$

Table 1 gives a view of all the context information in order of identifier number.

In environmental context information, Distance Information using Wi-Fi RSSI (Received Signal Strength Indicator) as reference: the stronger the RSSI is, the nearer the distance is. And because calendar schedules always contain the plans of users, the higher degree of similarity of a Theme main content and calendar schedulers is, the bigger possibility of users attending this Theme. Besides, Context-aware Business Card Tags always contain users' special characteristics that are frequently done in user's daily life, such as interests and habits, so the more times Tags appear in a Theme's main content, the bigger possibility of Actor joining in this Theme. Furthermore, Theme Join History is the reference for devices to learn users' habits, interest and favors, therefore the more frequently a Theme joined in the past, the bigger possibility of Actor joining in this Theme.

The personal context information includes friends' recommendations, whether offer souvenirs or not, whether have famous persons attend or not, and other participants' satisfaction grades. Also according to common senses, persons always desire to attend the social activity that has many acquaintances, so the more friends' recommendation comes from a Theme, the bigger possibility of users taking part in a Theme. People are always drawn by souvenirs to participate in social activities, hence, the more souvenirs offered, the more possibility for a user to attend a Theme. Moreover, persons are also affected by celebrity effect, the more famous persons attend, the bigger effects on users. Furthermore, people always take others' experiences into consideration, so the higher satisfaction degree of a Theme is, and the bigger possibility for users to join into this Theme.

As discussed above, the reference variables are different in different context information. The Table 1 summarizes all the reference variables in context information.

Table 1. Context Information List

Context Information Identifier	Context Information	Reference Variable	Variable Description
1	Distance Information (DIS)	r_i $i = 1,2,3 \ldots m$	The received signal strength indicator of Theme $i(\mathcal{T}_i)$
2	Calendar Schedulers (CAL)	s_i $i = 1,2,3 \ldots m$	The similar degree between this Actor's calendar schedulers and Theme $i(\mathcal{T}_i)$
3	Context-aware Business Card Tags (TAG)	n_i $i = 1,2,3 \ldots m$	The number of words of the Actor's tags in Context-aware Business Card appears in Theme i $(\mathcal{T}_i)$
4	Theme Join History (HIS)	t_i $i = 1,2,3 \ldots m$	The times of similar Themes with Theme $i(\mathcal{T}_i)$ appears in Theme Join History
5	Friend Recommendation (REC)	m_i $i = 1,2,3 \ldots m$	The times of recommendations of Theme $i(\mathcal{T}_i)$
6	Souvenir (SOU)	k_i $i = 1,2,3 \ldots m$	The kinds of souvenirs of Theme $i(\mathcal{T}_i)$
7	Famous Person Join (FAM)	f_i $i = 1,2,3 \ldots m$	The number of famous persons join in Theme $i(\mathcal{T}_i)$
8	Theme Satisfaction (SAT)	d_i $i = 1,2,3 \ldots m$	The degrees of satisfaction about Theme $i(\mathcal{T}_i)$

The quantitative method based on these reference variables of context information is expressed by Equation 2.

Let V_{ij} denotes Theme j 's reference variable values based on i_{th} context information, and supposing there are m available Themes near this user.

$$Q_{ij} = \frac{V_{ij}}{V_{i_{sum}}} = \frac{V_{ij}}{\sum_{j=1}^{m} V_{ij}}$$

$$i{=}1,2,3...8; j = 1,2,3 \ldots m; V \in \{r,s,n,t,m,k,f,d\} \tag{2}$$

After calculating Q_{ij}, the weight values (W_i) of context information should be used to calculate Sum_j together, following introduces the weighted mechanism in Context-driven Mobile Social Network Discovery System.

At the beginning, $W_1 = W_2 = \cdots = W_8 = 0.125$. Then once user rejects the recommendatory Theme, which means these weight values cannot correctly infer user desired Themes and W_i should be adjusted, the new W_i will be used to calculate in next calculation. Equation 3 presents the adjustment process of W_i.

Supposing this is the num time user rejected recommendatory Theme. There are m available Themes near this user. And after rejection, user chose Theme k as choice, so

$$W_i = \frac{W_i + \frac{W_i * Q_{ik}}{Sum_k}}{num}$$

$$i = 1,2 \ldots 8;\ k = 1,2,3 \ldots m;\ num \geq 1 \tag{3}$$

Applying this proposed Theme Awareness procedure, Context-driven Mobile Social Network Discover System can provide more intelligent recommendation service to users, and be ready for later interconnections in system.

5 System Implementation

The implementation of this system is executed on Android Platform, which is an operating system for mobile devices such as smartphones and tablet computers.

5.1 Interface Integration

This Context-driven Mobile Social Network Discovery System is implemented on Android 2.2.3(Motorola XT800W). Following Figure 5(a) is a menu view of this system, and Figure 5(b) shows the classification interface when users browse all the on-going Themes in this system. Figure 5(c) is a map view of user's current location and recommending an optimum.

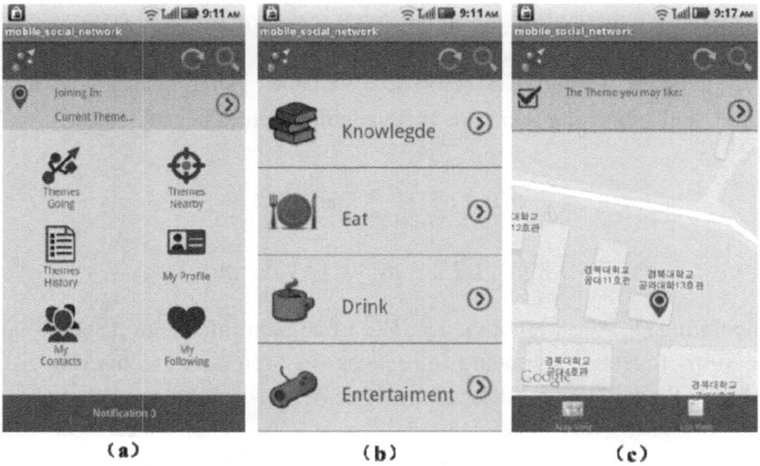

Fig. 4. System Screenshots on Android Platform

Also the implementation of exchanging Context-aware Business Card is shown in Figure 6. At exchanging time, both sides of exchange just click the cards on own mobile screens, system can intelligently complete exchange process, collect and save the related exchange information including exchange time, exchange place and exchange person, which can be used to manage numerous social relationships in the future. Figure 6(a) shows a screenshot of Context-aware Business Card, Figure 6(b) presents the screenshot of exchange procedure, and the last screenshot (Figure 6(c)) is a view of received cards.

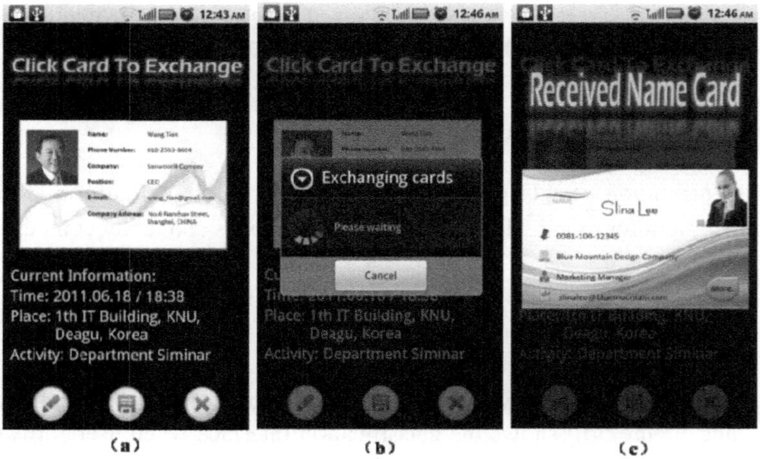

Fig. 5. Screenshot of Context-aware Business Card Exchanging

6 Conclusion and Future Work

This paper presents a Context-driven Mobile Social Network Discover System, and it takes full advantage of mobile devices' mobility to discover dynamic social networks nearby users. It is aimed to help users discover the potential social resources and become a convenient communication platform for users exchanging mind and provide more opportunities to create new social relationships in realistic social activities.

However, this system is not totally completed yet. In the future, we will complete this system, execute many tests, and then evaluate this Context-driven Mobile Social Network Discover System.

Acknowledgment. This work was supported by the second stage of the Brain Korea 21 Project in 2011.

References

1. Tong, C.: Analysis of Some popular Mobile Social Network System. Helsinki University of Technology (2008)
2. Dixit, J.: The artfu-l and mobile-dodger (location-based social networking). IEEE Sepectrum 3, 59–60 (2005)
3. Miluzzo, E., Lane, N.D., Fodor, K.: Sensing meets mobile scoail networks the design, the implemention and evaluation of CenceMe application. In: Proceedings of the 6th ACM Conference on Embedded Network Sensor Systems, NY, USA (2008)
4. Lin, Y., Sundaram, H., Kelliher, A.: Summarization of Social Activity over Time: People, Actions and Concepts in Dynamice Networks. In: Proceeding of the 17th ACM Conference on Information and Knowledge Management, NY, USA (2008)
5. Kao, K., Liao, I., Lyu, J.: An Indoor Location-Based Service Using Access Points as Signal Strength Data Collectors. In: 2010 International Conference on Indoor Positioning and Indoor Navigation (IPIN), pp. 1–6 (September 2010)
6. Meier, R., Cahill, V.: Steam: Event-based middleware for wireless ad hoc networks. In: Proceedings of 22nd International Conference on Distributed Computing Systems Workshops, pp. 639–644 (2002)
7. Chen, G., Kotz, D.: A survey of Context-Aware Mobile Computing Reaserch, Dartmouth College, Hanover, NH (2000)
8. Schmidt, A., Adams, N., Want, R.: Context-aware computing applications. In: Proceedings of IEEE Workshop on Mobile Computing System and Application, Santa Cruz, California, pp. 85–90 (December 1994)
9. Chang, Y., Liu, H., Chou, L., Chen, Y., Shin, H.: A General Architecture of Mobile Social Network Services. In: Interational Conference on Convergence Information Technology, pp. 151–156 (November 2007)

An Energy Efficient Filtering Approach to In-Network Join Processing in Sensor Network Databases*

Kyung-Chang Kim and Byung-Jung Oh

Dept. of Computer Engineering, Hongik University
Seoul, Korea
{kckim,obj}@hongik.ac.kr

Abstract. In processing join queries in a sensor network it is important to minimize communication cost, which is the main consumer of battery power, among sensor nodes. Shipping only relevant data involved in join result to the sensor nodes that is responsible for the final join means reduction in the size of data transmitted and hence lowers battery consumption. In this paper, we present algorithm SBJ which uses bloom filter and algorithm RFB which uses bit vector to filter unnecessary data during join processing in a sensor database. We compare our algorithms with the existing synopsis join (SNJ) algorithm in terms of the communication cost associated with processing BEJ (Binary Equi-Join) queries. The query performance results show that both the SBJ and the RFB algorithms outperform the SNJ algorithm. In addition, the RFB algorithm generally performs better than the SBJ algorithm.

Keywords: Sensor network, in-network join processing, sensor database, query performance, communication cost.

1 Introduction

Recent developments in hardware technology have enabled the widespread use and deployment of sensor networks. A sensor network consists of a large number of sensor nodes that combine physical sensing capabilities such as temperature, noise, light, or seismic sensors with networking and computation capabilities. Each sensor node is capable of observing the environment using sensors, storing the observed values, processing them and exchanging them with other nodes over the wireless network.

This motivates visualizing sensor networks as a distributed database system [6] and the data present in a sensor network as relational data streams. Like a database, queries are sent to the nodes in the sensor network to collect the sensed data tuples. We are interested in the scenario where join queries are used to correlate data stored in different regions of a sensor network, and due to the large volume of data, it is prohibitive to ship all the data to the base station (i.e. central server) for joining.

The main query performance criterion in a sensor network is the total communication cost incurred, since each sensor node has limited battery power and

* This work was supported by 2010 Hongik University Research Fund.

T.-h. Kim et al. (Eds.): MulGraB 2011, Part II, CCIS 263, pp. 116–122, 2011.

transmitting data is the main consumer of battery energy. Thus an energy efficient approach to distributed join query processing is to minimize the communication cost incurred.

There are many applications of sensor networks including monitoring and surveillance systems in both civilian and military contexts and warehouse management. For example, in a vehicle tracking system, we may be interested in vehicles that entered and exited a designated length of a road to monitor the traffic volume and speed. To deal with such a problem domain, an ad-hoc query can be specified. A naïve way to answer an ad-hoc query for such application is to ship the sensor readings back to the base station, and perform the join at the base station. As already mentioned, this approach is prohibitive since transmitting all sensor readings to the base station for the join would incur prohibitive communication cost.

A better approach is to transmit only those readings that are likely to contribute to the join results. In addition, we are interested in in-network implementation strategies whereby the join is implemented within the sensor network and not at the base station. The filtering techniques we propose only transmit those data involved in the join result to the join region near the base station. An approach similar to ours is the synopsis join (SNJ) algorithm [6]. The key idea is to use synopsis of sensor readings to prune those readings that are irrelevant to join results. The main difference between our approach (RFB, SBJ algorithm) and SNJ algorithm is that we use bloom filters and bit vectors instead of synopsis to prune irrelevant data. We discuss the query performance results of the proposed algorithms and compare communication costs with the SNJ algorithm.

The rest of the paper is organized as follows. We discuss related join processing techniques for sensor databases in Section 2. In Section 3, we present two join algorithms that use filtering approach for sensor databases. Experimental results are given for the query performance of proposed algorithms including comparison with existing SNJ algorithm in Section 4. The conclusion is given in Section 5.

2 Related Work

A technique to handle simple joins in sensor networks is proposed in [5]. It supports joining sensor readings stored in the same sensor, or between a sensor and a global data stream. The technique cannot handle joins across arbitrary pair of sensors. An adaptive algorithm for finding the optimal join operation placement was proposed in [2]. The paper focused on the continuous join of pairs of sensors and the join operation is carried out by a single sensor. Another work is path join [3] which selects an optimal set of join nodes to minimize communication cost. In [1], a combination of localized and centralized implementation for a join operation is considered in which one of the operands is a relatively small static table which is used to flood the network. However, the problem of distributed and communication efficient implementation for general join operation has not been addressed in the context of sensor networks.

The general join strategies in sensor networks can be classified as naïve join, sequential join, and centroid join depending on the location of the join region in the sensor network [4]. The main problem with these general approaches is the communication cost overhead associated with low join selectivity. Tuples that are not candidates for join can be transmitted to the join region. The most related work is synopsis join (SNJ) algorithm [7], which is an in-network join strategy for evaluating join queries in sensor networks with communication efficiency. In this strategy, data not contributing to the join results are pruned in the early stage of the join processing reducing unnecessary communication overhead.

3 In-Network Join Processing in Sensor Databases

The proposed in-network join strategies are energy efficient since they reduce data transmission cost by pruning and not sending those data (tuples) not involved in the join result. By shipping only relevant data involved in the join to the join region, the number of bytes t is drastically reduced resulting in lower battery consumption.

In this paper, we focus on the processing of BEJ (Binary Equi-Join) queries. A BEJ query is initiated at the sensor node called query sink and the query result is also collected at query sink. Since the memory size at each node is limited, the sink node is unable to perform the join locally. The join has to be performed through the collaboration of several nodes called the join region.

3.1 SBJ (Semi Bloom Join) Algorithm

The SBJ algorithm is a hybrid algorithm that reduces the size of data to be transmitted to the join region using bloom filters and semi joins. Figure 1 shows the join strategy of the SBJ algorithm for the join of data in sensor nodes in region R and region S. For simplicity, we reduce the problem to be a distributed join between table R and table S. We assume that table R and table S are distributed.

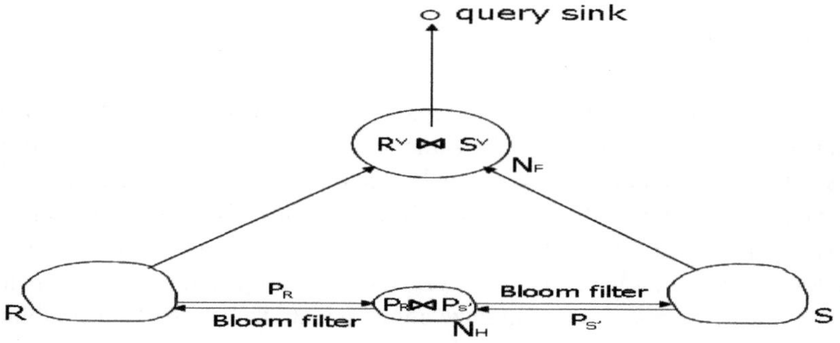

Fig. 1. SBJ join strategy

The SBJ algorithm consists of the semi table creation step, semi table join step and the final join step. In the semi table creation step, a semi table P_R is created for the sensor nodes in R region (i.e. table R) using the join attribute values. The semi table P_R is a projection of R on the join attributes of R and S.

The semi table join step is implemented as follows. The semi table P_R is shipped to the semi table join region N_H. A hash based Bloom filter is created using P_R in which join attribute values of R are hashed to some address in the Bloom filter whose corresponding bits are set to 1. A zero bit after hashing indicate that no join attribute values that hashes to that bit participates in the join. The Bloom filter is then shipped to sensor nodes in region S (i.e. table S). A semi table $P_{S'}$ is created and shipped back to region N_H. The semi table $P_{S'}$ is a projection of S on the join attributes of R and S. The semi table P_R and $P_{S'}$ are joined in region N_H and the resulting semi table $P_{R'}$ is used to create a Bloom filter to be shipped back to table R.

The final join step is implemented as follows. After the semi table join step is executed, those candidate tuples in table R and table S that participate in the join can be obtained. Those join candidate tuples are then shipped to the join region N_F for final join. The R^V (S^V) in N_F is the set of candidate join tuples in R (S) for the join attribute v. The join region N_F is chosen to reduce the cost of transmitting data from region R and region S to the query sink. The final join result is sent to the query sink.

3.2 RFB (Record Filtering Using Bit-Vector) Algorithm

The RFB algorithm is a hybrid algorithm that reduces the size of data to be transmitted to the join region using bit vectors. Figure 2 shows the join strategy of the RFB algorithm for the join of data in sensor nodes in region R and region S.

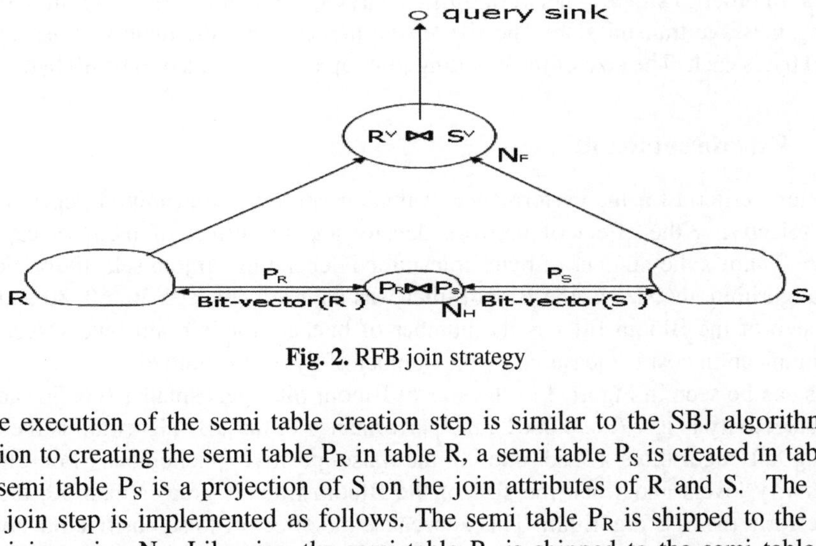

Fig. 2. RFB join strategy

The execution of the semi table creation step is similar to the SBJ algorithm. In addition to creating the semi table P_R in table R, a semi table P_S is created in table S. The semi table P_S is a projection of S on the join attributes of R and S. The semi table join step is implemented as follows. The semi table P_R is shipped to the semi table join region N_H. Likewise, the semi table P_S is shipped to the semi table join region N_H. A bit vector is created after the join of P_R and P_S in region N_H. A Bit-vector(R) contains one bit for every tuple in P_R. That bit is set to 1 if it is in P_S. Likewise a Bit-vector(S) contains one bit for every tuple in P_S. That bit is set to 1 if it is in P_R. Bit-vector(R) and Bit-vector(S) is shipped back to table R and table S respectively.

After the semi table join step is executed, those candidate tuples in table R and table S that participate in the join can be obtained. The final join step is identical to the SBJ algorithm.

4 Performance Analysis

To test the cost-effectiveness of the join algorithms presented in this paper in terms of the communication cost, including the number of bytes transmitted and processed to get the join result, a performance comparison is made with the SNJ algorithm.

4.1 Experiment Environment

In our experiment, 10,000 sensor nodes were created and distributed uniformly in a 100 by 100 grid. We placed each node at the center of each grid. The query sink was placed at the center of the grid. Region R and region S were placed at the bottom right and bottom left of the grid respectively with each region containing 800 sensor nodes each. The cardinality of table R consists of 2000 tuples or records and table S contains 1000 tuples.

The additional assumptions made for the experiment are as follows. The number of hops required to route a single message from the source node to the final node was assumed to use the distance and the communication radius between the two sensor nodes. In order to simplify network traffic analysis, we assumed that no failure occurs during message transmission. The size of the message and the tuple was assumed to be 40 bytes each. The size of the resulting join tuple was assumed to be 80 bytes.

4.2 Experiment Result

The three criteria for the performance evaluation are bytes transmitted depending on join selectivity, the effect of network density and the effect of memory capacity. Figure 3 shows the number of bytes transmitted depending on join selectivity. For the SBJ algorithm, the size of the Bloom filter was adjusted between 50, 60, 80 and 100. The size of the Bloom filter is the number of buckets for join attribute values. The communication cost is measured by the number of bytes transmitted.

As can be seen in Figure 3 as the size of Bloom filter gets smaller (i.e. 50) and the join selectivity is low (i.e. 0.0001), the performance of the SBJ algorithm is the worst among all algorithms tested due to the false positive phenomena. For all join selectivity levels and when the size of the Bloom filter is greater than 50, the SBJ outperform the SNJ algorithm. This is because the effect of false positive phenomena decreases with the increase in the size of the Bloom filter. Comparing RFB algorithm and SNJ algorithm, bytes transmitted are drastically lower in the RFB algorithm compared to the SNJ algorithm. The RFB algorithm performs better than the SBJ algorithm when the Bloom filter size is less than 100. If the Bloom filter size increases to 100 and up, the effect of false positive is minimal.

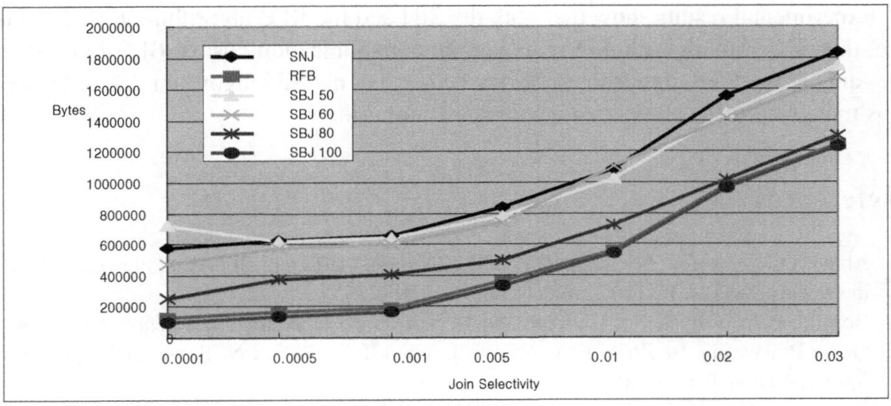

Fig. 3. The effect of join selectivity on bytes transmitted

Figure 4 shows the effect of changes in memory capacity on the number of bytes transmitted. In our experiment, we set the communication range to be 4units, and the join selectivity was set at 0.0001. In all the join algorithms tested, the increase in memory capacity did not affect the communication cost. As in previous experiment, both the SBJ and the RFB algorithms outperformed the SNJ algorithm.

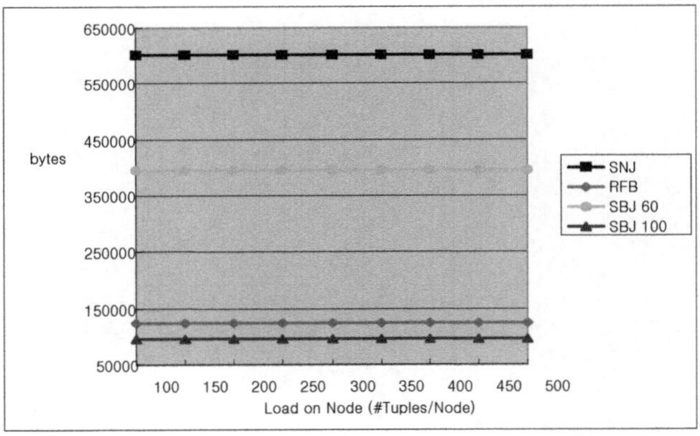

Fig. 4. The effect of memory capacity on bytes transmitted

5 Conclusion

The main focus of the existing join strategies in sensor network databases was how to select the sensor nodes in the join region to perform the final join. Few research results were reported on the use of some filtering techniques to prune unnecessary tuples before shipping the candidate tuples to the join region. In this paper, two join algorithms using some filtering approach were presented. The SBJ algorithm uses Bloom filter and the RFB algorithm uses bit vector to filter out tuples not involved in the join result.

Experimental results show that both the SBJ and the RFB algorithm outperform the existing SNJ join algorithm in reducing the communication cost of BEJ join queries. In general, the RFB algorithm performs better than the SBJ algorithm due to the false positive phenomena associated with using Bloom filter.

References

1. Abadi, D.J., Madden, S., Lindner, W.: REED: robust, efficient filtering and event detection in sensor networks. In: Proceedings of the VLDB (2005)
2. Bonfils, B.J., Bonnet, P.: Adaptive and Decentralized Operator Placement for in-Network Query Processing. In: Zhao, F., Guibas, L.J. (eds.) IPSN 2003. LNCS, vol. 2634, pp. 47–62. Springer, Heidelberg (2003)
3. Pandit, A., Gupta, H.: Communication-Efficient Implementation of Range-Joins in Sensor Networks. In: Li Lee, M., Tan, K.-L., Wuwongse, V. (eds.) DASFAA 2006. LNCS, vol. 3882, pp. 859–869. Springer, Heidelberg (2006)
4. Coman, A., Nascimento, M., Sander, J.: On join location in sensor networks. In: Proceedings of MDM (2007)
5. Madden, S.: The Design and Evaluation of a Query Processing Architecture for Sensor Networks. Ph.D. Thesis, UC Berkeley (2003)
6. Yao, Y., Gehrke, J.: Query processing for sensor networks. In: Proceedings of CIDR (2003)
7. Yu, H., Lim, E., Zhang, J.: On In-network Synopsis Join Processing for Sensor Networks. In: Proceedings of MDM (2006)

A Genetic Programming Approach to Data Clustering*

Chang Wook Ahn[1], Sanghoun Oh[1], and Moonyoung Oh[2]

[1] School of Information & Communication Engineering
Sungkyunkwan University, Suwon 440-746, Korea
cwan@skku.edu,oosshoun@gmail.com
[2] Department of Medical Administration
Busan College of Information Technology, Korea

Abstract. This paper presents a genetic programming (GP) to data clustering. The aim is to accurately classify a set of input data into their genuine clusters. The idea lies in discovering a mathematical function on clustering regularities and then utilize the rule to make a correct decision on the entities of each cluster. To this end, GP is incorporated into the clustering procedures. Each individual is represented by a parsing tree on the program set. Fitness function evaluates the quality of clustering with regard to similarity criteria. Crossover exchanges sub-trees between parental candidates in a positionally independent fashion. Mutation introduces (in part) a new sub-tree with a low probability. The variation operators (i.e., crossover, mutation) offer an effective search capability to obtain the improved quality of solution and the enhanced speed of convergence. Experimental results demonstrate that the proposed approach outperforms a well-known reference.

1 Introduction

Clustering refers to the operation of grouping objects/data with similar patterns in given data sets [1,2]. This is an important task in many applications such as information retrieval, web data analysis, bio-informatics, text mining, and so on [2]. If the number of clusters obtained by a clustering algorithm is equal to the actual number of clusters and each cluster does not contain any object (i.e., member) in different groups, then the clustering result becomes optimal. In essence, the accurate clustering involves the following two measures [3]: *Cluster-validity* and *Cluster-purity*. The former is the ratio of the discovered number of clusters to the optimal number of clusters, the latter is the ratio of the correctly categorized objects to the genuine objects of clusters.

Note that the cluster-validity is intimately related to the cluster-purity; thus, the purity deteriorates significantly when the incorrect number of clusters is returned. In other words, the discovery of the optimal number of clusters is primary, and the categorization of their members is secondary.

* This research was supported by the MKE, Korea under the ITRC NIPA-2011-(C1090-1121-0008).

T.-h. Kim et al. (Eds.): MulGraB 2011, Part II, CCIS 263, pp. 123–132, 2011.

Many existing clustering algorithms employ partitioning or machine-learning techniques [1,2]. In the K-means algorithm as the partitioning approach, for instance, the predicted number of clusters (K) is a very crucial parameter that directly influences the clustering results. However, the threshold K is usually determined in a trial and error manner. As the machine-learning approach, genetic algorithm-based clustering techniques give a change to adjust the threshold to some extent [3]. But there is a problem such that the threshold should be effectively transformed into a specific, related variable. Note that the existing approaches are ultimately confronted with a common task, viz., *deciding the threshold*. In other words, the threshold must be properly specified in advance, which is related to the number of clusters. It is noteworthy that an appropriate decision on the threshold is crucial to the success of clustering [1]. But the threshold is *a priori* unknown/unavailable in real-world applications.

This paper proposes a genetic programming (GP) based clustering algorithm that is not hampered by the threshold decision problem. It returns the accurate number of clusters and maintains the high quality in cluster-purity. It can be achieved by discovering and consulting a regularity function about cluster patterns. The rest of the paper is organized as follows. Section 2 describes the procedures of GP. The similarity criteria (i.e., intra-similarity and inter-dissimilarity) for (numerical) data sets are presented in Section 3. After presenting the proposed approach Section 4, a comparative study follows in Section 5. The paper concludes with a summary in Section 6.

2 Genetic Programming: GP

Genetic Programming (GP) suggested by Koza was embraced as the subject in his book "Genetic Programming" (1992) [4]. Many researchers have applied GP to various systems by employing linear strings, non-linear trees or graphs. Some even blend GP with linear regression or context free grammars (CFGs) while others use GP to model ontogeny and organism [4,5,6]. Fig. 1 illustrates the overall procedures of GP.

The most significant difference of GP to other evolutionary algorithms lies in the representation which for GP employs a tree structure [4,5,6]. The trees consist of two types of elements; *nodes* and *leaves*. Nodes are functional elements which connects other elements using the functions assigned to the nodes. On the other hand, leaves are end points consisting of values or inputs, and have no further connections below. An example shown in Fig. 4 (see Section 4.1) contains 3 nodes and 4 leaves and the expression reads as $\{(X_1/X_2) - (0.1 + X_1)\}$. Here the leaves normally take any real numbers or input variables.

Fitness function is the quantitative measure of how well a program has learned to predict the output(s) in terms of the input(s) [5]. It gives a feedback to the learning algorithm regarding which individuals should have a higher probability of being allowed to survive. Thus, the definition of fitness function is very important. Generally, fitness function is designed for fully reflecting the physical object of problems.

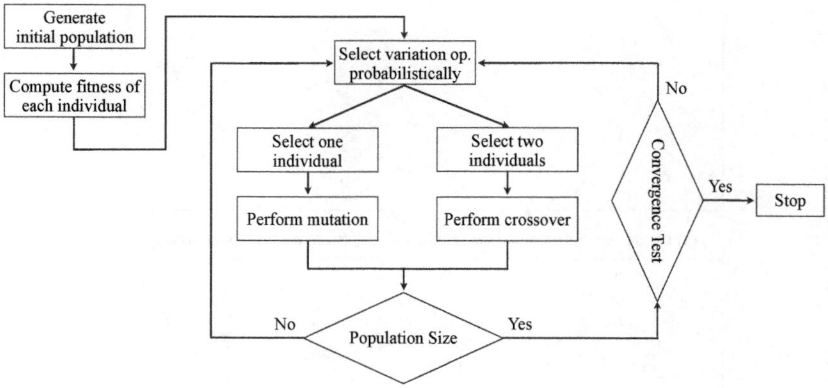

Fig. 1. Overall procedure of GP

After evaluating the quality of individuals, we have to decide which individuals are maintained and how new individuals are created. This task can be carried out GP operators; selection, crossover, and mutation. There are various selection operators. Selection focuses on the exploration of promising regions in the search space [4,5]. In other words, selection is responsible for the speed of evolution as well as the premature convergence. As such, a decision on the type of selection to be applied is one of the most important tasks. In general, ordinal selection methods are preferable [3].

Due to the uniqueness in the representation (i.e., tree) of GP, crossover is different from that of usual evolutionary algorithms [4,5]. The simplest way to perform crossover on the tree-type structure is to use *branch cutting and splicing* as shown in Fig. 5 (see Section 4.3). The method of exchanging proper sub-trees (of parents) is very effective in increasing the exploratory power of GP. Unlike crossover, mutation is performed on only a single individual with a small probability [4,5]. It plays an important role in maintaining search diversity of GP. When an individual has been selected for mutation, a point (i.e., node) in the tree is randomly chosen, and then the existing sub-tree at that point is replaced with a newly generated sub-tree. Fig. 6 (see Section 4.3) shows an example of mutation. The mutated individual is then placed back into the population.

3 Similarity Criteria

This section describes the similarity criteria for (numerical) data sets [3]. They are distance-based similarity measures; *intra-similarity* and *inter-dissimilarity.* They are the main constituents of fitness function described in Section 4.

3.1 Intra-similarity

The intra-similarity is related to the distance between each centroid and the objects within the cluster. To properly measure the intra-similarity, the intra-cluster distance is defined by

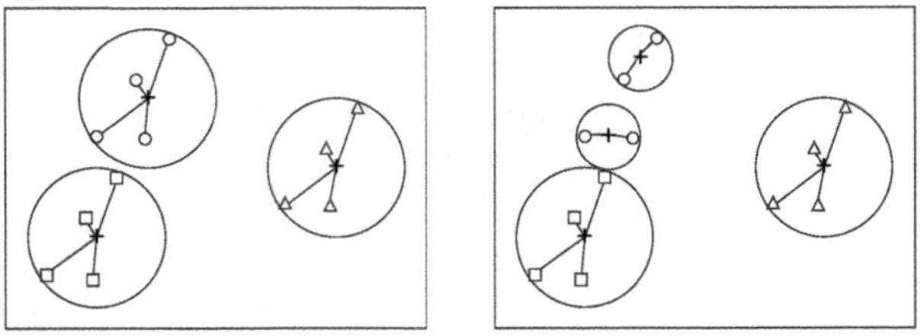

(a) Clustering results derived by intra-similarity (from three to four clusters)

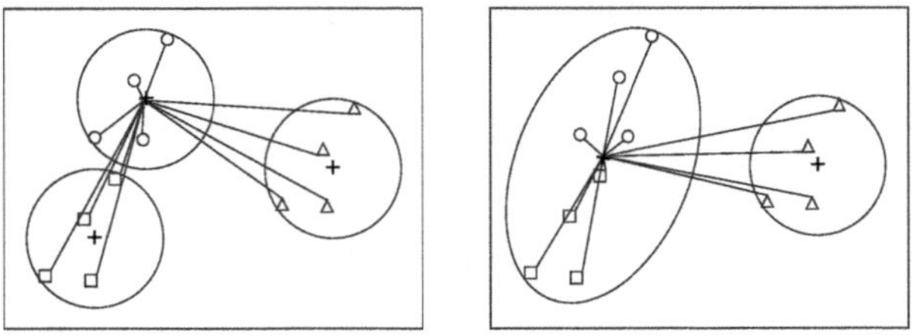

(b) Clustering results derived by inter-dissimilarity (from three from two clusters)

Fig. 2. Examples of intra-similarity and inter-dissimilarity

$$\mathcal{D}_{intra} = \sum_{k=1}^{K} \sum_{i=1}^{N_k} ||c_k - x_{k,i}|| \tag{1}$$

where N_k is the number of objects in cluster k, c_k is the centroid (of cluster k), x_i is the ith object in the data sets, $x_{k,i}$ denotes the entity (i.e., actual value) of the ith objects in cluster k, K is the (promising) number of clusters. In this measure, a higher value is preferable. As shown in Fig. 2(a), the intra-cluster distance of four clusters is larger than that of three clusters. That is, four clusters are more favorable in accordance with the intra-similarity. It denotes that the intra-similarity leads towards a larger number of clusters.

3.2 Inter-dissimilarity

The inter-dissimilarity is measured by the distance between centroids of clusters and all the objects encountered in clustering. With this in view, the inter-cluster distance for clusters is defined as follows:

$$\bar{\mathcal{D}}_{inter} = \sum_{k=1}^{K} \sum_{i=1}^{N} ||c_k - x_{k,i}|| \tag{2}$$

where K, c_k and $x_{k,i}$ are the same as those of eqn. (1), and N is the total numbers of objects in specific data sets. It computes the sum of distances between every centroid and all the objects. A larger value is also preferable. For instance, the inter-cluster distance of two clusters is larger than that of three clusters (see Fig. 2(b)). Definitely, two clusters are more favorable in terms of the inter-dissimilarity. It implies that the inter-similarity yields a smaller number of clusters.

Note that a trade-off exists between intra-similarity and inter-dissimilarity. It is important to strike a balance between two measures for getting accurate clustering results. Further details are explained in Section 4.2.

4 GP-Based Clustering Algorithm

This section presents the GP-based adaptive clustering algorithm. The aim is to automatically perform accurate clustering in terms of discovering the exact number of clusters and identifying their genuine members for the given data sets. This is achieved by discovering a regularity function on the pattern of clusters by employing GP. A promising pattern may be related to the distribution of centroids of clusters. The proposed algorithm consists of two phases in this regard. In the first phase, GP returns the number of clusters as well as the centroids of clusters. Here the information is provided by a mathematical function. In the second phase, a greedy procedure is performed such that each object is classified into the nearest centroid. A pseudocode is presented in Fig. 3. Operational procedures in the second phase is very straightforward. Thus, GP modules in the first phase are minutely described below.

4.1 Encoding

Each individual is encoded by a tree structure. Given two predefined sets – the *terminal* and *functional* sets – an initial population is created by stochastically choosing symbols from the two sets and then assembling them into a valid tree structure [4,5]. There are many variants, primarily aimed at biasing the shape of the trees produced. Generally, the terminal set consists of input variables and some constants, while the functional set is composed of the (unary or binary) functions of programs. The proposed algorithm employs GP in order to effectively traverse the space of computer programs. Specifically, GP is used for discovering a mathematical function that models the centroids (of clusters) in terms of given inputs. In this algorithm, the terminal set consists of some constants (R) and variables (X_k) which indicate the data of the k-th attribute (i.e., dimension). Thus, the terminal set is defined over $\{R, X_1, X_2, \cdots, X_{Dim}\}$ where Dim is the dimension of data sets and R is a random number between 0 to 1. Moreover, the functional set consists of unary and binary operators defined over $\{+, -, \div, \times, \sin, \cos, \log, \exp\}$. Each individual returns the values in terms of the input data (i.e., centroid candidates). The value can be used for finding the number of clusters as well as the centroids of clusters. The input data can be prepared by randomly sampling the data set to be clustered.

An example is illustrated in Fig. 4. The tree-type individual expresses a function such as $\{(X_1/X_2) - (0.1 + X_1)\}$. For the 2-dimensional input data $\{(X_1, X_2)\} = \{(1,4), (2,4), (2,2), (4,1), (4,2)\}$, the individual returns the integer values of $\{0, -1, -1, 0, -2\}$. It denotes that the individual offers the number of clusters as well as the centroids of clusters. In other words, it discovers three groups of $\{(1,4), (4,1)\}$, $\{(2,4), (2,2)\}$, $\{(4,2)\}$. Moreover, their representative

```
GP-BASED CLUSTERING ALGORITHM
[PARAMETERS] 𝒫: Population, p_c: Crossover probability
             p_m: Mutation probability, N: Number of objects
             K: Number of clusters, c: Centroids, d: distances
[OUTPUT] 𝒞: Clustering results

/*-----THE FIRST PHASE-----*/
𝒫:=initialize(); /*Initialize the population*/
while(termination criteria are not met) {
   evaluate_fitness(𝒫); /*Evaluate the fitness of population*/
   𝒫^(s):=selection(𝒫); /*Select superior individuals*/
   𝒫^(c):=GP_crossover(𝒫^(s)); /*Perform GP crossover*/
   𝒫^(m):=GP_mutation(𝒫^(c)); /*Apply GP mutation*/
   𝒫:=𝒫^(m); /*Replace the old population*/
}
/*Extract the information on K and c from the best individual*/
[K,c] := extract_info(𝒫_best);

/*-----THE SECOND PHASE-----*/
for i := 1 to N { /*For all the objects*/
   for j := 1 to K /*For all the centroids*/
      /*Compute a distance between i-th object and j-th centroid*/
      d_j := distance(x_i, c_j);
   /*Find the cluster index of the minimum distance*/
   idx := index_min(d_1, ···, d_j, ···, d_K);
   𝒞_idx ⟵ x_i; /*Add i-th object into idx-th cluster*/
}
return(𝒞); /*Return the clustering result*/
```

Fig. 3. Pseudocode of the proposed clustering algorithm

points can be used as the centroids for clustering, viz., $(2.5, 2.5)$ for $\{(1,4),(4,1)\}$, $(2,3)$ for $\{(2,4),(2,2)\}$, and $(4,2)$ for $\{(4,2)\}$.

4.2 Fitness Function

Fitness function must accurately evaluate the quality of individuals on the basis of intra-similarity and inter-dissimilarity since it plays an important role in performing better clustering [3]. The proposed fitness function makes an attempt to simultaneously optimize both cluster-validity (i.e., the actual number of clusters) and cluster-purity (i.e., the accuracy of discovering cluster members). The (*Euclidean*) distance-based similarity measures described in Section 3 is used here. The fitness function is designed by the proper combination of intra-similarity and inter-dissimilarity measures, defined as follows:

$$fitness = c_1 \cdot \left(\mathcal{D}_{intra}\right)^{\alpha} + c_2 \cdot \left(\bar{\mathcal{D}}_{inter}\right)^{\beta} \tag{3}$$

where $\mathcal{D}_{intra}$ and $\bar{\mathcal{D}}_{inter}$ represent intra-similarity and inter-dissimilarity respectively, c_1 and c_2 are problem-dependent scaling factors, and α and β play an

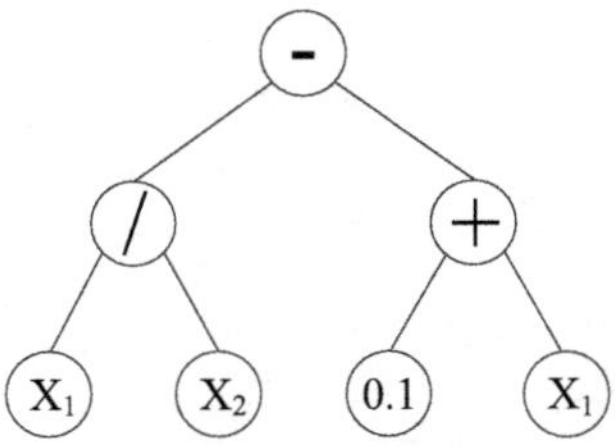

Fig. 4. A tree structure of individual

important role in striking a balance between two similarity measures regarding the dimension of data sets. There is a tradeoff between $\mathcal{D}_{intra}$ and $\bar{\mathcal{D}}_{inter}$ terms. If $\mathcal{D}_{intra}$ alone is involved in the fitness function, it always favors the larger number of clusters. Conversely, if $\bar{\mathcal{D}}_{inter}$ alone is employed, it forms the fewer number of clusters. This conflicting property can be compromised by a proper combination of two measures. To this end, α and β are set to $\alpha = \log_{10}(10 \cdot Dim)$, $\beta = \log_{10}(10 + Dim)$ where Dim is the dimension of data sets. Obviously, a smaller fitness value is favorable.

4.3 GP Operators

In essence, an initial population has a low average fitness. Evolution proceeds by transforming the initial population by the use of genetic operators.

Selection

Selection chooses a computer program from the current population (of programs) based on fitness values. Physically, better individuals are more likely to survive and to be copied into the next generation [4,5,6]. The proposed algorithm applies tournament selection as it is effective in keeping the selection noise as low as possible [3]. A number of individuals, called the tournament size, is selected randomly, and a selective competition takes place. The traits of better individuals are then allowed to replace those of the worse individuals.

Crossover

Crossover offers some variation to the population by combining the genetic materials of two parents by exchanging a part of one parent with another part of the other [4,5,6]. Tree-based crossover is shown in Fig. 5. Given two parents obtained by selection, the crossover is performed by randomly selecting a sub-tree in each parent and then swapping the selected sub-trees of the two parents.

The crossover is quite effective in searching around solution spaces; for some intricate structures, however, it is possible to give rise to a complicated scenario. For instance, it happens when the sub-tree of the donor is not suited to be placed

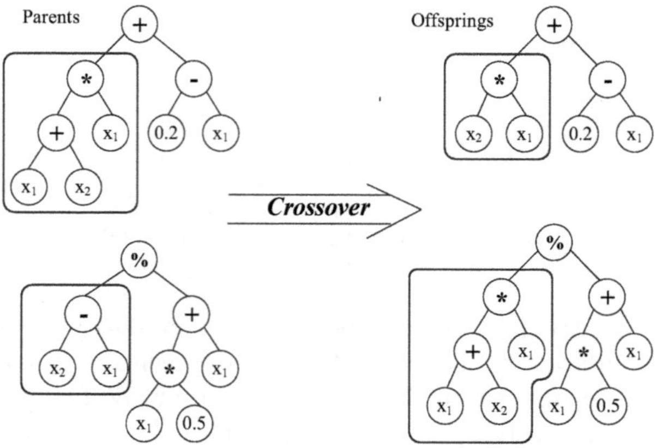

Fig. 5. An Example of GP Crossover

at the desired splice in the recipient. There are two possible solutions: either the input set for the nodes are extended until they can accept any expression in the trees, or the crossover is performed restrictedly in order to only permit to crossover the sub-trees of the same data type. The latter is incorporated with the proposed algorithm.

Another important issue in GP crossover lies in the size of trees since the size may grow exponentially unless any constraint is imposed. A possible solution is to only permit the crossover for the sub-trees of the same depth in the parental trees in order not to exceed the maximum tree depth. This approach is also employed in this regard.

Mutation

Mutation operates on only a single individual. Usually, each offspring (produced by the crossover) undergoes mutation with a low probability [4,5,6]. It introduces a certain amount of randomness, in order not to stagnate the exploratory power. Given one individual, the mutation is performed by replacing a selected sub-tree in the parent with a newly created sub-tree. A proper example is given in Fig. 6. To obtain the offspring, the selected sub-tree on the left-hand side is replaced by the newly generated sub-tree on the right-hand side. The altered individual is then placed back into the population.

5 Experimental Results

This section tests the proposed GP-based clustering algorithm. As described in Section 1, the clustering results can be evaluated by *cluster-validity* and

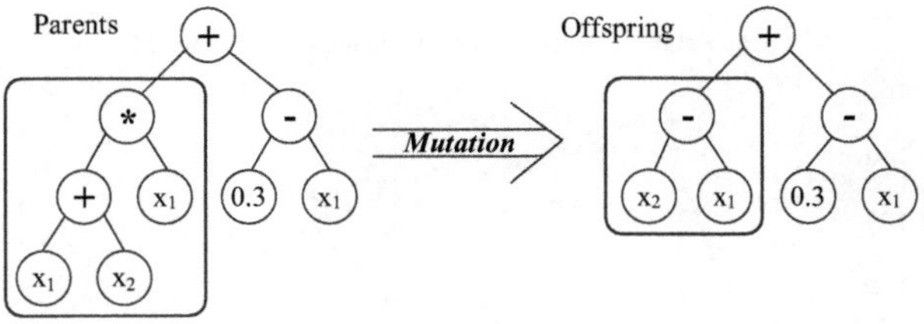

Fig. 6. An Example of GP Mutation

cluster-purity [3]. The cluster-validity is measured by the found number of clusters as compared with the optimal number of clusters. The cluster-purity evaluates how correctly the cluster members are discovered, viz., the number of objects correctly classified. In GP, pair-wise tournament selection (i.e., tournament size is 2) is employed due to its ability to keep the selection noise as low as possible. Crossover with $p_c = 0.75$ is used for exchanging the sub-trees of individuals. Mutation with $p_m = 0.1$ is used for escaping from the local optimum. The population size is set to the number of objects (N). The GP iterates until the number of generations reaches the half of objects ($N/2$). All the results are averaged over 100 runs.

Comparative studies have been performed with two synthetic data sets and one real-world data set [3]. The synthetic data sets have 2 and 3 dimensions (i.e., attributes), and all the sets consist of four clusters. Moreover, each attribute is normally distributed. *Ruspini* is used as the real-world data set. It also contains four clusters. Experimental results are shown in Table 1. As to the K-means algorithm, the cluster-purity is only presented since the number of clusters has been already set to the optimal value in advance (i.e., $K = 4$). It is seen that the proposed algorithm returns the optimal number of clusters while correctly discovering cluster members. In other words, it achieves the near-perfect validity and purity. Clearly, the proposed approach is more effective than the K-means. High efficiency and no need of deciding the threshold K (i.e., the number of clusters) are noteworthy features of the proposed approach. Moreover, it offers a regularity function on the pattern of cluster centroids. That is, it can mathematically predict some spatial arrangement of data sets. Fig. 7 illustrates an example about *Ruspini* data. The bold line indicates a mathematical function found by GP, which models the pattern of four groups.

Table 1. Performance comparison of algorithms

Date sets	*K-means Algorithm*		*Proposed Algorithm*	
	k	Purity	Validity	Purity
2D-data	4	0.9829	1.0	0.9999
3D-data	4	0.9844	1.0	0.9999
Ruspini	4	0.9840	0.98	0.9999

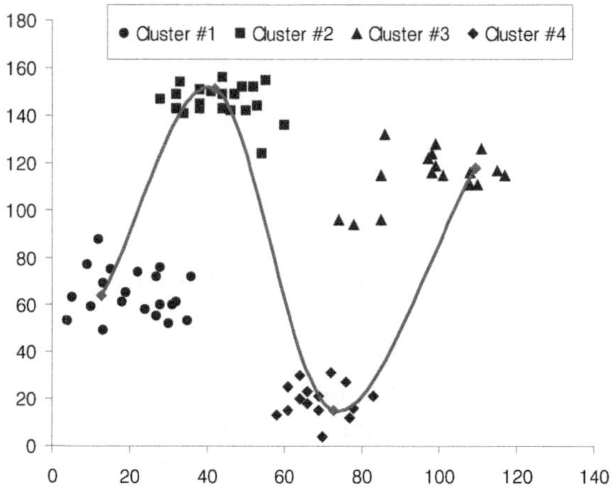

Fig. 7. Example: A mathematical function (found by GP) about *Ruspini* data

6 Conclusion

This paper has proposed a GP-based clustering algorithm for numerical data sets. It automatically discovers the number of genuine clusters and accurately categorizes data sets. Experimental studies with synthetic and real-world data sets have shown that the proposed algorithm performs better than K-means algorithm. Also, it yields a predictive function of clustering patterns in data sets. It seems that the GP approach works well on other types of data and with other types of fitness function. Also, a multi-criteria approach would be quite promising to handle the tradeoff between similarity measures.

References

1. Jain, A.K., Murty, M.N., Flynn, P.J.: Data Clustering: A Review. ACM Computing Surveys 31(3) (September 1999)
2. Han, J., Kamber, M.: Data mining: Concepts and techniques. Morgan Kaufmann Publishers, San Francisco (2001)
3. Park, N.H., Ahn, C.W., Ramakrishna, R.S.: Adaptive Clustering Technique Using Genetic Algorithms. IEICE Trans. Inf. and Syst. E88-D(12), 2880–2882 (2005)
4. Koza, J.R.: Genetic Programming On the programming of Computers by Means of Natural Selection. The MIT Press (1992)
5. Langdon, W.B.: Genetic Programming + Data Structures = Automatic Programming. The Kluwer International Series in Engineering and Computer Science. Kluwer Academic Publishers (1998)
6. Mitchell, T.M.: Machine Learning. Computer Science Series. McGRAW-HILL International Editions (1997)

Design and Implementation of a Hand-Writing Message System for Android Smart Phone Using Digital Pen

Jong-Yun Yeo[1], Yong Dae Lee[2], Sang-Hoon Ji[3], and Gu-Min Jeong[1,*]

[1] School of Electrical Engineering, Kookmin University, Seoul, Korea
[2] The Institute of Webcasting, Internet Television and Telecommunication, Korea
[3] KITECH Institute, Seoul, Korea
gm1004@kookmin.ac.kr

Abstract. In this paper, we propose a hand-writing message system for smartphone using digital pen. Existing messaging systems can only send a message through MMS and cannot utilize various SNS (Social Network Service) because it uses feature phone environment. A proposed messaging system based on smartphone can utilize SNS and can create new systems. We verify usefulness of it by implementation.

Keywords: Digital Pen, Android, Bluetooth, MMS, E-mail.

1 Introduction

There have been needs for hand-writing message system which saves and shares a message created by handwriting using digital pen in mobile device. Nokia's Digital pen is a representative system of hand-writing message system. Nokia's Digital pen can only share messages by SMS and MMS because it is used with feature phone[1]. Therefore, this system cannot share message by SNS (Social Network Service) such as Kakaotalk and Facebook. In addition, it is difficult to design new service model utilizes Internet and digital pen because of limits of feature phone.

In this paper, we propose a hand-writing message system for smartphone using digital pen. The Proposed system can share a message created by digital pen through Kakaotalk and update a message in Facebook because this system based on smartphone. Furthermore, if we use this system with Database server and Internet Connection, we can create new service, e.g. a submitting Report system for salesman. In this paper, we propose a hand-writing message system for Android phone and implement it.

* Corresponding author.

T.-h. Kim et al. (Eds.): MulGraB 2011, Part II, CCIS 263, pp. 133–138, 2011.

2 Digital Pen

In this chapter, we show two kinds of representative digital pen and explain how to save the written data using digital pen.

2.1 Nokia Pen and InterlliPen

Nokia has been developed digital pen used mobile phone and Bluetooth in 2003. To recognize handwriting, it utilizes the Anoto technology. This technology uses a paper on which Anoto pattern was printed and a camera to capture Anoto pattern[2]. Therefore, to use this pen, we need a special paper. In contrast, EPOS's InterlliPen don't need special paper because it uses ultrasonic and infrared light to recognize the position of digital pen as shown Fig. 1. [3][4].

In this paper, we implement an application by using digital pen which uses ultrasonic and infrared light to recognize handwriting.

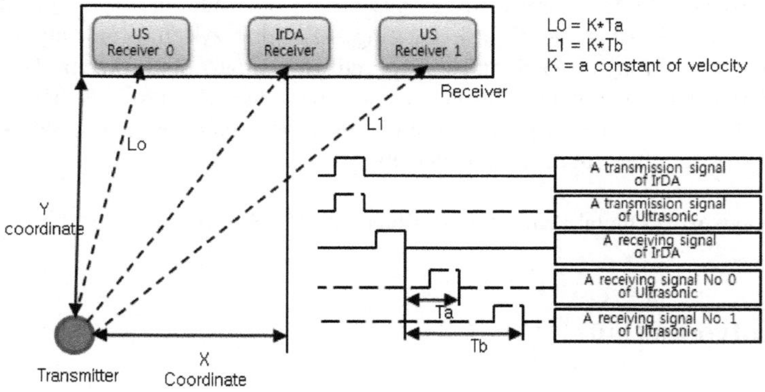

Fig. 1. The principle of coordinates calculation

3 Design and Implementation of a Hand-Writing Message System for Android Smart Phone

Figure 2 is system diagram of proposed handwriting message system based on smartphone. In this system, coordinates of digital pen are transmitted to smartphone through Bluetooth. The smartphone that receive coordinates of pen draws image for message. We can send created image through MMS or E-mail. In addition we can use the image in SNS. For example we send it by Kakaotalk to receiver. And we can update our Facebook by using it.

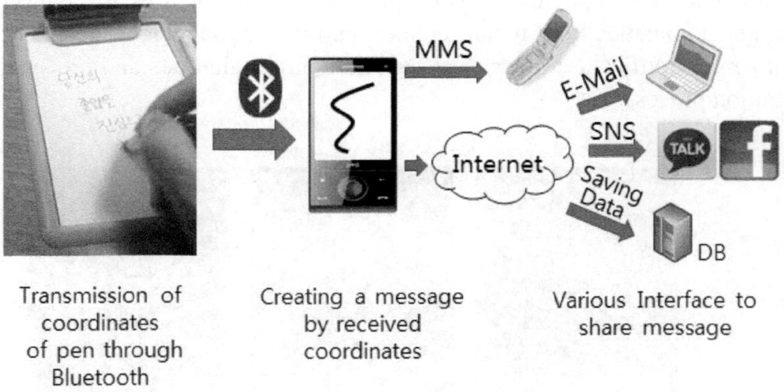

Fig. 2. Hand-writing message system based on smartphone

Especially, when we use this service in conjunction with Database Server, we can create a variety of services are available. For instance, we can design a business report system for salesman who has a lot of outside work by using mobility of smartphone. If this system used, we can report in real-time our work by creating message using digital pen and thus work efficiency can increase. Figure 3 is a submitting report system for salesman, which is used hand-writing message system based on smartphone with Database server.

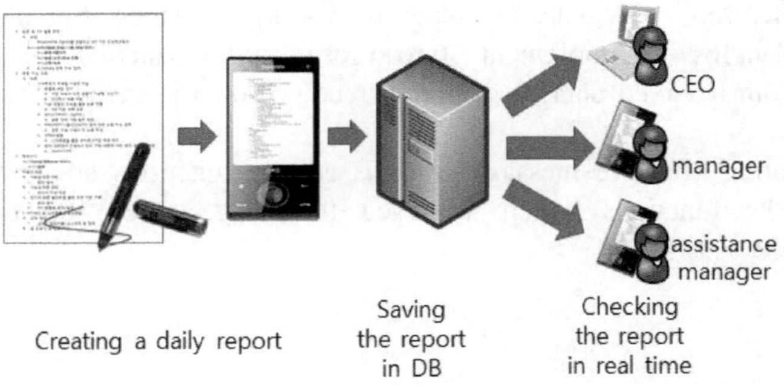

Fig. 3. A submitting Report system for salesman

The proposed messaging system is implemented based on Android phone. We explain major parts of this messaging system in next subchapter.

3.1 Connection with Digital Pen

To create a message, the connection between Android phone and the digital pen should be made. In our application the digital pen is enrolled when you operate application for the first time. When you operate later, it tries to connect enrolled digital pen automatically. If it can't connect enrolled digital pen or there is no enrolled digital pen, it notifies user to request registration of digital pen and proceeds with the registration process.

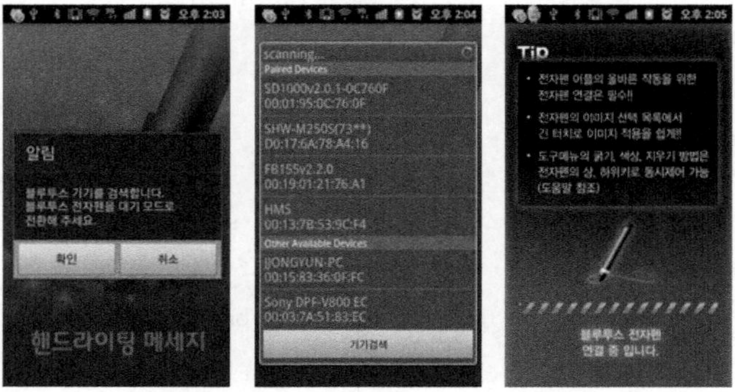

Fig. 4. Screen shot of electronic pen connection

3.2 Creating and Editing a Message Using Digital Pen

Android phone receives coordinates of digital pen. The digital pen supports wide handwriting area approximately 290cm in horizontal and vertical. We can't display original image from digital pen because the size of display of Android phone is limited. Therefore, we create an image to display on phone. For handling without incoming data loss, we implement a thread for receiving data and a thread for creating message from received data. In addition, received data is saved at ring buffer as in Fig. 5.

For creating effective message, various editing functions are implemented. For example, the functions which are used to change color and background are implemented.

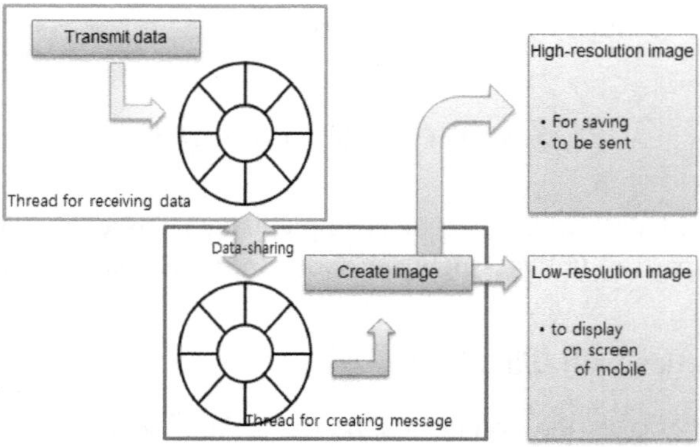

Fig. 5. Real-time image processing with ring buffer and Thread

3.3 Message Sending though E-mail or Internet

We can send the created message through MMS or Internet. Especially, we can utilize social network service.

Fig. 6. Screen shot of MMS and E-mail transfer functions

4 Result of Implementation

After creating message by digital pen and android phone, we sent the created message by using implemented application. We can verify that created image is accurately displayed on screen of android phone. It is possible to send the created message by SNS and MMS.

Fig. 7. Comparison images

5 Conclusion

In this paper, we have proposed a hand-writing message system for smartphone using digital pen. We could utilize various SNS by using proposed messaging system different with previous it. Furthermore, we have verified that we can extend functionality of this system if it is used with database server such as a submitting report system for salesman in chapter 3.

In the future, we will adopt recognition algorithm such as neural network in our application to improve the rate of recognition of handwriting.

References

1. Nokia Digital Pen, `http://www.nokiaaccessibility.com/digPen.html`
2. Anoto Technology, `http://www.anoto.com/`
3. Epos, `http://www.epos-ps.com/`
4. Jaejun, L., Yunmo, C.: Design of a wireless handwriting input system for mobile devices. In: Consumer Electronics 2005 (ISCE 2005), pp. 222–225 (September 2005)

Robust Blind Watermarking Scheme for Digital Images Based on Discrete Fractional Random Transform

Youngseok Lee[1] and Jongweon Kim[2,*]

[1] Dept. of Electronic Engineering, Chungwoon University,
San 29, Namjang-Ri, Hongsung-Kun, Hongsung-Eup, Chungnam, 350-701, Korea
yslee@chungwoon.ac.kr
[2] Dept. of Copyright Protection, Sangmyung University,
20, Hongjmoon 2 Rd, Jongno-gu, Seoul 110-743, Korea
jwkim@smu.ac.kr

Abstract. This paper proposes a robust blind watermarking scheme for digital images based on discrete fractional random transform, a generalization of the discrete fractional Fourier transform with intrinsic randomness. The proposed watermarking scheme can be easily used to embed and extract a watermark and it provides strong information security because of its inherent randomness. Experimental results obtained by subjecting the watermark to several types of attacks reveal that it is robust against frequency and geometric attacks, thus verifying its effectiveness.

Keywords: blind watermarking scheme, discrete fractional random transform, information.

1 Introduction

Digital watermarking is a process in which digital content such as image, video, audio, and even text is protected by embedding information such as a hidden copyright message into the content. Such a watermark should be imperceptible to others while being perceptible to the copyright holder who possesses the proper private information key [1].

In the case of image content, digital watermark signals are commonly embedded in the spectral or frequency domain. In particular, several researchers have reported that embedding a watermark in the spectral domain is more robust. Various spectral domain approaches have been used to transform a host image to spectral domains such as the discrete cosine transform (DCT) domain, discrete wavelet transform (DWT) domain, discrete Fourier transform (DFT) domain, and discrete fractional Fourier transform (DFRFT) domain. The watermark is then embedded into the transformed image using certain algorithms. Finally, the watermarked image is transformed back to the spatial domain.

* Corresponding author.

T.-h. Kim et al. (Eds.): MulGraB 2011, Part II, CCIS 263, pp. 139–145, 2011.

Recently, a watermarking algorithm based on discrete fractional random transform (DFRNT) was reported [2], this algorithm exploits the inherent randomness of the transform itself. Generally, intrinsic randomness improves the robustness of the watermarking against attacks. However, this algorithm requires a copy of the original image to extract the embedded watermark. Such a non-blind watermarking algorithm is unsuitable for industrial applications.

In this paper, we propose a novel DFRNT-based watermarking scheme. The proposed algorithm does not require a copy of the original image to extract the watermark, and it provides strong security through the use of a random kernel matrix. We have demonstrated that the proposed blind watermarking scheme is highly secure on account of the inherent randomness of DFRNT and that it is robust under several geometric and frequency attacks.

2 Short Review of Discrete Fractional Random Transform

It has been reported that a DFRNT can essentially be derived from the DFRFT [3]. The randomness is generated by using a random matrix. The overall process is quite similar to that by which the transform matrix of the DFRFT is obtained. The DFRNT can be defined by a diagonal symmetric random matrix. The matrix Q is generated by an $N \times N$ real random matrix P that satisfies the following relation

$$Q = \left(P + P^T\right)/2 \tag{1}$$

where $Q_{lk} = Q_{kl}$. We define the kernel matrix of the DFRNT R^α in such a way that Q commutes with R^α, i.e.,

$$R^\alpha Q = Q R^\alpha \tag{2}$$

In Eq. (2), these two matrices have the same eigenvectors. By the characteristic of a symmetric matrix, the eigenvectors of the matrix $\{V_{Rj}\}$ ($j = 1, 2, \cdots, N$) are real-orthonormal to each other. The eigenvector matrix $\{V_R\}$ is obtained by combining these column vectors:

$$V_R = [V_{R1}, V_{R2}, \cdots, V_{RN}] \tag{3}$$

The coefficient matrix that corresponds to the eigenvalues of the DFRNT is defined as

$$D_\alpha^R = diag\left[1, \exp\left(-j\frac{2\pi\alpha}{M}\right), \cdots, \exp\left(-j\frac{2(N-1)\pi\alpha}{M}\right)\right] \tag{4}$$

where M and α indicate the periodicity and the fractional order of the DFRNT, respectively. Then, the kernel transform matrix of the DFRNT can be expressed as

$$R^\alpha = V_R D_\alpha^R V_R^T \tag{5}$$

and the DFRNT of a two-dimensional image X is expressed as

$$X_R = R^{\alpha} X (R^{\alpha})^T \tag{6}$$

The DFRNT is linear, unitary, index additive, and energy conserved. However, its kernel transform matrix is random, and this affords high security in information security applications such as digital watermarking.

3 Proposed Blind Watermarking Scheme

The proposed watermarking algorithm is blind in that it does not require a copy of the original image or any characteristic of the original image for extraction. All embedding and extraction processes are simply carried out in the DFRNT domain. For the same random number β, a change in the value of fractional order α produces an entirely different transformed image and can make the watermark undetectable. A binary image is utilized as a watermark message and its pixels are embedded invisibly into the DFRNT pair of the host image. The fractional order α of the DFRNT and the random seed β used to generate the random kernel matrix are used as secret keys.

3.1 Watermark Embedding Process

Step 1: The host image X is transformed to Y by the DFRNT, where the fractional order α of the DFRN and the random seed β used for the generation of the random kernel matrix are used as secret keys.

Step 2: Extract the non-overlapping blocks from the DFRNT pair of the host image. The size of the block is decided according to the contents of the watermark. If the size of the host image X is $n=N \times N$ and that of the binary watermark image is $m= M \times M$, then the transformed image Y is divided into $b = Kn/M$ blocks, where K is a square number.

Step 3: The blocks to embed the watermark are randomly selected using the random number β. Random block selection can reduce the correlation between elements of the transformed image.

Step 4: For each pixel in the block, the j-th least significant bits LSB_j are selected and set to a value of 1 or 0 by watermark bit as follows:

$$\begin{array}{ll} if \quad watermark \quad bit = 1 & LSB_j = 1 \\ else & LSB_j = 0 \end{array} \tag{7}$$

Step 5: After embedding all the bits of the watermark, inverse DFRNT is applied to the watermarked coefficients of the transformed image Y to obtain the final watermarked image. The watermark embedding process is illustrated in Fig. 1.

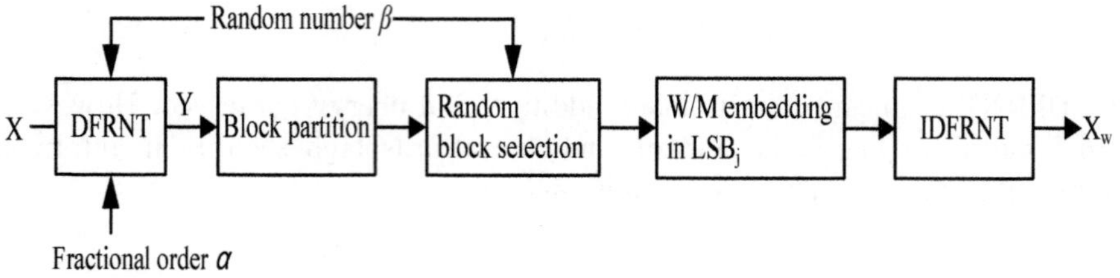

Fig. 1. Watermark embedding process

3.2 Watermark Extraction Process

The extraction process is almost exactly the reverse of the embedding process. Both the fractional order α and the random number β used in the embedding process are used in the extraction process as well.

Step 1: The watermarked image X_w is transformed to Y_W by a DFRNT whose kernel matrix is generated by the random number β.

Step 2: Y_W is divided into blocks, and several of these blocks are randomly selected.

Step 3: The least significant bit LSB_j of the coefficients in each block are extracted and their mean value is calculated. Then, the watermark bit is extracted according to the threshold value T as

$$\begin{array}{llll} If & mean(LSB_j) > T & then & watermark \;\; bit = 1 \\ else & & & watermark \;\; bit = 0 \end{array} \tag{8}$$

where the threshold value T is the mean value of the block number. The watermark extraction process is illustrated in Fig. 2.

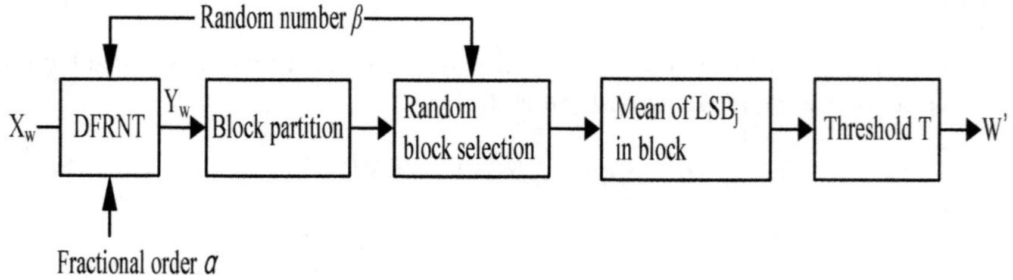

Fig. 2. Watermark extracting process

4 Experimental Results

To test the performance of the proposed algorithm, we calculated the bit error rate (BER) between the original watermark and the extracted watermark by the following expression;

$$BER\ (\%) = \frac{\sum_i \sum_j (W(i,j) \oplus (W'(i,j))}{\sum_i \sum_j W(i,j)} \times 100 \tag{9}$$

As host images, standard images such as "Lena," "Mandrill," "Gold hill," and "Ships" (256 × 256 pixels, 8-bit gray level) in fig. 3 were used to demonstrate the performance of the proposed algorithm. The values of the other parameters are as follows: fractional order $\alpha = 2.215$, size of block = 2×2. The bit position j in LSB_j is selected such that the PSNR of the watermarked image is 40 dB; this is imperceptible to the human visual system (HVS) in the absence of an attack. The obtained experimental results are compared with those of spread spectrum-based watermarking algorithms that are applied in the DCT and DWT domains [5].

Because of the randomness of DFRNT, the proposed algorithm provides very strong security. Even if a very small error occurs in the fractional order α used in the DFRNT, a meaningful image cannot be retrieved from the transformed image. Although the value of α is known, it remains difficult to retrieve the watermark. Because the kernel matrix of DFRNT has $N(N + 1)/2$ independent elements, more than $2^{N(N+1)/2}$ steps are required to try and find the right matrix.

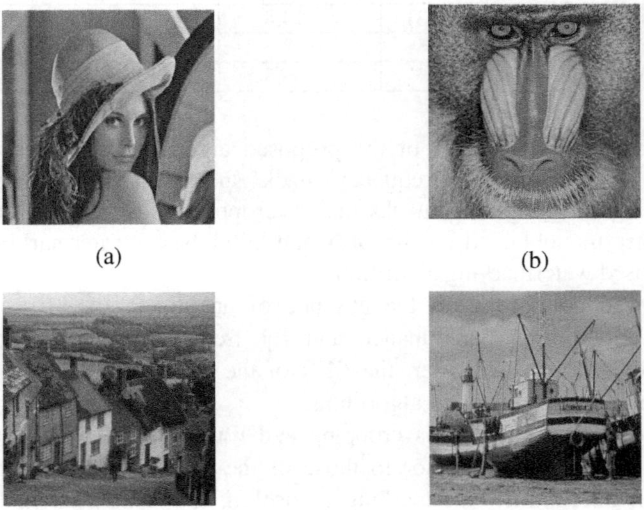

(a) (b)

(c) (d)

Fig. 3. Test sample images for experiment, (a) Lena, (b) Mandrill, (c) Gold hill, (d) Ships

Table 1. Comparison of PSNR and BER under frequency and geometric attacks for standard images when PSNR of watermarked image = 40 dB

Host images	Attacks	BER		
		DCT method	DWT method	Proposed method
Lena	No attack	0.63	0.12	0.0
	JPEG(50%)	7.2	6.2	5.2
	Gaussian noise(10%)	19.6	14.8	12.6
	Median filter(3×3)	14.2	10.2	8.6
	Cropping(10%)	10.4	10.2	5.6
	Rotation(10°)	62.3	56.2	22.5
Mandrill	No attack	0.52	0.11	0
	JPEG(50%)	11.2	8.6	6.2
	Gaussian noise(10%)	23.6	14.1	5.8
	Median filter(3×3)	15.2	13.6	9.4
	Cropping(10%)	22.3	13.2	6.5
	Rotation(10°)	44.8	38.8	20.3
Gold hill	No attack	0.58	0.11	0
	JPEG(50%)	7.8	5.6	3.2
	Gaussian noise(10%)	10.6	6.4	5.8
	Median filter(3×3)	12.6	10.2	6.8
	Cropping (10%)	14.8	12.6	6.3
	Rotation (10°)	66.2	58.8	26.9
Ships	No attack	1.32	0.52	0
	JPEG (50%)	8.6	7.3	5.8
	Gaussian noise(10%)	12.5	10.5	6.6
	Median filter(3 × 3)	14.8	10.9	7.2
	Cropping (10%)	18.6	12.8	6.6
	Rotation (10°)	66.5	59.6	36.0

We evaluated the robustness of the proposed algorithm when the watermarked image is subjected to different frequency attacks such as JPEG, Gaussian noise, and median filtering and geometric attacks such as cropping and rotation. Table 1 lists the experimental results obtained for the DCT and DWT based watermarking algorithms and the proposed watermarking algorithm.

Under normal conditions, in the absence of an attack, the BER of the three algorithms yielded high performance and for frequency attacks such as JPEG, Gaussian noise, and median filter, the BER of the proposed algorithm was slightly superior to those of the other two algorithms.

For geometric attacks such as cropping and rotation, the BER of the proposed algorithm was noticeably superior to those of the other two algorithms. It is well known that a bit-control watermarking algorithm, like that used in the proposed algorithm, is resilient to geometric attacks whereas a transform domain watermarking algorithm is resilient to frequency attacks.

As a result, the proposed algorithm is robust to frequency attacks because of the use of DFRNT and to geometric attacks because of the embedding of a bit-controlled watermark.

5 Conclusions

In this paper, we propose a novel blind watermarking scheme for digital images based on DFRNT.

The fractional order α and random seed β are used as the secret keys required to access the watermarked image in the proposed algorithm. The experimental results indicate that the proposed algorithm is robust against frequency and geometric attacks relative to DCT and DWT based watermarking algorithms and it can provide very strong security because of the inherent randomness of DFRNT.

Acknowledgments. This research project was supported by Ministry of Culture, Sports and Tourism(MCST) and from Korea Copyright Commission in 2011.

References

1. Cox, I., Kilian, J., Shammon, T.: Secure spread spectrum watermarking for images, audio and video. In: Proc. ICIP 1996, Lausanne, pp. 243–246 (1996)
2. Guo, J., Liu, Z., Liu, S.: Watermarking based on discrete fractional random transform. Optical Communications 272(2), 344–348 (2007)
3. Liu, Z., Zhao, H., Liu, S.: A discrete fractional random transform. Optical Communications 255(4-6), 357–365 (2005)
4. Vatsa, M., Singh, R., Noore, A., Houck, M.M., Morries, K.: Robust biometric image watermarking for fingerprint and face template protection. IEICE Electron Express 3(2), 23–28 (2007)
5. Chun-Shien, L.: Multimedia security: Steganography and digital watermarking techniques for protection of intellectual property. IGP, London (2004)

Performance Evaluation of DAB, DAB+ and T-DMB Audio: Field Trial

Myung-Sun Baek, Yonghoon Lee, Sora Park,
Geon Kim, Bo-mi Lim, Yun-Jeong Song, and Yong-Tae Lee

Electronics and Telecommunications Research Institute (ETRI),
Daejeon, Korea
{sabman,Lee.Y.H,parksora,kimgeon,blim_vrossi46,yjsong,
ytlee}@etri.re.kr

Abstract. This paper presents the field trial results of digital audio broadcasting (DAB), DAB+ and terrestrial-digital multimedia broadcasting (T-DMB) audio systems to provide useful information about each digital radio broadcasting standard. Although the all methods are representative digital radio broadcasting standards based on Eureka-147, they have different parts from each other. This field trial results describe a reception performance of each method in various practical reception environments. To evaluate reception performance, various measurement routes are considered. These test results are able to give basic information for the choice of digital radio standard in many countries.

Keywords: DAB, DAB+, T-DMB audio and field trial.

1 Introduction

Since digital radio broadcasting techniques can give highly enhanced performance and quality (e.g. CD like audio quality, single frequency network, slide show, etc), many countries pay attention to converting their analog radio broadcasting services into digital services. However, to choice most proper digital radio standard is very knotty problem for each country.

To evaluate the performance of digital radio broadcasting technologies in practical reception environment of Korea, field trials were performed in 2010. This paper deals with the field trial results of digital audio broadcasting (DAB), DAB+ and terrestrial digital multimedia broadcasting (T-DMB) technologies. Since DAB, DAB+ and T-DMB audio technologies are the representative digital radio standards operating in band III, and are based on Eureka-147 standard [1], most parts are very similar. However, to develop the performance of the system, they have some different parts [2], [3]. Because of the different parts, performance differences are observed.

The objective of the field trials is to measure and analyze the reception performance and service coverage in various practical reception environments. The

T.-h. Kim et al. (Eds.): MulGraB 2011, Part II, CCIS 263, pp. 146–152, 2011.

rest of the paper is organized as follows. Section II describes the test bed (transmitter and test vehicle). Field trial parameters and routes are addressed in section III. Field trial results are presented in section IV. And finally, concluding remarks is given in section V.

Table 1. Transmitter characteristics for field trials

Parameter	Value
Location	37°42'29.81"N, 129°00'0.62"E
Altitude	325 meters
Tower height	40 meters
Modulation	DAB, DAB+, T-DMB audio
Frequency	195.008MHz (CH. 10B)
Transmit Power	100W

Fig. 1. Receiver vehicle for field test

2 Test Bed for Field Trial

For the field trial, test bed has been built in Gangwon-do, Korea. This transmitter is located at the Gangwon Television Broadcasting (GTB) tower in Mt. Gwebang of Gangneung-City, Gangwon-do, Korea. Table 1 shows the transmitter feature of the trial. As Table 1, the DAB, DAB+ and T-DMB audio signals are transmitted through band III CH. 10B with 100W. In this test, the DAB, DAB+ and T-DMB audio signals are multiplexed in one ensemble and transmitted simultaneously. Furthermore, in this test, test vehicle is designed to evaluate the mobile reception performance as Fig. 1. The test van can receive multiplexed ensemble, and separate the ensemble into three digital radio signals.

3 Field Test Parameters and Routes

3.1 Test Parameters

The objective of our digital radio field trials is to measure the performance and to analyze the robustness and coverage of each method. To measure audibility, the main service channel (MSC) character error rate (CER) is adopted. CER means the corrected bit rate after Viterbi decoding. Snce the decoder has specific error correction capability, higher error value might induce miss operation of decoder or imperfect error correction. Therefore, high CER results in signal distortion, which causes packet loss. Through the laboratory test, the threshold values are determined for each system as follows:

- DAB : CER = 0.06
- DAB+ : CER = 0.084
- T-DMB Audio : CER = 0.09.

Fig. 2. Location and distance from transmitter of each route

3.2 Test Routes

The field trials were performed in Gangneung-City, Gangwon-do. Fig. 2 and Fig. 3 describe the measurement routes. The field test is executed according to the reception environments and distance. Gangneung city urban/rural routes and Jumunjin city urban/rural routes are considered in this test. Fig. 2 describes the location and distance from transmitter of each route. As Fig. 2, the Gangneung city is nearer from the transmit site than Jumunjin city. The distances of Gangneung city and Jumunjin city from transmit site are 10km and 25km, respectively. And among the environment measurement routes, the urban routes have many buildings and stores, while rural routes have many paddy fields and dry fields and a few houses. The features of the test routes are illustrated in Fig. 3.

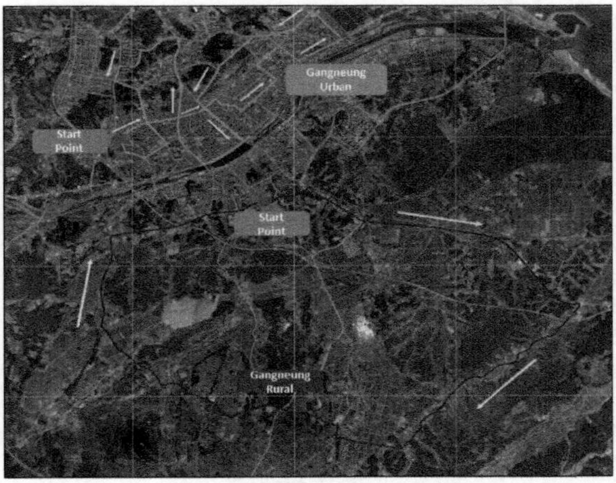

(a) Gangneung city

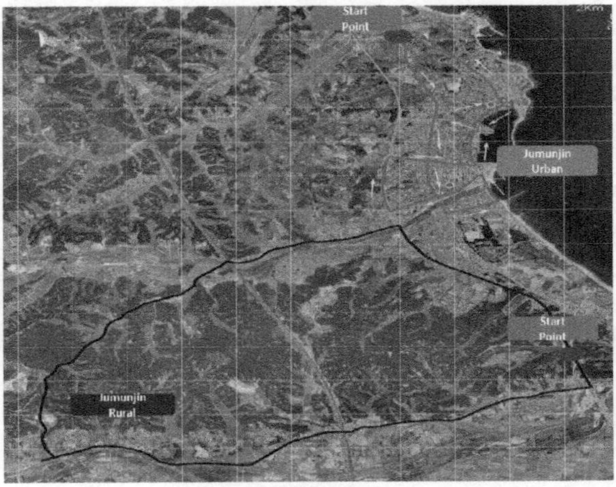

(b) Jumunjin city

Fig. 3. Field trial routes

4 Field Trial Results

Received field strength of environment test routes are showed in Fig. 4 and Fig. 5. Since the distance between transmit site and Gangneung city is shorter than that of Jumunjin, the field strength of Gangneung city is higher. In the case of play success rate of Gangneung city (Fig. 6), since both urban and rural routes are high field strength area, urban and rural routes have high play success rates. In the case of Jumunjin city (Fig. 7), since the urban route has line-of-sight, its play success rate is very high and similar to the performance of Gangneung city. However, because the rural route of Jumunjin city has a high mountain in the centre of the route, the received field strength of behind the mountain is very low, and the play success rate is worse than that of other routes.

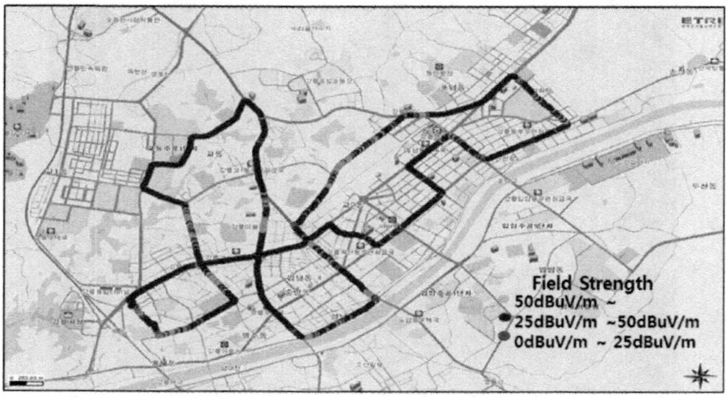

(a) urban

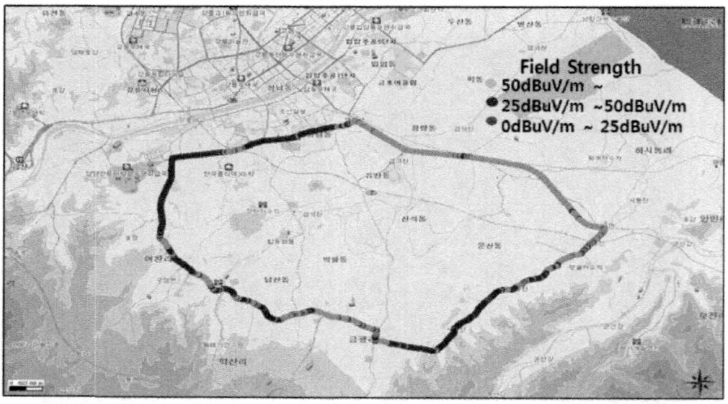

(b) rural

Fig. 4. Received field strength of Gangneung city

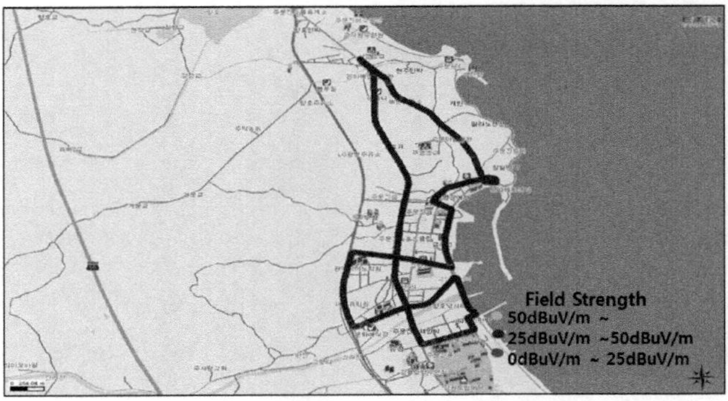

(a) urban

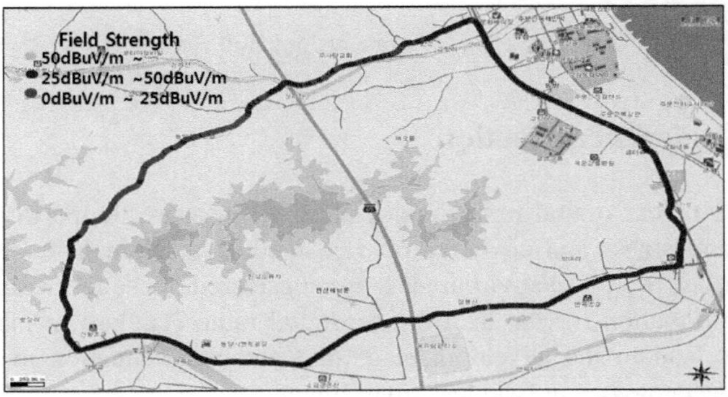

(b) rural

Fig. 5. Received field strength of Jumunjin city

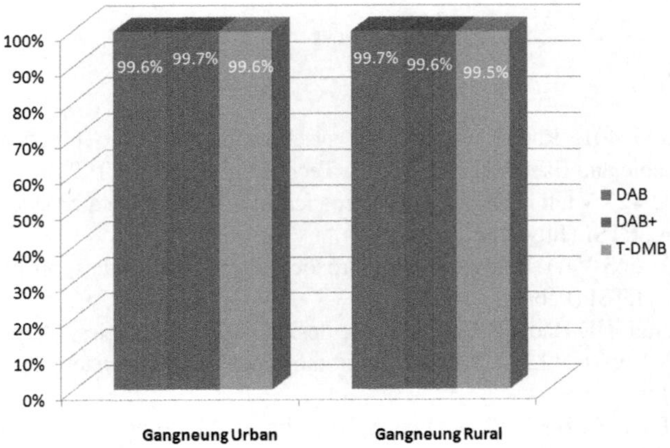

Fig. 6. Play success rate of Gangneung city routes

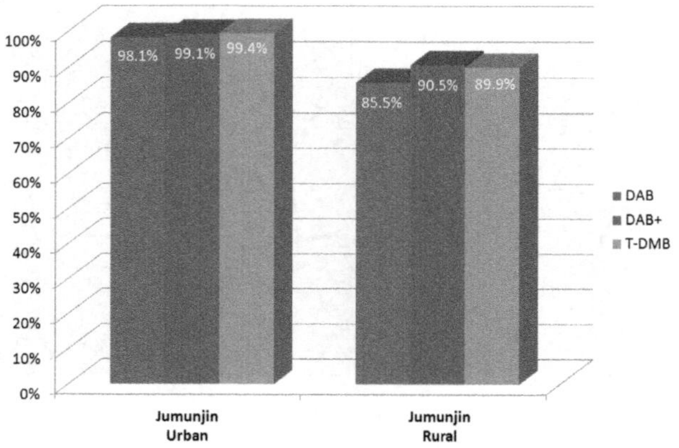

Fig. 7. Play success rate of Jumunjin city routes

5 The References Section

The objective of our digital radio field trials is to measure the performance and to analyze the robustness and coverage of each method in Korean field environment. Since the various reception environments are considered, these test results are able to give basic information for the decision of digital radio standard in many countries, and our tests lead to the development of performance evaluation method of each digital radio technologies in field test environment.

Acknowledgments. This research was supported by the KCC(Korea Communications Commission), Korea, under the R&D program supervised by the KCA(Korea Communications Agency)"(KCA-2011-11912-02002).

References

1. ETSI EN 300 401, Radio broadcasting systems: digital audio broadcasting (DAB) to mobile, portable and fixed receivers, ETSI, Tech. Rep. (February 1995)
2. ETSI TS 102 427 V1.1.1, Digital audio broadcasting (DAB); Data broadcasting - MPEG-2 TS streaming, ETSI (July 2005)
3. ETSI TS 102 563 V1.1.1, Digital audio broadcasting (DAB); Transport of advanced audio coding audio, ETSI (February 2007)
4. iBiquity Digital, HD RadioTM air interface design description series, (August 2007)
5. ETSI ES 201 980 V2.2.1, Digital radio mondiale (DRM) system specification, ETSI (August 2009)
6. Lee, Y.-T., Park, S., Baek, M.-S., Lee, Y.-H., Lim, B.-M., Song, Y.-J.: Field trials of digital radio technologies: DAB, DAB+, T-DMB audio, HD Radio and DRM+. In: Proceeding of NAB BEC 2011, pp. 255–262 (April 2011)

A Case Study on Korean Wave: Focused on K-POP Concert by Korean Idol Group in Paris, June 2011

Hyunhee Cha[1] and Seongmook Kim[2]

[1] Department of Broadcasting, Visual and Performing Arts,
JeongHwa Arts University, Korea
[2] Graduate School of IT Policy,
Seoul National University of Science and Technology, Korea

Abstract. The study dealt with Korean Wave focusing on K-POP and analyzed its success factors, the changes in Korean Wave and the future directions for development. Also the study has compared the results of the idol groups' performance, held by SM Entertainment in June 2011 in Paris, and the perspective of Korean and French media. Key reasons were examined to analyze what led K-POP to play a crucial part in spreading the Korean Wave: The expansion of the age of its takers ranging from teens to females in their 20s; the fusion of a variety of cultural elements including oriental dance and occidental pop; the systematic system of idol training; marketing activities based on social media, etc.

For the expansion of Korean Wave including K-POP and its successful positioning in the world market, there are several suggestions to make which are inventing the differentiated contents and highly appealing stories, approaching the local customers while considering local features, operating co-marketing with other cultural products.

Keywords: Social Media, K-POP, Korean Wave, Idol Group.

1 Introduction

1.1 Background and Purpose of Study

Korean Wave covers the cultural phenomena of people in China, Japan or the regions of East Asia following and learning the Korean pop culture, such as music, drama, movies, etc.[1] This was conceptualized in the late 1990s when Korean pop culture was acknowledged in China, Southeast Asia and "Globalization," the national policy, was launched.[2] The range of Korean Wave has been expanded to the traditional Korean culture such as Hansik (Korean food), Hangul (Korean alphabet), Hanok (Korean

[1] Yongsoo Oh (2010), The changes in Korean Wave and The creation of competitiveness of tourism of Korean Wave, Korean Tourism Policy 2010, Winter, No.42, Korean Culture and Tourism Institute, P78.

[2] Woongjae Rhyu (2009), The eclectic globalization and the political discourse of country, Korean Media Journal, No. 53, Issue 5

T.-h. Kim et al. (Eds.): MulGraB 2011, Part II, CCIS 263, pp. 153–162, 2011.

traditional house), Hanbok (Korean traditional clothing), and so on. However, the Korean Wave market has been limited to China, Japan, Southeast Asia and Central Asia, and it is recognized only by a few dramas and stars.

Nevertheless, in the late 2010s, the flow which was represented by the performances of Korean celebrities including K-POP idol group, has been clearly different from the existing features, the stretch of Korean Wave and the target market. Different marketing approaches have been implemented in the way that the contents were not localized and Korean Wave focusing on new cultural icon was carried out simultaneously in the U.S., the Middle East, and South America. Consequently, the difference in time and place has decreased. In this sense, 'SM Town World Tour' in June 2011 was meaningful in many aspects. As the performance of Korean idol was held for the first time in the center of Europe, the effects on the European market and the strategies of Korean Wave need to be examined.

This study focuses on the performance of idols from SM Entertainment in Paris. Also, this study has analyzed the idol group, which is regarded as a key player, and its performance and strategy. Regarding the perspective that Korean Wave targeted the European market, the study has tried to analyze the outcome of the performance while comparing the Korean and European media in an objective manner. Furthermore, this study will suggest the supportive policies and activities that are essential for the development of Korean Wave in the future.

1.2 The Precedent Studies

It seems that the academic study of Korean Wave is not sufficient in terms of quantity and quality. Most studies cover the whole Korean Wave or its contents, such as movies, drama and Korean pop. One example is journals based on the general understanding of Korean Wave, including the evolutionary process. Sungsoo Kim (2010) summarizes the development stage of Korean Wave and suggests "Glocal" convergence for sustainable development of Korean Wave. Hyejung JoHan (2003) analyzes the meaning of Korean Wave depending on articles, commentaries and reviews regarding the early stage of Korean Wave.

The other example is analyzed based on the success factors and the directions for the spread of Korean Wave. In the early 2000, there were many studies predicting the potential for development and evaluating the success factors of early Korean Wave (Hyoojong Kim, 2002; Buhyung Lee, 2004; Sangchul Jung and others, 2001). And there are studies on Korean Wave from a political perspective. Woongjae Rhyu (2009) analyzes ideology regarding globalization and explains Korean Wave with a frame of globalizing Korea and neo-liberalism. Jungah Rhyu and others (2003) analyze Korea Wave in a political view of cultural exchange policy in Northeastern countries.

Since 2010, idol group has been analyzed as a new icon of Korean Wave (Taesoo Jung, 2010). There are suggestions on the triggers and barriers of Korean Wave, expansion strategies beyond Asia and successful future plans based on trend analysis (Philsoo Kim, 2011; Sohyun Park, 2011).

1.3 Methodology

As a turning point of new Korean Wave, 'SM Town World Tour' in June 2011 was noteworthy. Thus, this study aims to evaluate the perspective of looking at Korean Wave based on the analysis on performance, analyze the recent changes in Korean Wave and its limitations, and seek the future directions of Korean Wave.

First, the process of Korean Wave focusing on contents of pop culture is discussed. The perspective of interpreting Korean Wave and the supportive policies are examined as well. Second, the evolution of Korean Wave turning into K-POP is covered focusing on the changes for the recent 1 or 2 years. Third, the perspective of looking at the performance in Paris in June 2011 as an example by the Korean and European media, namely the French media, is compared and analyzed. Based on this analysis, the perspective of examining Korean Wave is discussed in a balanced manner.

In order to support the study, several methods such as examining the precedent study, analyzing the cultural industry and the data on cultural policy, and analyzing the comparison of Korean and French media will be used.

2 Development of Korean Wave Popular Culture Contents

Although researchers or theses have differences, it appears to be that most of them agree the following spread process.

2.1 The Beginning of Korean Wave (Formation Period, Initial Stage)

With its starting point of Korean Dramas' export to China in 1996 and export of Korean songs in 1998, the year of 2000 was the first time appearance of the term 'Korean Wave' with HOT's Beijing performance. At first it was discounted as temporary phenomenon and it was focused within China, Taiwan, and Hong Kong.

2.2 The Spread of Korean Wave (Developing Period, Secondary Stage)

This is the period of early 2000 to mid-2000, spreading from Chinese area to Japan, Singapore, Taiwan, Mongolia, Russia, and India. Also the contents was diversified into Popular music (Clone, HOT, BOA, etc.), Drama (Winter Sonata, Great Janggeum, etc.), and Online games. Furthermore, it showed the outcome which consumers of Korean Wave spread from teenagers, who mainly consume Albums and Dramas, to 40~50s middle ages with the popularity of Bae Yongjun (Yon sama) and the success of drama Great Janggeum. From this period, Korean Wave expanded to Hansik (Korean food) and traditional culture, connecting tourism packages, and produced outcome in Korean Wave related industry, making the appearance of term New Korean Wave.[3]

[3] Jiyoung Chae and others (2005), Basic research for developing studies on Korean Wave, P.4. After that, few words such as Korean Wave 2.0, the first Korean Wave were presented but confusion was worse. This dissertation is focused on the fundamental value 'Commercial success of Korean pop-culture product' of Korean Wave.

2.3 The Division of Korean Wave (Diversification, Tertiary Stage)

This is the period of mid-2000 to 2010. After reaching peak in 2005, Korean Wave went slow down for a short while in China and Japan. The reason lied in firstly, cultivating material-insufficient culture contents with various stories, depending on a few Korean Wave stars, settling for early success. Second reason was that with emerging sentiment of one-sided encounter, not a mutual exchange of culture, there was a flow named by anti-Korean Wave.[4] As a result, films, broadcasts, music and other exports were actually showed poor results.[5] Nevertheless, in Southeast Asia, the popularity continues mainly with popular music, and the Middle East, the United States and Europe have increased the interests in it. Especially idol groups' entrance to Southeast Asia and Japan played a key role in re-spreading Korean Wave.

Table 1. Reanalysis of Korean Wave changes

	Initial stage	Secondary stage	Tertiary stage
Target market	China, Taiwan, Hong Kong	Japan, Southeast Asia, India, Russia	China, Japan, Middle East, America, Europe
Product	Drama, Popular music, Early idols	Drama, Movie, Game, Popular music	Popular music, Movie, Game, Non-verbal performance
Marketing	Separate marketing of dramas, and singers	Co-marketing of Korean Wave stars and idols – Synergy by movies, dramas, music, and advertisement	Standardized package based on project and system, simultaneous provision of idol groups
Effect of industry	Pop songs, Drama	Expand to Hansik (Korean food), Traditional culture, Broadcasting and Game	Expand to Beauty, Medical, Fashion, Hangeul (Korean language)

2.4 Korean Pop (K-POP) and Korean Wave

There is Korean popular music, so called "K-POP". In initial and secondary stage, early idol was in charge of one axis of Korean Wave. HOT, Clone and JaeWook Ahn were active in the Chinese country market, and BOA and SES has entered Japan. Until this time, the popularity of idol groups were not high when compared with Korean Wave stars like YongJoon Bae(Yon sama), and the popularity of TV dramas such as Great JangGeum. However, in tertiary stage, idol groups largely entered Southeast Asia and Japan, emerging as key players in re-spreading Korean Wave.[6]

---

[4] Jeongmin Ko (2007), Shrinking Korean Wave, SERI. Anti-Korean Wave, For analysis on current state and alternatives, referenced Jiyoung Chae and others (2009).

[5] Jeongmin Ko (2007), Pilsoo Kim (2011), New Korean Wave, is it sustainable?, Hyundai Research Institute, P2.

[6] Sohyun Park (2011), P147.

Table 2. Main cases of idol groups' entrance by each country

Japan	Girls' Generation, 'Oricon' monthly 4th (2010.9), Kara, 'Oricon' weekly 2nd (2010.9)
Taiwan	Super Junior, Taiwan music site 'KKBOX KOR, JAP Chart' 30 weeks consecutively 1st (2009.11)
Thailand	Super Junior, Girls' Generation, monopolized high rank in 'V Channel International Chart', 'MTV International Chart', etc. (2010)
U.S.A	Wonder Girls, ranked 76th in Billboard Single Chart 'Hot 100' (2009.10), Held SM Town Performance in LA, brought 15,000 people (2010.9)

With the spread of imitating South Korean idol groups' dancing, singing, and fashion, called 'Cover' phenomenon, there were emerging groups which mimicked Korean idols exactly.[7] There were several reasons for idol groups' rise. First, it was the multi-cultural fusion power, which resolves various cultures. Western pop and choreography have been stylishly modified into like East Asian, removing reluctance from both Western and Eastern. In fact, it is known as both composer and choreographer have knowledge base for the U.S. POP. Second, it is systematic idol training system. Over the years, they made idol groups to the highest level, training thoroughly with singing, dancing, foreign languages and performance. Large agencies' long-term investment was essential. Third, it is using Social Media to maximum. They alerted the world with the individual's ability with SNS, such as YouTube and other media, and induced the network's support of the Korea-American and students studying in abroad (Taesu Jeong, 2010).

Whereas, looking at the process of development of Korean Wave until now, the constraints become also clear.

First, barrier to experiences between Korea and Asia, and Asia and non-Asia might be a main constraint of spread of Korean Wave. Barrier to cultural experiences should be overcome in order to spread throughout the America, Europe, and so one apart from Asia. Second, ability of producing appropriate contents to global standard or killer contents beyond the barrier of cultural experiences is not enough. If the spread of Korean Wave is developed by trend of pop-culture, purchase of derivative Korean product, and preference of Korea, producing contents which suit the America and Europe and strategy of distribution should be vigorously carried forward.[8]

3 Analysis on Tendency of the Recent K-POP of Korean Wave

The performance of Korean idol group of SM Entertainment in Korea, held on 10 and 11 June 2011 in Paris as part of "SM Town World Tour", was a typical event which

[7] Pilsoo Kim (2011), New Korean Wave, is it sustainable?, P1. Taesu Jeong (2010), New Korean Wave, idol group. P3.

[8] Park Sohyun and the others (2011), Trend of Culture and Art in 2011, Korea Culture and Tourism Institute, P.145, re-referenced. Jeongmin Ko (2010), Korea, China and Japan overcome the crisis of Pop-culture, Herald Economy, 2010.10.31.

has showed the factors of the success and the limit of Korean Wave. The performance of Korean idol groups such as Girls' Generation, Super Junior, SHINee and so on has been held in 'Le Zenith de Paris', all ticket for both days has been sold out and it was crowed of around 14,000 people. Not only Korean media but also French one including European one were very interested in the performance and they have reported it. It is regarded as symbolic incident in a sense that nationality of fans was consisted of 14 countries such as France, U.K and Spain etc. and they filled almost of seat despite the first live K-POP performance in Europe.

3.1 News of Korean Media

[Now, Korean Wave is begun to be transferred to western strong culture countries cross over Japan, several Asian countries. The audience of 14,000 for two days has song along with Korean songs which they had never spoken before. The youngster in Paris was enthusiastic with the huge idol group flied from a small oriental country. Le Monde and Le Figaro focused on the main of the enthusiasm and reported "K-POP, already succeeded in Asia, has entered the European market." At the same time, they have talked about the success of the performance and the spread of Korean Wave. After the performance for 2 days, Europe has focused on Korean Wave. The music of Korean idol group has satisfied the western emotion because of the perfect harmony amongst dance, song and looks and active recruiting of European and American composers. The performance is regarded as a myth of Korean Wave that K-POP was spread into the world through SNS.

The center of world pop-music is New York and that of western history and culture is Paris in France and London in U.K. It might be proud enough of culture that K-POP fascinated local European people not Korean living in Europe. If Big Band and 2NE1 do the performance following Girls' generation and DVSQ, it appears that the acclamation will be able to be continued.] [9]

In addition to this, it has been reported the reasons for success in the performance of K-POP. Firstly, there are no idol singers like Korean one. While English music is more about band and French one is more about appreciation of lyrics, singers specialized in dance, song, visual as Korean idol are rare in Europe. Secondly, planned idol training system is existed only in Korea not in Japan or China. SM Entertainment let composers in Europe and USA make emotional songs which can be impressive to western people. With combining making looks by stylist, Korean idol group became a cultural product which can be impressive in world. Thirdly, Youtube, Twitter or Facebook message contributed to the spread of K-POP. Idol singer has more advantage to put contents on Youtube rather than artist type of good singer because idol singer satisfies both vision and hearing.[10]

3.2 News of French Media

The study took Le Monde and Le Figaro as examples, represented conservative and progressive media of each in France. Their news about the performance of SM Town is not different from Korean media.

---

[9] Arrangement of Korean newspapers' reports on 13-16 June 2011, Herald Economy.
[10] Herald Economy, reported on 14 June 2011.

[Korean Wave, attack Zenith in France...French youngster is enthusiastic about Korean "Boy & Girl" groups which are already the mainstream in Seoul. K-POP groups which already conquered Asia and became strong as started taking European market. The best performance is definitely Girls' Generation, the age of early 20's of all members, they already became the best celebrities with long legs and short skirt in Japan, China, Thailand, and so on. The part of participant groups are recruited at their young age (at primary school) by agency and had been strictly trained to become all-round star (omitted)...everybody was surprised of the reaction of enthusiastic European youngster (omitted)... The strength of K-POP is perfect mix transforming western dance and music which can suit public taste in Asia, and perfect performance in stage [Le Figaro, reported on 10 June 2011].

[Korean Wave stood out in Europe... K-POP which already conquered Asian market has begun to take European market. The participant groups such as SHINee, f(x), Girls' Generation, and so on are Boy & Girl group organized by entertainment agency. The agency has succeeded the exports in music as cultural content actively supported by Korean government. This stems from the fact that Korean government expected K-POP can be a tool of promoting positive and dynamic image of Korea. [Le Monde, reported on 11 June 2011]

3.3 The Perspective of Korean Media about Korean Wave

Through the performance of SM Town in France, although there are pros and cons about commercial viability of K-POP, idol group as representative of Korean Wave, long period of group training system since adolescence, and so on, Korean media interpreted that this performance showed the confidence to succeed K-POP in western market. In interview with Teuk Lee, a member of Super Junior, "We just started but re-exportation of culture is wishful" was focused[11] also, Korean Wave should go forward the flow of world beyond that of Asia and 'Globalization of K-POP' was asserted. Through the interview with those are related to the area, for 'Globalization of K-POP', it is suggested several ways such as creating qualified contents, improving the market environment against outcome in short term, protecting creators by controlling illegal downloading, increasing collaboration with other countries and revitalizing Korean features.[12]

3.4 The Perspective of French Media About Korean Wave

French media paid attention to the fact that the main groups of the performance were completely organized and managed by training process for a long term. Le Monde, left tendency, in particular, introduced a strict selection process in which tens of thousands apply every year for audition and selected trainees take training usually for 3-5 years for taking classes of singing, dancing, acting, foreign language, and they confirm the concept to maximizing their personal character during training period of at least 2 years. It added also that the agency actively recruits foreign talents such as f(x) for entering the overseas market. Le Monde has reported that the range of

[11] Maeil Economy newspaper, reported on 16 June 2011.

[12] Sports Dong-a, reported on 16 June 2011.

investment in from training to launching the first record is approximately from US$ 130K to 180K and this careful plan includes the extreme tool such as plastic. Le Monde has also pointed out that the life of singers or groups produced by vigorous marketing strategy could be limited even if degree of completion is high and it has differentiated features.[13]

In regard of the opinion of certain European media, Korean media pointed out that European media do not correctly look Korean Wave and report a negative argument of Korean Wave so called "Abrupt attacking K-POP". BBC has reported that the reality of the other side of K-POP is based on the wrong practices of unequal exclusive contract so called "slave contract". Le Monde has also reported that Korean government uses idol singers as a tool of promoting its image, they are completely "vigorously planned and produced product."[14] About these perspectives, Korean media pointed out that it would be difficult to understand considering European history and culture and commercial calculation of large agencies should not be easily exposed. In addition to this, Korean media takes the position of SM Entertainment which claimed that "vigorously produced scientific idol system is the essential base of entering into global market".[15]

However, it needs to understand at the same time the background of European culture considering individual and autonomy. Also, it is thought to understand that Le Monde, left tendency, its negative perspective tried to consider the particular relation in idol group between "employer (Entertainment agency) and employee (singer/group)" rather than to devaluate and criticize Korean Wave.

3.5 Implications for K-POP Performance in Paris to Korean Wave

Although there are different perspectives about training idol groups and typical features of K-POP, there is no doubt that the performance is a turning point of perspective of Korean Wave.

Firstly, it was a launch of K-POP as core code of Korean Wave in the middle of European market. The performance in Europe was an opportunity to see the possibility of the success in world market passing by Chinese zone, Asia and the America. To do it, appropriate story for European and world market and sophisticated strategy are needed. Secondly, target of takers was expanded to the women of the age

---

[13] Le Monde, reported on 10 June 2011, otherwise, there was not negative tons at all in Le Figaro, conservative tendency. BBC was more critical than Le Monde. BBC has criticized 'vigorously produced system' in which the treatment of young singers is controversial for example, 'slave contract' of DVSQ, and these are commercially produced. BBC, referenced report titled "The dark side of Koran pop music" on 14 June 2011.

[14] Herald Economy, reported on 16 June 2011.

[15] The president of SM Entertainment, Suman Lee, invited 70 people of European composers and producers in conference on 11 June 2011 in Paris and claimed this opinion and added the explanation that simulation of changes in voice and looks in 3-7 years considering trainees' growth. It was reported that he has presented the theory of 3 steps of development of Korean. Herald Economy, reported on 13 June 2011. His theory of 3 steps of development is known as 1) Exports in cultural products of Korean Wave, 2) Local company, expanding market through collaboration of celebrities, 3) Establishment a joint-venture company and Transfer technology of Korean culture to local.

of 10's and 20's. The performance stimulated the main target of consuming cultural products which is young women because the members of the idol groups at the similar age of takers do performance having feminine emotion and boy group was shown up. Thirdly, the spread of Korean Wave can be affected by the Internet and SNS. K-POP quickly proliferated through Youtube video, Twitter and Facebook message. The performance of K-POP was asked mainly by 'Korean Connection Association' (association K-POP, known 100,000-130,000 members) and Facebook. They organized fan café and shared the latest music video each other and hold a dance contest.[16] Social media made easier for "netizens" to share contents through video on the Internet and mouth to word of mouth in advanced countries where IT culture is already popularized. And last, creating synergy with other contents of Korean Wave rather than exclusive marketing K-POP is important. Korean idol groups do already in various areas such as drama, TV, advertisement, and so on apart from dance and song. For example, in France, it is reported that people knew K-POP through manga, Korean cartoon and Korean TV series (drama). Also, as their lyrics are not localized and are transferred themselves, it would be easier to transfer Hangul (Korean alphabet), Korean tradition, and Korean spirit.

4 Conclusion

This study has taken K-POP which is a part of Korean Wave and analyzed the factors of its success, changes in its character and direction of development in the future. Recently, idol group has stood out as main factor of spread of Korean Wave. In particular, the performance of Korean idol group, held on June 2011 in Paris, can be a turning point of Korean Wave in many senses; Korean Wave has entered into European market; The K-POP performance has showed the cultural competitiveness of idol group which had not been found in Europe; Korean training system of idol group has begun to be exposed to world market.

Starting with the performance of K-POP which is represented as Korean Wave, certain points should be improved for successful positioning in global market.

Firstly, the competitiveness of contents should be strengthened. The various stories should be produced by development of pop-culture industry which includes cartoon, novel, music and so on. The capacity of creating contents which suit the global standard and are targeted in global market should be improved. Secondly, strategies should be planned considering market of target or country. Thirdly, connection of marketing with cultural products such as tourism product, Hansik (Korean food), fashion, Hangul (Korean alphabet) and so on apart from pop-cultural products is needed. This allows producing the synergy, enhancing the familiarity about Korea and improving the awareness of Korean brand. Fourthly, marketing of maximum use of the environment of social media such as Youtube, Facebook, Twitter and so on is required. As there is no obstacle between countries and the speed of spread between consumers are very fast, it can be very useful tool for spread of Korean pop-culture which uses vision and hearing. Also, as digital media has been developed, they can be a consumer of contents and marketer or cooperator and the same time, and their desire of communication is strong. Lastly, regarding governmental policies, it is appropriate

[16] Le Figaro, reported on 11 June 2011.

to sustainably support Korean Wave in long term rather than expecting direct outcome in short term. It is very important to improve the infrastructures for products of Korean Wave such as producing environment, protection of copyright, analysis on consumer in foreign market, support for media strategy and so on, and stimulate developing contents

References

Journal and Paper

Chae, J., et al.: A Basic Study for Korean Wave Study Development. Korea Culture and Tourism Policy Researcher (2005)

Chae, J., et al.: A Study for the Support Plan for Abroad Entrance of Culture Industry. Korea Culture and Tourism Policy Researcher (2006)

Jeong, S., et al.: A Study for the Support Plan for Abroad Entrance of Korea Popular Culture Industry. Korea Culture Policy Researcher (2001)

Jeong, T.: New Korean Wave Has Been Started. Samsung Economy Laboratory (2010)

JoHan, H.: Korean Wave Fever Being Read as the Sign of Global Upheaval. JoHan, H., et al.: Korean Wave and Asia's Public Culture. Yonsei Univ. Press (2003)

Kim, H.: Korean Wave is the Possibility. Chugye University for the Arts Cultural Industry Graduate School (2002)

Kim, P.: New Korean Wave, Sustainable?, VIP Report, 11-06 (Serial number 476), Hyundai Economy Researcher (2011)

Kim, P.: A Search for the Direction for Continuous Spread, VIP Report, 11-09 (Serial number 479) Hyundai Economy Researcher (2011)

Kim, S.: Re-evaluation on Korean Wave from Global Aspect, Liberal contents the 18th (2010)

Ko, J.: Korean Wave Sustainability and Utilization Plan for Corporate. Samsung Economy Laboratory (2005)

Ko, J.: Plan to Sustain Korean Wave. Samsung Economy Laboratory (2005)

Ko, J.: Holding Back Korean Wave. Samsung Economy Laboratory (2007)

Lee, B.: Korean Wave Phenomena and Culture Industrialization. Hyundai Economy Researcher (2004)

Oh, Y: The Change of Korean Wave and the Creation of Korean Wave Tourism Competitiveness, Korea Tourism Policy 2010, Winter Issue, No. 42. Korea Culture and Tourism Policy Researcher (2010)

Park, S., et al.: Culture and Arts Trend Analysis and Prospect in 2011. Korea Culture and Tourism Policy Researcher (2010)

Rhyu, J., et al.: A Search for the Plan for Vitalization of Northeast Asia Culture Exchange. Korea Culture and Tourism Policy Researcher (2004)

Ministry of Culture and Tourism: Cultural Industry White Paper 2003 (2003)

Rhyu, W.: Conciliatory Globalization and Country's Discourse Politics, vol. 53(5). Korea Press Paper (2009)

Press

Mae-Il Economy, Kyeong-Hyang Newspaper, Herald Economy, Sports Dong-Ah, ENS, Media Daum, etc. Pressed in 2011.6.10-17 (2011)

Le Monde (France), Le Figaro (France), BBC Broadcast (U.K), Pressed in 2011.6.11-16 (2011)

Design and Implementation of Emergency Situation System through Multi Bio-signals

Ki-Young Lee, Min-Ki Lee, Kyu-Ho Kim, Myung-jae Lim, Jeong-Seok Kang, Hee-Woong Jeong, and Young-Sik Na

Department of Medical IT and Marketing, Eulji University,
553, Sanseong-daero, Sujeong-gu, Seongnam-si, Gyeonggi-do, 461-713, Korea
{Kylee,khkim,lk04}@eulji.ac.kr,
{mklee0311,nedved0213,07jeong}@gmail.com, nys82@naver.com

Abstract. In this paper, We proposed a recognition system of user's emergency situation by measuring several bio-signal and applying technology of Wearable Computing. The main features and contributions of the proposed system are as follows. First, input basic bio-signal is based on user's movement, ECG-signal, and body temperature. Second, this allows you to process a variety of additional bio-signals in order to provide on-demand service to Users. Third, by analyzing each bio-signal's data for emergency situation, it then determines the priorities and threshold that applies multiplex class SVMs and this offer an optimized algorithm for emergency situation. We evaluated performance of proposed system about bio-signal's threshold and emergency situation decision algorithm. Finally it confirmed effectiveness.

Keywords: u-Healthcare, Sensor Network, Bio-signal, Emergency Situation.

1 Introduction

Recently, as the quality of life has been improved, people have interested with the health. According to Information and Communication Technologies's continuous growth, u-Healthcare System based on IT convergence technologies laid the research and commercialization stage.

The Wearable Computing technology of u-Healthcare system is very closely related to human and is user-friendly interface that is being researched in several areas [1]. In case of acute and chronic illness, ongoing management and prompt response are required. If users need ongoing management, the suitable and effective system is needed for users requiring ongoing management.

In this paper, the user's movement, ECG-signal and body temperature are the basic bio-signal. To offer users on-demand service, a variety of the bio-signal is added. So, it is possible to understand exception situations. Measurement signal are inputted by the Wearable Computing [1]. After making a decision on the emergency situation, the system is designed to handle them.

T.-h. Kim et al. (Eds.): MulGraB 2011, Part II, CCIS 263, pp. 163–168, 2011.

2 Related Works

In emergency situations, causing physical disability and severe changes in vital signs leads to death. In case that life can be threatened, rapid response is requested [2]. Therefore, emergency situation is required with real-time and high accuracy Medical Systems.

2.1 Bio-signal

To decide emergency situation, proposed system analysis several bio-signal. Like Table 1, sensors related with user's disease acquire bio-signal additionally. This bio-signal can decide exceptional emergency situation more accurately.

Table 1. Multi Bio Sensor and Signal

Sensor	Model	Measurement Purposes	Threshold
Spo2 Sensor	TP320	Oxygen saturation	Safe : 70mmHg~95mmHg
Electromyogram Sensor	DE2.1	Action potential and contraction	Safe : 75-170
Glucose Sensor	G8270	Glucose	Empty Stomach : 100mg/dl Danger : 140mg/dl over
Heart Rate Sensor	DT155A	Heart Rate	Safe : 60 ~ 80

Basic bio-signal : First, by recognizing the user's behavior patterns, it is intended to separate between normal and abnormal behavior and attempt to provide a solution to a given problem [3].

As a result, after separating between the normal pattern and abnormal behavior patterns, it prevents bigger damage through fast perceive of user's safety accidents. Second, ECG-signal that is electricity signals generated by the heart is important method used to decide to emergency situation [4][5][6]. Analyzing ECG-signal can know Veins, Angina, Myocardial Infarction, Hypertension and much information in emergency situation [6][7]. Third, our body always maintains a constant body temperature(36.5°C inside or outside). and, they balance the loss and gain of body temperature [8].

Body temperature is the most basic diagnostic information and indicators that reflect the different physiological changes. So for almost every disease, it must be measured [8].

2.2 Information Extraction Measurement System

Like Figure 1, Each different type of three analog sensors(ECG : 5kHz±10% , Temperature : 13-bit, 3-Axis : 0-100Hz) extracts data in forms of electricity signals of different frequency band. Next, it transmits to interface device(USM-ED0101A). To consolidate different frequency bands data, they are transmitted to USM-ED0101A.

USM-ED0101A goes through process for conversion of different signals integration and electricity signals into digital signals. And USM(Unified Messaging System)-ED0101A perform as a medium for transmit to Information Measurement

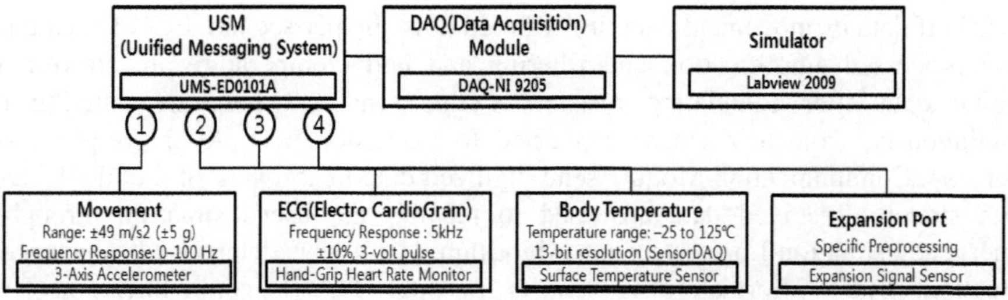

Fig. 1. Measure System Structure

Module(DAQ-Module). DAQ-Module goes through control process for testing and the programming, using integrated data transmitted from the interface device.

In this Paper, we used a LabView-based sensors(Hand-Grip Heart Rate Monitor(ECG), 3-Axis Accelerometer(Movement), Surface Temperature (Temperature)) that most closely similar to a micro sensors(Ps-2111(ECG), LM35DZ(Temperature), AM-GYRO_V02-Manua(Gyro)) to measure the user's bio-signals.

3 System Design and Implementation

To implement the propose system of this paper, we measured bio-signal using a NI's DAQ device and Labview and processed bio-signal. These bio-signal data are very important element in order to decide the emergency situation. Also, we use the extended data for responding to a variety of diseases. These extended data can measure Bio-Signals that correspond to certain diseases.

We explain the system for the efficient processing of these bio-signals' threshold calculation and that signals priorities weighting calculation.

3.1 System Design

Like Figure 2, Each sensor including an expansion port sensors measures the user's bio-signals in real-time and to analyze measured data, this data go through different pre-processing. bio-signals data are classified by these characteristics.

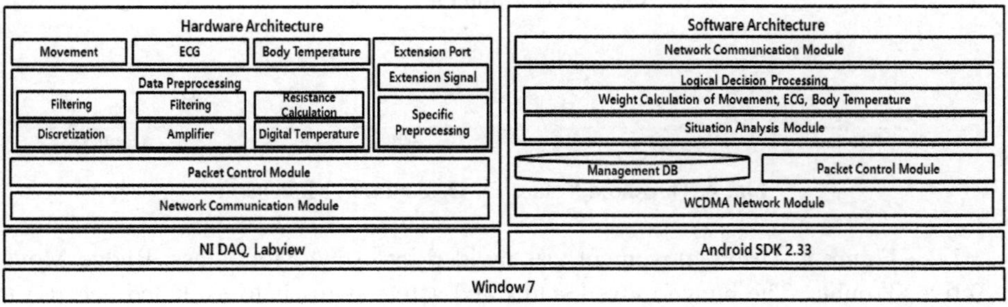

Fig. 2. System Structure

One if data us movement data, it is filtered noise by per second. ECG-signal data is also processed amplification and filtering and body temperature are converted to digital data after calculating resistor of this sensor. Others are entering data continuously, from any sensor connected to expansion port. After pre-processing, Network Communication Module send digitized data to software of mobile device as data stream. Received data are used to identify the user's situation through an emergency situation Logic Decision Algorithm. If a user is determined as emergency situation, user's information is sent to hospital TCP/IP communication. User's information include the user's code, location information and body temperature variations.

3.2 Emergency Situation Understanding Algorithm

Like Figure 3, It is an algorithms that can analyze the user's movement data, ECG-signal data, body temperature data and expansion data And determine an emergency situation. All data is configured to analyze the data of 60.0 seconds and the subsequent data of 60.0 seconds. Also, It is stored as a form of graph in Smart Phone's flash memory. First, The numerical data is respectively divided by the 0.1 per seconds queue control module and inserted into each queue. Second, It will assume a shock or a fall by analyzing the user's movement data. And if it will be assumed to be and emergency situation, it will change the weight of the priority of all data's signals. Third, Data of changed priorities is analyzed sequentially.

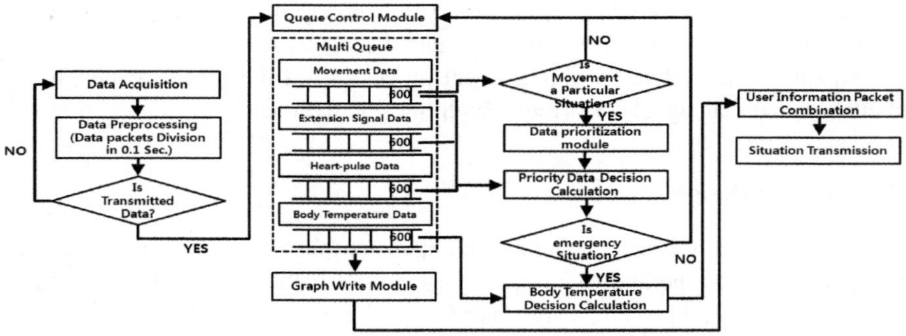

Fig. 3. Algorithm Flow Chart

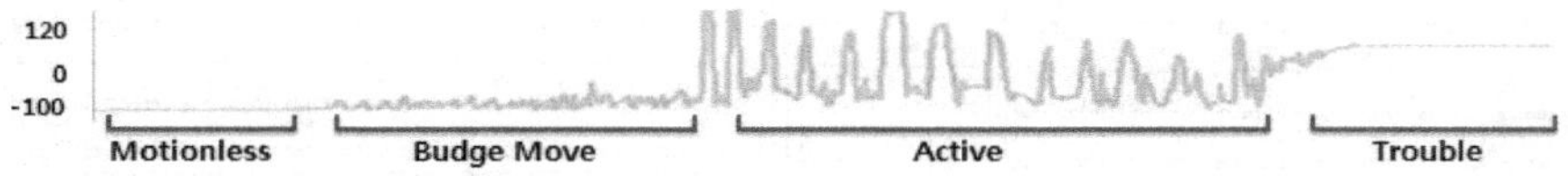

Fig. 4. Threshold Values for Detection of Movement

Like Figure 4, User's movement was divided into state Motionless, Budge Move, Active, Trouble. The budge moved status and active status is to excluded because to move status for determine of the emergency situation.

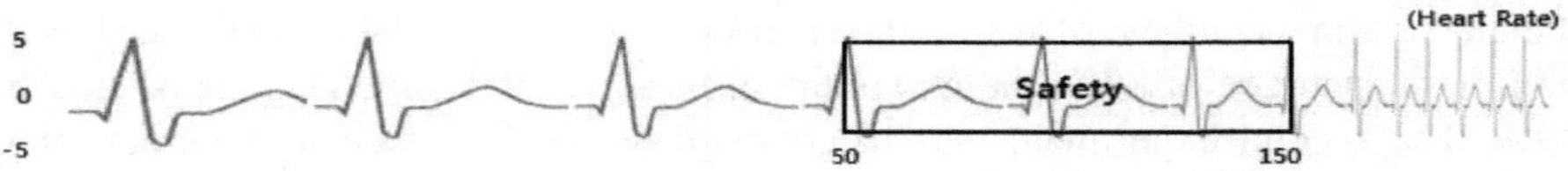

Fig. 5. Threshold Values for Detection of ECG-signal

ECG data needed to measure, heart rate depending on the amount of movement has many variations, the heart rate is to measured only state that does not move, As shown in Figure 5, threshold value is less than 50 to over 150.

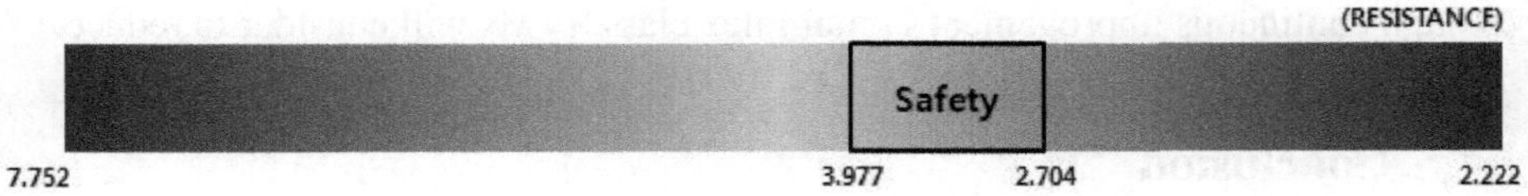

Fig. 6. Threshold Values for Detection of Body-Temperature

Temperature data through the sensor's resistance value, the operation is necessary, Like Figure 6, normal body temperature of the resistance value is the value of 3.977 or less than 2.704. This value is the threshold value. Extended signal data is calculated through the inputted threshold in accordance of each emergency situation. If all of the user's movement and ECG analysis are determined the emergency, It measures the amount of change by calculating the difference of a existing average temperature data of 60.0 seconds and a recent inputted temperature data. It was implemented to be transmit a user's information and a graphics bio-signals via TCP/IP.

4 Performance Evaluation and Analysis

The proposed system was used to evaluate the performance test using LabView 2009 and android 2.3.3 based on Windows 7 Home Premium. The total proposed system through two kinds of experiments.

The first experiment was to compare the performance to movement and ECG threshold. Data, a total of 10 times in 100 users who were measured in the experiments results shown in Figure 7. Movement is the minimum accuracy of 90%,

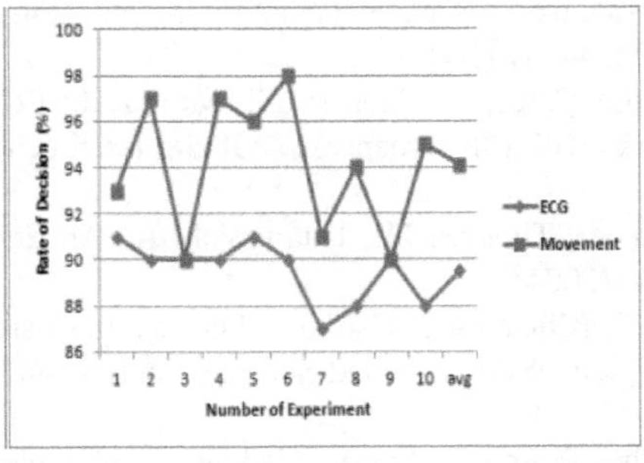

Fig. 7. Compare Data of Movement, ECG and Each Threshold

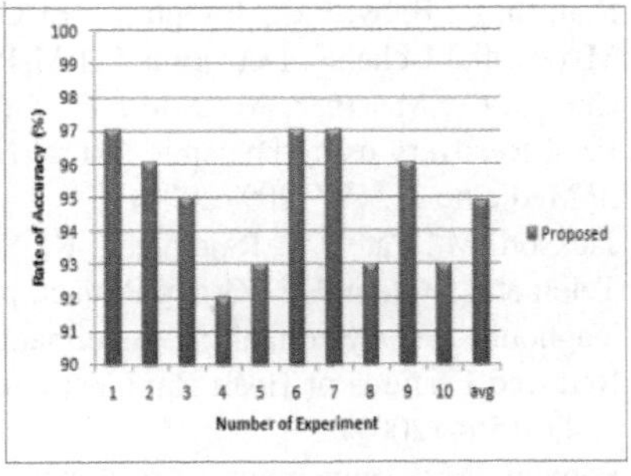

Fig. 8. Accuracy of Proposed System

the maximum accuracy of 98%, the average accuracy of 94%. and ECG is the minimum accuracy of 87%, the maximum accuracy of 91%, the average accuracy of 89%. The second experiment was to compare the performance to accuracy of the proposed system using algorithm. Data, a total of 10 times in 20 users who were measured in the experiments results shown in Figure 8, the minimum accuracy of 92%, the maximum accuracy of 97%, the average accuracy of 95%.

The evaluate the performance of approximately 98% over the accuracy of the overall satisfactory level is a fine. But error should be reduced due to the system characteristic of life or death. Because the error was caused a variety of exception situation, the setting of accurate threshold will be reduced an error. In this case, through continuous improvement of multiplex class SVMs will consider to reduce.

5 Conclusion

In this paper, We proposed the system by adding a variety of the bio-signals sensor can realize even exceptional emergency situations in order for users to provide on-demand service, based on the user's movement, ECG-signal and body temperature of three basic bio-signals data. Implemented to decide efficient emergency situation of user in real-time by giving priority of each bio-signals through providing emergency situation decision algorithm and shown a high accuracy.

In the future, according to each disease the high accuracy classification of emergency situation bio-signals will be apply, streaming formats for efficient data transfer will proceed in the related research. and user's other bio-signals to decision to priority of methods, also, much research is needed.

References

1. Fuller, S., Ding, Z., Sattineni, A.: A Case Study:using the Wearable Computer in the Construction Industry. In: Proceedings of the 19th ISARC, Washington, U.S.A, pp. 551–556 (2002)
2. Liu, H.: Biosignal Controlled Recommendation in Entertainment Systems, pp. 1–133. Technische Universiteit Eindhoven, Eindhoven (2010)
3. Perimutter, M.S.: A Tactical Fiber Optic Gyro with All-Digital Signal Processing. In: SPIE Fiber Optic and Laser Sensors Xl, vol. 2070, pp. 192–205 (1993)
4. Ranjith, P., Baby, P.C., Joseph, P.: ECG Analysis using Wavelet Transform:Application to Myocardial Ischemia Detection. ITBM-RBM 24, 44–47 (2003)
5. Camps, G., Martínez, M., Soria, E., G6mez, L., Calpe, J., Guerrero, J., Muñoz, J.: ECG Fetal Recovery using Dynamic Neural Networks with FIR Synapses. Artificial Intelligence in Medicine 31, 197–209 (2004)
6. Jackson, M., Patel, S., Rajaraman, R., Sharma, A., Thomas, M., Thurairajah, A.: An ECG Telemetry System, EE3 Group Project, pp. 1-40 (2004)
7. Yaghouby, F., Ayatollahi, A., Soleimani, R.: Classification of Cardiac Abnormalities using Reduced Features of Heart Rate Variability Signal. World Applied Sciences Journal 6(11), 1547–1554 (2009)
8. Pompei, M.: Temperature Assessment via the Temporal Artery: Validation of a New Method, Exergen Corporation, pp. 5–40 (1999)

Intelligent Music Recommendation System Based on Cloud Computing

Ki-Young Lee[1], Tae-Min Kwun[1], Myung-Jae Lim[1], Kyu-Ho Kim[1], Jeong-Lae Kim[2], and Il-Hee Seo[1]

[1] Department of Medical IT and Marketing, Eulji University, 553, Sanseong-daero, Sujeong-gu, Seongnam-si, Gyeonggi-do, 461-713, Korea
{kylee,lk04,khkim}@eulji.ac.kr, {jinro4,ilhee91}@gmail.com
[2] Department of Biomedical Engineering, Eulji University, Korea
jlkim@eulji.ac.kr

Abstract. In this paper, intelligent music recommend system is proposed based on clouding computer. User- selected music is classified to similar tendency by algorithm of music genre classification, after total of 12 musical feature extraction on cloud. This system classified using Thayer's model of mood and music was classified again suitable for current weather conditions. So, we suggested to music recommend system based on cloud computing system recommend for user and verified through simulation. The results of performance evaluation show that the proposed system can efficiently support weather condition and season information.

Keywords: Music Recommend System, Feature Extract, Cloud Computing, Thayer's Model.

1 Introduction

Recently, interest in media contents is growing to introduce the various smart device, and Device without the need to put music has been made available to synchronize as emerged cloud computing.

John C. Platt proposed every time to choose your own music to solve the problems how to learning through a Gaussian process [1]. This approach effectively creates a playlist of music. However, considering the regional situation of the current user does not exist disadvantages. Therefore, we suggested to music recommend system based on cloud computing system consider the user's current environment.

2 Related Works

2.1 Music Genre Classification

Currently, most of digital music is converted to using digital signals from analog signals. The study of digital signal is used to classify genres of music and Tzanetakis [2] of them for the music genre classification, for music features is used to compare to each other. 10 kinds combination of feature points is compared through various learning algorithm.

T.-h. Kim et al. (Eds.): MulGraB 2011, Part II, CCIS 263, pp. 169–174, 2011.

Tao Li, Mitsunori Ogihara, and Qi Li [3] proposed new musical extraction method based on DWCHs (Daubechies Wavelet Coefficient Histograms) rather than Fourier transform which was used to extract features. When using with the proposed method, Tzanetakis, the maximum had higher performance, 99%. Like Table1, feature elements of the music should be analyzed to compare the feature of the music.

Table 1. Music Features Elements

No.	Features elements	Description
1	Spectral Centroid	Measuring the brightness of the music
2	Spectral Roll off Point	Measuring the frequency change
3	MFCCs [4]	Quantification of the voice
4	Compactness	The ratio of spectrum as non-scale
5	Spectral Variability	The standard deviation of the spectrum
6	Root Mean Square	Quantified to measure the sound.
7	Fraction of Low Energy Windows	Measuring the degree of silence
8	Zero Crossings	Measuring the amount of noise
9	Strongest Beat	The most significant bit in the signal
10	Beat Sum	Sum of using bits
11	Strength of Strongest Beat	Degree of much Stronger than other bits
12	LPC	Evaluation of singer's vocalization and accent

2.2 Music Mood Classification

The most common method to classify music moods is the model of Thayer's music mood [5], which is Figure 1.

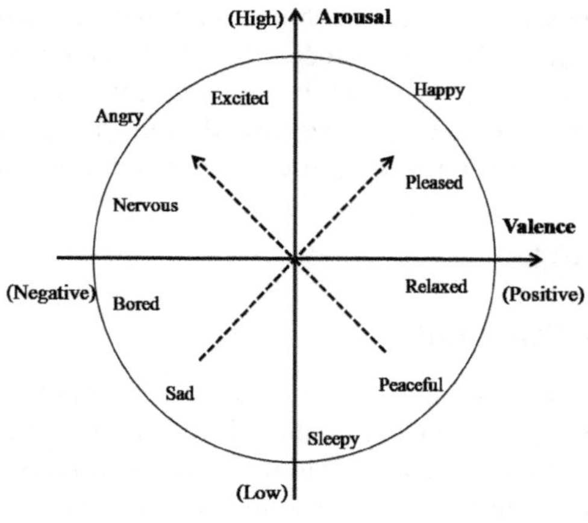

Fig. 1. Music Mood Model of Thayer

This model classifies two dimensional plain to Arousal and Valence. Arousal is used for tendency of Music, and Valence means brightness of music.

In this paper, Thayer's music mood classification will be used to classify the music depending on the weather condition. Four groups are randomly separated to response to each weather condition.

3 System Design and Implementation

The overall structure of this system is shown in Figure 2. The overall system consists of music classification module and music recommendation module. Each module works respectively, and it consists of particular modules again.

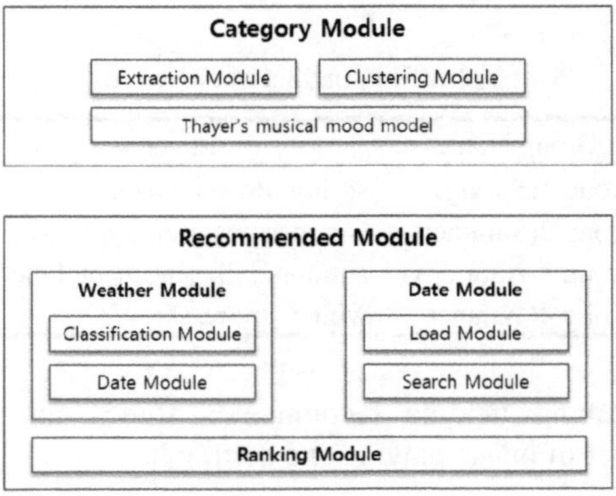

Fig. 2. System Structure

3.1 Music Feature Classification Module

The module which classifies features of music is aimed for extracting and clustering the music features when users or administrators enter the music.

As it's already explained in last research, all twelve features of music will be extracted, and the k-NN algorithm [6] will be used for clustering. The classified information will be stored in database.

3.2 Music Recommendation Module

The music recommendation module is divided to weather condition module, seasonal information module, and rank checking module.

First of all, weather condition module is verifying your local weather and playing a role of classifying the music suited for current weather situation. The weather group uses 4 groups consisting of Sunny, Cloudy, Rainy, and Snowy in Table 2, which is separated from prior music classification module.

Table 2. Music Mood Classification

Group Name	Elements
Group 1(Sunny)	lively, bright, humorous, happy
Group 2(Cloudy)	aggressive, peaceful, ominous
Group 3(Rainy)	sad, melancholy, gloomy
Group 4(Snowy)	dreamy, smooth, sentimental

Secondly, seasonal information module searches the suited keyword in music title for Spring, Summer, Autumn, and Winter, and it register the matching music on priority list. Separate sets of keyword should be formed to implement seasonal information module. Some parts of this keyword set that is used in this paper is shown in Table 3.

Table 3. Using Set of Keywords

Group Name	Elements
Group 1(Spring)	spring, flower, cozy...
Group 2(Summer)	summer, sea, rain, typhoon...
Group 3(Autumn)	autumn, fall, sentimental, book...
Group 4(Winter)	winter, snow, ski...

Lastly, rank checking module recommends some high ranking music after comparing the number of music playing and sorting it.

4 Performance Evaluation

In this paper, the experiment used PHP5 and Oracle 10g, and 144 tracks of music is also used for this experiment. In addition, 12 different features were extracted by using jAudio [7] in the experiment.

The experiment used total 10 data of experiment, and the recommendation result is confirmed when random music or weather is applied. As shown in Table 4 and Figure 3, K is sequentially applied from 4 to 6 to get gest result.

Table 4. Clustering Results of Musical Feature

Cluster Name	k=4	k=5	k=6
Cluster 1	58	35	28
Cluster 2	11	36	1
Cluster 3	50	2	38
Cluster 4	25	42	34
Cluster 5	-	29	24
Cluster 6	-	-	19

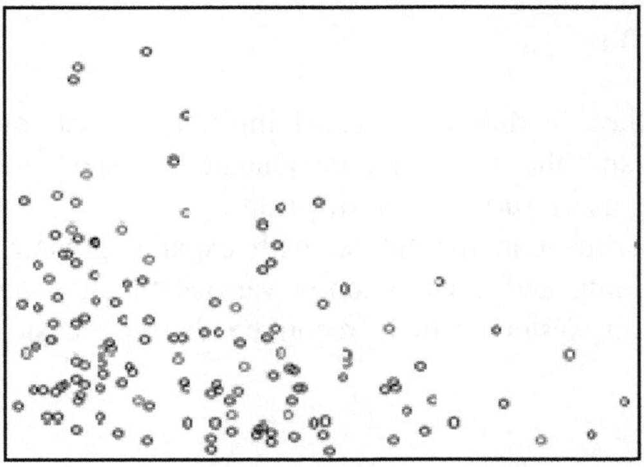

Fig. 3. Clustering Results of k=4

The experiment shows that the result of clusters is best when k is 4. As a next step, music mood group in which clusters are pre-classified is reapplied again like Table 5.

Table 5. The Result of Applying to Thayer's Model

Group	1	2	3	4
Group 1(Sunny)	50	18	25	71
Group 2(Cloudy)	15	78	37	23
Group 3(Rainy)	20	47	67	19
Group 4(Snowy)	82	23	33	47

After applying them, the result found best matching rate among group 1 to cluster 4, group 2 to cluster 2, group 3 to cluster 3, and group 4 to cluster 1. Finally, Table 6 shows the result of applying the seasonal information through three keywords. These three keywords consisted of 50 seasonal word, and experiment was processed by the cluster, which shows the best result to the each seasonal condition, and seasonal information in order to get diverse result of experience.

Table 6. The Result of Applying to Seasonal Information

Group	Sunny	Cloudy	Rainy	Snowy
Group 1(Spring)	7	6	3	5
Group 2(Summer)	6	3	5	2
Group 3(Autumn)	4	3	4	3
Group 4(Winter)	3	4	6	2
Unclassified	16	20	19	23

According to the result, 21 songs in spring, 16 in summer, 14 in autumn, and 15 in winter are confirmed. Other 78 songs were not suited for three keywords, and it's found that 54 percent of total songs were not classified by using limited number of keyword.

5 Conclusion

In this paper, weather conditions, seasonal information and ranking are added to existing play list, and the music recommendation system was verified through simulation reflecting user's surrounding situation.

As the next experiment in the future, with expanding three research keywords through opinion mining and smart phone's various function and technology, next study will focus on system which recommends the music considering user's environment.

References

1. Platt, J.C., Burges, C., Swenson, S., Weare, C., Zheng, A.: Learning a Gaussian Process Prior for Automatically Generating Music Playlist. In: Proc. NIPS, vol. 14, pp. 1425–1423 (2002)
2. Tzanetakis, G., Cook, P.: Musical Genre Classification of Audio Signals Speech and Audio Processing. IEEE Transactions 10(5), 293–302 (2002)
3. Li, T., Ogihara, M., Li, Q.: A Comparative Study on Content-Based Music Genre Classification. In: Proc. of the 26th Annual International ACM SIGIR Conference on Research and Development in Information Retrieval, pp. 282–289 (2003)
4. Rabiner, L.R.: Fundamentals of Speech Recognition. Prentice Hall (1993)
5. Thayer, R.E.: The Biopsychology of Mood and Arousal. Oxford University Press (1989)
6. Bishop, C.M.: Pattern Recognition and Machine Learning. Springer, Heidelberg (2006)
7. Extracting Features from Audio Files, `http://jmir.sourceforge.net`

Handling Frequent Updates of Moving Objects Using the Dynamic Non-uniform Grid

Ki-Young Lee[1], Jeong-Jin Kang[2], Joung-Joon Kim[3], Chae-Gyun Lim[1], Myung-Jae Lim[1], Kyu-Ho Kim[1], and Jeong-Lae Kim[4]

[1] Department of Medical IT and Marketing, Eulji University,
553, Sanseong-daero, Sujeong-gu, Seongnam-si, Gyeonggi-do, 461-713, Korea
{kylee,lk04,khkim}@eulji.ac.kr, fhdbrk@lycos.co.kr
[2] Department of Information and Comminication, Dong Seoul University,
76, Bokjeong-ro, Sujeong-gu, Seongnam-si, Gyeonggi-do, 461-714, Korea
jjkang@du.ac.kr
[3] Division of Computer Science and Engineering, Konkuk University,
1, Hwayang-dong, Gwangjin-gu, Seoul, 143-701, Korea
jjkim9@db.konkuk.ac.kr
[4] Department of Biomedical Engineering, Eulji University,
553, Sanseong-daero, Sujeong-gu, Seongnam-si, Gyeonggi-do, 461-713, Korea
jlkim@eulji.ac.kr

Abstract. For services related with the u-LBS and u-GIS, most previous works had try to solve frequent updates as a lot of moving objects by extending traditional R-tree. In related works, however, processing for a situation occurring partial denseness of many objects is so hard because these haven't considering the non-uniform distribution. Thus, we proposed new scheme to solve problems above by using the dynamic non-uniform grid. Due to its result of split isn't equal, our proposed scheme can allow distributed processing locally for dense moving objects. Also it has several in-memory buffers to handle frequent updates of massively moving objects lazily.

Keywords: Moving Object, Dynamic Non-uniform Grid, Frequent Updates, R-Tree.

1 Introduction

As the area of GIS is expanded, data of moving objects are more increased rapidly in the applications for u-LBS or u-GIS. To support precise information of these, the applications should be processed frequent update operations efficiently and considered a regional density of moving objects within data space. Traditional R-tree [1] index has been used to manage data of moving objects, but it isn't suitable for a case occurring frequent updates. So previous works such as FUR-tree [2], RUM-tree [3], R^R-tree [4] had aimed to handle many update operations frequently. This effort has solved one of problems, however, they didn't consider the density of massive objects.

T.-h. Kim et al. (Eds.): MulGraB 2011, Part II, CCIS 263, pp. 175–180, 2011.

Thus, we propose new index scheme called R^G-tree to allow frequent updates and non-uniform distribution of moving objects by using the dynamic non-uniform grid. Our proposed scheme has considering the distribution of moving objects dynamically so that unnecessary resource usage is decreased. Also it is able to reduce disk access because all operations such as insert, update, delete are accumulated to in-memory buffers and ran by batch-process.

2 Related Works

For processing and managing the n-dimensional spatial data, R-tree had been used traditionally. R-tree [1] is extended B-tree for spatial data, so it is balanced tree and has new concept of MBR(Minimum Bounding Rectangle) to simplify the complexity of n-dimensional data. However it has high cost for node split and merge when caused many frequent updates.

In FUR-tree [2] scheme, bottom-up approach is used to access leaf nodes directly. This approach can be realized by using a secondary index included all pointers of leaf nodes in memory. It is also having terms of extended MBR to process updates from objects moved zig-zag. Due to this concept, FUR-tree has more overlap between objects' MBR, so query operation is hard by increasing a set of candidate results.

Next, RUM-tree [3] is based on a structure of update memo. The update memo has saving operations of update and delete temporally, with a value of global stamp counter. In this scheme, the update operation just cause a insertion of new object except a deletion of old object. As the result, entries of same object are duplicated in the disk-based tree. Before a process of garbage cleaning to delete all old entries, these duplicated data have taking unnecessary large space in disk.

R^R-tree [4] has fundamentally same scheme with traditional R-tree. It uses additional operation buffer to annihilate corresponded operations for insert and delete. This annihilation can reduce the number of entire operations. Because this buffer has accumulated all operations simply, however, these data are required reconstitution when applying to disk-based tree. For such a reason, we think to require new scheme solving the problems above.

3 Proposed Scheme

The main idea of R^G-tree is to consider the data distribution by using dynamic non-uniform grid. Additionally, in-memory buffers for insert, update, and delete exist to improve performance of operations.

Fig. 1 shows the overall structure in our proposed scheme. In this Fig. 1, the moving objects of r1-r12 have existed in data space, and they are distributed into partitions respectively. Next, partition tree is a structure of tree to store each PN(Partition Node) corresponding to single partition. This has each pointer of MR(Main R-tree) created with partitions. Splitting of partition is dynamic depending on the distribution of moving objects in current based on the non-uniform grid.

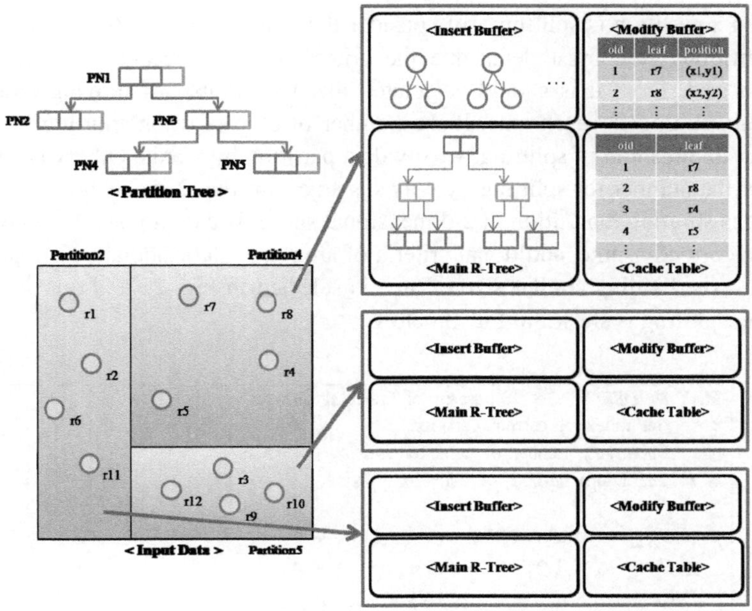

Fig. 1. Overall Structure of R^G-tree

For the efficiency of operations, Insert Buffer and Modify Buffer are used like temporary storage. These accumulate several operations; the insert operation is stored into Insert Buffer, or the update and delete operation are stored into Modify Buffer. Especially, to support frequent operations of update, the pointers of recent referenced object are saved into Cache Table. Traditional approach of update is top-down, so this operation occurs many I/O costs to find target object in disk-based MR. In contrast, R^G-tree is able to process update operations by bottom-up approach because it has the cache data including pointers of leaf nodes referenced repeatedly.

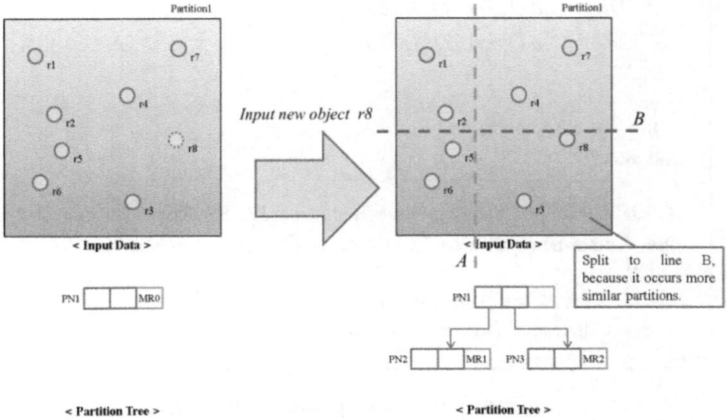

Fig. 2. Criteria of Partition Splitting

When a partition is splitting, we consider the number of objects to create effective two partitions. We must determine the criteria of split because we use the non-uniform grid. First, it is should calculated that the number of moving objects after partition splitting for each axis. If the number of objects when splitting by x-axis is adjacent to threshold of splitting, we divide a partition by x-axis. Otherwise, we check whether the number for splitting by y-axis is adjacent. Fig. 2 shows how our proposed scheme is splitting a partition in 2-dimensional space. If the numbers for x-axis and y-axis are correctly same, additional criteria of area size is considered. That is, it means that the axis dividing similar size of area is selected in Fig. 2. And our algorithm of partition splitting is shown in Fig. 3 below.

```
MAX_NODES ← Get 10-percent of the total objects.
k ← Get index of current partition.
n ← Maximum number of cells for x-axis
m ← Maximum number of cells for y-axis

if (PO^k_ALL > MAX_NODES)
  AO^k_X ← 0;  AO^k_Y ← 0;  a ← 0;  b ← 0;
  DF_X ← ∞;  DF_Y ← ∞;  N_X ← 0;  N_Y ← 0;

  while (a < n-1)
    AO^k_X ← AO^k_X + PO^k_X(a);
    if (DF_X > |AO^k_X − (PO^k_ALL/2)| )
      DF_X ← |AO^k_X − (PO^k_ALL/2)| ;
      N_X ← a;
    end if;
    a ← a + 1;
  end while;

  while (a < m-1)
    AO^k_Y ← AO^k_Y + PO^k_Y(b);
    if (DF_Y > |AO^k_Y − (PO^k_ALL/2)| )
      DF_Y ← |AO^k_Y − (PO^k_ALL/2)| ;
      N_Y ← b;
    end if;
    b ← b + 1;
  end while;

  if (DF_X − DF_Y < 0)  Create new partitions P1, P2 divided by N_X of x-axis;
  else  Create new partitions P1, P2 divided by N_Y of y-axis;
  end if;
  Add P1 and P2 into Partition Tree;
  Re-insert divided objects into P1 and P2;
end if;
```

Fig. 3. Partition Splitting Algorithm

4 Performance Evaluation

To evaluate cost for each operation, it is very hard to consider all experimental variables in real-world. Hence, we just consider I/O cost to access any leaf node in disk-based tree, and use following parameters shown in Table 1. The values of bold are used default in our experiments.

Table 1. Experimental Parameters and Value Used

Parameters	**Value Used (Increasement)**
Number of nodes	**1M** ~ 10M (1M)
Maximum distance per update	0 ~ **0.1** (0.01)
Buffer size	0 ~ **50%** (1%)
Data distribution	Uniform, **Non-uniform**
Experimental steps	100 ~ **1000** (100)

Actually it is impossible to create the data reflecting all variables in real-world. So we use two types of distribution; the uniform distribution, and the non-uniform distribution included dense objects regionally. This data of moving objects are created by GSTD(Generating Spatio-Temporal Datasets). Our experiments are evaluated based on Intel(R) Core(TM)2 Duo CPU T9300 2.5 GHz and 4GB RAM in Windows system.

Our result of experiments is shown in Fig. 4; (a) is I/O cost for update operations, (b) is I/O cost for query operations. According to the result in Fig. 4, our R^G-tree is mostly good performance both update and query operations. But, our scheme is shown low efficiency when the interval of update is so small value. It means that this interval should adjust to improve the performance of R^G-tree depending on system environments.

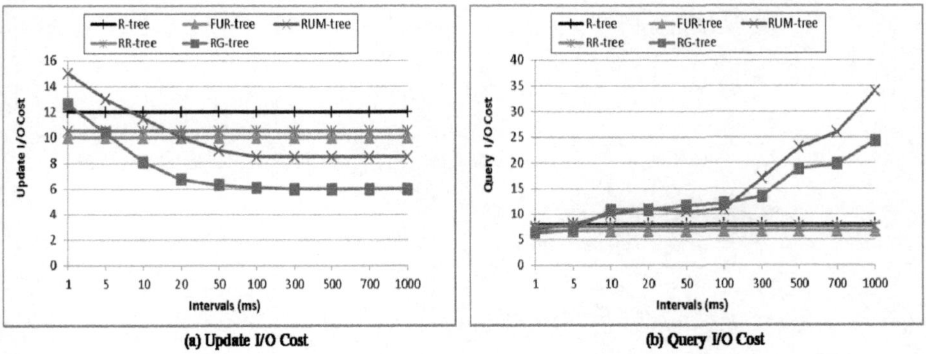

Fig. 4. Evaluation Results

5 Conclusion

We proposed the R^G-tree index to solve significant two problems in the area of GIS; one is adapting distribution of dense objects regionally, and another is supporting frequent updates for massively moving objects. Our scheme improved these by using the dynamic non-uniform grid and in-memory buffers such as Insert Buffer, Modify Buffer and Cache Table.

In the future, we will research to find the more effective methods for handling stored data of in-memory buffers. And we will also upgrade our processing algorithms to reduce the costs.

References

1. Guttman, A.: R-Trees: A Dynamic Index Structure For Spatial Searching. Association for Computing Machinery (1984)
2. Lee, M.L., Hsu, W., Jensen, C.S., Cui, B., Teo, K.L.: Supporting Frequent Updates in R-Trees: A Bottom-Up Approach. In: Proceedings of the 29th VLDB Conference, Berlin, Germany (2003)
3. Xiong, X., Aref, W.G.: R-Trees with Update Memos, CSD TR #05-020 (2005)
4. Biveinis, L.: Towards Efficient Main Memory Use For Optimum Tree Index Update. In: PVLDB 2008, Auckland, New Zealand, pp. 23–28 (2008)

The Guaranteed QoS for Time-Sensitive Traffic in High-Bandwidth EPON*

Jeong-hyun Cho[1] and Yong-suk Chang[2]

[1] Dept. of Mobile Internet, Yeungnam College of Science & Technology
170 Hyeonchung-ro, Nam-gu Daegu, 705-703 Korea
petercho@ync.ac.kr
[2] Representative Director, DAOOLDNS co. ltd
Dongbyeon-dong, Buk-gu, Daegu, 702-882 Korea
ysjang@daooldns.co.kr

Abstract. Recently many countries have kept studying on the methods of constructing high speed networks. Task Force team for IEEE 802.3ah has accomplished the standardization of EPON which is the next generation subscriber access network. EPON doesn't still have the bandwidth wide enough to support the new service which demands high bandwidth. Therefore 10G EPON is the next generation subscriber access network which expanded the up-down bandwidth range of 1G EPON 10 times in order to support a next generation multimedia service demanding high bandwidth and which is proceeding the standardization of physical layer in IEEE 802.3av Task Force. This paper has designed the model which can accommodate IEEE 802.1 AVB traffics smoothly in 10G EPON and suggesting the Intra-ONU scheduling model which makes this model operate effectively.

Keywords: 10G EOON, QoS, DBA Algorithm.

1 Introduction

The high speed network becomes an important indicator of national power in information society where the demand for multimedia service based on internet is increasing. Because of this reasons, many developed countries are accomplishing a number of projects in order to construct high speed networks. As the communication network, there are two types. One is the Local Area Network(LAN) which is composed of terminals, switches and links in short distance. The other is the subscriber access network which connects countries or LANs with the backbone network. In order to construct high speed communication network, all the above mentioned LAN, subscriber access network and backbone network should be able to transfer high bandwidth. As the backbone network, its speed has been increased up to Tbps class. The transfer rate of LAN has reached to 100Gbps class due to Carrier Sense Multiple Access/Collision Detection (CSMA/CD). However, as the subscriber access network, many researches have been studied but actual transfer rate is just a

* This research was supported by the Yeungnam College of Science & Technology Research Grants in 2009.

T.-h. Kim et al. (Eds.): MulGraB 2011, Part II, CCIS 263, pp. 181–190, 2011.

couple of tens of Mbps class. The construction of FTTH is still in the early stage due to the high cost for large scale network and approaching in various ways according to the communication environment of each country. These ways include xDigital Subscriber Line (DSL), cable modem, Fiber-to-the-Curb/Cabinet (FTTC), Fiber-To-The-Building (FTTB) and Gigabit Ethernet (GE)/10GE technologies.

The Final goal of Ethernet over Passive Optical Network (EPON) which appeared on the way to FTTH, is next generation subscriber access network [1]. The EPON has started the Ethernet in the First Mile Study Group which is targeted for the deployment of Ethernet in the First Mile (between house of a subscriber and a neighboring station or a neighboring connecting nodes). The concept of EPON is low price subscriber access tool accommodating the general subscriber in IEEE 802 LMSC(LAN/MAN Standards Committee). In May 2004, the Task Force of IEEE 802.3ah completed the standardization of EPON, the next generation subscriber access network.

The EPON has been set up in many places in the world as a new alternative for subscriber access network, but it doesn't still have enough bandwidth to support new services such as the HD level IPTV which needs a high bandwidth, and the Video On Demand (VoD), video conferences, IP Video surveillance systems and online games which demands higher interaction. Additionally the demand for Tripe-Play Service which can support internet service along with broadcast data and voice data is so high that the service to secure sure delay and jitter should be provided in order to satisfy it.

The 10G EPON has a maximum bandwidth up to 10Gbps, it covers the drawback of 1G EPON due to a bandwidth shortage. It can perfectly support strict realtime service based on IEEE 802.1 AVB which is the protocol operating based on reservation and acceptance control[2]. Because it basically communicates data between OLT(Optical Line Terminator) and ONU (Optical Network Unit) using optical fibers on the physical layer as one type of FTTH, there is no weakness for distances. Also it can permit various multimedia services that have their strict characteristics as its MAC layer to adopt the proper bandwidth allocation algorithm.

So we propose the effective Bandwidth Allocation Algorithm in order to support IEEE 802.1 AVB in 10G EPON. We introduce the basic concept of PON in chapter 2, the configuration and bandwidth allocation algorithm of 10G EPON to support IEEE 802.1 AVB traffic explained in chapter 3 and the experimental results of the scheduling method described in chapter 4. Finally, chapter 5 will summarize the result of this paper.

2 Relate Work

2.1 The Structure of the EPON

We explain the fundamentals of the operation in EPON. Figure 1 shows the EPON system structure, as suggested by the IEEE 802.3 EFM SG. The OLT and the ONU are located at the End Point of a Passive Star Splitter (PSS), each of which is connected by an optical fiber. The PON is either distributed into several identical optical signals or united into one signal according to the transfer direction of the optical signal. PSSs are economical as they have low construction, maintenance, and repair costs, plus since a PSS is a passive component, it does not require any extra power supply. In addition, between the OLT and the ONU are connected by a Point-to-Multipoint form, the installment cost of the optical fiber is lower than that of a Point-to-Point form.

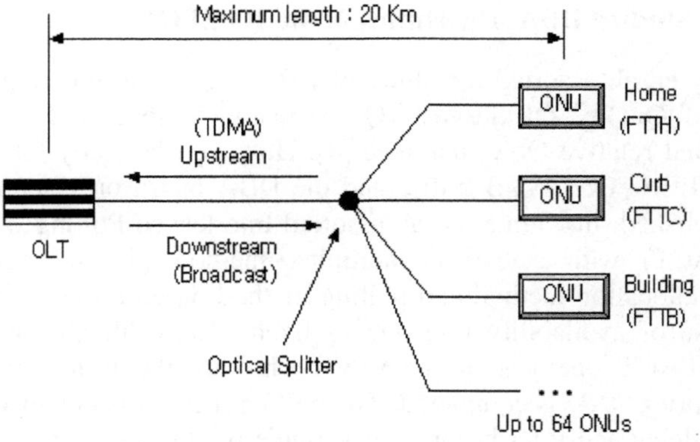

Fig. 1. The structure of Ethernet PON is proposed in IEEE 802.ah

2.2 10G EPON

The 10G EPON is a next generation subscriber access network with 10 times faster speed in the upstream and downstream than 1G EPON. So it can transmit easily multimedia data which requires a high bandwidth using its improved data transmission rate without shortage of the bandwidth such as installation cost and adaptability from the aspect of its simple structure and operation than Wavelength Division Multiplexing PON (WDM-PON) which allocates ONU's bandwidth for each wavelength [3].

Although the physical layer of 10G EPON is different from the physical layer of 1G EPON, because both MAC layers have analogous functionalities, 10G EPON can use the control protocol and MAC protocol of 1G EPON without the modification. But the existing Dynamic Bandwidth Allocation (DBA) algorithms of 1G EPON seem unsuitable to accommodate 802.1 AVB traffic with the strict time-sensitive property. This paper suggests a DBA algorithm that consists of Inter-ONU scheduling and Intra-ONU scheduling to support 802.1 AVB traffic. Inter-ONU scheduling allocates each ONU's bandwidth and Intra-ONU scheduling allocates a bandwidth for each traffic class consists of voice, video and data. The 10G EPON uses the traffic class 4, 5 and each priority queue for IEEE 802.1 AVB traffic while it introduces and utilizes the scheduling structure used in 1G EPON.

As for bandwidth allocation method, there are two types. One is the single level model which allocates bandwidth by reporting the scheduling information of each queue to ONU through GATE message. The other is the hierarchical model in which ONU makes notice to the length of the entire queue to REPORT and arranges the priority through the queue scheduler of its own bandwidth allocated in the DBA of OLT. The single level model provides convenience for maintenance because all the information can be controlled in OLT by reducing the load of the queue scheduling in ONU. However it can't cope with input traffics while each ONU transfers REPORT message and receives GATE message. On the other hand the hierarchical model can flexibly deal with input traffics in the queue of ONU between REPORT message and GATE message even though the price of ONU goes up due to scheduling function.

2.3 The Studied DBA Algorithms in the 1G EPON

In McGarry et. al. assorted the study of DBA algorithm into statistical multiplexing method and Quality Of Service (QoS) guarantee that is divided again absolute guarantee and relative QoS guarantee [4]. However the study for acceptance control to handle IEEE 802.1 AVB traffic and the DBA based on resource reservation was not accomplished. In Kramer et. al. assorted Interleaved Polling with Adaptive Cycle Time (IPACT) with statistical multiplex method [5]. Kramer suggested fixed bandwidth allocation method and polling method based on OLT in order to improve the decrease of availability rate due to fixed bandwidth allocation method [5][6]. Basically IPACT operates in the way of polling the following ONU before the transfer of prior ONU is completed. The polling method is not adequate to the service delicate to delay and jitter because of variable polling cycle time although it enables the statistical multiplex and has excellent capability. As for bandwidth allocation by polling, there are Fixed, Limited, Gated, Const, Linear and Elastic method. Fixed method is the static allocation method which allocates the same bandwidth to every ONU and Limited method allocates bandwidth which each ONU demands within the range not beyond maximum transmission window. Gated method allocates all bandwidth ONU demands. Const method allocates fixed credit to demanding bandwidth by adding the time slot and Linear method decides the size of credit according to demanding bandwidth. Finally Elastic method is the one which transfers bandwidth of ONU to demanding ONU which requires smaller amount than MTW does beyond the maximum bandwidth.

Ma and Zhu suggested the bandwidth guaranteed polling which shares upward traffic based on SLA between Internet Service Provider (ISP) and subscriber [7]. This algorithm provides the best effort service to general subscribers while it guarantees bandwidth to premium subscribers who contracted SLA. This model classifies ONU in network into two types of class. One is ONU to which bandwidth guarantee service is secured and the other is ONU to which the best effort service is secured. In Kramer et. al. minimum bandwidth is secured and the bandwidth beyond limitation is distributed fairly [8]. However it takes quite a few times to receive GATE message because allocating is possible only after bandwidth of all ONUs are reported. Therefore this study decreased the time between receiving of REPORT message and GATE message by dividing them into 2 groups but it was not solved perfectly. So it has limitation to provide QoS to traffic arriving during the time between REPORT message and GATE message.

3 The Method for Supporting Synchronous Ethernet

3.1 Inter-ONU Scheduling

The Inter-ONU scheduler in the OLT will allocate a bandwidth (start time and granted transmission time) within one cycle to each ONU based on REPORT messages. Inter-ONU scheduling can be expressed in (1), at (1) RB_i is required bandwidth as input, GB_i is the Granted Bandwidth as output. RB_i is consists of Booking information(B_i) for the reservation of IEEE 802.1 AVB traffic and Queuing information(R_i) for non-time sensitive traffic. Because AVB traffic is constant, once Inter-ONU scheduler permits B_i to ONU_i, it continues until ONU requests to terminate the connection. So, OLT keeps each ONU's B_i summation. But R_i is a variable per a cycle, therefore each ONU requests R_i every cycle.

$$GB_i = InterDBA(RB_i),\quad RB_i \in \{B_i, R_i\},\ GB_i \in \{T_i^{start}, G_i\} \tag{1}$$

GB_i that is notified to each ONU is consists of a start time (T_i^{start}) and a transmission duration (G_i). Each ONU initiates to transmit their traffic in queues accodring to their priority and allocated quantities at T_i^{start} in time next cycle and continues to T_i^{stop} as expressed in (2). B_{max} is the maximum transmission rate and equal to 10Gbps in the 10G EPON model.

$$T_i^{end} = T_i^{start} + G_i / B_{max} \tag{2}$$

Our system must accommodate two kinds of class 4 and class 5 traffic as defined in the IEEE 802.1 AVB to support synchronous Ethernet traffic. Each class has constraints of the maximum delay and jitter. The maximum delay of class 4 and class 5 is 1ms and 125μs respectively. Therefore we chose the class 5 which is limited to 125μs in upstream. One cycle can be expressed in (3). G_{BAND} is Guard Band in expression (3) that transmits data laser transmitter in ONU_i. This is used to prevent ONU_{i+1} transmitting before the nature signal disappeared after a short period. G_{BAND} uses 512ns which is the same in the existing EPON. M_{report} represents bit unit in length of a REPORT message

$$T_{cycle} = \sum_{i=1}^{N} (G_i / B_{max} + (G_{BAND} + M_{report} / B_{max})) \tag{3}$$

Our Inter-ONU scheduler operates in a transmission procedure based on IPACT made by Kramer et. al. IPACT operates as figure 2. Each ONU reports its queue information and OLT transmits the GATE message to each ONU used by DBA. This process increases the throughput by reducing the bandwidth of the uplink stream. We chose Limit method within IPACT methods to support synchronous Ethernet traffic.

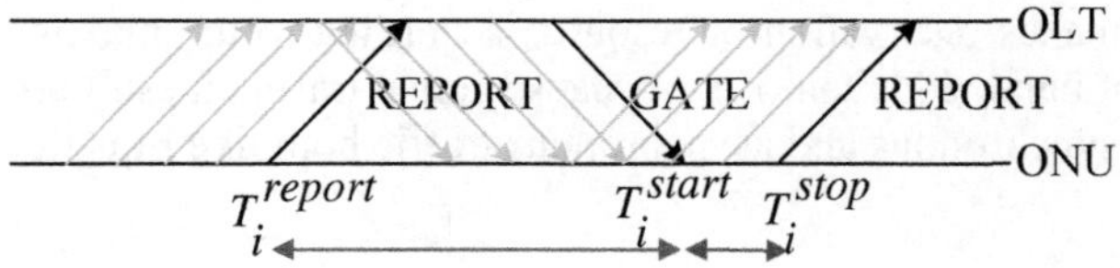

Fig. 2. IPACT mechanism

G_i and T_i^{start} are specified by Inter-ONU scheduler based on equation (4).

$$G_i = \begin{cases} R_i - B_i, & R_i + B_i < W_{max} \\ W_{max} - B_i, & R_i + B_i \ge W_{max} \end{cases} \tag{4}$$

$$W_{max} = (T_{cycle} / N - G_{BAND}) \times B_{max} - M_{report}$$

3.2 Intra-ONU Scheduling

Inter-ONU scheduling allocates transmission starting time (T_i^{start}) and transmission allowance quantity (G_i) based on queue information indicated in the REPORT message from ONU so that the conflict between each ONU may not occur. Intra-ONU scheduling is carried out for transmission window (W_i) which is the sum of the bandwidth G_i allocated from OLT and reserved bandwidth B_i in each ONU. B_i is classified into class 5 and class 4, which are defined in IEEE 802.1AVB. The bandwidth G_i allocated from Inter-ONU scheduler indicates the total quantity of 3 classes which are high, medium and low priority. We describe W_i, B_i, G_i in Equation (5).

$$W_i = B_i + G_i \,,\quad B_i = B_i^{T4} + B_i^{T5} \,,\quad G_i = W_i^H + W_i^M + W_i^L \tag{5}$$

Intra-ONU scheduling has the queue which has 5 priorities and its structure is like figure 4. It accomplishes the role of deciding the size of the transmission window and the transmission starting time with G_i which is carried out and allocated in ONU and Bi recorded on resource reservation table. In GATE message, $T_i^{T5,start}$, $T_iT4,start$, $T_i^{H,start}$, $T_i^{M,start}$ and $T_i^{L,start}$ indicates the transmission time while W_i^{T5}, W_i^{T4}, W_i^H, W_i^M, and W_i^L are the size of the transmission window.

Intra-ONU scheduler consists of 5 priority queues, priority manager and queue scheduler. Intra-ONU scheduler sorted each Ethernet frame according to priority and input in the queue matching priority. Priority manager classifies Ethernet frame into 5 priority queues based on Priority code point (PCP) in Virtual LAN (VLAN) tag of input frame.

As IEEE 802.1 AVB frame of class 4 and class 5 operate based on resource reservation, it is considered that the resource for incoming frame is available if there is reservation on resource table. If reservation is success state on resource table, incoming frame is stored in queue, but if reservation is not success, incoming frame is discarded. The transaction time is allocated in order according to priority from high one to low one after bandwidth of synchronous data and IEEE 802.1 AVB data are allocated.

3.3 The Method of Allocating Bandwidth

IEEE 802.1 AVB traffic specifies the resource it requires on the field of TSPEC in SRPDU. As resources are specified variably like minimum and maximum number of frame, ONU makes reservation of resource according to the maximum number. So as the waste of bandwidth can occur because actual traffic doesn't arrive, it calculates bandwidth of synchronous and asynchronous traffic both like Equation (6).

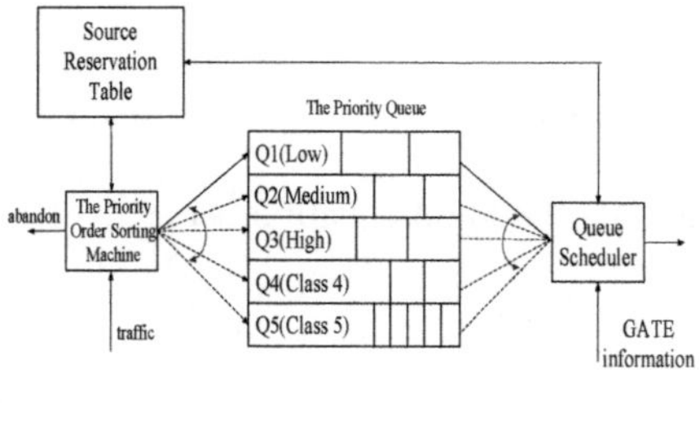

Fig. 3. The structure of Intra-ONU scheduler

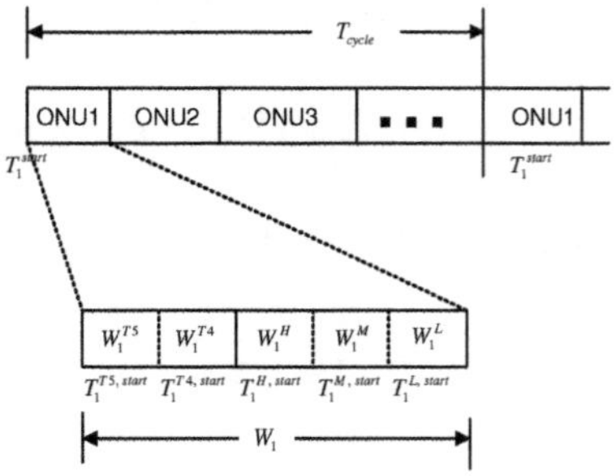

Fig. 4. The example of 5 classes of traffic transmission

In Equation (6), for the size(B_i^{T5}) and transmission of bandwidth reserved for class 5 traffic, the minimum value of traffic size (Q_i^{T5}) is designated as the transmission window size. Likewise it is applied to traffic of class 4.

$$W_i^{T5}=MIN(B_i^{T5}),\ W_i^{T4}=MIN(B_i^{T4},Q_i^{T4}),\ W_i^{NR}=G_i+(B_i^{T5}-W_i^{T5})+(B_i^{T4}-W_i^{T4}) \quad (6)$$

The asynchronous traffic transmits the data of subscriber with SLA contract which doesn't support synchronous traffic. It can be classified into 3 types. They are Expedited Forward (EF) class which is high priority traffic, Assured Forward (AF) class which is medium priority and Best Effort (BE) class which is low priority traffic. It is the QoS method which has been studied in 1G EPON and the service that should be provided for exchangeability with conventional EPON. When ONU_i makes REPORT message, the entire demanding bandwidth of asynchronous traffic can be expressed as R_i in Equation (7). After GATE message is received, the status of queue which stores asynchronous data at the transmission start time can be expressed as Q_i^{NR}.

$$R_i = R_i^H + R_i^M + R_i^L\ ,\quad Q_i^{NR} = Q_i^H + Q_i^M + Q_i^L \quad (7)$$

The reason why Equation (7) is needed, the packet which arrived during TWT can be delayed for more than a cycle since only the length of packet which arrived during Treport is reported to OLT through REPORT in IPACT method like figure 5. As the load of network is higher, its delay is larger. So quality of high priority traffic which has the lowest delay among asynchronous traffics could be lowered[5].

In order to guarantee QoS of high priority traffic, traffic which arrives during TWT should be transmitted faster than traffic of other class. The most basic method is to use Strict Priority Queuing (SPQ). The shortage of SPQ is that delay is increased for low priority traffic. The second method is the way additional Credit is allocated as expecting high priority traffic during TWT. The shortage of credit is waste of additional bandwidth because Credit method is hard to estimate credit, so entire cycle can increase. As it couldn't accommodate synchronous traffic, high priority traffic must deal first. So the paper was focused on minimizing delay of high priority traffic. However, as 10G EPON can accommodate synchronous traffic, the efficiency of asynchronous traffic like abolition rate of traffic rather than capability of high priority traffic is important. So this paper suggests Adaptive Guarantee Bandwidth Allocation (AGBA) which takes consideration in characteristics of 10G EPON which supports synchronous Ethernet traffic based on WFQ. The WFQ doesn't occur the disadvantage for QoS of high priority traffic. As AGBA is a WFQ method which sets weight dynamically, weight is an important standard for capability. To decide weight, we consider maximum delay, maximum jitter and characteristics of traffic quantity stored in queue of each class.

The maximum delay and jitter of high priority traffic(EF) and medium priority traffic(AF) is defined as 10ms and 100ms in IEEE 802.1Q but there is no definition in low priority traffic(BE). However excessive delay can cause Time out in TCP, a high protocol layer. The value which decides time-out of timer is RTO (Retransmission Time-Out) and it is calculated based on RTT. So it is decided dynamically for each TCP.

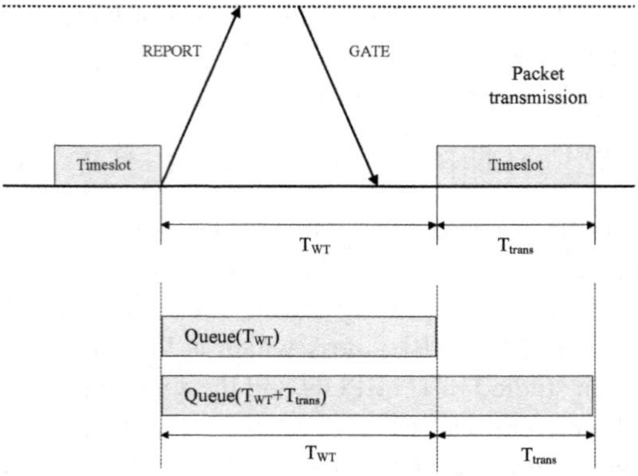

Fig. 5. The structure of Intra-ONU scheduler

So in this paper the maximum delay value of BE is designated 1s, 10 times of AF. The ratio for EF, AF and BE becomes 1:10:100 when considering the max delay time of them. As the max value of cycle in 10G EPON is 125□, we can conclude that the max delay can be guaranteed only if EF can transmit 80 cycles, AF can do 800 cycles and BE can do 8000 cycles for traffic which arrives within one cycle. Therefore the quantity for traffic of each class, which arrived within a cycle, can be estimated. The period of a cycle is divided into Ttrans and TWT.

The following 3 cases happen if compare the sum of $W_{i,t}^{min}$ of minimum guarantee bandwidth with allowed bandwidth, G^{i} before additional bandwidth is allocated. So the additional bandwidth is allocated according to 3 cases.

$W_{i,t}^{min} = G_{i,t}$: the minimum guarantee bandwidth becomes the size of transmission window.

$$W_{i,t}^{c,add} = 0 \tag{8}$$

$W_{i,t}^{min} > G_{i,t}$: the minimum guarantee bandwidth of all classes is decreased by the ratio of sum of allocated bandwidth and minimum guarantee bandwidth.

$$W_{i,t}^{c,add} = \left(G_{i,t} - W_{i,t}^{min}\right) \times \frac{W_{i,t}^{c}}{W_{i,t}^{min}} \tag{9}$$

$W_{i,t}^{min} < G_{i,t}$: Like Equation (10) it calculates out and allocates the additional bandwidth calculated by multiplying average and the ratio in queue on sum of weight for the excess bandwidth which subtracts the sum of minimum guarantee bandwidth from allocated bandwidth.

$$W_{i,t}^{c,add} = W_{i,t}^{\alpha} \times \frac{1}{2} \times (Q_{i,t}^{c,ratio} + \omega^{c}) \quad , \quad Q_{i,t}^{c,ratio} = \frac{Q_{i,t}^{c}}{Q_{i,t}^{NR}} \quad , \quad W_{i,t}^{\alpha} = W_{i,t}^{NR} - \sum_{\beta \in c} W_{i,t}^{\beta,min} \tag{10}$$

4 Experimental Results

This section has implemented the 10G EPON model that supports IEEE 802.1 AVB traffic in order to analyze the capability of bandwidth allocating method this study suggests by use of OPNET and is analyzing capability of Intra-ONU scheduling method. Intra-ONU scheduling accomplishes the role to allocate bandwidth allocated by Intra-ONU scheduling method to each class as described in section 3. This experiment compared Par and DBA2 of the method this paper suggests with those of SPQ, WFQ, and Credit method. Each experiment model of bandwidth allocation system has 3 10Mbits priority queues [9]. Under asynchronous experiment model, we allocated 30 % of whole traffic produced to synchronous traffic and kept the ratio of EF, AF and BE with 1:1:2 and increased 10 % each time from 10% to 100%.

Figure 6 and 7 shows average delay of terminal to terminal and queue size of EF traffic in each bandwidth allocation method. Under load below 70%, delay of terminal to terminal was lower in order of Par, the suggested method, DBA2, SPQ and WFQ method. When traffic load goes over 70%, end-to-end delay changed in order of SPQ, WFQ, the suggested method, DBA2 and Par method. The queue size showed the same order with average end-to-end delay. However SPQ which showed the lowest delay, had no large difference end-to-end delay and queue size while it showed delay low enough to accommodate EF traffic. We have analyzed capability of asynchronous traffic under synchronous allocation system with max end-to-end delay, average end-to-end delay and queue size.

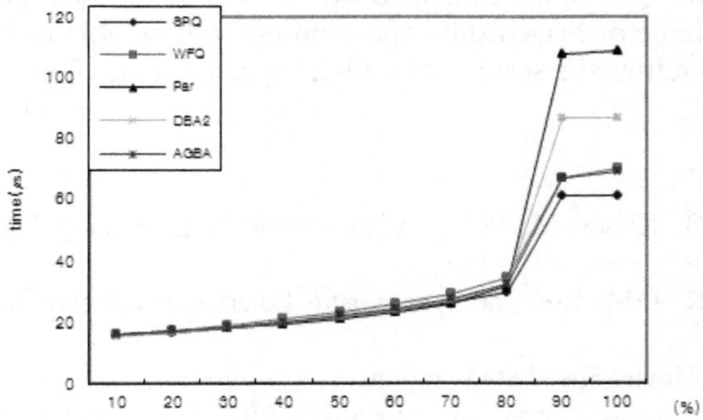

Fig. 6. Average end-to-end delay in EF traffic

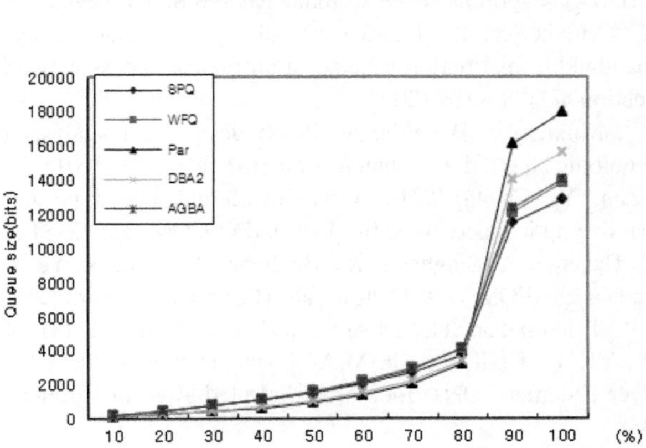

Fig. 7. Queue size which stores EF traffic

5 Conclusion

As the demand for multimedia service increases, many research and investment on bandwidth expansion of network has been accomplished. The backbone network and LAN enabled the transfer of multimedia data with large quantity as it developed a lot as a result of a long time research and investment. However the subscriber access network which connects backbone network and short distance network still remains the area that is insufficient to transmitting multimedia data between high bandwidth of backbone network and short distance network.

In this situation the EPON technology that can provide higher transmission rate than various subscriber access networks appeared. But as its transmission rate is just maximum 1Gbps, its bandwidth is not enough to serve Internet Protocol TeleVision (IPTV) that has more than 100 channels, Video on Demand (VoD) of High Definition (HD) class and online games of large capability in the future. So now 10G EPON is considered to be an alternative. As 10G EPON not only can support high bandwidth but also traffic of IEEE 802.1 AVB that requires strict delay and jitter, it can support all services customers want. We designed the model that can accommodate IEEE 802.1 AVB traffic in those 10G EPONs and suggested Intra-ONU scheduling model to allocate bandwidth more effectively. Our Intra-ONU scheduling model showed lower end-to-end delay for class 5 traffic. Also we suggested AGBA to to accommodate for QoS of multimedia traffic in 10G EPON. The suggested 10G EPON is not just the issue of bandwidth expansion but will be able to a solution which can accommodate multimedia service with high capacity in the future.

References

1. Pesavento, G., Kelsey, M.: PONs for the Broadband Local loop. Lightwave 16(10), 68–74 (1999)
2. Rodrigues, S.: IEEE-1588 and Synchronous Ethernet in Telecom. In: ISPCS, pp. 138–142 (2007)
3. IEEE 802.1 Higher Speed Study group, `http://grouper.ieee.org/groups/802/3/hssg/index.html`
4. McGarry, M.P., Maier, M., Reisslein, M.: Ethernet PONs: A Survey of Dynamic Bandwidth Allocation (DBA) Algorithms. IEEE Communications Magazine 42(8), 8–15 (2004)
5. Kramer, G., Mukherjee, B.: Interleaved polling with adaptive cycle time (IPACT): a dynamic bandwidth distribution scheme in an optical access network. Photonic Network Communication 4(1), 89–107 (2002)
6. Kramer, G., Mukherjee, B.: Ethernet PON: design and analysis of an optical access network. Photonic Network Communication 3(3), 307–319 (2001)
7. Ma, M., Zhu, Y., Cheng, T.H.: A bandwidth guaranteed polling MAC protocol for Ethernet passive optical networks. In: IEEE INFO-COM, pp. 22–31 (2003)
8. Kramer, G., Banerjee, A., Singhal, N.K., Mukherjee, B., Dixit, S., Ye, Y.: Fair Queueing With Service Envelopes (FQSE): A Cousin-Fair Hierarchical Scheduler for Subscriber Access Networks. IEEE Journal on Selected Areas In Communications 22(8), 1497–1513 (2004)
9. Assi, C.M., Ye, Y., Dixit, S., Ali, M.A.: Dynamic Bandwidth Allocation for Quality-of-Service Over Ethernet PONs. Journal of Selected Area in Communication 21(9), 1467–1477 (2003)
10. IEEE P802.1Qat/D4.2: Draft Standard for Local and Metropolitan Area Networks, Virtual Bridged Local Area Networks, Amendment 9: Stream Reservation Protocol (SRP) (2009)

Robust Vehicle Tracking Multi-feature Particle Filter

M. Eren Yildirim[1], Jongkwan Song[1], Jangsik Park[1],
Byung Woo Yoon[1], and Yunsik Yu[2]

[1] Department of Electronics Engineering, Kyungsung University,
Daeyeon3-dong, 110-1, Nam-gu, Busan, 608-736, Korea
jsong@ks.ac.kr
[2] Convergence of IT Devices Institute Busan, Gaya-dong, San 24, Busanjin-gu, Busan,
614-714, Korea
nz90nz@deu.ac.kr

Abstract. Object detection and tracking have been studied separately in most cases. Particle filtering has proven very successful for non-linear and non-Gaussian estimation problems. This paper presents a new method for tracking moving vehicles with temporal disappearance. The proposed method can continue tracking after disappearance. Color distribution of objects is integrated into particle filtering algorithm. As the color of an object can vary over time dependent on the illumination, a likelihood model is used including color cue and detection cue. Color cue is provided by using Bhattacharyya distance, and detection cue is provided by Euclidean distance. Tests are made by using highway cameras that are located on bridge.

Keywords: Particle filtering, Color distribution, Euclidean distance, Bhattacharyya distance.

1 Introduction

Object tracking is required by many vision applications such as human-computer interfaces [1], video communication/compression [2] or surveillance [3, 4, 5]. On the other hand, achieving this task efficiently and robustly in clutter environment is a challenging problem. In this context, particle filters provide a robust tracking framework as they are neither limited to linear systems nor require the noise to be Gaussian.

Particle filtering is a sequential Monte Carlo methodology where the basic idea is the recursive computation of relevant probability distributions using the concepts of importance sampling and approximation of probability distributions with discrete random measures. The particle filtering method has become an important alternative to the extended Kalman filter. With particle filtering, continuous distributions are approximated by discrete random measures, which are composed of weighted particles, where the particles are samples of the unknown states from the state space, and the particle weights are "probability masses" computed by using Bayes theory. In the implementation of particle filtering, importance sampling plays a crucial role and,

T.-h. Kim et al. (Eds.): MulGraB 2011, Part II, CCIS 263, pp. 191–196, 2011.

since the procedure is designed for sequential use, the method is also called sequential importance sampling. The advantage of particle filtering over other methods is in that the exploited approximation does not involve linearization around current estimates but rather approximations in the representation of the desired distributions by discrete random measures.[6]

Color histograms in particular have many advantages for tracking non-rigid objects as they are robust to partial occlusion, are rotation and scale invariant and are calculated efficiently. A target is tracked with a particle filter by comparing its histogram with the histograms of the sample positions using the Bhattacharyya distance.

Color histogram can change over time by illumination, so more reliable method is required. We used the Euclidean distance between target object and observation in order to make a more accurate tracking.

The outline if this paper is as follows. In section 2 we briefly describe particle filtering and how color histograms are used as object models. Moreover, Euclidean distance and its integration for tracking is described. In section 3 experimental results are shown. The conclusion is delivered in section 4.

2 Proposed Particle filter with Color Histogram and Euclid Distance

2.1 Particle Filtering

Particle filtering [7, 8] was originally developed to track objects in clutter. The state of a tracked object is described by the vector X_t while the vector Z_t denotes all the observations $\{z_1,\ldots\ldots z_t\}$ up to time *t*. Particle filters are often used when the posterior density $p(X_t \mid Z_t)$ and the observation density $p(Z_t \mid X_t)$ are non-Gaussian.

The key idea of particle filtering is to approximate the probability distribution by a weighted sample set $S = \{(s^{(n)}, \pi^{(n)}) \mid n = 1\ldots\ldots N\}$. Each sample *S* represents one hypothetical state of the object, with a corresponding discrete sampling probability π, where $\sum_{n=1}^{N} \pi^{(n)} = 1$.

The evolution of the sample set is described by propagating each sample according to a system model. Each element of the set is then weighted in terms of the observations and *N* samples are drawn with replacement, by choosing a particular sample with probability $\pi^{(n)} = p(z_t \mid X_t = s_t^{(n)})$. The mean state of an object is estimated at each time step by

$$E[S_t] = \sum_{n=1}^{N} \pi^{(n)} s^{(n)} \tag{1}$$

2.2 Color Distribution Modeling

Color information is remarkably persistent and robust to changes in pose and illumination. The histograms are produced with the function $h(x_i)$, that appoints the color information at the location x_i to its corresponding bin. In our experiments, the histograms are typically calculated in the RGB space using 8x8x4 bins.

We determine the color distribution inside an upright elliptic region with half axes H_x and H_y .To increase the reliability of the color distribution when boundary pixels belong to the background or get occluded, smaller weights are assigned to the pixels that are further away from the region center by employing a weighting function

$$k(r) = \begin{cases} 1 - r^2, & r < 1 \\ 0, & else \end{cases} \tag{2}$$

where r is the distance from the region center. Thus, we increase the reliability of the color distribution when these boundary pixels belong to the background or get occluded. It is also possible to use a different weighting function, for example the Epanechnikov kernel [9,10].

The color distribution $p_y = \{p_y^{(u)}\}_{u=1...m}$ at location y is calculated as

$$p_y^{(u)} = f \sum_{i=1}^{I} k\left(\frac{\| y \quad x_i \|}{a}\right) h[(x_i) - u] \tag{3}$$

where δ is the Kronecker delta function. I and m is the number of pixels in the region and number of bins respectively.

The parameter a is used for adapting the region size and it is equal to $a = \sqrt{H_x^2 + H_y^2}$ and f is the normalization factor that is defined as

$$f = \frac{1}{\sum_{i=1}^{I} k\left(\frac{\| y - x_i \|}{a}\right)} \tag{4}$$

In a tracking approach, the estimated state is updated at each time step by taking the new observations into account. Therefore, we need a similarity measure which is based on color distributions. A popular measure between two distributions p(u) and q(u) is the Bhattacharyya coefficient [11, 12]

$$\rho[p,q] = \int \sqrt{p(u)q(u)}du \tag{5}$$

and we define one more term that is Bhattacharya distance which is as follows

$$d_B = \sqrt{1 - \rho[p,q]} \tag{6}$$

Finally, the likelihood weights are specified by Gaussian distribution with variance σ_c

$$\pi_{color}^{(i)} = \frac{1}{\sqrt{2\pi\sigma_c}} e^{\left\{\frac{-d_B^2}{2\sigma_c^2}\right\}}, \quad i = 1,2...,N \tag{7}$$

where N is number of samples.

Each particle of the distribution represents an ellipse and is given as

$$s = \{x, y, H_x, H_y\} \tag{8}$$

where (x, y) refers to the center location and (H_x, H_y) refers to the half axes lengths of the ellipse.

2.3 Implementation of Euclidean Distance to Particle Filtering

Usage of only color cue is not sufficient in cases where illumination changes. We needed to implement an extra likelihood model to get similarity between the target and observations. Euclidean distance is defined as

$$d_E = \sqrt{(x - \hat{x})^2 + (y - \hat{y})^2} \tag{9}$$

Usage where (x, y) is the center of the target ellipse and $(\hat{x}, \hat{y})$ is the center of the ellipse corresponding to each particle.

We can define our likelihood model dependent on Euclidean distance as

$$\pi_{Euclid}^{(i)} = \frac{1}{\sqrt{2\pi\sigma_d}} e^{\left\{\frac{-d_E^2}{2\sigma_d^2}\right\}} \tag{10}$$

Our final likelihood model is combination of distributions dependent on color and detection cue as follows[13]

$$\pi_{total}^{(i)} = \pi_{euclid}^{(i)} \pi_{color}^{(i)} \tag{11}$$

where i is the sample index.

3 Experimental Results

We have demonstrated our system on videos of road on the bridge. Besides the illumination handicap, vibration of the camera and bridge was also another problem. Our test video had a frame rate of 59frames/sec and a size of 720x480 pixels.

Figure 1 shows some examples frames that our algorithm tracks a target vehicle on the bridge effectively. As it is seen, there are occlusions on the background of the image caused by lighting poles near the road. So, as the target object is moving forward, it is occluded for a short period behind the poles. After that short period, our system detects and continues tracking the target. We used N=100 samples and RGB color space with 8x8x4 for our tests.

4 Conclusion

In this study, we have proposed an efficient system which integrates color distributions and Euclidean distances into particle filtering. Our results shows that this system tracks moving objects under occlusion and illumination changes. Our next goal is to improve our detection and tracking algorithms to a faster one.

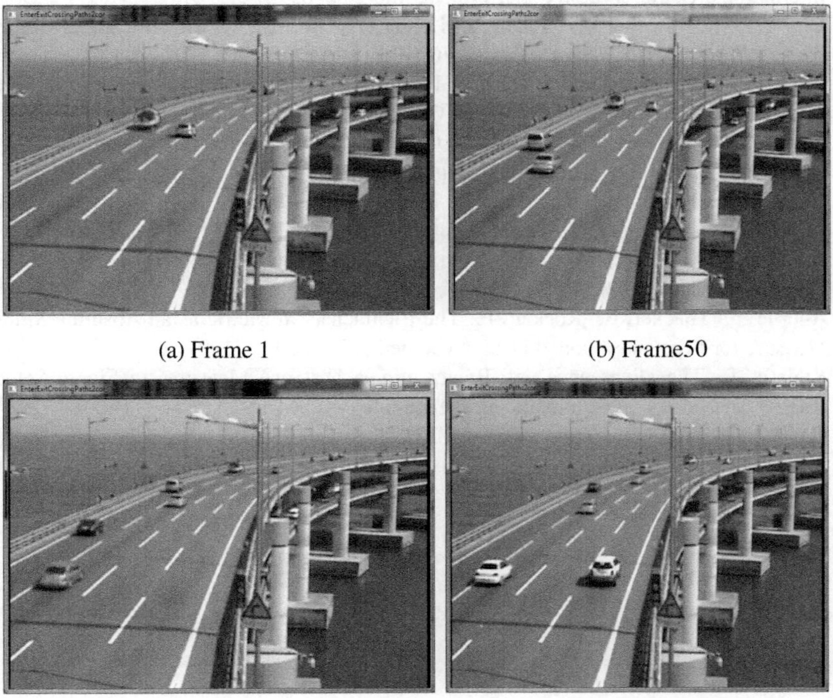

(a) Frame 1 (b) Frame50

(c) Frame 70 (d) Frame 100

Fig. 1. Visual tracking results a) frame 1; b) frame 50; c) frame 70; d) frame 100 shows the successful tracking after temporal disappearance

Acknowledgement. This work was supported in part by MKE(NIPA), Busan Metropolitan City and Dong-Eui University.(08-GIBAN-13, Convergence of IT Devices Institute Busan).

References

1. Black, M.J., Jepson, A.D.: A Probabilistic Framework for Matching Temporal Trajectories: CONDENSATION-Based Recognition of Gestures and Expressions. In: Burkhardt, H.-J., Neumann, B. (eds.) ECCV 1998. LNCS, vol. 1406, pp. 909–924. Springer, Heidelberg (1998)
2. Beymer, D., McLauchlan, P., Coifman, B., Malik, J.: A Real-time Computer Vision System for Measuring Traffic Parameters. In: Computer Vision and Pattern Recognition, pp. 495–501 (1997)
3. Greiffenhagen, M., Ramesh, V., Comaniciu, D., Niemann, H.: Statistical Modeling and Performance Characterization of a Real-Time Dual Camera Surveillance System. In: Computer Vision and Pattern Recognition, pp. 335–342 (2000)
4. Menser, B., Brünig, M.: Face Detection and Tracking for Video Coding Applications. In: Asil omar Conference on Signals, Systems, and Computers, pp. 49–53 (2000)
5. Segen, J., Pingali, S.: A Camera-Based System for Tracking People in Real Time. In: International Conference on Pattern Recognition, pp. 63–67 (1996)
6. Djuric, P.M., Kotecha, J.H., Zhang, J., Huang, Y., Ghirmai, T., Bugallo, M.F., Miguez, J.: Particle Filtering. IEEE Signal Processing Magazine (2003) 1053-5888/03
7. Isard, M., Blake, A.: Contour Tracking by Stochastic Propagation of Conditional Density. In: European Conference on Computer Vision, pp. 343–356 (1996)
8. Isard, M., Blake, A.: CONDENSATION – Conditional Density Propagation for Visual Tracking. International Journal on Computer Vision 1(29), 5–28 (1998)
9. Comaniciu, D., Ramesh, V., Meer, P.: Real-Time Tracking of Non- Rigid Objects using Mean Shift. In: Computer Vision and Pattern Recognition, pp. 142–149 (2000)
10. Nummiaro, K., Koller-Meier, E., Gool, L.V.: An Adaptive Color-Based Particle Filter. Elsevier Science (2002)
11. Aherne, F., Thacker, N., Rockett, P.: The Bhattacharyya Metric as an Absolute Similarity Measure for Frequency Coded Data. Kybernetika 32(4), 1–7 (1997)
12. Kailath, T.: The Divergence and Bhattacharyya Distance Measures in Signal Selection. IEEE Transactions on Communication Technology COM 15(1), 52–60 (1967)
13. Jia, Y., Qu, W.: Real-Time Integrated Multi-Object Detection and Tracking in Video Sequences Using Detection and Mean Shift Based Particle Filters. IEEE, 978-1-4244-6359-6/10

Computationally Efficient Vehicle Tracking for Detecting Accidents in Tunnels

Gyuyeong Kim[1], Hyuntae Kim[2], Jangsik Park[3], Jaeho Kim[4], and Yunsik Yu[1]

[1] Convergence of IT Devices Institute Busan, Gaya-dong, San 24, Busanjin-ku, Busan, 614-714, Korea
nz90nz@deu.ac.kr

[2] Department of Multimedia Engineering, Dongeui University, Gaya-dong, San 24, Busanjin-ku, Busan, 614-714, Korea
htaekim@deu.ac.kr

[3] Department of Electronics Engineering, Kyungsung University, Daeyeon3-dong, 110-1, Nam-gu, Busan, 608-736, Korea
jsipark@ks.ac.kr

[4] Department of Electronics Engineering, Pusan National University, Kumjeong-gu, Busan, 609-735, Korea
jhkim@pusan.ac.kr

Abstract. It is becoming increasingly important to construct tunnel for transportation time and space utilization. To avoid the large scale of damages of vehicle accident in the tunnel, it is necessary to have a tunnel accidents monitoring system to minimize and discover the accidents as fast as possible. In this paper, a moving and stopped vehicle detection algorithm is proposed. It Detecting vehicle based on morphological size information of object according to distance and Adaboost algorithm. Kalman filter and LUV color informations of rear lamp are used to detect stopped vehicles. Results of computer simulations show that proposed algorithm increases detection rate more than other detection algorithms.

Keywords: Background estimation, Adaboost Algorithm, Kalman Filter, LUV color.

1 Introduction

In countries around world, it has mountainous terrain characteristic. In this reason, the construction of tunnel is essential to avoid traffic congestion and to make be traffic flow smoothly. The rate of construction tunnel has shown an increase of 3.4 times since last 10 years. The long tunnel usually has been built. Accordingly, the risk of an accident in the tunnel has been increased[1]. The disastrous fires in the Mont Blanc and St. Gotthard Tunnels, led to a major reappraisal of tunnel safety. Full video surveillance with road tunnels is now mandatory, not just in a country but throughout much of the world, and the latest video surveillance technologies are being deployed to ensure the highest levels of safety and fast reaction to emergencies.

T.-h. Kim et al. (Eds.): MulGraB 2011, Part II, CCIS 263, pp. 197–202, 2011.

Usually, speeding, lane change, a traffic accident for carelessness of driving or deficiency of vehicle causes accident in the tunnel and huge accident such as fire in it may occur serious human, material damage. Therefore, it is becoming more and more important that image recognition systems can detect these elements being the cause of accident in the tunnel using CCTV in advance and can early prevent it as an accident occurs[2].

Most detecting approach works Adaboost[2, 3] for visual class detection are using Haar-like features. It is to build a strong classifier, assembling weighted weak classifiers, those being obtained iteratively by making use of weighting in the training set. We also make use of Adaboost algorithm in this paper.

The previous approaches of object tracking algorithm address optical flow [4], template matching [5], and Kamlam Filter [6]. Optical flow estimation has much computational costs that computation is done in every pixels of the frame. It is not very roubust against noise and illumination and hard if objects with large homogeneous area in motion. Template matching method has been used for simple implementation and quick detection. But it is difficult to track as resizing problem of between template image and detected image. Also if many cars appear in video stream, a lot of complexity will increase.

There are various affecting factors, such as locations of CCTV camera, lightings, road conditions and vehicle status, in tunnels. Therefore, robust to the surroundings and computationally efficient algorithm is required. Detection of moving and stopped vehicles is mainly discussed in this paper. Morphological features and Adaboost algorithm is used to detect vehicles. It is proposed that stopped vehicle detection algorithm using Kalman filter tracks rear lights. It is shown that the proposed algorithm can be utilized to detect accidents in tunnels.

2 Proposed Algorithm

The block diagram of the proposed vehicle detection and tracking system is shown in fig. 1. The proposed system consists of two steps. The first step consists of detecting vehicles make use of background estimation and Adaboost algorithm. The second step consists of tracking rear lights of vehicle using Kalman filter.

2.1 Background Estimation and Moving Vehicle Detection

In this paper, running Gaussian average(RGA) is used to detect vehicles. The model is based on ideally fitting a Gaussian probability density function(pdf) on the last n pixel's values[8]. In order to avoid fitting the pdf from scratch at each new frame time, t, a running average is computed instead as:

$$\mu_t = \alpha I_t + (1-\alpha)\mu_{t-1} \quad (1)$$

Where I_t is the pixel's current value and μ_t the previous average; α is an empirical weight often chosen as a trade-off between stability and quick update. Range of α is between 0 and 1.

A each t frame time the I_t pixel's value can then be classified as a foreground pixel if the inequality:

$$|I_t - \mu_t| > k\sigma_t \tag{2}$$

I_t can be classified as background. Fig. 2 shows the results of detecting vehicles and people using RGA

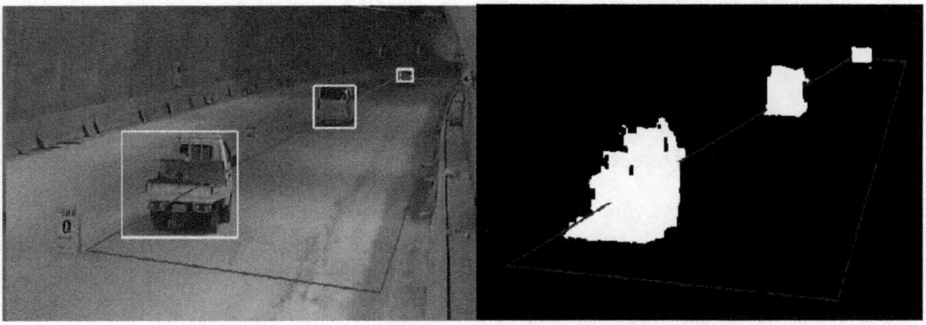

(a) Results of detecting vehicles using RGA

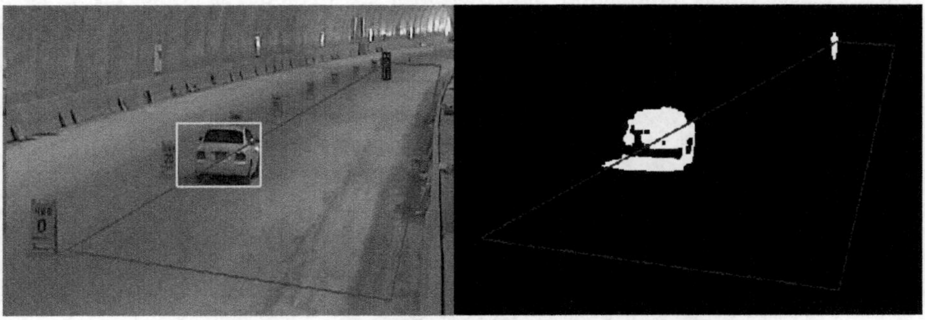

(b) Results of detecting vehicles and people using RGA

Fig. 1. Results of background estimation

Detected objects are considered as candidates. Adaboost algorithm is used to decide vehicles from candidates. Adaboost algorithm makes strong classifier, combined by weak one linearly, which has high detection performance. A Weak classifier to create a strong classifier is generated by the Haar-like features shown in equation (3), an indication of characteristic of the vehicle.

$$h_j(x) = \begin{cases} 1, & if \;\; p_j f_j(x) < p_j \theta_j \\ 0, & otherwise \end{cases} \tag{3}$$

In equation (3), subscript j is number of specific group, f_j is detected feature value, θ_j is a threshold value, p_j is the sign determination parity. Each stage classifier was trained using the Adaboost algorithm. The idea of boosting is selecting and ensemble a set of weak learners to form a strong classifier by repeatedly learning processing over the training examples.

In t stage, T numbers of weak classifiers $h_t(x)$ and ensemble weights α_t are yielded by learning. Then a stage strong classifier $h_j(x)$ is shown i n equation (4). In this paper, we trained the classifier using haar classfier which build a boosted rejection cascade. We do this with OpenCV "*haartraining*" application, which creates a classifier given a training set (372 vehicle images and 1000 non-vehicle images).

$$\cdot\, h_j(x) = \begin{cases} 1, & \sum_{t=1}^{T} \alpha_t h_t(x) \geq \frac{1}{2} \sum_{t=1}^{T} \alpha_t \\ 0, & otherwise \end{cases} \quad (4)$$

2.2 Tracking and Detecting Stopped Vehicles

Adaboost algorithm is very effective to detect vehicle located within 100 m. However, it didn't detect vehicle at the long-distance. We analyzed color information of rear lights of vehicles at the long-distance and proposed to track vehicles using Kalman filter.

Generally, lights of vehicles are turned on entering tunnels. To track vehicles at the long-distance, color information of lights with LUV model is used. Fig 2 is U component of lights of vehicles. It is shown that U component of rear lamp can be used to classify vehicles from background.

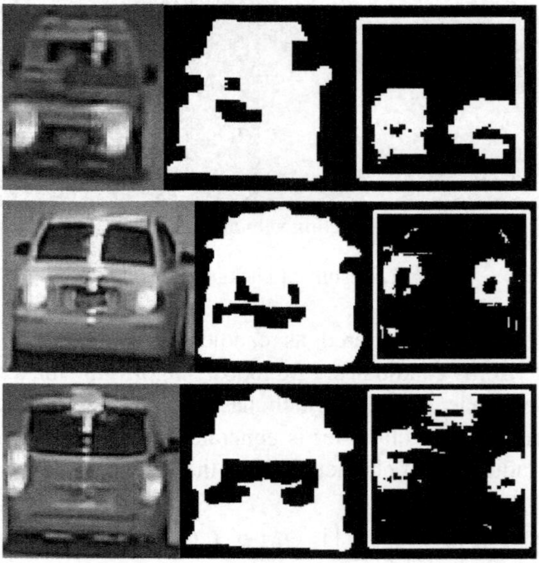

Fig. 2. Detection results of rear lamp using LUV color space

The Kalman filter is well-knowing tracking algorithm and instead recursively conditions the current estimate on all of the past measurements. It consists of two phases. In the first phase, typically called the prediction phase, we use information learned in the past to further refine tracking model for what the next location of vehicles will be. In the correction phase, we make a measurement and then reconcile that measurement with the predictions based on previous measurements.

3 Experimental Results

Computer simulation is conducted to evaluate the performance of the proposed detection and tracking algorithm. In order to implement the proposed algorithm, we used Visual Studio 2010 tool and open source library OpenCV. This algorithm is running the Multiprocessor PC having a 2.5 GHz Intel Core2 Quad Processor with 2 GB of RAM and Windows 7 as the operating system. The number of moving vehicles in the videos of tunnels is 4,255 and the number of stopped vehicles is 1,254. experiment showed that detection rates of moving vehicles are about 95.1%, 97.3% and 93.2% within 60 m, 100 m and 150 m, respectively. Average of detection rates of stopped vehicles is 96.4%. Fig. 3 shows simulation results of vehicle tracking and stopped vehicle detection.

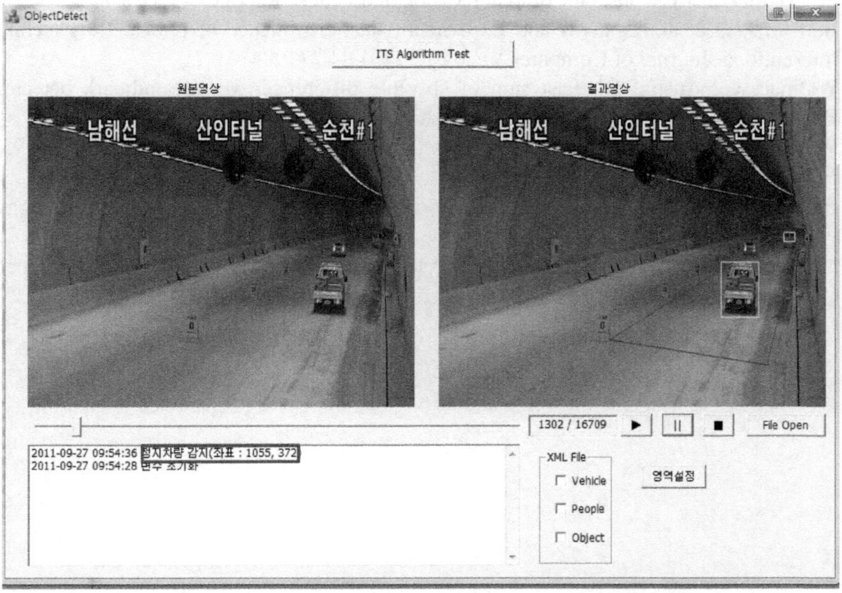

Fig. 3. Detection and Tracking results of the proposed algorithm

4 Conclusions

It is difficult to track in the tunnel because of noise, reflection of lights and a lot of motion. In this paper, moving and stopped vehicle detection algorithm is proposed using the video of tunnels. Running Gaussian estimate is used to search candidates of vehicles and Adaboost algorithm is used to decide ones. LUV color model is introduced to detect and track vehicles at the long-distance. As results of simulations, it is shown that the proposed algorithm can be applied to detect and track vehicles in the tunnel. Because various situations are occurred in tunnels, it is required to update detection and tracking algorithm corresponding complex events.

Acknowledgement. This work was supported in part by MKE(NIPA), Busan Metropolitan City and Dong-Eui University.(08-GIBAN-13, Convergence of IT Devices Institute Busan).

References

1. Kim, G., Kim, H., Park, J., Yu, Y.: Vehicle Tracking Based on Kalman Filter in Tunnel. In: Kim, T.-h., Adeli, H., Robles, R.J., Balitanas, M. (eds.) ISA 2011. CCIS, vol. 200, pp. 250–256. Springer, Heidelberg (2011)
2. Freund, Y., Schapire, R.E.: A short introduction to boosting. Journal of Japanese Society for Artificial Intelligence 14(5), 771–780 (1999)
3. Viola, P., Jones, M.: Rapid object detection using a boosted cascade of simple features. In: Proceedings IEEE Conf. on Computer Vision and Pattern Recognition (2001)
4. Barron, J.L., et al.: Systems and Experiment In: Performance of optical flow techniques. International Journal of Computer Vision 12(1), 43–77 (1994)
5. Watman, C., Austin, D.: Fast sum of absolute differences visual landmark detector. In: Proceedings IEEE Conf. on Robotics and Automation (2004)
6. Welch, G., Bishop, G.: An introduction to the Kalman filter. UNC-Chapel Hill, TR 95-041, July 24 (2006)
7. Rad, R., Jamzad, M.: Real time classification and tracking of multiple vehicles in highways, vol. 26, pp. 1597–1607. Elsevier (2005)
8. Massimo, P.: Background subtraction technique: a review. In: IEEE International Conference on Systems, Man and Cybernetics, pp. 3099–3104 (2004)

Development of an Android Application for Sobriety Test Using Bluetooth Communication

Jangju Kim[1], Daehyun Ryu[2], Jangsik Park[3], Hyuntae Kim[1], and Yunsik Yu[1]

[1] Convergence of IT Devices Institute Busan, Dongeui University
Gaya-dong, San 24, Busanjin-ku, Busan, 614-714, Korea
{jangju,htaekim,ysyu}@deu.ac.kr
[2] Faculty of Information Technology, Hansei University, Dangjung-dong, 604-5, Kunpo city, Kyunggi Province, 435-742, Korea
dhryu@hansei.ac.kr
[3] Department of Electronics Engineering, Kyungsung University, Daeyeon3-dong, 110-1, Nam-gu, Busan, 608-736, Korea
jsipark@ks.ac.kr

Abstract. Drinking is one of the most prominent causes for social problems like domestic violence, drinking and driving, and health problems. If who drunken can check promptly how much blood alcohol content, abstain from drunken driving or successive drinking schedule. In this paper, how to develop an effective application for transmission and expression of drunken report from digital portable breathalyzer to Android Smartphone using Bluetooth module were suggested. A simple user friendly GUI is also implemented for user. The user can check the report for his present blood alcohol level promptly using this App. And then he can decide whether to continue or stop drinking immediately.

Keywords: Bluetooth Communication, Android Application, Portable breathalyzer, Alcohol sensor.

1 Introduction

Drinking and driving is dangerous and illegal. Most countries have a legal threshold of about 0.08 BAC (blood alcohol content). That means you are legally drunk; but you can be under the influence with far less alcohol. Most experts note that 0.0% BAC is the only safe driving level. National averages show that a healthy liver can metabolize (get rid of) 0.015 BAC per hour. How much alcohol is in a drink? Glass of wine is usually 5 ounces and 12% alcohol, the alcohol is mixed through the entire volume so the 5 ounces is the volume. Beer often in 12 ounce cans or bottles, pints are 16 ounces. Like wine the alcohol is mixed throughout the entire drink so the volume to enter is the 12 or 16 or whatever the drink volume is.

Famous blood alcohol test methods are chromatography and spectrophotometry. But these are not proper to insert in portable device. Recently, alcohol sensors based on MEMS were introduced. A variety of portable breathalyzers included with the sensors are released. And also blood alcohol checking Apps were introduced. Most of

T.-h. Kim et al. (Eds.): MulGraB 2011, Part II, CCIS 263, pp. 203–209, 2011.

them consist with game type. It can be check the condition of a participant through earning the score at each stage of the game. But portable device linked with Smartphone is not yet.

In this paper, we propose an Android Application for sobriety test linked with portable breathalyzers using Bluetooth module.

2 Development of Android Application for Sobriety Test

2.1 Bluetooth Architecture

Bluetooth is a new wireless protocol that allows devices of any kind to discover them and communicate without need of user. Two Bluetooth units just have to be less than 10 meters away to be able to exchange information. This affords a wireless world, especially in: keypads, mice, printers, notebooks, mobile phones, PDAs, faxes, keys, headsets, mobile phones, and navigation platforms, etc. Besides cable replacement (e.g. between an application running on a PC and a modem), Bluetooth also provides numerous services as auto-detection, service browsing (discovering of available services delivered by the devices) and so on [1, 2]. It supports numerous protocols, and allows multiplexing (i.e. numerous links at the same time). Bluetooth devices are organized in mini-networks, where one device plays the role of master and all other ones the role of slave.

Between devices either data or voice can be exchanged.OSI 7 layers are defined fully in Bluetooth [3] . Detail architecture is shown in Fig. 1.

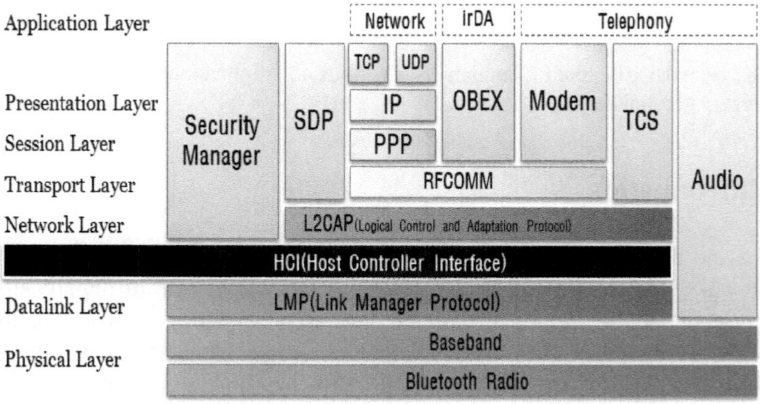

Fig. 1. Bluetooth Architecture

2.2 Android Bluetooth

Android can communicate with Bluetooth devices using Bluetooth protocol. If Bluetooth API were used, a variety of tasks like as, other Bluetooth device searching, local Bluetooth adaptor query for paired Bluetooth devices, setting RFCOMM channel, etc. could be performed.

2.3 Program Configuration

2.3.1 Class Configuration

The program consisted with three Classes. These are 'main.java', 'DeviceListActivity.java' and 'BluetoothService.java'. When the program executed, 'main.java' can be activated at first and then 'DeviceListActivity.java' and 'BluetoothService.java' activated if necessary.

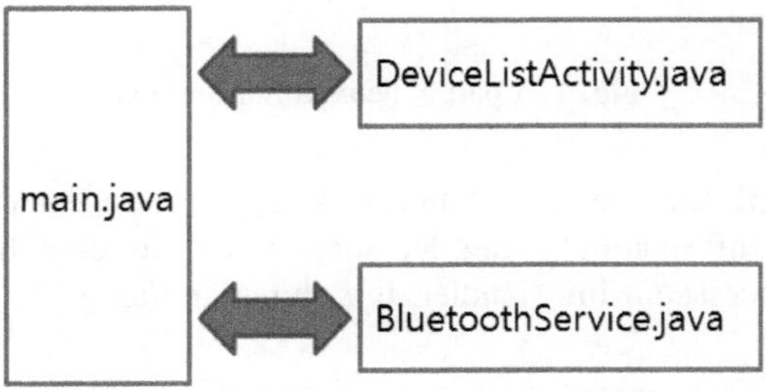

Fig. 2. Connection between classes

2.3.2 Function of Class

① main.java

Checking devices equipments, whether or not available Bluetooth, if not, open alarm message and stop. It is shown in Fig. 3.

```
public void onCreate(Bundle savedInstanceState) {
    super.onCreate(savedInstanceState);
    setContentView(R.layout.main1);

    //현재 장비의 블루투스 Adapter 얻기
    mBluetoothAdapter = BluetoothAdapter.getDefaultAdapter();

    //현재 장비에 블루투스 Adapter가 없다면 프로그램 종료
    if (mBluetoothAdapter == null)
    {
        Toast.makeText(this, "Bluetooth 통신을 사용할 수 없는 장비입니다", Toast.LENGTH_LONG).show();
        finish();
        return;
    }else
    {
        viewDeviceList();
    }
}
```

Fig. 3. A part of checking availability of Bluetooth

Checking Bluetooth device whether or not activated state, if not, activate it. It is shown in Fig. 4.

```
public void onStart() {
    super.onStart();
    if(D) Log.e(TAG, "++ ON START ++");

    // 블루투스가 on상태가 아니면, 가능하게 요청한다.
    if (!mBluetoothAdapter.isEnabled()) {
        Intent enableIntent = new Intent(BluetoothAdapter.ACTION_REQUEST_ENABLE);
        startActivityForResult(enableIntent, REQUEST_ENABLE_BT);
    // Otherwise, setup the chat session
    } else {
        if (mChatService == null)
            setupChat();
    }
}
```

Fig. 4. A part of activating Bluetooth

There are several functions that connecting state, message receive, currently connected Bluetooth information using Handler. Received data from 'BluetoothService.java' were processed using Handler. It is shown in Fig. 5.

```
private final Handler mHandler = new Handler() {
    public void handleMessage(Message msg) {

        switch (msg.what) {

        case MESSAGE_STATE_CHANGE:

            if(D) Log.i(TAG, "MESSAGE_STATE_CHANGE: " + msg.arg1);
            switch (msg.arg1) {
            case BluetoothChatService.STATE_CONNECTED:
                break;

            case BluetoothChatService.STATE_CONNECTING:
               /* mTitle.setText(R.string.title_connecting);*/
                addText("장비와 연결 중");
                break;

            case BluetoothChatService.STATE_LISTEN:

            case BluetoothChatService.STATE_NONE:
                /*mTitle.setText(R.string.title_not_connected); */
                addText("장비 연결 실패");
                break;
            }
            break;
        case MESSAGE_WRITE:
```

Fig. 5. A part of data receiving using Handler

② DeviceListActivity.java
DeviceListActivity.java can be called by sub activity of startActivityForResult() method in main( ). It is shown in Fig. 6.

```
private void viewDeviceList()
{
    Intent serverIntent = new Intent(this, DeviceListActivity.class);
    startActivityForResult(serverIntent, REQUEST_CONNECT_DEVICE);
}
```

Fig. 6. Call DeviceListActivity.java

③ BluetoothService.java

When devices were connected with each other, one of them should be activated as a server using 'BluetoothServerSocket' object. Proposed system consisted of a client linked with alcohol sensor and ODROID (hardware based on Android) as a server.

```
private class AcceptThread extends Thread {
    // The local server socket
    private final BluetoothServerSocket mmServerSocket;

    public AcceptThread() {
        BluetoothServerSocket tmp = null;

        // Create a new listening server socket
        try {
            tmp = mAdapter.listenUsingRfcommWithServiceRecord(NAME, MY_UUID);
        } catch (IOException e) {
            Log.e(TAG, "listen() failed", e);
        }
        mmServerSocket = tmp;
    }
```

Fig. 7. 'BluetoothServerSocket' generation

2.4 GUI Configuration

When the proposed Application activated, selected Bluetooth device were shown in Fig. 8.

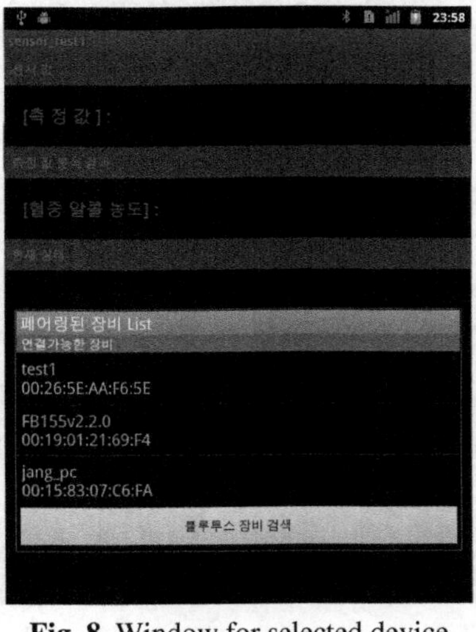

Fig. 8. Window for selected device

3 Experimental Results

We test with portable breathalyzer with Bluetooth module and Android phone. It is shown in Fig. 9. After connected with sensor, the phone displays the numerical value

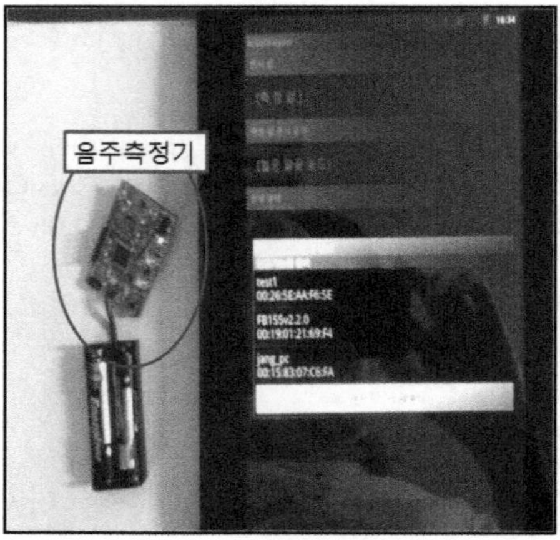

Fig. 9. Test device and activated test screen

Fig. 10. Three stage GUI for different blood alcohol levels

of sensor. It is shown in Fig. when alcohol density changed, proposed system activated well. Detected results in Smartphone GUI are illustrated in Fig. 10.

4 Conclusions

In this paper, how to develop an effective application for transmission and expression of drunken report from digital portable breathalyzer to Android Smartphone using Bluetooth module were suggested. A simple user friendly GUI is also implemented for user. The user can check the report for his present blood alcohol level promptly using this App.

Acknowledgement. This work was supported in part by MKE(NIPA), Busan Metropolitan City and Dong-Eui University.(KI002044, Convergence of IT Devices Institute Busan).

References

1. Bluetooth Consortiums: Specification of the Bluetooth System. Specification Vol. 2 (1999)
2. Sang-Wook, S., Hyun-Chang, Y., Kwee-Bo, S.: Behavior Learning of Swarm Robot System using Bluetooth Network. International Journal of Fuzzy Logic and Intelligent Systems 9(3), 10–15 (2009)
3. Lan, Z.-P., Tao, X.-H., Zhao, X.: Parsing the Security of Bluetooth. In: MITA 2006, pp. 653–656 (2006)

Performance of Collaborative Cyclostationary Spectrum Sensing for Cognitive Radio System

Yoon Hyun Kim[1], In Hwan Park[1], Seung Jong Kim[2], Jeong Jin Kang[3], and Jin Young Kim[1]

[1] Department of Wireless Communications Engineering, Kwangwoon University, Wolgye-Dong, Nowon-Gu, Seoul, 447-1 Korea
{inhwan623,yoonhyun,jinyoung}@kw.ac.kr
[2] LSIS, Samsung-ri, Mokchen-eup, Cheonan-si, Chungcheongnam-do 330-845, Korea
sjkime@lsis.biz
[3] Dong Seoul University, Department of Information and Communication, Seongnam-City, 461-714, Korea
iwit2000@gmail.com

Abstract. In this paper, we propose and simulate a collaborative cyclostationary spectrum sensing for the advanced television systems committee digital television (ATSC DTV) signals. In order to enhance the spectrum sensing performance, we employ collaborative sensing system. And an equal gain combining (EGC) scheme is adopted for combining local decision results. A wireless communication channel considered in this paper is a Gaussian channel. For evaluating the spectrum sensing performance, a detection probability is derived. We consider two kinds of decision rules which are AND and OR decision rule. From simulation results, it is confirmed that in case of OR decision rule, the spectrum sensing performance is improved as the number of collaborative sensing point increases, while AND decision rule is decreased. The results of this paper can be applied to implement cognitive radio (CR) systems.

Keywords: Cognitive radio, spectrum sensing, cyclostationary, ATSC TV.

1 Introduction

Spectrum sensing plays an important role in cognitive radios, of which a feasible method that fulfills both detection agility and users' mobility requirement remains unknown [1]. In recent years since Joseph Mitola coined the term "cognitive radio," many researchers devote themselves to developing and mining new technologies to promote the spectrum sharing level in the apparent spectrum scarcity situation [2].

In this paper, we propose and simulate a collaborative cyclostationary spectrum sensing for the advanced television systems committee digital television (ATSC DTV) signals. In order to enhance the spectrum sensing performance, we employ collaborative sensing system. And an equal gain combining (EGC) scheme is adopted for combining local decision results. A wireless communication channel considered in

T.-h. Kim et al. (Eds.): MulGraB 2011, Part II, CCIS 263, pp. 210–219, 2011.

this paper is a Gaussian channel. For evaluating the spectrum sensing performance, a detection probability is derived. We consider two kinds of decision rules which are decision rule. From simulation results, it is confirmed that in case of OR decision rule, the spectrum sensing performance is improved as the number of collaborative sensing point increases, while AND decision rule is decreased.

The rest of this paper is organized as follows. In Section 2, we briefly describe DTV signals. A collaborative cyclostationary spectrum sensing considered for ATSC DTV signals in this paper is illustrated in Section 3. In Section 4, we analyze the system performance. Finally, concluding remarks are given in Section 5.

2 ATSC Signal

The terrestrial broadcast mode, which is known as 8- vestigial side band (VSB), will support a payload data rate of 19.28 Mbps in a 6 MHz channel. A functional block diagram of a representative 8 VSB terrestrial broadcast transmitter is shown in Fig 1.

Fig. 2 shows how the data are organized for transmission. Each data frame consists of two data fields, each containing 313 data segments.

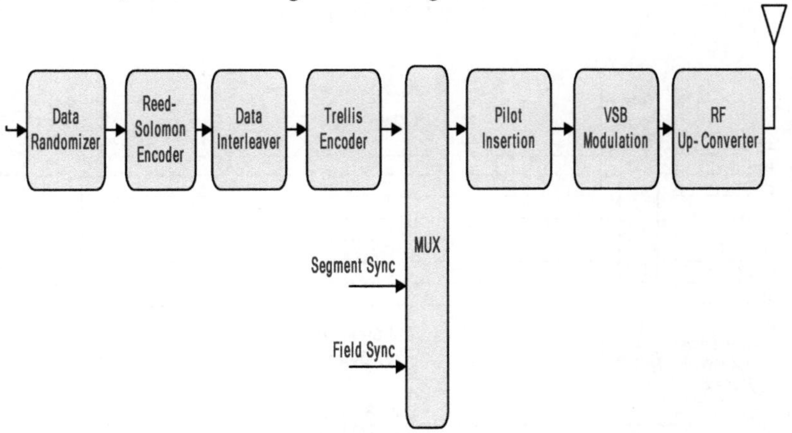

Fig. 1. VSB transmitter model

The first data segment of each data field is a unique synchronizing signal (data field sync) and includes the training sequence used by the equalizer in the receiver. The remaining 312 data segments each carry the equivalent of the data from one 188-byte transport packet plus its associated FEC overhead. The actual data in each data segment comes from several transport packets because of data interleaving.

Each data segment consists of 832 symbols. The first 4 symbols are transmitted in binary form and provide segment synchronization [3]. A two-level (binary) 4-symbol data segment sync shall be inserted into the 8-level digital data stream at the beginning of each data segment. The data segment sync embedded in random data is illustrated in Fig. 3.

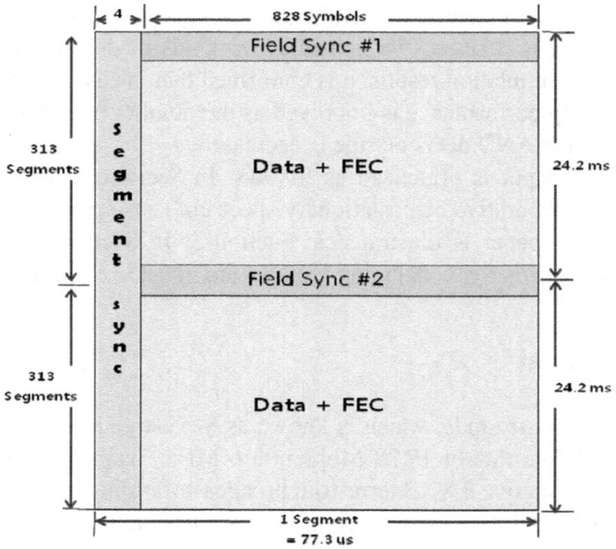

Fig. 2. VSB data frame

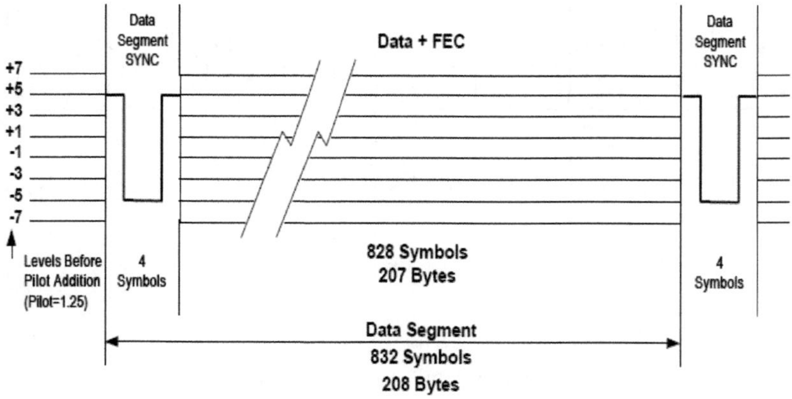

Fig. 3. VSB data segment

A complete segment shall consist of 832 symbols: 4 symbols for data segment sync, and 828 data plus parity symbols. The data segment sync is binary (2-level). The same sync pattern occurs regularly at 77.3 ms intervals, and is the only signal repeating at this rate. Unlike the data, the four symbols for data segment sync are not Reed-Solomon (RS) or trellises neither encoded nor are they interleaved. The data segment sync pattern shall be a 1001 pattern. The data are not only divided into data segments, but also into data fields, each consisting of 313 segments. Each data field (24.2 ms) shall start with one complete data segment of data field sync. Each symbol represents one bit of data (2-level). The 832 symbols in this segment are defined below as shown in Fig. 4.

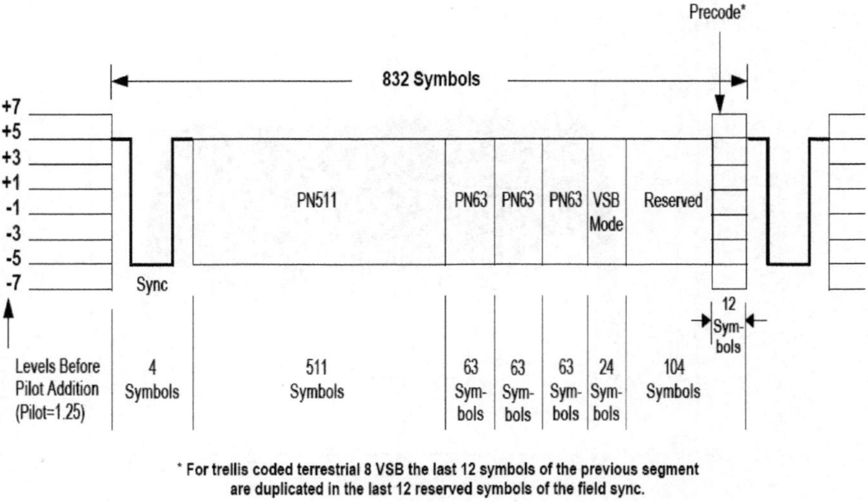

Fig. 4. VSB data field sync.

3 Spectrum Sensing

3.1 Cyclostationary Spectrum Sensing

It has been recognized that many random time series encountered in the field of signal processing are more appropriately modeled as cyclostationary, rather than stationary, duo to the underlying periodicities in these signals. Another reason to use cyclostationary signal model is that random signals such as white Gaussian noise are not cyclostationary. Thus, cyclostationary provides us a way to separate desired signals from noise. According to [3], ATSC DTV data are VSB modulated. Before VSB modulation, a constant of 1.25 is added to the 8-level pulse amplitude modulated signal (8-PAM). Therefore, there is a strong pilot tone on the power spectrum density (PSD) of the ATSC DTV signal [4-5] which is presented by Fig 5.

Let $s(t)$ be this pilot tone is located at frequency f_0,

$$s(t) = \sqrt{2P}\cos(2\pi f_0 t + \theta) \otimes h(t) \quad , \tag{1}$$

where P and θ are power and the initial phase of the sinusoidal function, respectively. The function $h(t)$ is the channel impulse response and $\otimes$ is the convolution operator. The received signal must contain the signal,

$$x(t) = s(t)e^{-j2\pi vt} + w(t)\,, \tag{2}$$

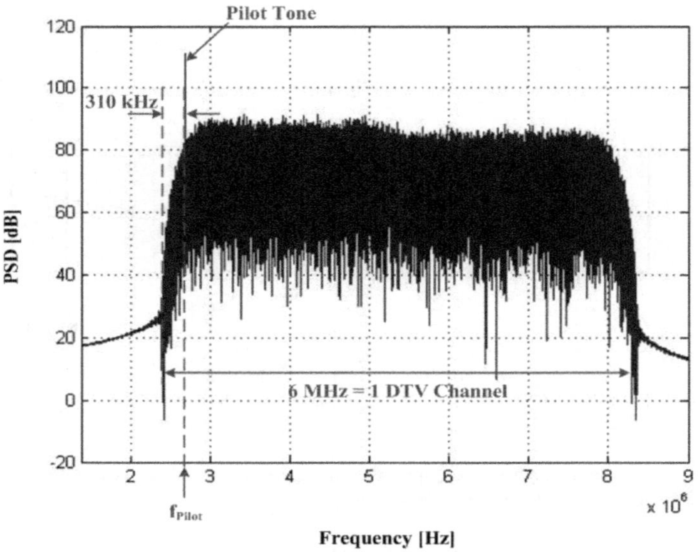

Fig. 5. ATSC DTV signal

where $w(t)$ is the additive white Gaussian noise (AWGN) and v is the amount of frequency offset in the unit of Hz. We will assume that $w(t)$ is zero-mean with autocorrelation function.

$$R_w(\tau) = E[w(t)w^*(t-\tau)] = \sigma^2\delta(\tau)\,. \tag{3}$$

The cyclic spectrum of received signal must contain the cyclic spectrum of $x(t)$ which is given by

$$S_x^\alpha(f) = \begin{cases} \frac{P}{2}[\delta(f-f_0-v)+\delta(f+f_0+v)]|H(f)|^2+\sigma^2 & \text{for } \alpha=0 \\ \frac{P}{2}\delta(f)H(f-f_0-v)H^*(f+f_0+v) & \text{for } \alpha=\pm 2(f_0+v)\,, \\ 0 & \text{otherwise} \end{cases} \tag{4}$$

where $H(f)$ is the frequency response of the channel. The parameter α is the cyclic frequency. From (3), ideally, the noise does not contribute to the cyclic spectrum of $x(t)$ when cyclic frequencies $\alpha = \pm(2f_0+v)$. Thus, performing spectrum sensing by detecting the peaks on the cyclic spectrum of the signal should be better than that of using PSD

The condition to detect DTV signals is that noise floor value is -174dBm/Hz and whole noise figure of receiver from low noise amplifier (LNA) noise figure (NF), coupling loss and RF switch loss is assumed by 8dB. In receiver, we calculated power density function (PDF) of noise.

$$\overline{N} = N_0 + NF \\ = -166 dBm / Hz . \tag{5}$$

And average power of included noise in 6MHz bandwidth of ATSC DTV is calculated.

$$\overline{P}_{Noise} = -166 + 10\log(6\times10^6) \ . \\ \approx -98.22 dBm \tag{6}$$

But the signal power of ATSC DTV is presented by 116dBm. So, we calculated signal to noise (SNR) in case of the spectrum presence in frequency band.

$$SNR = -116 - (-98.22) . \\ = -17.78 dB \tag{7}$$

From this result, ATSC DTV power lower about 18dB than noise power. Therefore performance of ATSC DTV signal detection has to satisfy ATSC DTV required condition when SNR value is under 18dBm.

3.2 Collaborative Sensing

CR must constantly sense the spectrum in order to detect the presence of the primary user (PU) and use the spectrum holes without causing harmful interference to the PU.

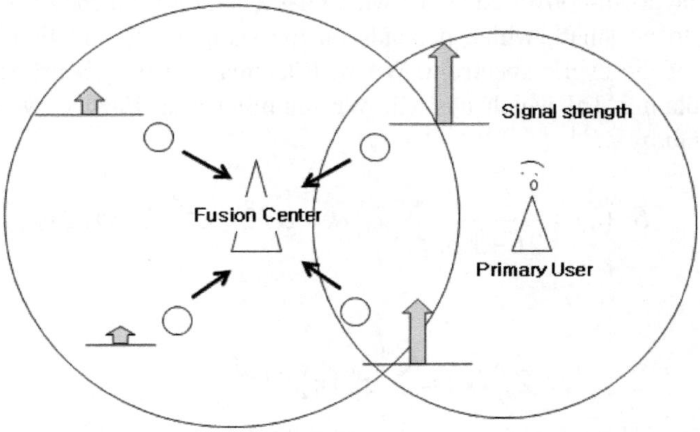

Fig. 6. Collaborative spectrum sensing diagram

Hence, efficient spectrum sensing constitutes a major challenge in cognitive networks. For sensing the presence of the PU, the secondary users (SU) must be able to detect the signal of the PU. Various kinds of detectors can be used for spectrum sensing such as matched filter detectors, energy detectors, cyclostationary detectors or wavelet detectors [6]. However, the performance of spectrum sensing is significantly affected by the degradation of the PU signal due to path loss or shadowing (hidden terminal).

It has been shown that, through collaboration among SU, the effects of this hidden terminal problem can be reduced and the probability of detecting the PU can be improved [7–9]. For instance, in [7] the SUs collaborate by sharing their sensing decisions through a centralized fusion center in the network. This centralized entity combines the sensing bits from the SUs using the OR decision rule and AND decision rule for data fusion and makes a final PU detection decision which is presented by Fig 6. A similar centralized approach is used in [8] using different decision-combining methods.

4 Simulation Results

The radio frequency (RF) ATSC DTV signal for a given DTV channel is first filtered and down-converted to a given intermediate frequency (IF). The IF signals are usually sampled at a rate that is multiple times of the symbol rate. The samples can be expressed as

$$y[n] = x[n] + w[n] \tag{8}$$

where $x[n]$ are samples of the transmitted DTV signal. The noise $w[n]$ is assumed to be zero-mean with variance σ^2. Then, $y[n]$ is used to perform cyclostationarity based sensing algorithms.

We use a proper narrow band-pass filter to filter $y[n]$ and obtain a small frequency bands which contains the pilot tone. Then, $y[n]$ is down-converted to have lower central frequency. Note that we will perform down-conversion for multiple times. Let $z_l[n]$ denote the down-converted signal which has a central frequency $f_{IF}+lf_\Delta$. Note that f_Δ is chosen to be small, which depends on the sample rate and FFT size used in computation of the cyclic spectrum. We will decimate $z_l[n]$ by a proper decimation ratio D to obtain $z_l^D[n]$ which has a lower sampling rate. Finally, we compute the cyclic spectrum by

$$S_z^\alpha(k) = \frac{1}{2L+1}\frac{1}{\Delta t}\sum_{l=-L}^{L} Z_l^D(k+\alpha/2)\cdot Z_l^{D^*}(k-\alpha/2), \tag{9}$$

where

$$Z_l^D(k) = \sum_{n=0}^{N-1} z_l^D[n]e^{-j2\pi kn/N} . \tag{10}$$

We use below formula as our decision statistic.

$$T = \max_\alpha \left|S_z^\alpha(0)\right| . \tag{11}$$

We consider two kinds of decision rules which are AND decision rule and OR decision rule. Also we analyze the system performance in accordance with the number of collaborative sensing points. And the wireless channel is modeled as Gaussian channel.

The performances of the collaborative cyclostationarity based algorithm were demonstrated using computer simulations according to the spectrum sensing simulation model [3]. The band-pass filter used to filter the pilot tone has a bandwidth of 40 KHz and f_{IF} is 17 KHz. The decimation factor is 200 and the decimation filter is a ±50 KHz low-pass filter. The size of FFT is 2048. And according to threshold value, false alarm rate is presented by Fig. 7 [5]. In this paper, threshold is calculated based on constant false alarm rate (CFAR) algorithm [10]

Fig. 8 and Fig. 9 show the detection probability versus signal to noise ratio (SNR) performance for different numbers of collaborative sensing point when false alarm is set to be 10 %.

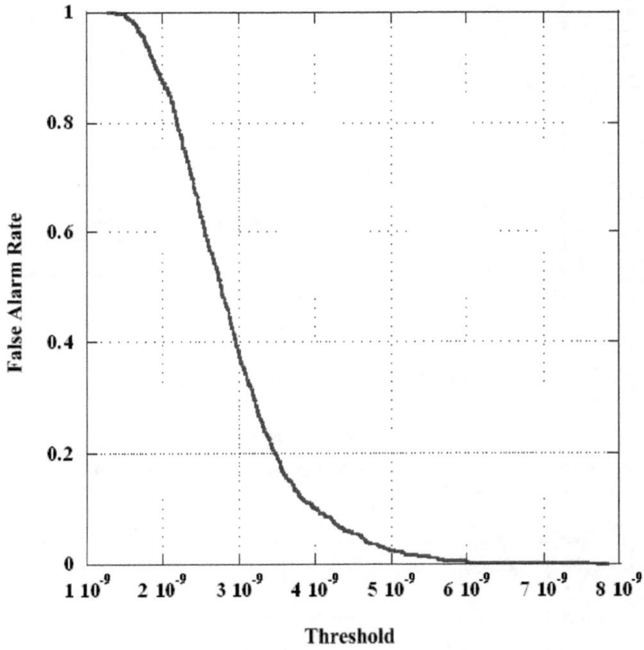

Fig. 7. False alarm rate according to threshold value

In case of single sensing, we consider the general cyclostationary spectrum sensing scheme and in case of multi-point spectrum sensing, the collaborative spectrum sensing is adopted.

From simulation results, it is confirmed that in case of OR decision rule, the spectrum sensing performance is improved as the number of collaborative sensing point increases, while AND decision rule is decreased.

In case of single sensing, we think that this case is basic cyclostationary spectrum sensing, and in case of multi distributed sensing, the collaborative sensing system is adopted. AND decision rule can be thought as multiplication of each bit so detection probability is decreased in accordance with the number of distributed sensing points.

While OR decision rule can be thought as summation of each bit so detection probability is increased in accordance with the number of distributed sensing points.

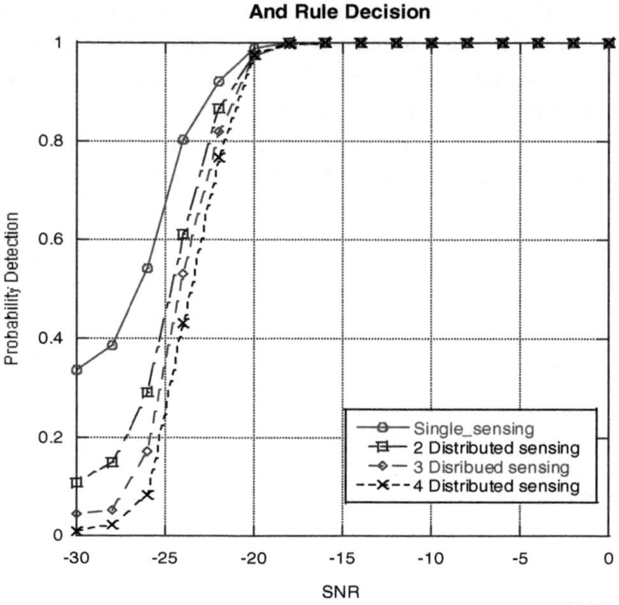

Fig. 8. And rule decision result

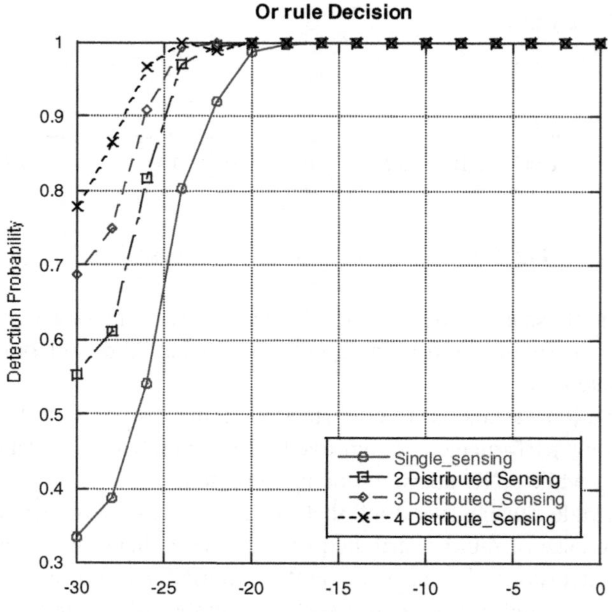

Fig. 9. Or rule decision result

5 Conclusions

In this paper, we propose based on collaborative cyclostationary spectrum sensing for ATSC DTV signals and evaluate the system performance in term of a detection probability. A threshold value is determined by using the constant false alarm rate (CFAR) algorithm. A wireless communication channel considered in this paper is a Gaussian channel. From simulation results, it is confirmed that in case of OR decision rule, the spectrum sensing performance is improved as the number of collaborative sensing point increases, while AND decision rule is decreased. The result of this paper can be applied to implement CR systems.

Acknowledgments. "This work was supported by Basic Science Research Program through the National Research Foundation of Korea(NRF) funded by the Ministry of Education, Science and Technology(MEST)"(No. 2011-0025983).

References

1. Sun, H., Jiang, J., Lin, M.: Adaptive cooperation algorithm for cognitive radio networks. In: WiCOM 2006, pp. 1–4 (September 2006)
2. Kim, J.Y.: Cognitive Radio Communications. Gyobo Publishers, Seoul (2008)
3. McKinney, J.C., Hopkins, R.: ATSC digital television standard (September 1995)
4. Gardner, W.A.: Exploitation of Spectral Redundancy in Cyclostationary Signals. IEEE Signal Processing Magazine 8(2), 14–36 (1991)
5. Chen, H., Gao, W.: Text on cyclostationary feature detector-for informative annex on sensing techniques. IEEE 802.22-07/0283r0 (June 2007)
6. Cabric, D., Mishra, M.S., Brodersen, R.W.: Implementation issues in spectrum sensing for cognitive radios. In: Proc. Asilomar Conference on Signals, Systems, and Computers, Pacific Grove, CA, USA, pp. 772–776 (November 2004)
7. Ghasemi, A., Sousa, E.S.: Collaborative spectrum sensing for opportunistic access in fading environments. In: IEEE Symp. New Frontiers in Dynamic Spectrum Access Networks, Baltimore, USA, pp. 131–136 (November 2005)
8. Visotsky, E., Kuffner, S., Peterson, R.: On collaborative detection of TV transmissions in support of dynamic spectrum sensing. In: IEEE Symp. New Frontiers in Dynamic Spectrum Access Networks, Baltimore, USA, pp. 338–356 (November 2005)
9. Zhang, W., Letaief, K.B.: Cooperative spectrum sensing with transmit and relay diversity in cognitive networks. IEEE Trans. Wireless Commun. 7, 4761–4766 (2008)
10. Minkler, G., Minkler, J.: CFAR. Magellam Book Company (1990)

Novel Spectrum Sensing for Cognitive Radio Based Femto Networks

Kyung Sun Lee, Yoon Hyun Kim, and Jin Young Kim

447-1, Wolgye-Dong, Nowon-Gu, Seoul, Korea,
Kwangwoon University
{sub3344,yoonhyun,jinyoung}@kw.ac.kr

Abstract. In this paper, we propose spectrum sensing technique in TV white space (TVWS) for cognitive radio (CR) based femto networks. The spectrum sensing is performed based on digital watermarking technique. The performance is analyzed and simulated in terms of detection probability. From the simulation results, it is confirmed that the proposed scheme achieves better detection performance compared with other sensing algorithm.

Keywords: Cognitive radio, spectrum sensing, femto network, TV white space.

1 Introduction

As wireless technologies have been rapidly developed, more spectrum resources are needed to support considerable and various wireless services. However, limited spectrum resources are assigned only to licensed users. A recent survey on spectrum utilization made by FCC (federal communications commission) has indicated that the actual licensed spectrum is largely under-utilized in vast temporal and geographic dimensions [1]. In additional to that, there is a spectrum shortage problem due to explosive increase of data traffic in femto network by smart phones. In order to solve the spectrum scarcity and inefficient spectrum utilization, cognitive radio (CR) was recently proposed in [2-4]. Especially, use of TV white space (TVWS) based on the CR has been researched on the various fields [5].

In this paper, to solve a spectrum shortage problem in femto network, we analyze and simulate the TVWS sensing algorithm for CR based femto networks. We employ digital watermarking algorithm to improve sensing probability compared with the other conventional sensing algorithms. Also, the proposed algorithm has capabilities which detect and classify the various low power CR based femto devices such as smart phones. The performance is evaluated in terms of detection probabilities with various false alarm (FA) probabilities.

This paper is organized as follows. In Section 2, we describe the CR based femto network model, proposed digital watermarking algorithm and the system performance. In Section 3, simulation results are presented. Finally, concluding remarks and applications of proposed algorithm are provided in Section 4.

T.-h. Kim et al. (Eds.): MulGraB 2011, Part II, CCIS 263, pp. 220–224, 2011.

2 System Model

In this section, we describe the system model and the proposed algorithm. Fig. 1 shows the system model composed of a TV broadcasting tower (primary user) and a CR based femto network (secondary user). In the femto network, a lot of smart devices are linked to a femto based station. It is assumed that each smart device has the sensing capability which knows whether TVWS is occupied by other smart phone or not. Also, all the smart phones in the femto network can support CR standard of IEEE 802.22 WRAN (wireless regional area network) [6]. In this system model, data traffic of the femto network is increased by a lot of smart devices, so a spectrum shortage problem for the femto network is getting worse. Therefore, in this paper, we propose a novel TVWS spectrum sensing algorithm using digital watermarking sequence to increase the efficiency of spectrum usage and the spectrum sensing probability. Fig. 2 shows the proposed spectrum sensing algorithm with digital watermarking sequence. First, a watermarking sequence is added up to each transmitter data in the femto network. The power level of the watermarking sequence is about -27~ -21dB lower than transmitter data power in order to maintain system bit error performance. Selection of the watermarking sequence level is based on bit error rate (BER) performance.

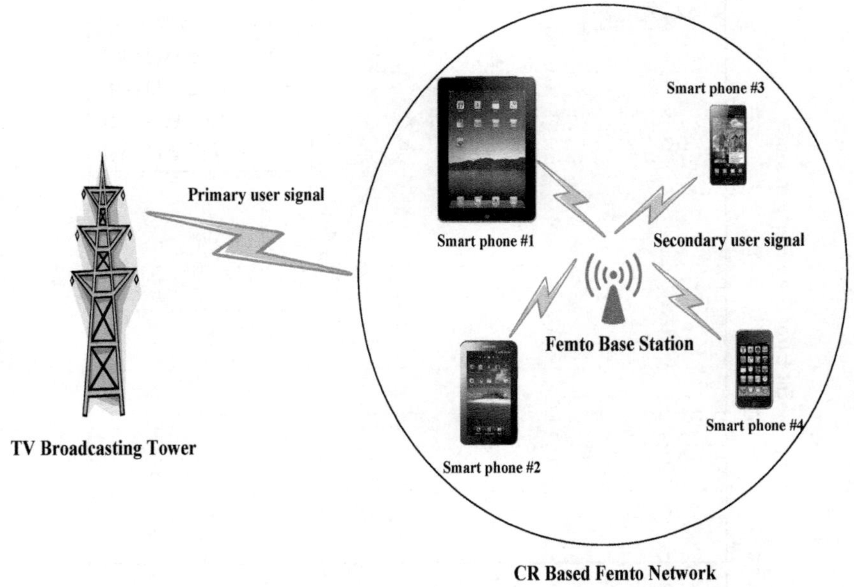

Fig. 1. System model with a TV broadcasting tower and a CR based femto network

Fig. 3 shows the BER performance with different watermarking sequence level. As seen in Fig. 3, water marking sequence levels between -27dB and -21dB have almost same BER performance.

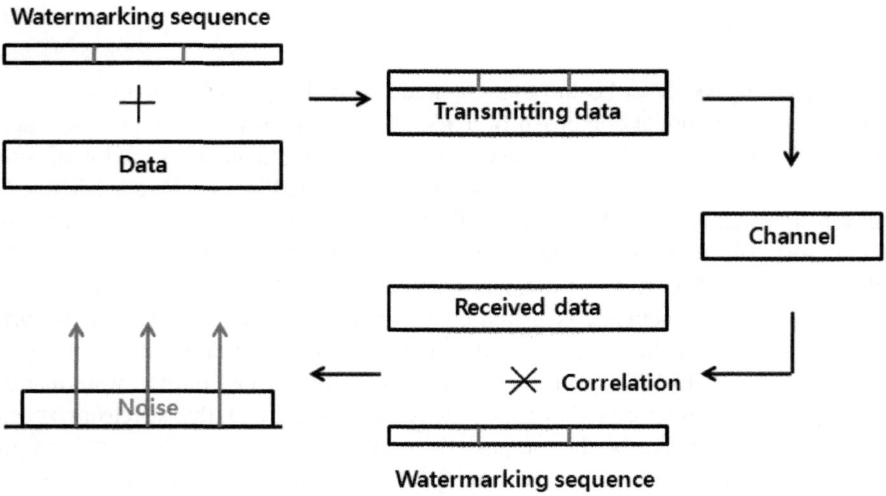

Fig. 2. Block diagram of proposed algorithm with watermarking sequence

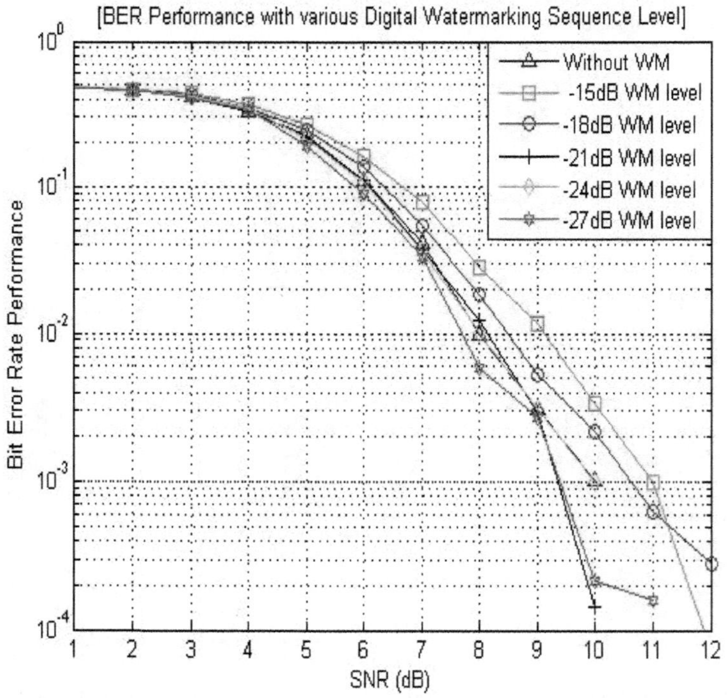

Fig. 3. BER performance with different water marking sequence level

At the receiver, when the transmitted signals are received, a log-likelihood function of received signals is given by

$$L(S) = \ln p(r(n)), \tag{1}$$

where $r(n)$ is received signal and $p(r(n))$ denotes probability density function (PDF) of $r(n)$.

From (1), we obtain the maximum likelihood (ML) estimation of S given by

$$\begin{aligned}\hat{S} &= \arg\left\{\max_{S} L(S)\right\} \\ &= \arg\left\{\max_{S} \sum_{n=0}^{i-1} \ln\left(p\left(r(n)\right)\right)\right\} \\ &= \arg\left\{\max_{S} \sum_{n=0}^{2i-1} r(n)\, w_{seq}(\tau-n)\right\},\end{aligned} \tag{2}$$

where $w_{seq}(n)$ is the watermarking sequence which is added up to the transmitter signal. By correlating the received signal with the watermarking sequence, ML estimation finds the maximum value of the correlator outputs.

3 Simulation Results

In this section, the performance of proposed algorithm with digital watermarking sequence is simulated in terms of detection probabilities. Kasami sequence is chosen

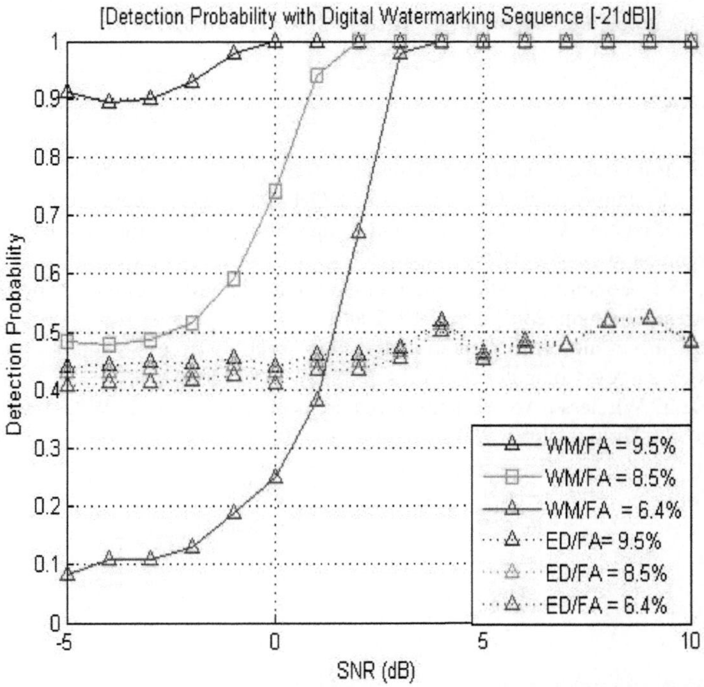

Fig. 4. Detection probabilities vs. SNR performance for the proposed algorithm with various FA probabilities (9.5%, 8.5%, 6.4%)

(WM : Watermarking / ED : Energy detection)

as watermarking for good autocorrelation property. It is assumed that the base station of the CR femto network knows watermarking sequences of each smart phone.

Fig. 4 shows detection probabilities for the various FA probabilities. We compare the proposed algorithm (solid line) with the energy detection algorithm (dotted line) for the same FA probabilities. We confirm that detection probabilities with proposed digital watermarking algorithm are far better than the conventional energy detection scheme. Also, in the range of SNR (signal-to-noise ratio) above 0dB, detection probabilities of proposed algorithm are almost approaching to the detection probability of "1".

4 Conclusions

In this paper, we proposed the novel TVWS spectrum sensing algorithm with digital watermarking sequence in order to improve sensing probability for the CR based femto network. From the simulation results, the performance of detection probabilities of proposed algorithm is pretty better than the conventional energy detection schemes. The results of the paper can find their applications in solving the spectrum shortage problem in femto-cell networks.

Acknowledgments. "This work was supported by Basic Science Research Program through the National Research Foundation of Korea(NRF) funded by the Ministry of Education, Science and Technology(MEST)"(No. 2011-0025983).

References

1. FCC, Spectrum Policy Task Force Report, No. 02-155 (November 2002)
2. Kim, J.Y.: Cognitive Radio Communications. Gybo Publishers, Seoul (2008)
3. Mitola, J., Maguire, G.Q.: Cognitive radio: making software radios more personal. IEEE Pers. Commun. 6, 13–18 (1999)
4. Haykin, S.: Cognitive radio: Brain-empowered wireless communications. IEEE J. Select.Areas Commun. 23(2), 201–219 (2005)
5. Akyildiz, I.F., et al.: Next generation/dymamic spectrum access/ cognitive radio wireless networks: a survey. Computer Networks 50, 2127–2159 (2006)
6. IEEE 802.22 Wireless LAN, Functional requirements for the 802.22 WRAN standard, IEEE 802.22-05/0007r46 (October 2005)

Efficient Transmission Scheme Using Transceiver Characteristics for Visible Light Communication Systems

In Hwan Park, Yoon Hyun Kim, and Jin Young Kim

Kwangwoon University, Department of Wireless Communication Engineering, Wolgye-Dong, Nowon-Gu, Seoul, 447-1, Korea
{inhwan623,yoonhyun,jinyoung}@kw.ac.kr

Abstract. Visible Light Communication (VLC) systems are considered as a future green convergence communication technology because of it used for not only illumination devices, but also indoor communication device. In this paper, RGB LED (light emitting diode) characteristics of transmission and receiving are analyzed for VLC systems. The red, green and blue light wave which used for communication in VLC systems have different characteristic of transmission and receiving. For example, the red light wave has good transmission characteristic for transmission power and distance. Also the blue light wave has good transmission characteristic for data rate likewise red light wave. However, the green light wave has low SNR (Signal-to-noise ratio) characteristic compared with red and blue light waves. Therefore, VLC systems take in SNR to make the green LED. In this case, system performance such as data rate, transmission power and bit error rate (BER) are seriously deteriorated to VLC systems. To resolve these problems, in this paper, we used optical filter to separate RGB light waves and then, transmit the main data such as image, video, and etc. using red and blue light waves. Using this method, we obtain the SNR gain for main data transmission and receive, in additional, without increase of system complexity, we transmit additional data. From simulation results, it is confirmed that the proposed scheme is very effective to enhance system performance of VLC.

Keywords: Visible Light Communication (VLC), RGB light wave, Optical bandpass filter, Transceiver.

1 Introduction

Recently, light emitting diode (LED) has been emerging as a new growth technology which is expected to replace existing illumination infrastructure. LED is known to be more advantageous than the existing incandescent in terms of long life expectancy, high tolerance to humidity, low power consumption, and minimal heat generation lighting, etc. Their diverse applications include numeric displays, flashlights, liquid crystal backlight, vehicle brake lights, traffic signals and the ubiquitous power-on indicator light [1-7].

Currently, interests in LED communication using white LEDs are gradually growing as needs for indoor communication systems increase because there are many

T.-h. Kim et al. (Eds.): MulGraB 2011, Part II, CCIS 263, pp. 225–233, 2011.

devices using the lightings in our offices, home, the lightings on roads, traffic signals, home appliances including TVs, and etc. The typical LED has special characteristics to light on and off very fast at ultra high speed. By using visible light for the data transmission, most of problems related to radio communications are resolved or relieved. The visible light communication is known to have characteristics to be ubiquitous, transmitted at ultra high speed and harmless for human body and electronic devices, compared to those by radio communications. The human eye would not be able to follow these variations, and, hence, the lighting will not be affected. As a consequence, simple off-the-shelf LEDs can be used to develop cheap transmitters [6-11].

The LED visible light communication is interpreted as a convergence communication technology which is not only used as a lighting device, but also to be used as communication device [12]. It is a kind of indoor optical wireless communication that uses 'visible light' ray as communication medium. However, it is also facing challenges such as using appropriate techniques to construct cheap processing units and high brightness LEDs.

The objectives of this paper are to analyze the transmission and receive characteristic for RGB LEDs and provide efficient data transmission scheme for VLC. For LED communication systems, each red, green and blue LED has different transmission/receive characteristic. The red LED has good transmission characteristic in the transmission power and distance aspects. Similarly, the blue LED has good transmission characteristic in the data rate aspects. However, the green LED has low SNR (Signal-to-noise ratio) and transmission power characteristic in comparison with red and blue LEDs. In the middle of this paper, the transmission characteristic of each RGB LEDs is introduced detail. As a result, LED communication systems take in SNR to make the green LED. So, system performance such as data rate, transmission power and bit error rate (BER) are deteriorated for LED communication systems. For this reason, in this paper, we use optical filter to separate RGB colors and then, send the main data (image, video, etc.) using red and blue LEDs.

This paper is organized as follows. In section 2, VLC channel model and characteristic of RGB are described. And, in section 3, we introduce the proposed transmission scheme for VLC. In section 4, simulation results are presented, and the application is drawn in section V. Finally, concluding remarks are given in section 6.

2 VLC System

2.1 Channel Model

For rigorous analysis of the proposed system, a suitable channel model is highly required for exact estimate of system performance in VLC. Background noise is assumed to be AWGN (additive white Gaussian noise). In VLC systems, the LEDs are usually installed in a ceiling and they have has large superficial area. Therefore, VLC has particular impulse response other than that from infrared communication. To consider reflection effect correctly, both reflex and diffusion characteristics are also taken into account for more practical approach. Lambertian reflector model has been known be a well-fitting one for modeling of indoor diffusion characteristics of representative materials such as plaster wall, acoustic-tiled walls, carpets, unvarnished woods, and etc [13]. Therefore, the wall or ceiling can be interpreted as Lambertian reflector in VLC.

The channel of LED-ID systems can be modeled with an additive white Gaussian noise (AWGN) model. In optical channels, quality of transmission is typically dominated by shot noise because receiver employs a narrow band optical filter. However, the system can neglect the shot noise caused by signals. Accordingly, the received signal can be expressed as

$$y(t) = r \cdot x(t) \otimes h(t) + G_n , \tag{1}$$

where *y(t)* represents received signal, *x(t)* embodies transmitted optical pulse, G_n depicts AWGN noise, the symbol ⊗ denotes convolution, and r denotes an optical/electric (O/E) conversion efficiency. In this paper, we employ impulse response channel with bounces of ninth times. Considering reflected signal by reflectors, the impulse response can be written as

$$h(t;S,R) = \sum_{k=0}^{\infty} h^{(k)}(t;S,R) , \tag{2}$$

where *h(k)(t)* is response of the reflected impulse signals k times.

Higher order terms, at *k>0*, can be calculated recursively. It is given by

$$h^{(k)}(t;S,R) = \int_S h^{(0)}(t;S,\{r,\hat{n},\frac{\pi}{2},dr^2\} \otimes \mathrm{h}^{(\text{k-1})}(t;\{r,\hat{n},1\},R) . \tag{3}$$

The equation (3) can be rearranged and be written as

$$h^{(k)}(t;S,R) = \frac{m+1}{2\pi} \int_S \frac{\rho_r \cdot \cos^m(\psi) \cdot \cos(\theta)}{R^2} \cdot rect(\frac{\theta}{FOV}) \cdot h^{(k-1)}(t - \frac{R}{c};\{r,\hat{n},1\},R)dr^2 . \tag{4}$$

2.2 Characteristic of RGB

Fig. 1 shows the voltage value of red, green and blue LEDs according to distance between transmitter and receiver. In case of the blue LED, almost voltage value is fixed until about 40cm and it has good reception performance in comparison with other LEDs. In contrast, voltage value of the green LED is degraded rapidly after 30cm. Thus, in the case that the distance between transmitter and receiver is about 1m, the green LED cannot be used for main data transmission such as audio and video data. LED communication systems take in SNR to make the green LED. So, system performance such as data rate, transmission power and bit error rate (BER) are deteriorated for LED communication systems. Therefore, in this paper, additional data such as simple text information and location information etc. is transmitted by the green LED. Using this method, we obtain the SNR gain for main data transmission and receive, in additional, without increase of system complexity, we transmit sub-data.

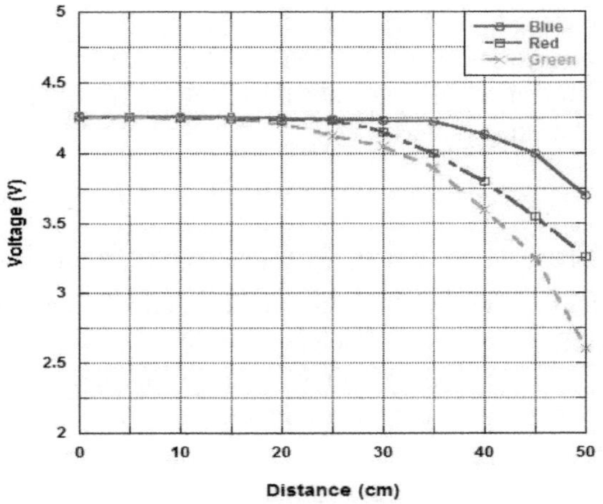

Fig. 1. RGB characteristic for VLC transmission

3 Proposed System Model

In this section, the proposed scheme is described for LED-ID systems. Block diagram of the proposed LED-ID system is illustrated in Fig. 2. Main data such as audio and

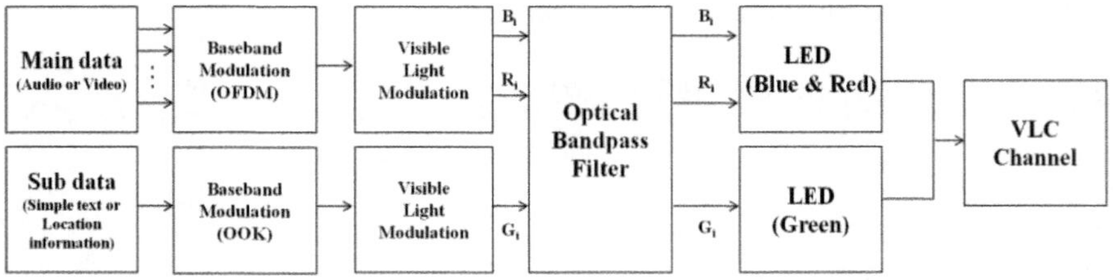

(a) Transmitter

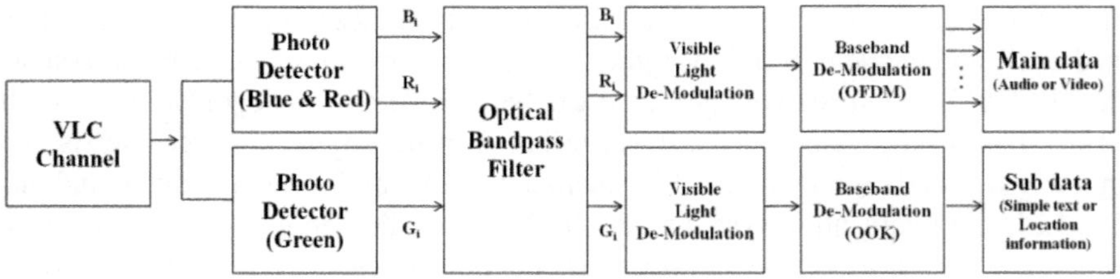

(b) Receiver

Fig. 2. Block diagram of proposed scheme

video data is modulated in baseband by OFDM block because it must be transmitted with high data rate. On the other hand, sub data such as simple text or location information is modulated by on off keying (OOK) in baseband. In this paper, we assume that main and sub data which is modulated by OFDM and OOK are orthogonal each other. As shown in Fig. 2 (a), the main data in baseband are transferred to visible light band of blue and red, however, the sub data are transferred to visible light band of green. In Fig. 2, B, R and G are each stand for blue, red and green. Also sub-script i is denoted as i^{th} data. Finally, using optical bandpass filter, the main data are transmitted by blue and red LED and sub data are transmitted by green LED.

The main data which are passed by OFDM modulation block with i^{th} data, $x^i{}_{OFDM}(n)$, is given by,

$$x_{OFDM}{}^{i}(n) = \left(\frac{1}{N_c}\right)\sum_{k=-K}^{K} X_k^i \exp\left(j\frac{2\pi kn}{N_c}\right), \tag{5}$$

where $n = 0,1,\ldots,N_c - 1$ with $N_c \geq 2K+1$ and N_C is number of sub-carrier. The multipath effect causes the inter-symbol interference (ISI) in time dispersive channels. And the orthogonality of the OFDM signal is distorted. In order to maintain the orthogonality of the OFDM signal in multipath channel, a guard interval is inserted in front of each OFDM block. The last N_g samples of the OFDM signal are copied and appended as a preamble to compose an OFDM frame. This is known as a cyclic prefix. The main data which are passed by OOK modulation block with i^{th} data, $x^i{}_{OOK}(n)$, is given by,

$$x_{OOK}^i(n) = 1 \; or \; 0 \quad 0 \leq n \leq T\,, \tag{6}$$

where, T is symbol duration.

At the receiver, first photo detector receives only blue and red visible light band data, but second photo detector receives only green visible light band data. Each data is divided into blue, red and green visible light band by optical bandpass filter. The each data of blue, red and green visible light band are transferred to baseband, and through the OFDM / OOK de-modulation, we obtain original data.

4 Simulation Results

In this section, the proposed scheme is simulated for LED-ID system. The simulation parameters of the LED-ID system are listed in Table 1.

As referred to former, the conventional scheme is to transmit the same data using all RGB. Thus, it has only sent the signal with low SNR because green LED has bad SNR property. However in case of using the supposed algorithm in this paper, this

Table 1. Simulation Parameters

Parameter	Value
Number of FFT points	512
Modulation	QPSK/OOK
The receiver O/E conversion efficiency	0.53[A/W]
Detector physical area of PD	1.0[cm^2]
Transmitted optical power	1[W]
FOV at the Tag	60[deg.]
Distance between Tag and Reader	50cm
Channel	VLC channel

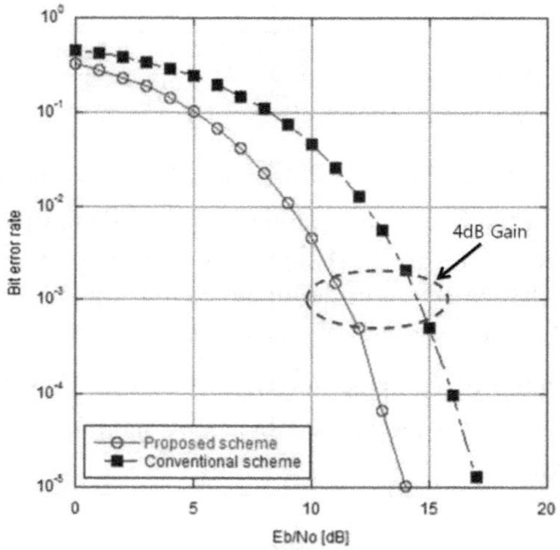

Fig. 3. BER performance (Distance between Tx & Rx is 50cm)

system can send the data to maintain high SNR as compared with conventional scheme by sending the main data signal using blue LED and red LED.

Fig. 3 shows the proposed system's BER performance in the case that the distance between transmitter and receiver is 50cm. High SNR gain is achieved when we used the supposed scheme. The reason of this simulation results is that the voltage property of green LED is significantly reduced as the distance is farther. In the case that BER is 10^{-3}, we are able to confirm the system has about 4dB SNR gain compared with existing scheme.

Fig.4 is shown the relation between data rate and received SNR when distance between Tx and Rx is 50cm. In order to achieve bit error probability of 10^{-4}, the received SNR is about 13.6dB in the OFDM modulation scheme. Therefore, the proposed transmission scheme makes it possible to transmit at the maximum data rate of about 5.8Mb/s. Since the transmit power for lighting and the distance between communication equipment can vary, the proposed system can obtain high efficiency of transmission.

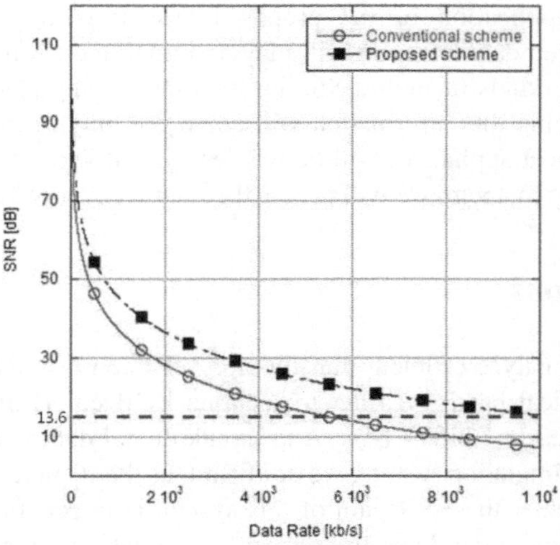

Fig. 4. SNR vs. data rate performance (Distance between Tx & Rx is 50cm)

5 Applications

One application of the proposed system is for LED traffic lights. Nowadays, high brightness LEDs are increasing being used in traffic lights. This is mainly due to the low power consumption and minimal maintenance required for LED-based traffic lights. The LED traffic light can be used as a communications device, in addition to their normal function of being an indication and signaling device. This allows a concurrent use of traffic lights because it can broadcast local traffic information, vehicle location, road and navigation information, and at the same time perform its normal function of being a traffic signaling device. The LED traffic light becomes a new kind of short-range beacon to support roadside-to-vehicle communications.

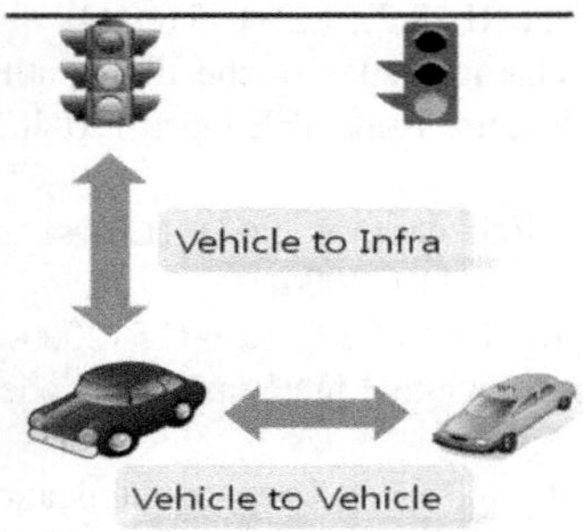

(a) LED traffic system

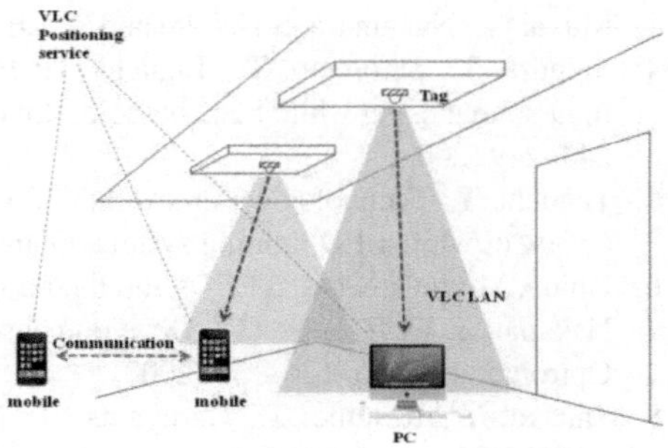

(b) VLC Wireless home link

Fig. 5. Variable applications of the proposed system using VLC

And another application of the proposed system is for wireless home link. Recently, high speed data transport will play an important roll in our life. We will be able to have many kinds of multimedia information, in any place at any time. High speed data containing this information will come not only to offices but also to our homes. The electrical appliances will be wireless linked with each other by VLC and PLC system. Using by them, we will access the internet everywhere in our home.

6 Conclusions

In this paper, we analyze efficient transmission scheme using RGB characteristic for VLC. We use optical bandpass filter to separate RGB colors and then, transmit the main data using red and blue LEDs. And an additional data is transmitted by green LEDs. From the simulation results, we confirm that the distance between transmitter and receiver is farther the SNR gain of this system is larger. In consideration of the VLC environment with the distance between transmitter and receiver is 50cm~1m, if it use the proposed scheme with VLC system, it is able to achieve better transmission efficiency. Consequently, it is confirmed that the proposed scheme is very effective to enhance system performance of VLC systems based on the home network.

Acknowledgments. This work (Grants No. 00046504) was supported by Business for Cooperative R&D between Industry, Academy, and Research Institute funded Korea Small and Medium Business Administration in 2011.

References

1. Kim, J.Y.: LED Visible Light Communication Systems. Hongreung Science Publishers, Seoul (2009)
2. Nakamura, S.: Present performance of InGaN based blue / green /yellow LEDs. In: Proc. of SPIE Conf. on Light-Emitting Diodes: Research, Manufacturing, and Applications, San Jose, CA, vol. 3002, pp. 24–29 (1992)
3. Mukai, T., Nakamura, S.: White and W LEDs. OYO BUTURI 68(2), 152–155 (1999)
4. Tamura, T., Setomoto, T., Taguchi, T.: Fundamental characteristics of the illuminating light source using white LED based on InGaNse miconductors. Trans. IEE Japan 120-4(2), 244–249 (2000)
5. Taguchi, T.: Technological innovation of high-brightness light emitting diodes (LEDs) and a view of white LED lighting system. Optronics 19(228), 113–119 (2000)
6. Ishida, M.: InGaN based LEDs and their application. Optronics 19(228), 120–125 (2000)
7. Nakamura, T., Takebe, T.: Development of ZnSe-based white Light emitting diodes. Optronics 19(228), 126–131 (2000)
8. Tanaka, Y., Komine, T., Haruyama, S., Nakagawa, M.: Indoor visible communication utilizing plural white LEDs as lighting. In: Proc. of IEEE PIMRC 2001, vol. 2, pp. F81–F85 (October 2001)
9. Komine, T., Nakagawa, M.: Fundamental analysis for visible-Light communication system using LED lights. IEEE Trans. on Consumer Elec. 50, 100–107 (2004)

10. Komine, T., Tanaka, Y., Haruyama, S., Nakagawa, M.: Basic study on visible-light communication using light emitting diode illumination. In: Proc. of 8th International Symposium on Microwave and Optical Technology (ISMOT 2001), pp. 4548 (2001)
11. Komine, T., Nakagawa, M.: Intergrated system of white LED visible light communication. IEEE Trans. on Consumer Electronics 49(1), 71–79 (2003)
12. Haruyama, S.: Visible light communication. IEEE Trans. on IEICE J86-A(12), 1284–1291 (2003)

Modification of Feed Forward Process and Activation Function in Back-Propagation

Gwang-Jun Kim[1], Dae-Hyon Kim[1], and Yong-Kab Kim[2]

[1] Chonnam National University, Department of Computer Engineering
Yeosu, 550-749, Korea
{Kgj,daehyon}@jnu.ac.kr
[2] Wonkwang University, School of Electrical Information Engineering,
Iksan, 570-749, Korea
ykim@wku.ac.kr

Abstract. Research on neural networks has grown significantly over the past decade, with valuable contributions made from many different academic disciplines. While there are currently many different types of neural network models, Back-propagation is the most popular neural network model. However, the input vectors in the Back-propagation neural network model usually need to be normalized and the normalization methods affect the prediction accuracy. In this study, a new method is proposed in which an additional feed-forward process was included in the Back propagation model and a sigmoid activation function was modified, in order to overcome the input vector normalization problem. The experimental results showed that the proposed approach might produce a better training and prediction accuracy than the most current common approach using input vector normalization and that it has the potential to improve performance in machine vision applications.

Keywords: Backpropagation, Normalization, Feed-forward Process, Sigmoid Activation Function, Machine Vision.

1 Introduction

Research on neural networks has grown significantly over the past decade, due to the remarkable ability of neural networks to be able to derive meaning from complicated or imprecise data. Valuable contributions on research into neural networks have been made within many different academic disciplines.

Kim[1] theoretically studied the requirement of normalization for the input vectors on Back propagation, and different normalization methods were considered, in order to determine the effects of the normalization method for input vectors. He has shown that a normalization method for input vectors could affect the predictive performance of a Back propagation neural network in a pattern recognition problem. Even though the input vector normalization does affect the convergence in training and predictive accuracy in testing, it is not always a prerequisite to normalize input vectors.

Instead of using normalization methods for input vectors, another approach was proposed in this research, which is based on activation function modification, in order

T.-h. Kim et al. (Eds.): MulGraB 2011, Part II, CCIS 263, pp. 234–240, 2011.

to cope with the problem occurring due to the property of the sigmoid activation function in the Back propagation neural. The predictive performance from two different approaches, those of a current common approach which is to normalize input vectors and a new approach proposed in this paper, will be compared on the real world traffic scene analysis in which the task is to detect vehicle image patterns.

2 Back-Propagation Neural Network Model

General network architecture and an individual neuron of the Back propagation model are shown in Figure 1. The layers include an input layer, a hidden layer, and an output layer, with a one-directional flow of information from the input to the output. The symbol x denotes an input, y denotes an output, and w denotes a synaptic weight.

As can be seen in Figure 1 (b), each processing unit receives signals from its input links and computes a new activation level that it sends along each of its output links. The computation of the activation level is based on the values of each signal previously received from other nodes, and the weights on each input link. The computation is split into two components; the first is a linear component that computes the weighted sum of the unit's input value (Σ), and the second is a non-linear component that transforms the weighted sum into an output value using an activation function, $f(\,)$.

While the computation for output of each neuron works forward from the input to the output layer, the error at the output is propagated back to the previous layer, and the weights are changed so as to decrease that error.

Mathematically, the net input to the ith unit can be written as

$$Net_i = \sum_j x_j w_{ij} \,, \tag{1}$$

Once the net input is calculated, we can determine the output value by applying an activation function. The activation function, denoted by $f(\,)$, defines the output of a neuron in terms of the activity level at its input.

$$Out_i = f(Net_i) \,, \tag{2}$$

There are three common types of activation functions; the Threshold, the Piecewise-linear, and the Sigmoid function [2]. However, the sigmoid function is the most common form of activation function used in the construction of a Back propagation neural network. It is defined as a strictly increasing function that exhibits smoothness and asymptotic properties. An example of the sigmoid is the logistic function which is the most popular type of activation function in Back propagation, defined by

$$f(Net) = \frac{1}{1+\exp^{-Net}} \,, \tag{3}$$

One of the advantages of the sigmoid is that it is differentiable. This property had a significant impact because it has made it possible to derive a gradient search learning algorithm for networks with multiple layers. The sigmoid activation function is also popular for other reasons. For example, many applications require a continuous valued output rather than the binary output produced by a step function. Whereas a step-threshold function assumes the value of 0 or 1, a sigmoid function assumes a continuous range of values from 0 to 1. In addition, it is particularly efficient for pattern recognition problems because it produces an output between 0 and 1, which can often be interpreted as a probability estimate.

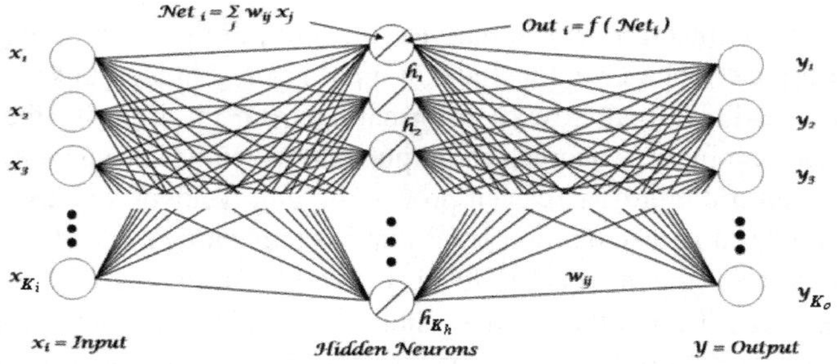

(a) A three-layered Back propagation network architecture

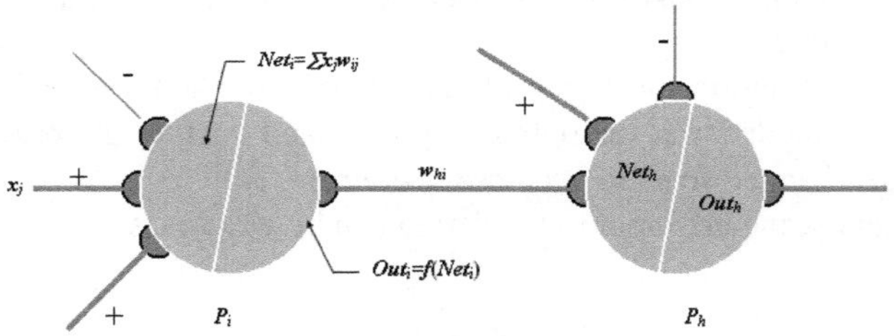

(b) Diagram of a generalized processing element in Back propagation

Fig. 1. Network architecture and a generalized processing element in Back propagation

3 Input Vectors Normalization and Activation Functions

3.1 Flat Spot Problem

Due to the properties of the sigmoid function, output units may become stuck in a bad state for some training patterns in the standard Back propagation training. From Eq.(2), the derivative of the sigmoid function is given by

$$Out_i\,(1 - Out_i\,)\,, \tag{4}$$

Eq. (4) approaches 0 as Out_i approaches either 1 or 0. Since the error term for the output unit i is the product of derivative of the sigmoid function and the difference between the target vector and output vector, weight changes are minimal even though the errors are maximal. This places severe limitations on the learning convergence of the Back propagation model. This phenomenon is known as the Flat Spots Problem.

A solution to the Flat Spots Problem is to ensure that the derivative function does not approach zero. Fahlman[3] proposed that this could be accomplished by simply adding a small value of constant to the derivative of the sigmoid function before using it to scale the error. Fahlman[3] reported a significant speed-up of the network convergence by using this additional constant parameter on the sigmoid-prime function.

Kim[4] also showed that the parameter of the Prime-offset, which has been used for Quickprop [4], could be useful for the Back propagation with Momentum[5]. This model is an enhanced Back propagation model proposed by Rumelhart, et al. [5] to speed up learning by adding a Momentum term to the standard Back propagation model [5].

3.2 Modification of Feed-Forward Process and Activation Function

Up to now, input vectors have been normalized prior to training in order to avoid the problem which may occur due to the property of the general Sigmoid activation function in the Back propagation model. However, the requirement of input vector normalization could be omitted if the feed-forward process and the most commonly used activation function have been modified properly. The proposed method used in this study differs from that of the general Back propagation neural network model in two ways. Firstly, the proposed model includes an extra feed-forward process for learning. Figure 2 shows a diagram of a modified processing element in Back propagation. In feed-forward processes, an additional process step in Back propagation involves making the net input to the ith unit smaller than 1. Mathematically, it can be written as

$$NNet_i = \frac{1}{Net_i}, \tag{5}$$

Secondly, the network uses a modified activation function in order to include large values for inputs. The sigmoid activation function has been modified by including a slope parameter, α as in Eq. (6)

$$f(NNet) = \frac{1}{1 + \exp^{-\alpha * NNet}}, \tag{6}$$

By varying the parameterα, we obtain sigmoid functions of different slopes. In this study, a large value for the slope parameter, i.e. 1,000, has been used in order to reflect a wide range of *NNet*.

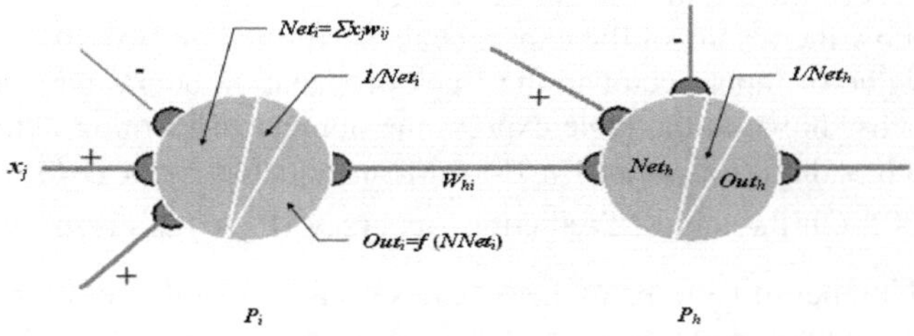

Fig. 2. Diagram of a modified processing element in Back propagation

4 Experiments and Results

4.1 Data Sets for Training and Test

In this study, the pattern recognition problem for traffic scene analysis has been used to examine the network performance, by the proposed approach, in terms of predictive accuracy and computing cost for training, as well as the current approach with input vector normalization.

The task is to classify three different patterns; Pattern A, Pattern B, and Pattern C (see Fig.3). This image data have been used by Kim [6]. A total of 930 data sets have been used, 400 sets for Pattern A, 400 sets for Pattern B and 130 sets for Pattern C. The data sets were split into two subsets, one for training and the other for testing (see Table 1).

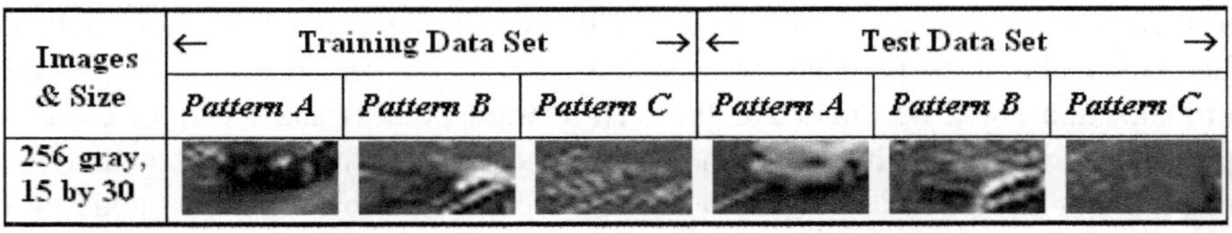

Fig. 3. Three patterns and image data used for training and testing

Table 1. Number of data sets for training and testing

	Training data	Test data	Total
Pattern A	100	300	400
Pattern B	100	300	400
Pattern C	30	100	130
Total	230	700	930

4.2 Experimental Results

It is known that the performance of the Back propagation model is sensitive to the initial weight configuration, and many trials on the same network need to be implemented at the same value of parameters, yet with different initial weights, in order to properly evaluate a model.

The results in this study were achieved from30 trials of experiments with different initial weights that are initialized to random values between +0.5 and -0.5, in order to avoid the effect of the initial value of the weights.

Table 2 show the results of the experiments performed on two different approaches for a large value of input vector in the Back propagation neural network model. The learning epochs shown in the table express the number of learning iterations until the network reaches the error goal of a Root Mean Squared Error (RMSE) of 0.01 and zero (0.00000). On the tables, Prediction Accuracy (P. A.) is given by $P.A = \frac{N}{P_{ts} \times K_o}$, where P_{ts} = Number of patterns in the testing sets, K_o = Number of output units, and N = Number of output patterns in which Diff is bigger than the Threshold Value,

Table 2. Performance on the proposed method

		Error goal of a RMSE for stopping network training	
		0.01	0.00000
Epochs	Min	37	38
	Max	597	598
	Average	136	137
RMSE	Min	0.03801	0.00000
	Max	0.09325	0.00000
	Average	0.05082	0.00000
Prediction Accuracy (%)	Min	86.57	86.67
	Max	92.0	92.67
	Average	89.74	89.85
	Variance	0.02	0.03

Note: Network reached error goal within maximum epoch number of 1,000, and the value of Average is an average of 30 trials.

$\text{Diff} = |\text{Desired Output Value} - \text{Computed Output Value}|$. The Threshold Value has been to determine prediction error, i.e. it is an error if Diff > Threshold Value of 0.1. Also, the RMSE(Root Mean Squared Error) is given by $\text{RMSE} = \sqrt{\text{SSE}/_{P_{tr} \times K_o}}$, where $\text{SSE(Sum Squarred Error)} = \sum_{p=1}^{P}\sum_{k=1}^{K_o}(y_{pk} - Out_{pk}^{o})^2$, and P_{tr} = Number of patterns in training data sets.

With a learning rate of 0.001, a very fast training convergence has been achieved on the proposed method than the Input Vector Normalization method (see Figure 4). Moreover, the value of RMSE on the proposed method rapidly reached to a value of zero (0.0000) within one epoch after the network reached the error goal of 0.01 in all of the trials. However, the network on the input vector normalization with a learning rate of 0.001 did not reach to the value of RMSE of zero (0.0000) and a higher learning rate, i.e. 0.1, allowed the network to reach it. Unfortunately, the network has failed 9 times to reach a zero RMSE within maximum epoch number of 1,000. These results imply that the proposed method could produce better performance for training than the current normalization-based method.

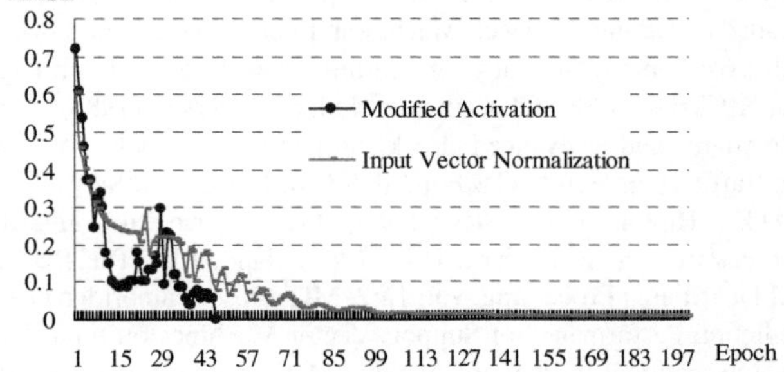

Fig. 4. Network convergence with learning rate of 0.001 on two approaches

The results from a current normalization-based method with 0.01 RMSE produced the correct recognition rate on the test sets ranging from 82.85% to 85.38% (average 84.08 %). For zero (0.00000) of training RMSE, the correct recognition rate on the test sets range from 85.52% to 91.10% (average 88.68 %).

The results from a proposed method with 0.01 RMSE produced the correct recognition rate on the test sets ranging from 86.57% to 92.0% (average 87.74 %). For zero (0.00000) of training RMSE, the correct recognition rate on the test sets range from 86.67% to 92.67% (average 89.85 %).

Experimental results obtained for this research imply that the proposed method might be useful in the application of the Back propagation neural network model in order to minimize the effort required to normalize input vectors. More importantly, the experimental results showed that the proposed approach might produce a better performance than the previous method, in which the input vectors were normalized even with the best normalization method.

5 Conclusions

In this study, a new approach has been proposed in order to overcome the normalization problem for input vectors. It has been conducted by including an extra mathematical operation in the feed-forward process and modifying the sigmoid activation function. The comparison of the two approaches was investigated and discussed in this research, and the experimental results showed that the proposed method might produce a better performance in terms of training and predictive accuracy than the current approach in which input vectors are normalized to use the Back propagation neural network model.

Consequently, the input vector normalization process could be omitted and the effort required to investigate the choices for a good normalization method could be reduced, if we use the method proposed in this paper. Moreover, the experimental results showed that the proposed approach might be competitive with any normalization method even if it produces a relatively good performance.

References

1. Kim, D.: Normalization Methods for Input and Output Vectors in Back propagation Neural Networks. International Journal of Computer Mathematics 71(2), 161–171 (1999)
2. Haykin, S.: Neural networks: a comprehensive foundation. Macmillan, New York, Maxwell Macmillan Canada, Toronto, Maxwell Macmillan International, New York (1994)
3. Fahlman, S.E.: An empirical study of learning speed in back propagation networks. Technical ReportCMU-CS-88-162, Carnegie Mellon University (1988)
4. Kim, D.: Standard and Advanced Back propagation models for image processing application in traffic engineering. ITS Journal 7(3-4), 199–211 (2002)
5. Rumelhart, D.E., Hinton, G.E., McClelland, J.L.: A general framework for parallel distributed processing. In: Rumelhart, D.E., McClelland, J.L., The PDP Research Group (eds.) Parallel Distributed Processing, vol. 1&2, MIT Press, Cambridge (1986)
6. Kim, D.: Prediction Performance of Support Vector Machines on Input Vector Normalization Methods. International Journal of Computer Mathematics 81(5), 547–554 (2004)

Influential Parameters for Dynamic Analysis of a Hydraulic Control Valve

Kyong Uk Yang[1], Jung Gyu Hur[1], Gwang-Jun Kim[1],
Dae Hyon Kim[1], and Yong-Kab Kim[2]

[1] Chonnam National University, School of Marine Technology
Yeosu, 550-749, Korea
{yangku,kgj,daehyon}@jnu.ac.kr, hurbond@gmail.com
[2] Wonkwang University, School of Electrical Information Engineering,
Iksan, 570-749, Korea
ykim@wku.ac.kr

Abstract. A numerical problem that has easily ignored in the dynamic analysis of hydraulic control valves is described, and an analysis of the effects of such problems on numerical modeling is provided. Previous studies have ignored the effects of changes in the flow coefficient in the orifice, the solenoid force along the spool movement in the valve and an ascending tendency of pressure during reach to the steady state. Thus, simulation results obtained in earlier studies have had numerical value errors. To eliminate these problems, this study employed a method to substantiate the nonlinearity of the pressure loss caused by passing between the orifice and port as well as that caused by interaction with the solenoid. Moreover, the movement of the spool and spring expressed using the time-delay-element (TDE). The proposed numerical model has been used in the Bond graph method of a hydraulic control valve and the simulation results have been shown to be accurate. It is known that differences between simulated and experimental results can have a considerable impact on the function of actual systems. The contribution of three factor mentioned in this paper was observed in TDE, Flow coefficient, solenoid order.

Keywords: Hydraulic Control Valve, Bond Graphs, Numerical Simulation.

1 Introduction

We conducted this study to analyze the dynamic characteristics of the proportional control valve in a hydraulic system using the Bond graphs modeling method. It is favorable to modeling of the valve expresses approximate to the experiment result for valve production and grasp the characteristics easily. However, the results obtained by numerical modeling cannot reproduce the experimental results exactly. This study analyzed the causes of differences between the results obtained by numerical modeling and experimental results. In general, models do not consider the electromagnetic forces of the solenoid that have nonlinear characteristics. Accordingly, it is necessary to use arbitrary quantitative values when forces with nonlinear characteristics are used.

T.-h. Kim et al. (Eds.): MulGraB 2011, Part II, CCIS 263, pp. 241–247, 2011.

The flow coefficient is used as an arbitrary constant value. The value of the flow coefficient changes depending on the flow rate through the port in the valve and the difference in pressure. In addition, Reynold's number changes according to the inertia or viscosity of the hydraulic oil. However, the flow coefficient used is commonly an arbitrary value that is used without considering these effects.

An ascending tendency of pressure is not considered during modeling. In practice, the position of the spool changes in response to the electromagnetic force of the solenoid, which results in changes in the interaction with the static frictional force of the spring and early compressive force. In addition, pressure loss occurs between the orifice and spool and sleeve according to displacement of the spool. These interactions are complex and result in the fluid having non-linear characteristics and non-laminar flow. At that point, the model does not consider the conversion of pressure loss to the second-delay element or the first-delay element. Many earlier studies have employed modeling to develop proportional pressure control valves in hydraulic systems[1-3]. However, these studies did not conduct modeling to approximate the experimental results while considering the non-linear elements using Bond graphs.

In this study, we considered these three problems in modeling and compared the results with those of a previous study using Bond graphs method [4]. specifically, when spool operating changes from the open state to the closed state or vice versa, the fluid loses pressure as it passes through the orifice and the sleeve. We were able to obtain better modeling results by considering variables that were not considered in the previous study.

2 Bond Graphs Modeling and Numerical Analysis

2.1 Bond Graphs

The subject of the modeling was a 3-port proportional pressure control valve (PPCV) (Fig. 1). The valve consisted of three systems, the electromagnetic system of the solenoid, the mechanical system of the spool and the spring and the hydrodynamic system of the fluid flowing through the orifice in the valve. In this study, the hydrodynamic force of the spool and pressure loss has been leaked to the outside of the valve were ignored.

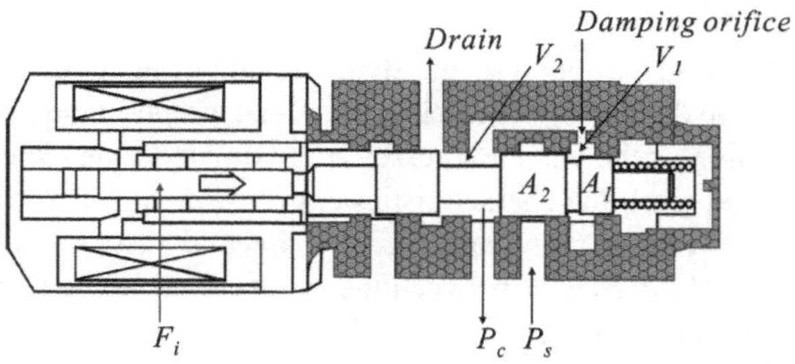

Fig. 1. Model of the proportional pressure control valve (PPCV)

The action of the valve occurs as follows. Supply-pressure (P_s) through the orifice is compressed in chamber 1 (V_1) and chamber 2 (V_2). When input voltage generates the electromagnetic force of the solenoid, displacement of the spool is changed to interact with the spring. In this process, the damping orifice acts as a buffer against the pressure impulse. At this time, pressure loss occurs in the gap between the orifice or the spool and the sleeve.

Bond graphs of the system are shown in Fig. 2. In this bond graphs, nodes 4-7 are connected with the 0-junction, which represents the control pressure (P_c) and compressibility of volume 2 (V_2). Each 1-junction connected with the 0-junction indicates pressure loss via flow through the gap of the spool and the sleeve in the valve. That is, the second-delay element of the orifice and the first-delay element of the gap have expressed nonlinear characteristics via the spool displacement. Nodes 6, 10, and 11 connected with the 1-junction represent the damping orifice and nodes 11-14 connected with the 0-junction represent volume 1 (V_1). The element TF between node 14 and node 15 represents the transformer factor. This element is used to connect the characteristics of the mechanical and fluid portions of the system. Nodes 15-20 connected with the 1-junction represent the mechanical characteristics of the spool and the spring in the valve. GY is the gyrator factor and nodes 22-30 connected with the 0-junction and the 1-junction represent the electromagnetic characteristics of the solenoid.

As shown in Fig. 2, the proportional pressure control valve based on TF and GY can be represented by the characteristics of the fluid, the mechanical system and the electromagnetic system. However, the elements of the effort and the flow in the system must be set to match the characteristics of each system [2,5].

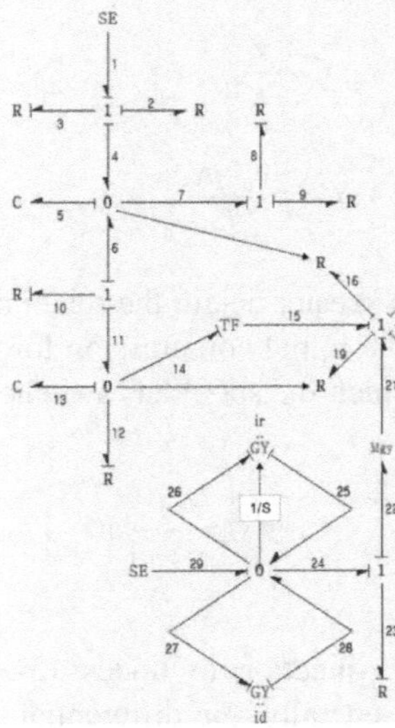

Fig. 2. Bond graphs of the proportional pressure control valve

2.2 Bond Graphs Modeling and Numerical

Nodes 1-13 represent the flow characteristics of the valve. The equation describing the relationship between flow and pressure can obtained from Expression (1) and (2).

$$Q = C_d A \sqrt{\frac{2}{\rho}(\Delta P)} \tag{1}$$

$$Q = \frac{\pi d h^3}{12\mu\delta}\Delta P \tag{2}$$

The Bond graphs model equation of nodes 1 to 13 in Fig. 2 are expressed by Expressions (3-10).

$$R_2 : \; f_2 = \frac{1}{R_2}\cdot e_2 \qquad R_2 = \frac{12\mu\delta}{\pi d h^3} \tag{3}$$

$$R_3 : \; e_3 = R_3 \cdot f_3^2 \qquad R_3 = \frac{\rho}{2(c\pi d h)^2} \tag{4}$$

$$R_8 : \; f_8 = \frac{1}{R_8}\cdot e_8 \qquad R_8 = \frac{\rho}{2(c\pi d)^2(\delta^2 + h^2)} \tag{5}$$

$$R_9 : \; e_9 = R_9 \cdot f_9^2 \qquad R_9 = 0 \tag{6}$$

$$R_{10} : \; {f_{10}}^2 = \frac{1}{R_{10}}\cdot e_{10} \qquad R_{10} = \frac{\rho}{2\left(c(\pi/4)d_0^2\right)^2} \tag{7}$$

$$R_{12} : \; f_{12} = \frac{1}{R_{12}}\cdot e_{12} \qquad R_{12} = \frac{12\mu\delta}{\pi d h^3} \tag{8}$$

$$C_5 : \; e_5 = \frac{1}{C_5}\int f_5 dt \qquad C_5 = \frac{V_1}{K} \tag{9}$$

$$C_{13} : \; e_{13} = \frac{1}{C_{13}}\int f_{13} dt \qquad C_{13} = \frac{V_2 - Ax}{K} \tag{10}$$

To express the nonlinearity in greater detail, the relational equation requires the TDE to express the interaction of the initial compression force and the static friction force of the spring at the point at which the spool has switched. The TDE can be described as follows:

$$y(s) = \frac{1}{\tau s + 1}u(s) \tag{11}$$

where, τ is the time constant.

As shown in Fig. 2, the 1-junction of nodes 15-20 represents the mechanical characteristics of the spool. Generally, the differential equation can be described by Expression (12).

$$F_i = m\frac{d^2x}{dt^2} + f_R\frac{dx}{dt} + f_S sign\left(\frac{dx}{dt}\right) + kx + F_0 \tag{12}$$

where, F_i is node 21 of Fig. 2.

$$R_{16}:\ e_{16} = R_{16} \cdot f_{16} \qquad R_{16} = f_R \tag{13}$$

$$I_{17}:\ f_{17} = \frac{1}{I_{17}}\int e_{17}dt \qquad I_{17} = m \tag{14}$$

$$C_{18}:\ e_{18} = \frac{1}{C_{18}}\int f_{18}dt \qquad C_{18} = k \tag{15}$$

$$R_{19}:\ e_{19} = R_{19} \cdot f_{19} \qquad R_{19} = F_0 \tag{16}$$

$$R_{20}:\ e_{20} = R_{20} \cdot f_{20} \qquad R_{20} = f_S \tag{17}$$

Expressions (13-17) express the Bond graphs modeling process of the mechanical characteristics of the valve. The electromagnetic characteristics of the solenoid are expressed as nodes 22-29 of Fig. 2.

Expression (18) describes a general solenoid model that does not consider the nonlinearity caused by the spool's displacement.

$$V_S = V_R + V_L = iR + L\frac{di}{dt} \tag{18}$$

where V_R and V_L are the resistance and the inductance caused by the supply voltage (V_S), i is the current, R is the resistance, and L is the inductance.

Overall, this study expressed the characteristics of the fluid, the mechanical and the electromagnetic systems in the valve using Bond graphs. As described above, modeling using Bond graphs can describe the characteristics of variables that are linked to each junction, and enable easy understanding of the overall system via a method that expresses the interaction between junctions using nodes[5-6].

3 Simulation and Consideration

We compared the response characteristics of this study with those of a previous study[4] and investigated the influence of each variable on the modeling results. Fig. 3 shows the step response obtained by modeling using the technique described herein and the results of a previous study. In addition to the three problems described above, the TDE was used to consider the spool's conversion condition and effect on the spring. This enabled improvement of the results of the previous study. The previous study, which revealed that there were many differences until steady state was reached, did not consider the ascending tendency of pressure. However, when the experimental result were compared with those of the present study, a similar increase in pressure was observed, and the same time was required (0.18s) to reach the steady state.

The cause that does not satisfy supply pressure (0.6MPa) of the experiment result because it is not considered effect of pressure loss, which is leak to the outside.

In improved modeling, the first delay time depends on the first compressive force and the static friction force of the spring, but the results can confirm the accuracy of the delay time according to the TDE. Moreover, when modeling is used to approximate an experiment, the size and slope of the pick pressure can be made up for by fine adjustment of the TDE, and the increase in pressure until steady state is reached can be related to the characteristics of the solenoid by the input voltage. The time constant of TDE is 0.0125±0.0008, and outside this range the experiment results are not satisfied.

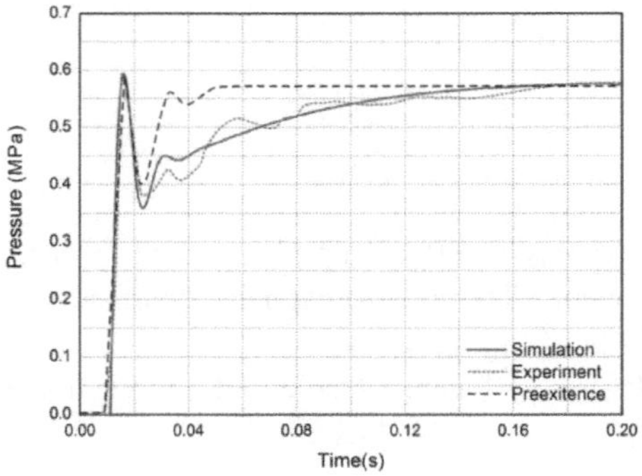

Fig. 3. Step response of PPCV

In Fig. 4, the investigation method of the level of contribution changes value of each variable by the range of ±10%, analyzed the response result. Analysis standard observed the first peak value, pressure increase to the steady state and the settling time in the response results. As see in Fig. 4, the contribution of three factor mentioned in this paper was observed in TDE, Flow coefficient, solenoid order.

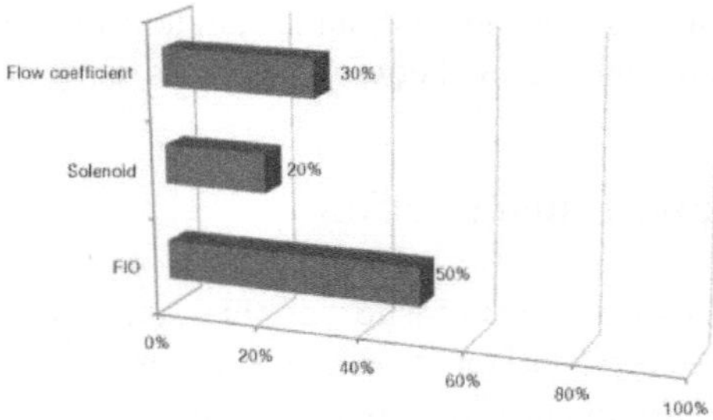

Fig. 4. The relative contribution of the three factors mentioned in this study on modeling

4 Conclusions

This study proved that the problems cause for make many errors in dynamic analysis of the hydraulic control valve. In addition this study analyzed pressure loss between the orifice and the gap, which are nonlinear using TDE. Therefore, we obtained a modeling result that was improved over the existing model.

In the characteristics analysis of the variable in modeling, it analyzed by comparison simulation to change of the variance (the section area of the spool, the spring constant, viscous friction coefficient, damping orifice diameter, mass of the spool and the chamber volume). Above all, we found that the viscosity change of the fluid shows each other response result in the steady state with transient state of the response results.

References

1. Borutzky, W.: A Dynamic Bond Graph Model of the Fluid Mechanical Interaction in Spool Valve Control Orifices. In: Bondgraphs for Engineers, pp. 229–236. Elsevier, North Holland (1992)
2. Mukherjee, A., Karmakar, R.: Modelling and Simulation of Engineering Systems through Bondgraph. Narosa Publishing House, New Delhi (2000)
3. Dasgupta, K., Chattapadhyay, A., Mondal, S.K.: Selection of fire resistant hydraulic fluids through system modeling and simulation. Simulation Modeling Practice and Theory 13(1), 1–20 (2005)
4. Suzuki, K., Nakamura, I., Thoma, J.U.: Pressure regulator valve by Bondgraph. Simulation Modeling Practice and Theory 7(5-6), 603–611 (1999)
5. Karnopp, D., Margolis, D.L., Rosenberg, R.C.: System dynamics: modeling and simulation of mechatronic systems, pp. 12–59, 400–423. Wiley (2000)
6. Dasgupta, K., Karmakar, R.: Dynamic analysis of Pilot operated pressure relief valve. Simulation Modeling Practice and Theory 10(1-2), 35–49 (2002)

Fixed-Width Modified Booth Multiplier Design Based on Error Bound Analysis

Kyung-Ju Cho[1], Jin-Gyun Chung[2], Hwan-Yong Kim[3], Gwang-Jun Kim[4], Dae-Ik Kim[4], and Yong-Kab Kim[3]

[1] Korea Association Aids to Navigation
kjcho@chonbuk.ac.kr
[2] Chonbuk National University
jgchung@chonbuk.ac.kr
[3] Wonkwang University
hykim@wku.ac.kr
[4] Chonnam National University
daeik@jnu.ac.kr, ykim@wku.ac.kr

Abstract. The maximum quantization error has serious effect on the performance of fixed-width multipliers that receive *W*-bit inputs and produce *W*-bit products. In this paper, the error bound offered-width modified Booth multiplier is analyzed. Then, we present a design method that can be used to reduce the maximum error. By simulations, it is shown that the performance of the proposed fixed-width multiplier is close to that of the multiplier with rounding scheme. Also, by an FIR filter example, it is shown that the proposed method can be successfully applied to many multimedia and DSP applications requiring fixed-width property.

Keywords: Fixed-width multiplier, Error bound, Quantization.

1 Introduction

In many multimedia and DSP applications, multiplications require their input and output products have the same bit width. For example, the $2W$-bit product obtained from W-bit multiplicand and W-bit multiplier is quantized to W-bits by eliminating the W-LSBs (Least-Significant Bits).

In typical fixed-width multipliers, the adder cells required for the computation of the W-LSBs are omitted and appropriate biases are introduced to the retained adder cells. To efficiently quantize the LSBs with reduced hardware, various fixed-width multiplier design techniques have been proposed for Baugh-Woolymultipliers[1-5], CSD (Canonic Signed Digit) multipliers[6] and modified Booth multipliers[7,8].

The above schemes are intended to reduce the average error with small hardware. However, the maximum error of a fixed-width multiplier can be critical in some applications. In general, the maximum error of fixed-width multipliers should be less than or equal to the weight of LSB (or, one unit in the last place), which is always true when the ideal $2W$-bit product is rounded or truncated to W-bits.

T.-h. Kim et al. (Eds.): MulGraB 2011, Part II, CCIS 263, pp. 248–256, 2011.

In this paper, the error bound of fixed-width modified Boothmultipliers [7] is first analyzed. Then, we present a design method that can be used to reduce the maximum error. By various simulations, it is shown that the maximum quantization error cans be reduced efficiently by the proposed approach at the cost of slightly increased hardware complexity.

2 Fixed-Width Multiplier Design

The modified Booth encoding has been widely used in parallel multipliers to reduce the number of partial products by a factor of two. Consider multiplication of *W*-bit two 2's complement numbers $X = -x_{W-1}2^{W-1} + \sum_{i=0}^{W-2} x_i 2^i$ and $Y = -y_{W-1}2^{W-1} + \sum_{i=0}^{W-2} y_i 2^i$.

By modified Booth coding is expressed as

$$Y = \sum_{i=0}^{W/2-1} y_i^{'} \cdot 2^{-2i}, \tag{1}$$

where

$$y_i^{'} = -2y_{2i+1} + y_{2i} + y_{2i-1}. \tag{2}$$

2.1 Fixed-Width Multiplier

The partial products for a modified Booth multiplier can be divided into *MP* and *LP* as shown in Fig. 1. To generate error compensation bias more efficiently, *LP* can be further divided into LP_{major} and LP_{minor}. In Fig. 1, *k* defines the number of the columns belonging to LP_{major}. Then, we can express 2*W*-bit ideal product P_I as

$$P_I = S\_MP + S\_LP, \tag{3}$$

where *S_MP* and *S_LP* represent the sum of the elements in *MP* and *LP*, respectively.

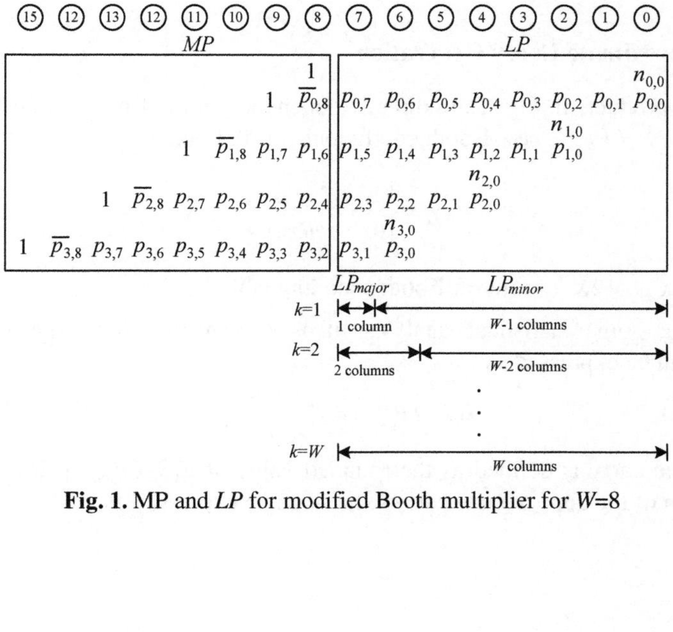

Fig. 1. MP and *LP* for modified Booth multiplier for *W*=8

In typical fixed-width multipliers, the adder cells required for S_LP are omitted and appropriate biases are introduced to the retained adder cells based on a probabilistic estimation. Thus, the W-bit quantized product P_Q can be expressed as

$$P_Q = S\_MP + \sigma \times 2^W, \tag{4}$$

where σ represents the error-compensation bias, which is the approximate carry signals propagated from LP to MP.

The quantized products by rounding and truncation schemes can be expressed as

$$\begin{aligned} P_R &= S\_MP + \sigma_R \times 2^W, \quad \sigma_R = \{S\_LP/2\}_r \\ P_T &= S\_MP + \sigma_T \times 2^W, \quad \sigma_T = \lfloor S\_LP/2 \rfloor \end{aligned} \tag{5}$$

where $\{t\}_r$ and $\lfloor t \rfloor$ mean round and floor operation for t, respectively.

From Fig. 1, S_LP can be expressed as

$$S\_LP = S\_LP_{major} + S\_LP_{minor}. \tag{6}$$

Then, for k=1, $S\_LP_{major}^{k=1}$ and $S\_LP_{minor}^{k=1}$ can be expressed as

$$\begin{aligned} S\_LP_{major}^{k=1} &= p_{0,7} + p_{1,5} + p_{2,3} + p_{3,1}, \\ S\_LP_{minor}^{k=1} &= 2^{-1}(p_{0,6} + p_{1,4} + \cdots + n_{3,0}) + 2^{-2}(p_{0,5} + p_{1,3} + p_{2,1}) + \cdots + 2^{-7}(p_{0,0} + n_{0,0}). \end{aligned} \tag{7}$$

Obviously, S_LP_{major} has dominant effect on the carry signals generated from LP since S_LP_{major} has the largest weight in the LP part.

In[7], the error compensation bias is defined as

$$\sigma_{[7]} = C_E[S\_LP_{major} + C_A[S\_LP_{minor}]], \tag{8}$$

where $C_E[t]$ and $C_A[t]$ mean the exact carry value and approximate carry value of t, respectively. Note that $C_A[S\_LP_{minor}]$ computes approximate carry value from LP_{minor} to LP_{major}.

2.2 Approximate Carry Generation

The partial products in Fig. 1 are directly dependent on the Booth encoder output. To approximate S_LP_{minor}, new Booth coefficient y_i'' is defined as

$$y_i'' = \begin{cases} 1, & if \ \ y_i' \neq 0, \\ 0, & otherwise, \end{cases} \tag{9}$$

where $y_i'' = X_{sel,i} \vee 2X_{sel,i}$ (refer to Booth encoding table[7]).

In[7], using some statistical analysis, it is shown that the expected value of S_LP_{minor} can be expressed as

$$E[S\_LP_{minor}] = 2^{-1} \cdot \sum_{i=0}^{W/2-1} y_i''. \tag{10}$$

Approximate carry is defined as the rounded value of $E[S\_LP_{minor}]$. It can be shown that the sum of the approximate carry values can be expressed as

$$\sum_{i=0}^{N_{AC}-1} a\_carry\_i = \left\{ \sum_{i=0}^{\{(k-k)/2\}_r -1} \frac{y_i^{"}}{2} \right\}_r , \tag{11}$$

where N_{AC} means the number of approximate carry signals which is defined as $N_{AC} = \lceil (W-k)/4 \rceil$ and k means the number of columns included in S_LP_{major}.

3 Error Bound Analysis

In this section, we analyze the error bound of the fixed-width modified Booth multipliers designed in[7]. Also, it is shown that the number of columns included in LP_{major} can be selected appropriately to satisfy the maximum error bound requirement for given W.

3.1 LP_{major} Part Keeping One Column(k=1)

For W=8, using (7) , the bounds on $S\_LP_{major}^{k=1}$ and $S\_LP_{minor}^{k=1}$ can be computed as

$$0 \le S\_LP_{major}^{k=1} \le W/2, \qquad 0 \le S\_LP_{minor}^{k=1} \le W/2. \tag{12}$$

Then, the bound on $S\_LP^{k=1}$ is expressed as

$$0 \le S\_LP^{k=1} \le W. \tag{13}$$

From (11), approximate carry value for $S\_LP_{minor}^{k=1}$ is bounded by

$$0 \le \sum_{i=0}^{N_{AC}-1} a\_carry\_i^{k=1} \le N_{AC}. \tag{14}$$

The maximum error occurs when the partial product bits in LP_{minor} are (a) all 0's (X=×0000000, Y=01010101) or (b) all 1's (X=××000000, Y=10101010) as shown in Fig. 2. Notice that in cases (a) and (b), by (2), all $y_i^{"}$ are 1's, Then, if the approximate error $\Delta_{minor}^{k=1}$ from S_LP_{minor} is defined as $\Delta_{minor}^{k=1} = S\_LP_{minor}^{k=1} - \sum_{i=0}^{N_{AC}-1} a\_carry\_i^{k=1}$, the bound on $\Delta_{minor}^{k=1}$ is computed as using Fig. 2

$$-N_{AC} \le \Delta_{minor}^{k=1} \le W/2 - N_{AC}. \tag{15}$$

From LP_{major}, only the carry signals are added to MP as compensation bias.

Let $\Delta_{major}^{k=1}$ be defined as

$$\Delta_{major}^{k=1} = \left[(S\_LP_{minor}^{k=1} + \sum_{i=0}^{N_{AC}-1} a\_carry\_i^{k=1})/2 - \left\lfloor S\_LP_{minor}^{k=1} + \sum_{i=0}^{N_{AC}-1} a\_carry\_i^{k=1} \right\rfloor /2 \right] \times 2. \tag{16}$$

Then, the error bound on LP_{major} is

$$0 \le \Delta_{major}^{k=1} \le 1. \tag{17}$$

Note that in (17), $\Delta_{minor}^{k=1}$ can actually take either 0 or 1.

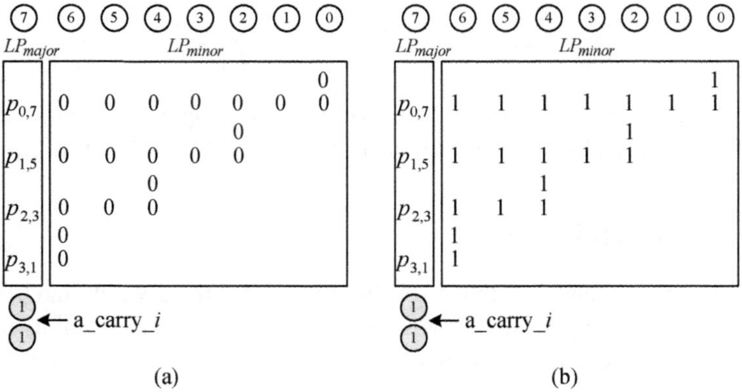

Fig. 2. Worst case approximation error with k=1: (a) X=×0000000, Y=01010101, and (b) X=××000000, Y=10101010

From (15) and (17), the total error bound $\Delta_{total}^{k=1}$ (defined as $\Delta_{total}^{k=1} = \Delta_{minor}^{k=1} + \Delta_{major}^{k=1}$) due to the approximation of LP can be computed as

$$-N_{AC} \le \Delta_{total}^{k=1} \le W/2 - N_{AC} + 1. \tag{18}$$

Then, the quantization error ε (defined as $\varepsilon = P_I - P_Q$) of fixed-width multiplier is bounded by

$$-2^{W-1} \cdot N_{AC} \le \varepsilon^{k=1} \le 2^{W-1}(W/2 - N_{AC} + 1). \tag{19}$$

For W=8, N_{AC} is 2 and the maximum absolute error ε_{max} (defined as $\varepsilon_{\max} = \max(|\varepsilon|)$) is 1.5×2^8. Notice that the weight of 2^W corresponds to that of the LSB. In addition, for $W \ge 12$, the maximum error is greater than or equal to 2^W. It may not be desirable in some cases since 2^{W+1} is larger than the weight of the LSB. Thus, some techniques are required to reduce the maximum error for $W \ge 8$.

3.2 LP_{major} Part Keeping Two Column (k=2)

From Fig. 1, for k=2, $S\_LP_{major}^{k=2}$ and $S\_LP_{minor}^{k=2}$ can be expressed as

$$\begin{aligned} S\_LP_{major}^{k=2} &= S\_LP_{major0}^{k=2} + S\_LP_{major1}^{k=2} = S\_LP_{major}^{k=1} + 2^{-1}(p_{0,6} + p_{1,4} + p_{2,2} + p_{3,0} + n_{3,0}), \\ S\_LP_{minor}^{k=2} &= 2^{-2}(p_{0,5} + p_{1,3} + p_{2,1}) + \cdots + 2^{-7}(p_{0,0} + n_{0,0}). \end{aligned} \tag{20}$$

It can be shown that $S\_LP_{major1}^{k=2}$ and $S\_LP_{minor}^{k=2}$ are bounded by

$$0 \le S\_LP_{major1}^{k=2} \le 2^{-1}(W/2+1), \quad 0 \le S\_LP_{minor}^{k=2} \le 2^{-1}(W/2-1). \tag{21}$$

From (11), approximate carry value for $S\_LP_{minor}^{k=2}$ is bounded by

$$0 \le \sum_{i=0}^{N_{AC}-1} a\_carry\_i^{k=2} \le 2^{-1} \cdot N_{AC}. \tag{22}$$

The maximum error of approximate carry values occurs when the partial product bits are (a) all 0's (X=××000000, Y=××010101) or (b) all 1's (X=×××00000, Y=××101010) as shown in Fig. 3.

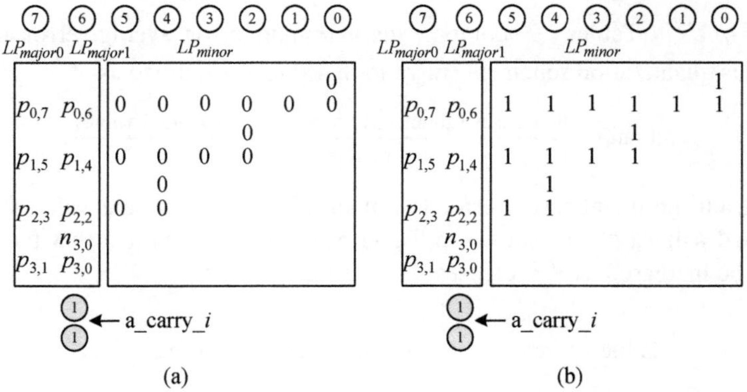

Fig. 3. Worst case approximation error with k=2: (a) X=××000000, Y=××010101, and (b) X=×××00000, Y=××101010

According to (21) and (22), the bound of approximate error is computed as

$$-2^{-1}\cdot N_{AC}\leq\Delta_{minor}^{k=2}\leq 2^{-1}\{(W/2-1)-N_{AC}\}. \tag{23}$$

Since rounding operation is performed within LP_{major}, the rounding error $\Delta_{major1}^{k=2}$ from $LP_{major1}^{k=2}$ to $LP_{major2}^{k=2}$ is bounded by

$$-2^{-1}\leq\Delta_{major1}^{k=2}\leq 0. \tag{24}$$

The total error bound $\Delta_{total}^{k=2}$ (defined as $\Delta_{total}^{k=2}=\Delta_{minor}^{k=2}+\Delta_{major1}^{k=2}+\Delta_{major}^{k=1}$) in LP, from (17), (23) and (24),can be computed as

$$-2^{-1}(N_{AC}+1)\leq\Delta_{total}^{k=2}\leq 2^{-1}\{(W/2-1)-N_{AC}+2\}. \tag{25}$$

Then, the quantization error (ε=P_I-P_Q) of fixed-width multiplier is bounded by

$$-2^{-(W-2)}(N_{AC}+1)\leq\varepsilon^{k=2}\leq 2^{(W-2)}\{(W/2-1)-N_{AC}+2)\}. \tag{26}$$

For general k, the total error and quantization error bound can be easily obtained by the same way as

$$\begin{aligned}&-2^{-(k-1)}(N_{AC}+2^{(k-1)}-1)\leq\Delta_{total}\leq 2^{-(k-1)}(W/2-\lfloor k/2\rfloor-N_{AC}+2^{k-1})\\&-2^{-(W-k)}(N_{AC}+2^{(k-1)}-1)\leq\varepsilon\ \leq 2^{-(W-k)}(W/2-\lfloor k/2\rfloor-N_{AC}+2^{k-1}).\end{aligned} \tag{27}$$

From (27), the maximum error can be computed as

$$\varepsilon_{\max}=\begin{cases}2^{W}(1+\lfloor(W-4)/4\rfloor\times 2^{-1}), & for\ \ k=1\\2^{W}(1+\lfloor(W-10)/4\rfloor\times 2^{-2}), & for\ \ k=2\\2^{W}(1+\lfloor(W-18)/4\rfloor\times 2^{-3}), & for\ \ k=3\\2^{W}(1+\lfloor(W-36)/4\rfloor\times 2^{-4}), & for\ \ k=4.\end{cases} \tag{28}$$

4 Simulation Results and DSP Applications

To evaluate the performance of fixed-width multiplier, we compute the maximum absolute error ε_{max} and the average absolute quantization error $\bar{\varepsilon}$ (defined as $\bar{\varepsilon} = (\sum|\varepsilon|)/2^{2W}$). Tables 1~3 compare the maximum error, average error and hit-ratio for various quantization schemes. Hit-ratio in Table 3 is defined as

$$\text{hit ratio} = \frac{\#\text{ of cases (quantized value = ideal rounded value)}}{\text{total }\#\text{ of cases}}. \quad (29)$$

To constrain the quantization error less than 2^W, the appropriate value for k can be determined using (28), as shown in Table 5. It should be notice that the value of k needs to be increased as W increases.

Table 1. Comparison of maximum absolute error ε_{max} ($\times 2^W$)

Method	W=6	W=8	W=10	W=12	W=14
σ_R	0.5	0.5	0.5	0.5	0.5
σ_T	0.9844	0.9961	0.9990	0.9998	1
$\sigma_{8\ k=1}$	1.3281	1.7305	2.1299	2.5300	2.9300
$\sigma_{prop,\ k=1}$	1	1	1.5	1.5	2
$\sigma_{8,\ k=2}$	0.9688	1.1641	1.3652	1.5649	1.7650
$\sigma_{prop,\ k=2}$	0.75	0.75	1	1	1.25

Table 2. Comparison of average absolute error $\bar{\varepsilon}$ ($\times 2^W$)

Method	W=6	W=8	W=10	W=12	W=14
σ_R	0.2461	0.2490	0.2498	0.2499	0.25
σ_T	0.4688	0.4902	0.4971	0.4991	0.4998
$\sigma_{8\ k=1}$	0.3375	0.4028	0.4590	0.5060	0.5470
$\sigma_{prop,\ k=1}$	0.3066	0.3302	0.3424	0.3527	0.3687
$\sigma_{8,\ k=2}$	0.2839	0.3113	0.3364	0.3592	0.3795
$\sigma_{prop,\ k=2}$	0.2578	0.2621	0.2681	0.2731	0.2753

Table 3. Comparison of hit-ratios

Method	W=6	W=8	W=10	W=12	W=14
σ_T	0.5	0.5	0.5	0.5	0.5
$\sigma_{8\ k=1}$	0.7432	0.6677	0.6080	0.5644	0.5303
$\sigma_{prop,\ k=1}$	0.7910	0.7680	0.7520	0.7328	0.7168
$\sigma_{8,\ k=2}$	0.8031	0.7931	0.7558	0.7240	0.6979
$\sigma_{prop,\ k=2}$	0.8945	0.9028	0.8970	0.8827	0.8726

We apply the proposed fixed-width modified Booth multiplier to 35-tap low-pass FIR filter implementation. Filter coefficients are obtained using Remezex change algorithm in MATLAB. For simulation, we take 1500 samples from the "voice signal" as shown in Fig.4(a). Input data and the filter coefficients are represented using the word-length of 12 bits. Also, we assume that the required output word-length is 12 bits. Fig.4(b) shows absolute error values of filtered output samples for each scheme for k=2. In this example, the average absolute error of the proposed method is about 37% of that of the scheme in[8].

Table 4. Relation between W and k for $\varepsilon_{max} \leq 2^W$

Method	$W < 8$	$8 \leq W < 14$	$14 \leq W < 22$	$22 \leq W < 40$
k	1	2	3	4

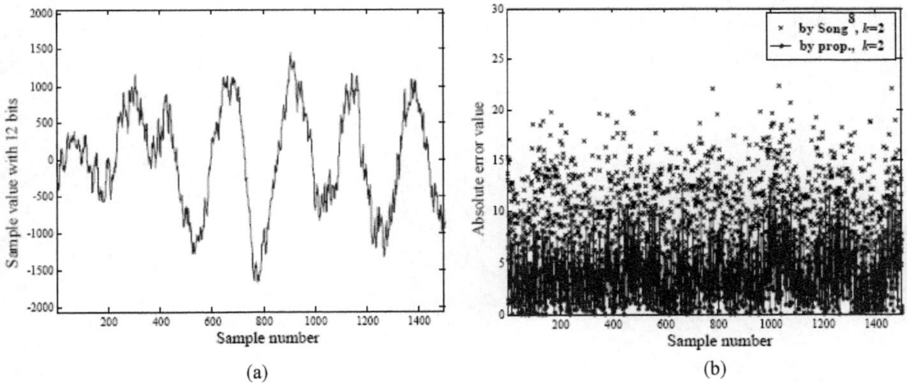

Fig. 4. FIR filter example: (a) input voice signal with 1500 samples and (b) comparison of absolute error for filter output

5 Conclusions

The error bound of fixed-width modified Booth multipliers was analyzed and the maximum quantization error was derived as a function of W and k. In addition, our methodology was extended to reduced-width multipliers. By an FIR filter example, it was shown that the proposed error bound on fixed-width modified Booth multipliers can be successfully used to estimate the performance of the fixed-width multipliers. Consequently, the proposed error bound can be used to decide appropriate quantization scheme for a given application.

References

1. Schulte, M.J., Swartzlander Jr., E.E.: Proceedings of the VLSI Signal Processing (1993)
2. King, E.J., Swartzlander Jr., E.E.: Proceedings of the 31st Asilomar Conference on Signals, Systems, Computers (1997)
3. Jou, J.M., Kung, S.R., Chen, R.D.: IEEE Trans. Circuits & Systems II (1999)
4. Van, L.D., Wang, S.S., Feng, W.S.: IEEE Trans. Circuits & Systems II (2000)
5. Jou, S.J., Wang, H.H.: The Proceedings of International Conference on Computer Design (2000)
6. Kim, S.M., Chung, J.G., Parhi, K.K.: IEEE Trans. Circuits & Systems II (2003)
7. Cho, K.J., Lee, K.C., Chung, J.G., Parhi, K.K.: IEEE Trans. VLSI Systems (2004)
8. Song, M.A., Van, L.D., Huang, T.C., Kuo, S.Y.: IEEE Trans. Circuits & Systems II (2005)

A Performance Enhancement for Ubiquitous Indoor Networking Using VLC-LED Driving Module

Geun-Bin Hong[1], Tae-Su Jang[1], Kwan-Woong Kim[2], and Yong-Kab Kim[1]

[1] Wonkwang University, School of Electrical Information Engineering, Iksan, 570-749, Korea
{Ghdrmsqls,ts-1stepjang}@nate.com, ykim@wku.ac.kr
[2] Korea Atomic Energy Research Institute, Deajeon, 305-353, Korea
kwkim@kaeri.re.kr

Abstract. This study aims to use LED, a representative runner in electric energy reduction as Green IT technology in the field of lighting and suggest visible communication for using ubiquitous Indoor networking system. As LED is excellent in its efficiency, the aim has to use such LED to access ubiquitous environment, a network that can be used remotely at any time anywhere and determine the possibility of its application into various applications that promote users' convenience. The communication performance by implementing a communication system for lighting in order to send a text message has been tested in ubiquitous environment within ~2.5m, 0.45V, 5% error rate, data rate Kbps and within disturbance light. We could confirm that the implementation of LED communication was possible in ubiquitous environment within ~2.25m, data rate ~Kbps, and 3% error rate, or more was weak or none where data transmission is seamlessly done indoors.

Keywords: Visible light communication, Illumination, Ubiquitous networking, LED, Control of Light.

1 Introduction

Until now, incandescent bulbs and fluorescent lights have been used widely for lighting. However, our current trend transits from incandescent bulbs and fluorescent lights into LED. The LED is ahead of incandescent bulbs in its efficiency of changing electricity into light or similar to fluorescent lights, and at the same time unlike the fluorescent lights that contain mercury, it does not contain mercury and it's eco-friendly, has a long life more than 50,000 hours, and electricity efficient 90% more than poor electricity efficient incandescent bulbs. LED technology expands its area starting from the field of lighting to LED, TV, and notebook and even to cellular phones[1, 2]. The lighting in the past has a function of giving us light, but now we have wireless visible light communication in the ubiquitous service environment where we can receive information there at any time anywhere wherever we can find LED lights.

Visible Light Communication has not received much attention until now as it was pushed behind by RF communication, but in current times, with the development of

T.-h. Kim et al. (Eds.): MulGraB 2011, Part II, CCIS 263, pp. 257–262, 2011.

LED technology it received much attention as it has LED fusion technology. Visible light communication is a way of communication that uses visible light wavelength ranging from 780nm~380nm(385THz~789THz if converted to frequency). If we look at the applications of this visible light communication, there are various areas of applications: ITS communication between traffic lights, Location Determination Technology that informs indoor location information, broadcasting communication that delivers information through display or digital multi signboard, and LED lighting or communication that utilizes display infra. The biggest advantage of visible light communication is that it does not need to establish an additional construction and utilize the infra for lighting, unlike RF. Besides, it does not have problems in allocation of frequency and is good to be convertible internationally; has no regulations about the use of visible light spectrum and thus has high degree of freedom; is simple and easy to be used in the areas sensitive to electromagnetic waves such as hospitals and airplanes as it is a way of communication that uses light rather than electromagnetic wave. And visible light itself basically does not pass through the wall, and thus it is easy to build a local network which is highly complementary. On the other hand, visible light communication may cause communication failure if there is interference from other light sources, but this is a task that can be solved from technical perspective. Based on these advantages, with the recent advent of necessity of indoor communication system and the appearance of LED, the interest on the visible light-based communication system has been increasing[3,4].

In this study, coupled by such increased demands for these lighting visible infrastructure and the necessity of wireless visible light communication technology with ubiquitous indoor networking system[5,6], we aimed to use remote controller, a medium of infrared communication used conveniently in everyday life, establish a visible light communication system with the fusion of lighting communication that LED lighting on the ceiling receives information signal and transmits to each room under remote control system[7] (i.e. lighting) in ubiquitous environment, and identify the potential of next-generation network applications in ubiquitous indoor networking environment.

2 VLC-LED Driving Module

In this LED switching module based indoor networking system, we used infrared remote controller as a medium of communication, and the system to send information is as shown in [Fig. 1]. In the visible light communication based VLC-LED driving module systems with ubiquitous indoor networking, the distance between receiver part and transmitter part is at least ~0.6m or more (limited ~2.50m), and we used infrared remote controller that has 6 modules consisting of 21 LEDs at luminous part and sends data information and even adjust lighting, and visible light sensor that can receive data signal at a receiver part.

Besides, to monitor if it performs exact communication for performance evaluation, we manufactured LED visible light communication data transmission program using Visual C++ computer programming language, input data with infrared remote controller, and made it communicate data with a computer, using ATmega16 chip, TSL250RD and ILX232N so that users can see the process of giving and receiving data in real time by the naked eye for ubiquitous indoor networking with driving module.

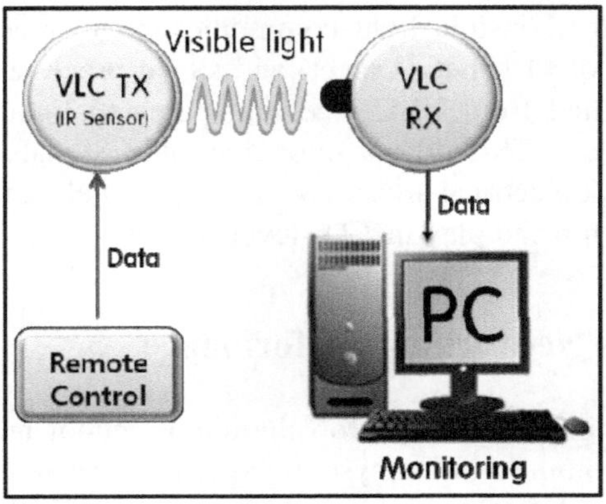

Fig. 1. VLC-LED driving module system architecture

The entire configuration of VLC-LED driving module system has shown as a data transmission with receiver and transmitter. The receiver and transmitter part of visible light communication using VLC-LED module system is as shown in [Fig. 2]. The major components for the indoor networking module that enter into the substrate of VLC receiver and transmitter part consist of Korea Kodenshi's IR sensor for optical parts, KSM60WLM, ATmel's MCU-ATmega16 chips, and TAOS's visible light receiving sensor TSL250RD chip, Good i-Tech's 6 modules consisting of 21 high-intensity white LEDs for white LED, TTL ILX232N chips for the conversion of signal level.

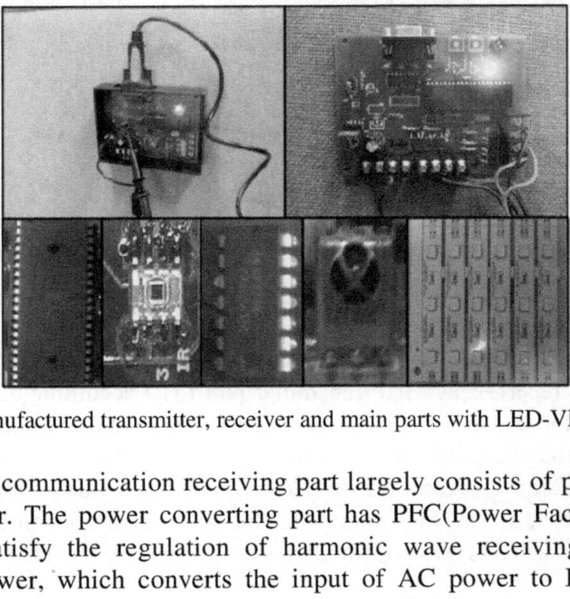

Fig. 2. Manufactured transmitter, receiver and main parts with LED-VLC module

Visible light communication receiving part largely consists of power converter and LED driver. The power converting part has PFC(Power Factor Correction) that tries to satisfy the regulation of harmonic wave receiving input of AC commercial power, which converts the input of AC power to DC power in a suitable form to drive LED. LED driver converts to Infrared remote controller sends data signal through IR sensor-KSM60WLM- and the signal is converted through ILX232N chip to TTL signal level and sent through micro-controller to LED emitting part.

The receiver part of visible light communication to receive data signal sent from LED consists of PD(Photo-Detect) and signal processing part. PD converts data signal transmitted from VLC receiving part and lights exposed to visible light receiving sensor TSL250RD into electronic signals, and in the signal processing part weak electrical signal converted photo electrically is amplified by op-amp, LM324N chip and play in TTL-level signals.

3 Ubiquitous Networking Performance

The real picture in implementation for ubiquitous indoor networking system, of LED visible light communication system experiment is as shown in [Fig. 3]. To measure the speed and data rate in communication to smooth communication and distance, two transceivers face each other from a certain level of distance as shown in [Fig. 3]. Monitoring computer conducts serial communication through USB port and observes data transmission and reception status. To check if it operates seamlessly, ø 5 bulb-typed LED is attached to see the transmission and reception status. In carrying out accurate communication in an indoor environment, we measured electrical pulse waveform received through visible light receiving sensor with an oscilloscope where it is not affected by extraneous light. In the experiment below, we could check the normally operating transmitting and receiving waveform as shown in [Fig.4]

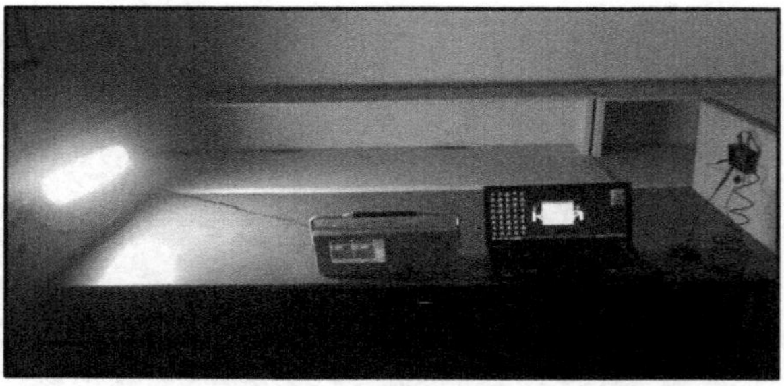

Fig. 3. The VLC experimental setup for ubiquitous indoor networking

[Fig. 4] shows optical oscilloscope pulse waveform of the visible light sensor measured at the receiver part and transmitter part LED according to the transmission of text file. As the distance between reception and transmission becomes distant, the signal level at the reception part is lower. In this experiment, communication at a distance of ~2.25m or more was weak or none, and maximum communication distance was 2m or so. In this experiment, for stable data transmission, the distance between two transceivers was ~1.5m, data was 8bit, and in the state of non-parity bit and flow control, the transmission speed was a few ~Kbps. At a distance of 0~2.25m or more with 5% error rate, it was difficult to receive data exactly due to weak intensity of light, but the data transmission process had no problem.

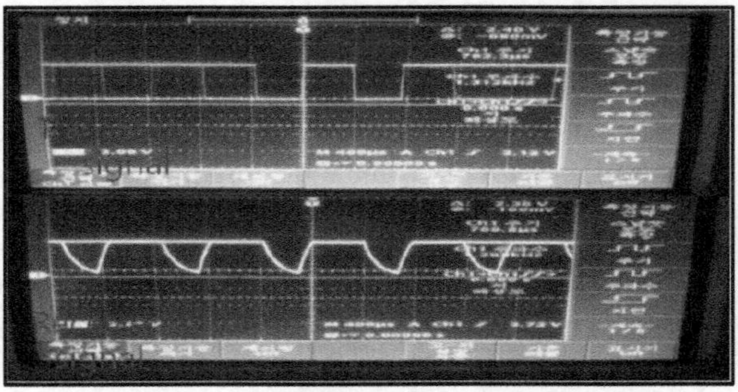

Fig. 4. For indoor networking transmitted and received waveform

[Fig. 5] shows a capture of monitoring screen for VLC communication with LED that observes the status of transmission using the program manufactured with computer programming language. Visual C++was manufactured with a computer programming language that ordinary users may use easily and we could see if transmission and reception between lighting and computer operates smoothly by inputting the letter. The PD has detected transmitted data signal via transmitter based on indoor networking system. The detected effectiveness within optical sensor has captured in ~2.50m and larger. We also could find that there was a loss of data by 0.450[v].

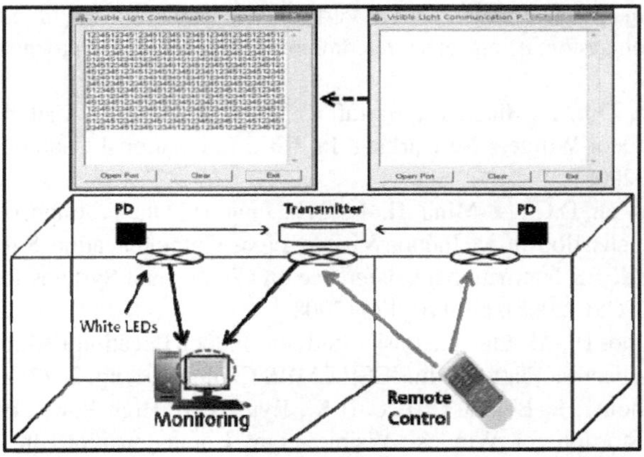

Fig. 5. The transmitting and receiving on-line monitoring status with communication data

How to use is that we can collect data transmitted in visible light and convert to electrical signals by opening the reception port program connected to monitoring computer and pressing the data information number key on the infrared remote controller at the transmission part. This signal is amplified by LM324N chip, converted to TTL-level signal, and then you can see if it is able to receive or transmit signals correctly from the implemented monitoring program. As a result, we could find that about ~2.0[m] maximum of data transmission occurred without loss of information. As it consists of basic number source values, but it is replaceable to desired manual source values at any time. For example, we can obtain information as wanted by accessing network in ubiquitous environment at anytime and anywhere.

4 Conclusions

We configured the overall system of visible light communication in ubiquitous indoor networking environment, has manufactured VLC-LED driving module system. The proposed maximum data rate distance was limited to ~2.50[m], ~0.45[v], data rate ~Kbps, and 5[%] error rate within interference effect. If we apply filter for light communication to reduce error rate by extraneous light, the communication distance will extend. We could confirm that the implementation of LED communication was possible in ubiquitous environment within ~2.25m, data rate ~9600bps, and 3% error rate, or more was weak or none where data transmission is seamlessly done indoors. The system is expected to spread dramatically in the next-generation networking applications such as smart phone, PDA, template PC as it has an advantage that it combines with lighting devices.

References

1. Hara, T., Iwasaki, S., Yendo, T., Fujii, T., Tanimoto, M.: A new receiving system of visible light communication for its. In: IEEE Intelligent Vehicles Symposium, pp. 474–479 (June 2007)
2. Lee, I.E., Sim, M.L., Kung, F.W.L.: Performance enhancement of outdoor visible-light communication system using selective combining receiver. IET Optoelectronics 3(1), 30–39 (2009)
3. Little, T.D.C., Dib, P., Shah, K., Barraford, N., Gallagher, B.: Using LED Lighting for Ubiquitous Indoor Wireless Networking. In: IEEE International Conference WIMOB 2008, pp. 373–378 (2008)
4. Zeng, L., O'Brien, D.C., Le-Minh, H., Lee, K., Jung, D., Oh, Y.: Improvement of Data Rate by Using Equalisation in an Indoor Visible Light Communication System. Accepted for publication in IEEE International Conference on Circuits and Systems for Communications 2008 (IEEE ICCSC 2008), pp. 170–173 (2008)
5. Liu, X., Makino, H., Maeda, Y.: Basic Study on Indoor Location Estimation using Visible Light Communication Platform. In: IEEE EMBS Conference, pp. 2377–2380 (2008)
6. Ryu, S.B., Choi, J.H., Bok, J.Y., Lee, H.K., Ryu, H.G.: High Power Efficiency and Low Nonlinear Distortion for Wireless Visible Light Communication. In: IFIP International Conference, pp. 1–5 (2011)
7. Ntogari, G., Kamalakis, T., Walewski, J., Sphicopoulos, T.: Combining Illumination Dimming Based on Pulse-Width Modulation With Visible-Light Communications Based on Discrete Multitone. IEEE/OSA Journal on Optical Communications and Networking, 56–65 (2011)

Improved Password Mutual Authentication Scheme for Remote Login Network Systems

Younghwa An

Division of Computer and Media Information Engineering
111, Gugal-dong, Giheung-ku, Yongin-si, Gyeonggi-do, 446-702, Korea
yhan@kangnam.ac.kr

Abstract. Password-based authentication schemes have been widely adopted to protect resources from unauthorized access. In 2008, Chang-Lee proposed a friendly password mutual authentication scheme to avoid the security weaknesses of Wu-Chieu's scheme. In this paper, we have shown that Chang-Lee's scheme is vulnerable to the forgery attack and password guessing attack, etc. Also, we proposed the improved scheme to overcome these security weaknesses, even if the secret information stored in the smart card is revealed. As a result of security analysis, the proposed scheme is secure against the forgery attack and password guessing attack, etc. And the performance of the proposed scheme is more efficient than that of Chang-Lee's scheme in terms of the computational complexities.

Keywords: Authentication, Forgery Attack, Password Guessing Attack.

1 Introduction

With the increasing of users using commercial services through networks, the user authentication scheme using smart card has been becoming one of important security issues. However, lots of vulnerabilities have been exposed in the authentication scheme due to the careless password management and the sophisticated attack techniques. Several schemes and improvements for remote user authentication schemes using smart card have been proposed[1-5].

In 2000, Sun[3] proposed a user authentication scheme based on one-way hash functions without using a password table. Wu-Chieu[4], in 2003, proposed a user authentication scheme with smart cards to improve the drawback of Sun's scheme. However, in 2004, Yang-Wang[6] pointed out that Wu-Chieu's scheme is vulnerable to password guessing attack and forgery attack. And, in 2008, Chang-Lee[7] proposed a friendly password mutual authentication scheme to avoid the security weakness of Wu-Chieu's scheme. Also, they claimed that their scheme is secure against the forgery attack, the password guessing attack, the replay attack, etc. and provides the mutual authentication between the user and the remote server.

In this paper, we analyze the security weaknesses of Chang-Lee's scheme and we have shown that Chang-Lee's scheme is still insecure against the forgery attack, password guessing attack, etc. To analyze the security of Chang-Lee's scheme, we

T.-h. Kim et al. (Eds.): MulGraB 2011, Part II, CCIS 263, pp. 263–269, 2011.

assume that an attacker could obtain the values stored in the smart card by monitoring the power consumption or analyzing the leaked information[8-10]. Also, we propose the improved scheme to overcome these security weaknesses, while preserving all their merits, even if the secret information stored in the smart card is revealed.

This paper is organized as follows. In section 2, we briefly review Chang-Lee's scheme. In section 3, we describe the security weaknesses of Chang-Lee's scheme. Our improved scheme is presented in section 4, and its security analysis and performance evaluations are given in section 5. Finally, the conclusions are made in section 6.

2 Review of Chang-Lee's Scheme

In 2008, Chang-Lee proposed a friendly password mutual authentication scheme for remote login network systems. This scheme is divided into three phases(i.e. registration, login, and authentication). The notations used throughout this paper are as follows:

- U_i : The user i
- PW_i : The password of user I
- $h()$: One-way hash function
- $\|$: Concatenation
- ID_i : The identity of user i
- S : The remote server
- $\oplus$: Exclusive-OR operation

2.1 Registration Phase

This phase works whenever the user U_i initially registers or re-registers to the remote server S.

1. U_i submits his ID_i and PW_i to S through a secure channel.
2. S computes $A_i=h(ID_i\|x)$ and $B_i=h(A_i\|h(PW_i))$, where x is a secret key of server.

S issues the smart card to the user through a secure channel, where the smart card contains $\{ID_i, A_i, B_i, h()\}$.

2.2 Login Phase

This phase works whenever the user U_i wants to login to the remote server S.

1. U_i inserts his smart card into a card reader, and enters his ID_i and PW_i^*.
2. The smart card computes $B_i^*= h(A_i\|h(PW_i^*))$, $C_1=h(T_1\oplus B_i)$ and $C_2= B_i^*\oplus h(A_i\oplus T_1)$.
3. U_i sends a message $m_1=\{ID_i, C_1, C_2, T_1\}$ to S, where T_1 is the current time stamp.

2.3 Authentication Phase

This phase works whenever the remote server S received the user U_i's login request.

1. S checks the validity of ID_i, and then verifies the validity of the time interval.
2. S computes $A_i=h(ID_i\|x)$, $B_i^*=C_2\oplus h(A_i\oplus T_1)$ and $C_1^*=h(T_1\oplus B_i^*)$.

3. S checks whether $C_1^*=C_1$ or not. If they are equal, the U_i's login request is accepted.
4. S sends a message $m_2=\{C_3, T_2\}$, where $C_3=h(h(A_i||B_i^*)\oplus T_2)$ and T_2 is the current time stamp.
5. Upon receiving the message, U_i verifies the validity of the time interval, and then computes $C_3^*=h(h(A_i||B_i)\oplus T_2)$.
6. U_i checks whether $C_3^*=C_3$ or not. If they are equal, the server is authenticated to the user.

3 Security Weaknesses of Chang-Lee's Scheme

In this section, we analyze the security of Chang-Lee's scheme. To analyze the security weaknesses, we assume that an attacker could obtain the values stored in the smart card by monitoring the power consumption or analyzing the leaked information[8-10].

3.1 Forgery Attack

In Chang-Lee's scheme, the attacker without knowing U_i's password can impersonate as the legal user U_i. After the attacker can extract the secret values A_i, B_i from the legal user's smart card by some means, the attacker can perform the user impersonation attack easily as the following steps.

1. The attacker computes easily $C_1^*=h(T_1^*\oplus B_i)$ and $C_2^*=B_i\oplus h(A_i\oplus T_1^*)$, where T_1^* is the current time stamp. Then, the attacker sends the forged message $m_1=\{ID_i, C_1^*, C_2^*, T_1^*\}$ to the remote server S.
2. Upon receiving the message m_1, the attacker can successfully impersonate as the legal user U_i, because the remote server will be convinced that the message m_1 is sent from the user U_i to login the system.

Hence, the attacker can perform the user impersonation attack and the server masquerading attack. Therefore Chang-Lee's Scheme does not provide the mutual authentication between the user and the remote server.

3.2 Password Guessing Attack

The attacker can extract the secret values A_i, B_i from the legal user's smart card by some means. Now, the attacker can easily find out PW_i by employing the password guessing attack, in which each guess PW_i* for PW_i can be verified by the following steps.

1. The attacker computes the parameter $B_i^*=h(A_i||h(PW_i^*))$ from the login phase.
2. The attacker verifies the correctness of PW_i^* by checking $B_i^*= B_i$.
3. The attacker repeats the above steps until a correct password PW_i^* is found. Finally, the attacker can derive the correct user's password PW_i.

Thus, the attacker can perform the off-line password guessing attack. Therefore, the attacker can successfully impersonate as the legal user with the user's password.

4 The Proposed Scheme

In this section, we propose an improved Chang-Lee's scheme which not only can withstand the password guessing attack and forgery attack, but also provide the mutual authentication between the user and the server. The proposed scheme is divided into three phases: registration phase, login phase and verification phase. The login and verification phase is illustrated in Fig. 1.

4.1 Registration Phase

This phase works whenever the user U_i initially registers or re-registers to the remote server S.

1. U_i submits his identity ID_i and $h(b \oplus PW_i)$ to S through a secure channel, where a random number b is generated by U_i.
2. S computes $A_i=h(ID_i \oplus x)$ and $B_i=h(A_i \oplus h(PW_i))$, where x is a secret key of server.
3. S issues the smart card to the user through a secure channel, where the smart card contains $\{ID_i, B_i, h()\}$.
4. U_i stores b into his new smart card so that U_i does not need to remember b.

4.2 Login Phase

This phase works whenever the user U_i wants to login to the remote server S.

1. U_i inserts his smart card into a card reader, and enters his ID_i and PW_i.
2. The smart card computes $A_i=B_i \oplus h(b \oplus PW_i)$, $C_1=h(B_i \oplus T_1)$, and $C_2=B_i \oplus h(A_i \oplus T_1)$.
3. U_i sends a message $\{ID_i, C_1, C_2, T_1\}$ to S, where T_1 is the current time stamp.

4.3 Authentication Phase

This phase works whenever the remote server S received the user U_i's login request. Upon receiving the message from the user, the server performs the following steps to identify the user.

1. S checks the validity of ID_i, and then verifies the time stamp T_1 with the current time T'. If $(T'-T_1) \leq \Delta T$, S accepts the login request, where ΔT denotes the expected valid time interval for transmission delay.
2. S computes $A_i^*=h(ID_i \oplus x)$, $B_i^*=C_2 \oplus h(A_i^* \oplus T_1)$, and $C_1^*=h(B_i^* \oplus T_1)$.
3. S checks whether $C_1^*=C_1$ or not. If they are equal, the U_i's login request is accepted.
4. S computes $C_3=h(A_i^* \oplus B_i^* \oplus T_2)$, where T_2 is the current time stamp, and then sends a message $\{C_3, T_2\}$to the U_i. Upon receiving the message from the remote server, the user performs the following steps to identify the remote server.
5. U_i verifies the time stamp T_2 with the current time T''. If $(T''-T_2) \leq \Delta T$, then the smart card computes $C_3^*=h(A_i \oplus B_i \oplus T_2)$.
6. U_i checks whether $C_3^*=C_3$ or not. If they are equal, the server is authenticated and allowed to access the smart card.

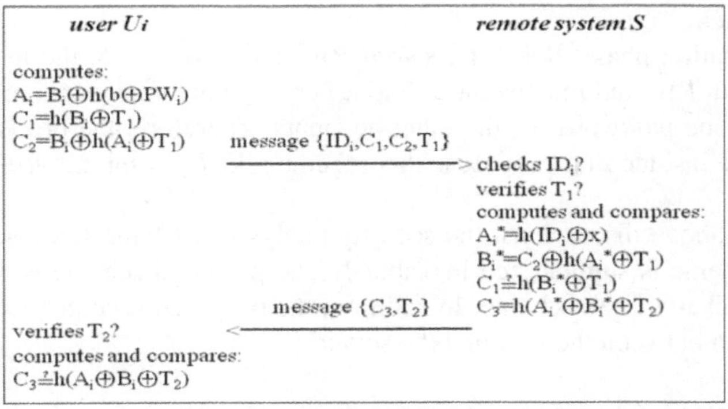

Fig. 1. Login Phase and Authentication Phase

5 Security Analysis and Performance Evaluations

In this section, we will analyze the security of the proposed scheme based on secure one-way hash function.

5.1 Security Analysis

To analyze the security of the proposed scheme, we assume that an attacker could obtain the values stored in the smart card by some means[8-10]. Here, we only discuss the forgery attack, password guessing attack, and the insider attack.

Forgery Attack

The attacker can extract the secret values B_i, b from the legal user's smart card by some means and intercept the login message $\{ID_i, C_1, C_2, T_1\}$ between the user and the remote server. Without knowing the U_i's password, the attacker attempts to make the forged message $\{ID_i, C_1^*, C_2^*, T_1^*\}$. However, the attacker cannot compute $C_2^*=B_i \oplus h(A_i \oplus T_1)$, because the attacker does not know the remote server's secret value x and the U_i's password PW_i. Hence, the attacker has no chance to login by launching the user impersonation attack. Also the attacker has no chance to authenticate by launching the server masquerading attack, because the attacker cannot compute the $C_3^*=h(A_i^* \oplus B_i^* \oplus T_2)$ for making the forged message $\{C_3^*, T_2^*\}$. Therefore, the proposed scheme is secure for the user impersonation attack and the server masquerading attack.

Password Guessing Attack

The attacker can extract the secret values B_i, b from the legal user's smart card by some means. Then the attacker attempts to derive the U_i's password PW_i using $B_i=h(A_i \oplus h(PW_i))$ in the registration phase. However, the attacker cannot guess the U_i's password PW_i using the secret values extracted from the legal user's smart card, because the attacker does not know the remote server's secret value x. Therefore, the proposed scheme is secure for the off-line password guessing attack.

Insider Attack

In the registration phase, if U_i's password PW_i is revealed to S, the insider of S may directly obtain PW_i and impersonate U_i to access U_i's other accounts in other server if U_i use the same password for the other accounts. Therefore, the proposed scheme is secure for the insider attack, because this scheme asks U_i to submit $h(b \oplus PW_i)$ instead of PW_i to S.

From the above discussions, the security analysis of Chang-Lee's scheme and the proposed scheme is summarized in Table 1. The proposed scheme is relatively more secure than Chang-Lee's scheme. In addition, the proposed scheme provides a mutual authentication between the user and the server.

Table 1. Comparison of Chang-Lee's scheme and the proposed scheme

Security Feature	Chang-Lee's scheme	The proposed scheme
forgery attack	Yes	No
password guessing attack	Yes	No
insider attack	Yes	No
mutual authentication	No	Yes

5.2 Performance Evaluations

In this section, we evaluate the efficiency of the proposed scheme in terms of the computational complexities by comparing with Chang-Lee's scheme. In Table 2, it is clear that the proposed scheme is more efficient than Chang-Lee's scheme.

Table 2. Comparison of Chang-Lee's scheme and the proposed scheme

Phase	Chang-Lee's scheme	The proposed scheme
Registration phase	3TH	2TH+3TX
Login phase	4TH+3TX	3TH+5TX
Authentication phase	7TH+5TX	5TH+8TX

* TH: the time for performing a one-way hash function, TX: the time for performing a exclusive-OR computation.

6 Conclusions

In this paper, we analyzed the security weaknesses of Chang-Lee's scheme. Although Chang-Lee's scheme overcame the vulnerability of Wu-Chieu's scheme, we have shown that Chang-Lee's scheme is still insecure against the forgery attack and password guessing attack, etc. Also, we proposed the improved scheme to overcome these security weaknesses, while preserving all their merits, even if the secret information stored in the smart card is revealed. As a result of security analysis, the proposed scheme is secure against the forgery attack and password guessing attack, etc. And the performance of the proposed scheme is more efficient than that of Chang-Lee's scheme in terms of the computational complexities.

References

1. Lamport, L.: Password Authentication with Insecure Communication. Communications of the ACM 24(11), 770–772 (1981)
2. Hwang, M.S., Li, L.H.: A New Remote User Authentication Scheme Using Smart Cards. IEEE Transactions on Consumer Electronics 46, 28–30 (2000)
3. Sun, H.M.: An Efficient Remote User Authentication Scheme Using Smart Cards. IEEE Transactions on Consumer Electronics 46(4), 958–961 (2000)
4. Wu, S.T., Chieu, B.C.: A User Friendly Remote Authentication Scheme with Smart Cards. Computers & Security 22(6), 457–550 (2003)
5. Yoon, E.J., Ryu, E.K., Yoo, K.Y.: Further Improvements of an Efficient Password based Remote User Authentication Scheme Using Smart Cards. IEEE Transactions on Consumer Electronics 50(2), 612–614 (2004)
6. Yang, C.C., Wang, R.C.: Cryptanalysis of a User Friendly Remote Authentication Scheme with Smart Cards. Computers & Security 223(5), 425–427 (2004)
7. Chang, C.C., Lee, C.Y.: A Friendly Password Mutual Authentication Scheme for Remote Login Network Systems. International Journal of Multimedia and Ubiquitous Engineering 3(1), 59–63 (2008)
8. Kocher, P.C., Jaffe, J., Jun, B.: Differential Power Analysis. In: Wiener, M. (ed.) CRYPTO 1999. LNCS, vol. 1666, pp. 388–397. Springer, Heidelberg (1999)
9. Messerges, T.S., Dabbish, E.A., Sloan, R.H.: Examining Smart-Card Security under the Threat of Power Analysis Attacks. IEEE Transactions on Computers 51(5), 541–552 (2002)
10. Brier, E., Clavier, C., Olivier, F.: Correlation Power Analysis with a Leakage Model. In: Joye, M., Quisquater, J.-J. (eds.) CHES 2004. LNCS, vol. 3156, pp. 16–29. Springer, Heidelberg (2004)

Context-Awareness Smart Safety Monitoring System Using Sensor Network

Joon-Mo Yang, Jun-Yong Park, So-Young Im, Jung-Hwan Park, and Ryum-Duck Oh*

Department of Computer science and Information Engineering
Chung-ju National University, Chungju-si, Korea
{greatyjm,pjy1418,gray474}@gmail.com,
jeyhpark@telecomland.co.kr, rdoh@cjnu.ac.kr

Abstract. In recent times, the human-centered information society is changing into Ubiquitous Sensor Network computing society, where information between objects can be combined organically and utilized. An accurate context awareness reasoning proceeds with use of the ontology with possible exact association with objects and meaning. This uses data of the users' surrounding environment to analyze or predict a situation and provides the basis for the accident prevention and the automation of the management system. Currently a variety of context awareness studies with many approaches are conducted in many fields. USN environment has been used in the field of context-awareness to reduce industrial accidents in various industrial settings and has proven to be effective as a precaution to frequent environmental disasters. This paper analyses many problems occurring in USN environment to prevent disasters at construction sites as part of industrial accidents and proposes measures to handle sensor nodes and wireless stream data. We also propose effective systems to reduce industrial accidents by showing industrial safety control system with smart objects and some detailed module structure.

Keywords: Ubiquitous Sensor Networks, Context-Aware, Stream Data High Speed Processing.

1 Introduction

In recent times, the human-centered information society is changing into Ubiquitous computing society, where information between things can be combined organically and utilized. USN refers to the possibility of ubiquitous computing system where sensors are attached to each object and sensed information is delivered using a wireless network. Such a USN technology is used to monitor various environments around us. In industrial settings, among them, USN technology is widely utilized to reduce industrial accidents. To apply such a USN technology in industrial settings,

* Corresponding author.

T.-h. Kim et al. (Eds.): MulGraB 2011, Part II, CCIS 263, pp. 270–277, 2011.

sensor nodes (which are used to collect data in industrial fields), middle wares (which are used to deal with the collected data), and GUI (Graphic User Interface: a control system which is available to provide a wealth of information to administrators) are required. In this paper, we propose industrial safety control system that can prevent industrial accidents and casualties using occupational safety smart objects with sensor nodes and cameras built in helmets or belts used in industrial settings. The requirements of the occupational safety control system using smart objects include high-speed sensor stream data technology (which is available to process in high speed sensor data in the form of stream coming from a number of sensors equipped in smart objects), management technology to manage objects in various industrial settings, and safety control system with intelligence service technologies combined using sensor data and context-awareness. This paper proposes the structure of industrial safety control system using smart objects and some detailed module structure and then proposes industrial safety control system-applied scenarios.

2 Related Research

2.1 Ontology

Ontology is a formal and explicit specification available to conceptualize a certain area of interest, which can be defined as 'a computational concept that specifies the clear statement and the relation of the conceptual structure.' It is a kind of data model that represents a specific area, which can be defined as a set of formal vocabularies that describe the relationship between concept and concept belonging to domain. In other words, it means to find a common thing from each object and explain in detail its meaning, use of the knowledge to demonstrate it in a set or category. The use of this characteristic of ontology enables an exact context aware computing as a basic data for context aware computing.

2.2 Context-Aware

The context aware computing was first discussed by Schilit and Theimer in 1994. Then it was defined as 'a software that is adaptive to the place of use, and a set of people or objects, and at the same time can accept such a change over time. At a later time, there were a number of definitions on it, but most of them focused on a particular aspect. Today, it is better defined as "a 'situation' in the process of providing appropriate information or service related to user's operation." The situations are, for example, image, temperature, humidity, or other data being sensed from industrial safety environment for the safety of workers. It gives an alarm or warning about dangerous environment to protect workers' safety, and for this, based on the data sensed, an alarm or warning sounds, which can be said as context awareness.

3 The Entire System Environment

The entire system environment can be divided into smart helmet (sensing information), smart belt (collecting the information sensed and sending the information to smart safety control system), and smart safety control system (sorting and sensing the information sensed and doing context-awareness). Sensors are attached to smart helmet to sense data around smart objects such as camera, temperature, humidity, etc. and the information sensed is sent to smart belt via Bluetooth. Smart belt is equipped with WLAN, which can send high-capacity battery and data that provide power to smart safety control system. At the heart of the system, there is a smart safety control system that classifies and processes data sensed from smart objects. The role of smart safety control system is to provide users with useful situational information and control information using sensed information and image data. For the flow of the entire data, various data around smart objects are sensed from smart helmets with sensors attached and the sensed data is collected and sent by smart belts. The sent data is sorted out and stored in smart safety control system, and those data are used as context-awareness data after an analysis. If the information analyzed is safe, it does not react, and if it is in danger, "caution" is alarmed or announced to the smart object. When a particular event occurs, it alarms the "accident" and informs the situation to the rescue team so that they can help to rescue victims. Besides, it allows administers to monitor the situation and thus they can determine danger in a passive way and make warnings and instructions.

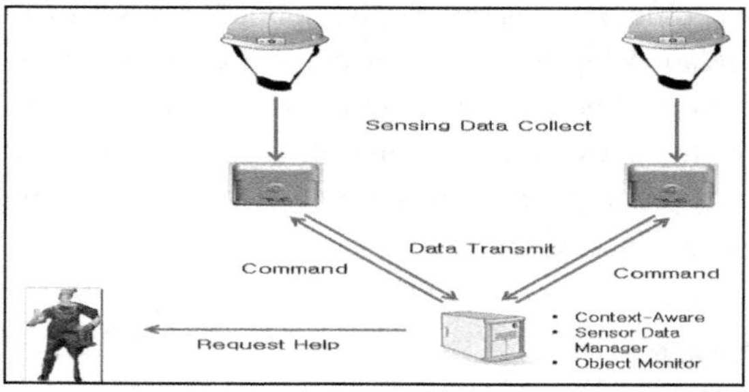

Fig. 1. The Entire System Environment

4 Smart Safety Monitoring System

Smart Safety Control System consists of interface manager(receiving sensed stream data from industrial safety setting using wireless communication system in a smart object worn by a worker in occupational safety environment), sensor data integration system (sorting stream data out and sending it to each processing module), image data processing, context-awareness system (doing situational awareness according to the relationship between each of the data), metadata manager (managing sensor node information), and GUI (industrial safety control that is used for administers to manage node information). For real-time processing, it is parallel processing in the form of thread.

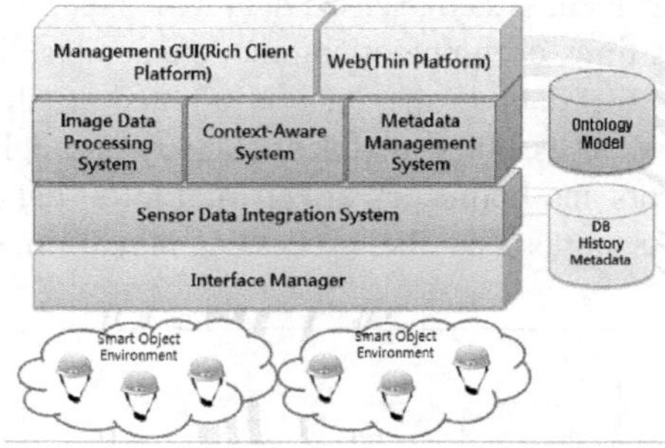

Fig. 2. Smart Safety Monitoring System

4.1 High-Speed Sensor Stream Data Processing Technology

In smart safety control system, data from various sensors in a large number of objects will occur from time to time. Such a continuous data stream requires high capacity processing and it causes a load of system memory and thus it is difficult to store and process the entire data. Therefore the control system, which needs to be processed in real time, requires high speed stream data processing technology. In this study, we use high speed sensor stream data processing technology that supports parallel processing, by the type of data, to handle various types of stream data in real-time and propose sensor data integration management system.

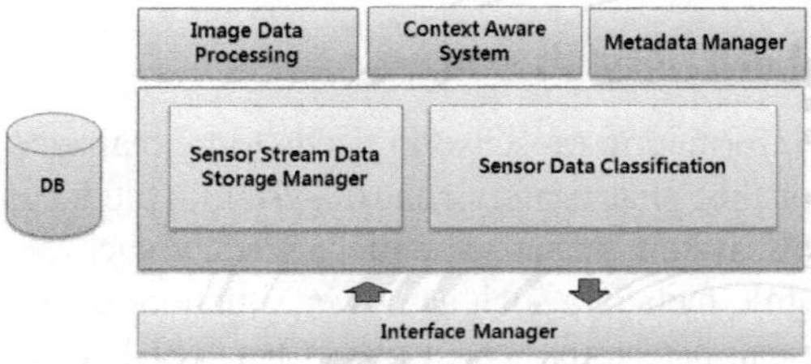

Fig. 3. Sensor Data Integration System

Sensor data integration management system acts to sort out and store smart object packets collected at smart belt, as shown in Figure 4 and processes image processing of classified data, situational awareness, and meta-data processing. It also has a separate sensor stream data storage administrator module, which is used to classify storage space and effectively store stream data continuously coming. At sensor data classifier, smart object packet, which is the stream data, is classified into each value depending on each type of sensor. The classified data is sent to image processing, context-awareness, and metadata management module.

High-speed sensor data processing technology is designed to be in parallel processing by configuring data processing module as independent type of thread in order to prevent bottleneck effect of stream data incoming in real time and delays, as shown in Figure 5. For data processing procedure, if stream data is classified at sensor data integration management system, sensed data will enter the queue according to the type of sensor. At this time, each processing module detects the data incoming in the queue and processes the data if the data is allotted to the queue. Multi-sensor processing technique reduces other modules' standby and delays in data processing caused by module errors and bottleneck effects of a lot of data sent from a variety of objects as each module supports parallel processing in real-time.

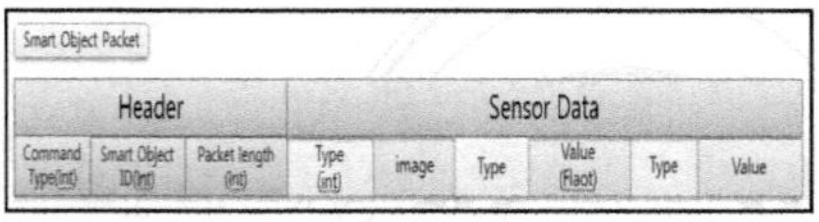

Fig. 4. Smart Object Packet

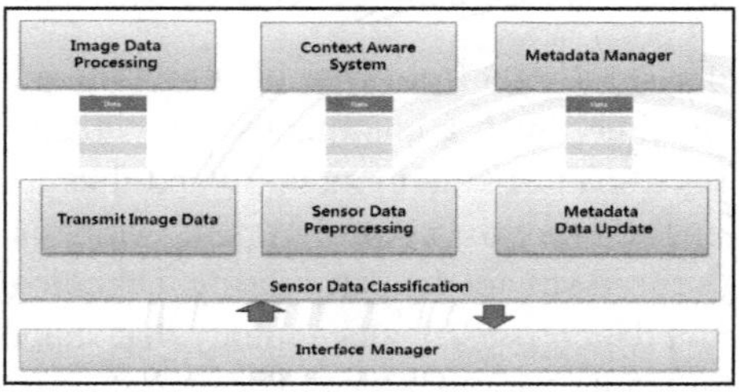

Fig. 5. Multi-sensor Data Processing Technique

4.2 Metadata Management System

Metadata (holding information on sensors) needs to be managed for the management of smart objects. For this, smart safety control system includes metadata management system module. This system manages static metadata such as object ID, hardware specs, etc and dynamic metadata such as power situation, object, GPS, etc. If we use static metadata, we can determine which object has which spec. and which function. The use of the dynamic metadata allows us to determine the region where an object is located and which object is located around. The management of such data provides an environment that can control smart object effectively. The metadata management system makes it possible to input static metadata and collect dynamic metadata, and it consists of modules to control storage and creation: Dynamic Metadata Collector module(collecting dynamic metadata), Static Metadata Console module(inputting static metadata), Metadata Storage Manager module(storing metadata and managing schema), and XML Generator module(creating metadata according to the standard specification). The industrial safety control system possesses such metadata management functions and we can use information on various objects and sensor nodes. From this, we can increase the accuracy of context-awareness data by increasing the quality of metadata.

4.3 Context-Aware System

This system uses a context-awareness system in order to cope with various accidents or disasters in industrial safety settings. The context-awareness aims to detect situational changes, provide users with appropriate information or service, and allow the system change its status by itself. The context-awareness system in Figure 5 uses sensed information entered by ontology model and inference rule to draw industrial safety situations. To do so, we need to have ontology model that is applicable in industrial safety settings and inference rule that is available to detect industrial safety situations. The typical examples of context-awareness in industrial safety situations are: if you get a sudden high value for the data sensed in the acceleration sensor at a staircase, it is considered as an accident in a fall or if you get a sudden high temperature in sharp change near the chemicals warehouse, it is estimated to be on fire. Like this, if we use a sensor, we can do an exact context-awareness based on inferences of an object's identification, place, and time and automate Safety Control.

5 Service Scenario

In industrial settings, we are always exposed to dangerous situations and serious accidents and disasters may occur. To prevent possible accidents, safety education, etc are held, but still they never stop and are not treated promptly. The application of smart safety control system may prevent possible accidents, treat accidents promptly, and prevent delays. The subsequent events are scenarios that can be expected by the application of smart safety control system: first situational awareness, warning to danger, and immediate dealing with the accident.

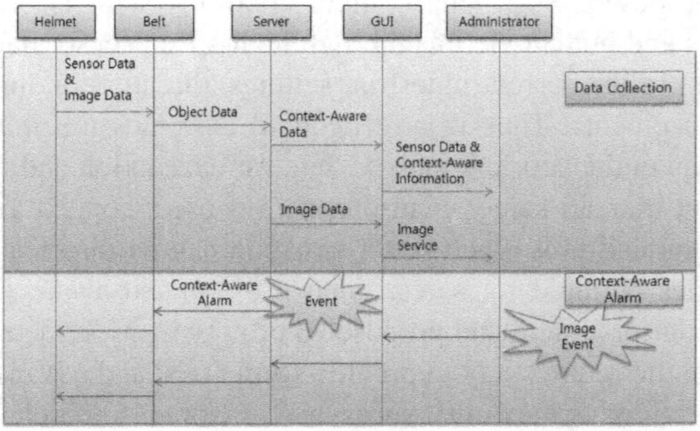

Fig. 6. Sequence

- Accident: The smart belt equipped in smart objects in industrial settings collects sensing data from many sensors attached to smart helmet and sends the data collected to smart safety control system. At this time, fire occurred, and data after accident is also sent to smart safety control system.

- Context Awareness and Introduction: If a packet is entered into smart safety control system, sensor stream storage administrator stores data. And it sends to image processing, context-awareness, and metadata manager module. If image data processed result is sent to industrial safety object monitor, image can be identified. Temperature sensing value continues to be over 90°C, and as a result of analysis in the context-awareness system it turned out to be a fire and should take a measure accordingly. If it may cause much damage in the surroundings such as gas leaks, GPS location can be identified at metadata manager and the danger is informed to a smart object in the adjacent field to the scene of the accident.
- Call for Help: We had casualties in industrial settings, and to rescue the injured, the accident location and the type of injury are informed to the rescue team based on the GPS data of the metadata transmitted from the injured and context-awareness. The rescue worker who received information on the injured from smart safety control system infers the approximate situation of the scene of the accident to rescue the injured and moves swiftly to the rescue.

6 Future Works and Conclusions

This work used USN and context-awareness and designed smart safety control system to guarantee the safety of smart objects in industrial settings. This work proposes high-speed sensor stream data processing technology that is available to process stream data in the industrial setting and modules subsequently in order to improve problems that might occur in the process of application of USN technology in Industrial Safety Control. The prototype of context-awareness technology in industrial settings is also proposed. Such smart safety control system is effective to reduce industrial disasters and human victims through high-speed sensor data processing and context-awareness. In the current industrial settings, directors or smart objects check the scene of the accidents. Thus it is difficult to take measure immediately. If gas leaks, smart objects in the surroundings are late for evacuation and thus can lead to a major accident, but if smart safety control system is used, context-awareness leads to an immediate action and thus much better situation can be directed. This paper used several technologies required for safety control of context-awareness system in the industrial safety control system and proposed a prototype. More detailed technologies should be added in the future study to provide specialized and advanced user interface in the industrial safety context-awareness and ongoing research will continue to improve the efficiency of industrial safety control.

Acknowledgement. The research was financially supported by the Ministry of Education, Science Technology (MEST) and National Research Foundation of Korea (NRF) through the Human Resource Training Project for Regional Innovation and the research was supported by a grant from the Academic Research Program of ChungJu National University in 2011.

References

1. Akyildiz, I.F., Su, W., Sankarasubramaniam, Y., Cayirci, E.: A survey on sensor networks. Computer Networks (2002)
2. Szewczyk, R., Mainwaring, A., Polastre, J., Culler, D.: An Analysis of a Large Scale Habitat Monitoring Application. In: Proc. ACM Conf. Embedded Netwoked Sensor Systems, pp. 214–226 (July 2004)
3. Chong, C.Y., Kumar, S.P.: Sensor Networks: Evolution, Opportunities, and Challenges. Proc. of the IEEE 91(8), 1247–1256 (2003)
4. Choi, J.-H., Park, Y.-T.: A Dynamic Service Supporting Model for Semantic Web-based Situation Awreness Service. KIISE Information Science 36(9), 732–748 (2009)
5. TTAK.KO-06.0168/R1 (USN Metadata Specification) (December 2009)
6. Dey, A.K.: Supporting the Construction of Context-Aware Applications. Dagstuhl seminar on Ubiquitous Computing (2001)
7. Korkea-Aho, M.: Context-Aware Applications Survey (2000), http://www.hut.fi/~mkorkeaa/doc/context-aware.html

Spectro-temporal Analysis of High-Speed Pulsed-Signals Based on On-Wafer Optical Sampling

Dong-Joon Lee, Jae-Yong Kwon, Tae-Weon Kang, and Joo-Gwang Lee

Center for Electromagnetic Wave, Korea Research Institute of Standards and Science, 1 Doryong-dong, Yuseong-gu, Daejeon 305-340, Korea
{dongjoonlee,jykwon,twkang,jglee}@kriss.re.kr

Abstract. We present a sampling technique that enables to explore transmission and reflection of fast electromagnetic pulses on a microstrip transmission line. Employing a minimally invasive optical sampling technique, temporal pulsed signals and the corresponding spectra are obtained for 20 GHz bandwidth.

Keywords: oscilloscope, electromagnetic pulse measurement, electro-optic sampling, pump-probe experiment.

1 Introduction

In accordance with the rapid growth of multimedia technology, the demands for high speed signal and bandwidth enhancement are consistently increasing. As higher speed signal transmission is advantageous for larger channel capacity and data throughput, modern communication and multimedia transmission lines evolve to more compact and faster schemes. To investigate the performance of high-speed devices or lines, vector network analyzers (VNA) or sampling oscilloscopes have been widely employed. These instruments are generally supposed to measure signals at specified terminals having connectorized interfaces. Not only such port-to-port analyses, in many cases, it is also important for system diagnosis to observe signals between ports. On-wafer probe measurement has served as a standard method for this but it still contains inherent limitations such as bandwidth and invasiveness due to the nature of metallic tip use. To address this issue, we present an optical sampling technique to realize significantly less invasive and advantageous measurement for higher bandwidth signal analysis in both time and spectral domains.

2 Optical Sampling System for High-Speed Pulsed Signals

To overcome the conventional bandwidth of electronic measurement systems, the electro-optic (EO) sampling technique has become a viable solution [1-4]. Figure 1 is our EO system optimized for 20 GHz bandwidth signals. The system employs a femto-second scale pulsed laser with ~0.1 ps duration and 80 MHz pulse repetition frequency (PRF). We split the pulses half and one is used as excitation beam to generate 20 GHz EM pulses through a fast photodiode. The other half pulses serve as

T.-h. Kim et al. (Eds.): MulGraB 2011, Part II, CCIS 263, pp. 278–283, 2011.

optical sampling beam which can be temporally overlapped with the EM pulses with a delay line. As the EM signal and optical sampling pulse reconcile in the EO sensor medium, the polarization of the original sampling pulse becomes modulated according to the EM pulse. This modulated polarization indicates the amount of EM-optical pulse interaction with respect to the temporal position of the sampling pulse. Translating the stepper motor in the sampling path, the sampling pulse can sweep the EM pulse across. Thus, the original EM pulse waveform can be plotted on a PC screen by reconstructing the sampled trace.

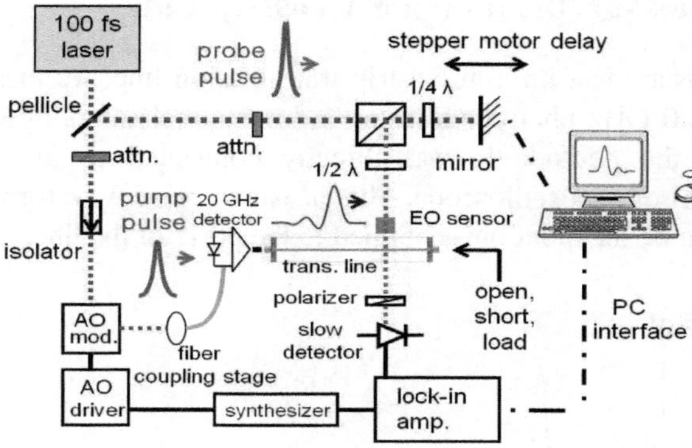

Fig. 1. Fast EM pulse measurement system based on electro-optic sampling

3 Spectro-temporal Pulse Analysis of a Transmission Line

We fabricated a wideband microstrip transmission line for 20 GHz signal transmission as illustrated in Fig. 2. The line is 200 mm long and designed to deliver up to 20 GHz signals. The generalized transmission field at l is expressed as Eq. (1).

$$T(l)=\frac{t_1 e^{ik(l)}\left(1-r_2 e^{2ik(L-l)}\right)}{1-\Gamma_{in} r_2 e^{2ik(L)}}. \tag{1}$$

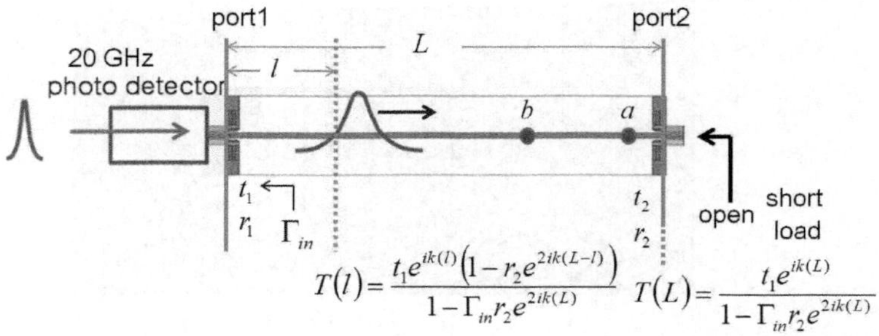

Fig. 2. Signal transfer in a microstrip transmission line. (t and r are the Fresnel field transmission coefficients at each port. Γ_{in} is an equivalent reflection coefficient to port1. $T(l)$ is the transmission fields at location l.) (a and b are points to be measured.)

The transmission field $T(l)$ is an infinite geometric series including multiple reflections from both terminals. However, in this case, port1 is well-matched with the source photodiode thus the t_l~1 and Γ_{in}~0. Hence, the main field component at the arbitrary point l is re-expressed as $1\text{-}r_2exp(2ik(L\text{-}l))$. It should be noted that the first term (i.e., 1) is the normalized incident pulse component and the rest is the reflective term from port2. These two are major field components that govern the both temporal and spectral responses over the transmission line at the points of interest.

4 Pulse Measurement on a Microstrip Line

Prior to the measurement on a microstrip transmission line, we measured the output pulse from the 20 GHz photodiode using a commercial sampling oscilloscope. The output port of the photodiode was directly connected to the 2.4 mm coaxial measurement port of the oscilloscope. The measured pulse waveform is shown in Fig. 3(a) and this is to be the input pulse applied to the port1 of the line.

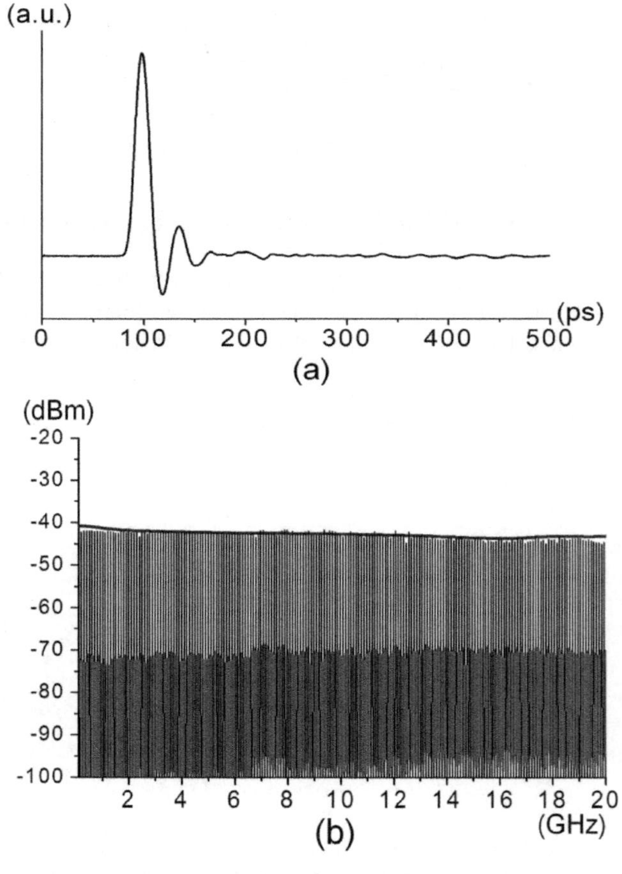

Fig. 3. Response of a 20 GHz photodiode. (a) temporal response (b) spectral response with FFT spectral envelope (solid line).

The rising and falling time of the pulse are 10.0 ps and 12.5 ps, respectively. Such fast transition time corresponds to 28~35 GHz of 3 dB bandwidth. In fact, the solid line in Fig. 3(b) is the calculated spectrum of the pulse by FFT algorithm. The spectrum basically matches well with the envelope of the measured one by a commercial spectrum analyzer. (The spectrum is filled with 80 MHz of fine RF comb which is due to the PRF of the laser.) Both spectra degrade less than 3 dB at 20 GHz as expected.

Verified from such a pulse-spectrum transform and measurement by certified instruments, now we can measure the pulses over the transmission line at arbitrary and portless points utilizing our EO system. First, we tried a point near port2 (point *a* in Fig. 2) with various port2 terminations. The pulse1, 2 and 3 are the respective case of 50 ohm, open and short terminations with a 2.4 mm calibration kit. In any cases, the primary incident pulses are identical whereas their reflections are quite different for terminations.

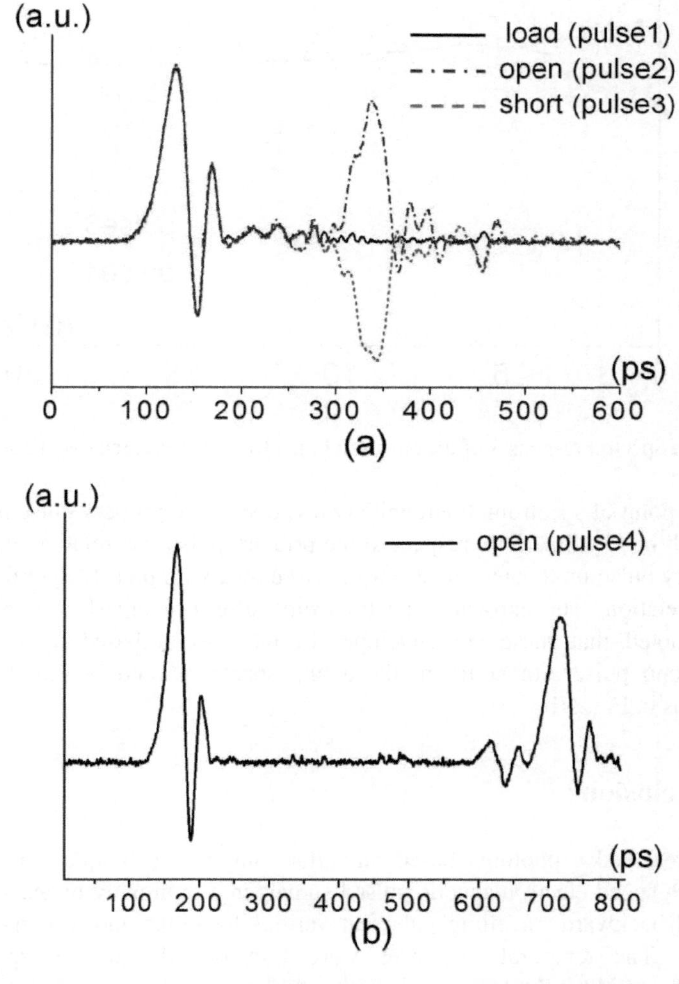

Fig. 4. Pulse measurements (a) at point *a* in Fig. 2 with various terminations (b) at point *b* in Fig. 2 with open termination

Figure 4 exhibits useful information of the transmission line. The waveform of the primary pulse – compared to the original pulse as in Fig. 3(a) – indicates dispersive characteristics of the line as propagates. For instance, the pulses measured at the closer position from port1 (point *b* in Fig. 2) is shown in Fig. 4(b). The incident pulse is less dispersive as it is closer to the original pulse in Fig. 3(a) while the reflected one becomes more separated and attenuated as it travels longer. In addition, the relative relations between primary and secondary (reflected) pulses – such as temporal separation, waveform broadening, amplitude contrast and phase difference – heavily influence the spectral response of the pulses.

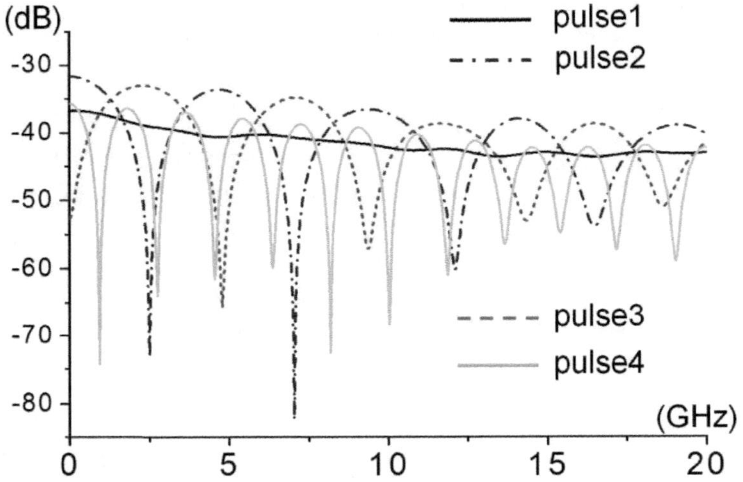

Fig. 5. Spectral responses of the pulses in Fig. 4 by FFT. (with relative dB scale)

From the point of spectrum, the relatively less dispersive primary pulse is in charge of the overall bandwidth. With respect to the primary pulse, the relative amplitude of the secondary pulse modulates the spectrum associated with their temporal separation and phase relation. The extracted spectra from pulse 1~4 are shown in Fig. 5. It should be noted that these are envelopes of the spectra based on primary and secondary-echo pulses. In addition, the actual spectra should be filled with PRF combs as was in Fig. 3(b).

5 Conclusions

We have presented a photonic based on-wafer sampling technique that enables to measure high-speed electromagnetic pulsed signals in a minimally invasive way. The forward and backward travelling pulses at various locations and terminations were investigated. The temporal responses were transformed into the spectra after presenting the validity of transform algorithm through certified instruments. Utilizing this technique to explore the pulse propagation along the transmission line with known standard terminations, more detailed data for transmission line analysis and unknown mismatch calculation are to be presented at the conference.

References

1. Williams, D.F., Hale, P.D., Clement, T.S., Morgan, J.M.: Calibrated 200-GHz waveform measurement. IEEE Trans. Microwave Theory Tech. 53, 1384–1388 (2005)
2. Seitz, S., Bieler, M., Spitzer, M.: Optoelectronic measurement of the transfer function and time response of a 70 GHz sampling oscilloscope. Meas. Sci. Technol. 16, L7–L9 (2005)
3. Ito, H., Minamide, H.: Ultra-broadband THz-wave generation and detection. In: Conference on Optoelectronics and Communications, pp. 528–529 (2010)
4. Ma, Z., Ma, H., Gong, P., Yang, C., Feng, K.: Ultrafast optoelectronic technology for radio metrology applications. J. Syst. Eng. 21, 461–468 (2010)

e-Test System Based Speech Recognition for Blind Users

Myung-Jae Lim*, Eun-Young Jung, and Ki-Young Lee

Department of Medical IT and Marketing, Eulji University,
553, Sanseong-daero, Sueong-gu, Seongnam-si, Gyeonggi-do, 461-713, Korea
lk04@eulji.ac.kr, wdd0523@naver.com, kylee@eulji.ac.kr

Abstract. The voice is the most basic means of interaction among people. If it is combined with computer, blind users are provided with more information and convenience. Also, it will develop e-learning, which is customized education in field of Internet-based services, to improve environmental education. The purpose of this paper is the employment in many different fields for blind users and provides e-learning education to overcome this terrible situation..

Keywords: Blind user, e-Lerning, Fourier transform.

1 Introduction

The voice communication is one of the tools to express your opinion. Also, It is superior to other methods in terms of convenience and economics. Phonetic features can provide more information to communicate between people and computers by combining the computers. If you are using to overcome the visual disadvantage, you will be able to expect great educative result to apply internet-based and related services sector. Therefore, the purpose of this paper is to design Question Answering System using a voice for blind users to expect educative result through e-learning system. And it is the employment in many different fields for blind users and provides e-learning education to overcome this terrible situation. Consequentially, we can see a higher level of participation by community.

According to the study related to blind user employment, if blind users are provided with appropriate system, environment, service support, and assistive technology, they will perform tasks well. Compared to people in general, the blind people have low levels of space judgment, shape perception, and physical intelligence. On the other hand, they possess similar or higher level of learning ability, linguistic skills, numeracy, and work perceptivity. In other words, blind users have advantage on task based knowledge such as learning ability, linguistic skills, numeracy, and work perceptivity.

One of the assistive technology, e-Test systems will be able to offer blind users with improved skill and convenience. Blind user takes an examination in braille or provided with expanded test paper. but, cheongsubeop is uncomfortable because of read several times over. However, the employment of the blinds are limited, such as to a massage service. Therefore, e-Test system provides wide range of opportunities for employment.

* Corresponding author.

T.-h. Kim et al. (Eds.): MulGraB 2011, Part II, CCIS 263, pp. 284–289, 2011.

2 Related Works

2.1 Voice Recognition Technology

Voice Recognition Technology has an intention of make the machines that can perform the appropriate actions to interpret human language. Recently, The development of this technology provides better interface environment than before. Especially, according to practical use of Speech Recognition System, application that can be useful in real life are being developed. Voice Recognition Technology recognizes many other words and has developed cognition performance. Therefore, developed country has conducted continuously various studies.

Since each person's voice is different, the program cannot possibly contain a template for each potential user, so the program must first be "trained" with a new user's voice input before that user's voice can be recognized by the program. During a training session, the program displays a printed word or phrase, and the user speaks that word or phrase several times into a microphone. The program computes a statistical average of the multiple samples of the same word and stores the averaged sample as a template in a program data structure. With this approach to voice recognition, the program has a "vocabulary" that is limited to the words or phrases used in the training session, and its user base is also limited to those users who have trained the program. This type of system is known as "speaker dependent." It can have vocabularies on the order of a few hundred words and short phrases, and recognition accuracy can be about 98 percent.

A more general form of voice recognition is available through feature analysis and this technique usually leads to "speaker-independent" voice recognition. Instead of trying to find an exact or near-exact match between the actual voice input and a previously stored voice template, this method first processes the voice input using "Fourier transforms" or "linear predictive coding (LPC)", then attempts to find characteristic similarities between the expected inputs and the actual digitized voice input. These similarities will be present for a wide range of speakers, and so the system need not be trained by each new user. The types of speech differences that the speaker-independent method can deal with, but which pattern matching would fail to handle, include accents, and varying speed of delivery, pitch, volume, and inflection. Speaker-independent speech recognition has proven to be very difficult, with some of the greatest hurdles being the variety of accents and inflections used by speakers of different nationalities. Recognition accuracy for speaker-independent systems is somewhat less than for speaker-dependent systems, usually between 90 and 95 percent.

2.2 FFT, Fast Fourier Transform

This document describes the Discrete Fourier Transform (DFT), that is, a Fourier Transform as applied to a discrete complex valued series. The mathematics will be given and source code (written in the C programming language) is provided in the appendices. For a continuous function of one variable f(t), the Fourier Transform F(f) will be defined as:

$$F(f) = \int_{-\infty}^{\infty} f(t)\, e^{-j2\pi ft}\, dt \tag{1}$$

and the inverse transform as

$$f(t) = \int_{-\infty}^{\infty} F(f)\, e^{j2\pi ft}\, df \tag{2}$$

where j is the square root of -1 and e denotes the natural exponent

$$e^{j\varnothing} = \cos(\varnothing) + j\sin(\varnothing). \tag{3}$$

2.3 e-Learning

E-learning comprises all forms of electronically supported learning and teaching. The information and communication systems, whether networked learning or not, serve as specific media to implement the learning process.
The term will still most likely be utilized to reference out-of-classroom and in-classroom educational experiences via technology, even as advances continue in regard to devices and curriculum.

E-learning is essentially the computer and network-enabled transfer of skills and knowledge. e-learning applications and processes include Web-based learning, computer-based learning, virtual education opportunities and digital collaboration. Content is delivered via the Internet, intranet/extranet, audio or video tape, satellite TV, and CD-ROM. It can be self-paced or instructor-led and includes media in the form of text, image, animation, streaming video and audio.

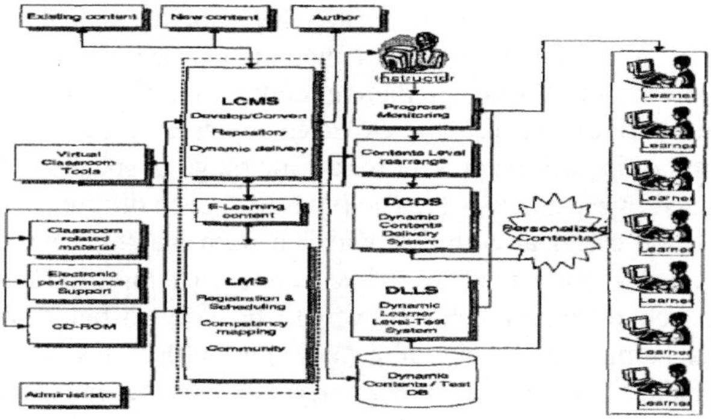

Fig. 1. e-Learning System

3 e-Test System

3.1 Outline of e-Test System

E-Test system is based on records voice information data to build the DB and provides effective training effect for users. E-Test system is the process like figure2. It goes through the process to receive basic information for users and to extract voice through conversion FFT spectrum. The data through conversion FFT spectrum is contributed to increase the accuracy of system owing to the many data through the saved DB data. The result of comparative analysis reduces margin of error and the user is reminded through translated voice. It will assist more effective imaginary answer papers for blind user and increase learning effect of e-learning through communication with computer.

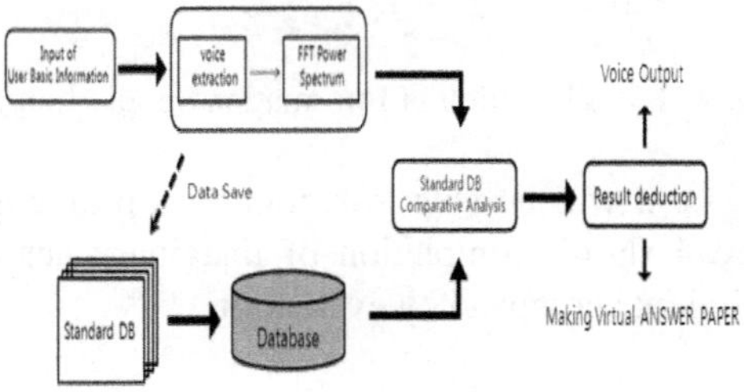

Fig. 2. e-Test System Process

3.2 e-Test System Design and Implementation

The voice input through microphone is manufactured into necessary information that is converted digital signal by use FFT method through A/D converter. The precondition that the noise does not occur for set up removal noise environment is needed. This way can progress e-Test through voice recognition information.

First of all, execution of e-Test has progressed to input user basic information to obtain the identity. Figure 3 shows interface about user basic information. The basic information is received through keyboard and results of input make sure that the input data is accurate as read system. Also, the degree of completion about imaginary answer papers increases as user saves basic information. After listening to the question or information, data can be collected by recording answer.

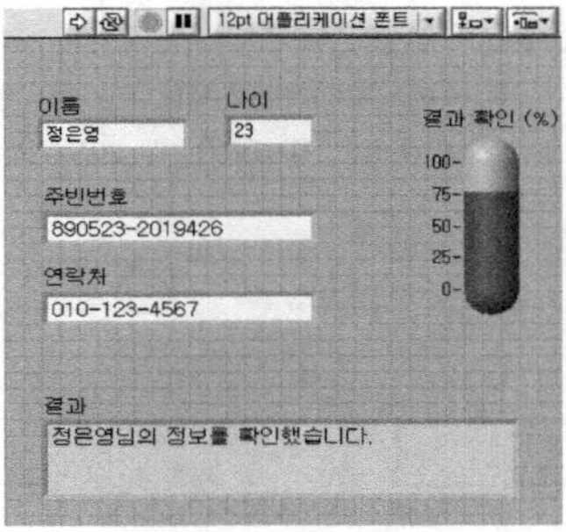

Fig. 3. Basic Information Interface

As you can see in figure 4, a correct answer was derived by adding buttons for adjusting the volume and replay to reduce mistakes on listening to question or information. It must input information required system because the answers are not always the ideal. In other words, e-Test system needs the role to remove unnecessary noise in recognition course.

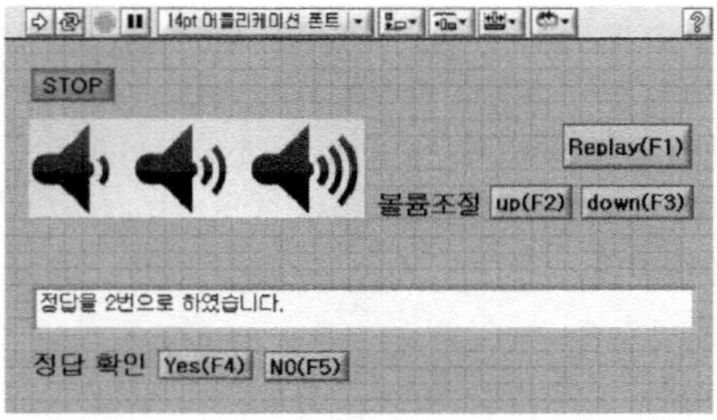

Fig. 4. Extra Function of Information Supply Interface

According to process, it will be able to recognize a problem and write imaginary answer papers. Figure 4 shows completion of imaginary answer paper. There is a possible ability of individual competency evaluation.

3.3 Consideration of e-Test System

If e-learning system is combined e-test system, it is effective aspect of tool for teachability estimation. Personal Security Environment has to be forged to secure the information written on imaginary answer paper through e-Test system. The plan has to draw up to prevent data spill because of saved personal information.

4 Experiment Process and Result

4.1 Experiment Process

As in this Figure 5, the system is proceeded through the following process. During the execution of system, the question about the visually impaired is being asked in part of study evaluation. The user feeds information to make basic information DB for imaginary answer paper. When you are finished entering information, it is possible to listen to question or information. The users can listen to by adjusting the volume and replay button to reduce mistake.

Introduction of e-Test system can increase the number of test-taker(the blind user) of licensing examinations or state examination and it will be provided with an improved environment.

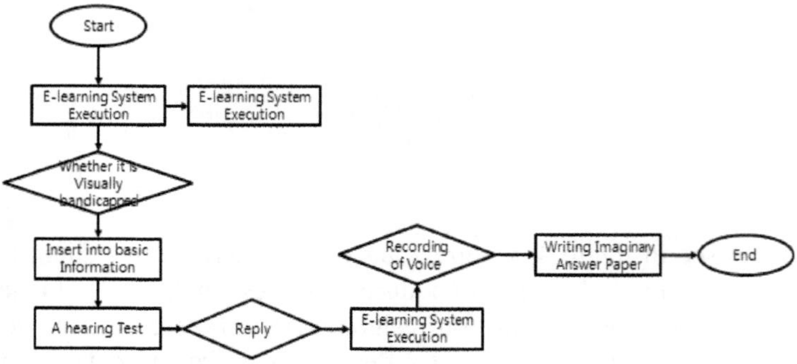

Fig. 5. Flow Chart of e-Test System

4.2 Result of Experiment

The table 1 shows that e-Test system has been improved over conventional methods. The braille book has weakness that users who have not learned braille can not take the test. Also, it weakens objectivity compared to ordinary person because it increases test time. If you are placed on probation by cheongsubeop, question awareness environment is dependent and inefficient methods.

Table 1. Comparative Analysis of System

	Braille Book	Cheong Subeop	e-test System
Problem Cognition Envirnment	Normal	Poor	Good
The incidence for Wrong Anser	Good	Normal	Normal
Test Time	Normal	Poor	Good
Judgment of Independence	Good	Normal	Good

5 Conclusion

E-Test system is speech recognition system for blind user to communicate with computer. Learning ability through obstacle is to be conquered by system based of voice recognition. Introduction of e-Test system can increase test-taker(the blind user) of licensing examinations or state examination and it will be provided an improve environment.

Consequentially, it is possible to method of individual learning although they are blind users. Also, it is increase of employment in many different fields for blind users and provides e-learning education for overcome this terrible situation.

References

1. Kerkman, L.: Convenience of Online Education Attracts Midcareer Students. Chronicle of Philanthropy 16(6), 11–12 (2004); retrieved from Academic Search Premier database
2. Nagy, A.: The Impact of E-Learning. In: Bruck, P.A., Buchholz, A., Karssen, Z., Zerfass, A. (eds.) E-Content: Technologies and Perspectives for the European Market, pp. 79–96. Springer, Berlin (2005)
3. Allen, I.E., Seaman, J.: Staying the Course: Online Education in the United States, 2008. Sloan Consortium, Needham (2008)
4. Allen, I.E., Seaman, J.: Sizing the Opportunity: The Quality and Extent of Online Education in the United States, 2002 and 2003. The Sloan Consortium, Wellesley (2003)
5. Adams, Russ: Sourcebook of Automatic Identification and Data Collection. Van Nostrand Reinhold, New York (1990); Yannakoudakis, E. J., Hutton, P. J.: Speech Synthesis and Recognition Systems. Ellis Horwood Limited, Chichester (1987)
6. Tavangarian, D., Leypold, M., Nölting, K., Röser, M.: Is e-learning the Solution for Individual Learning. Journal of e-learning (2004)
7. Assessment, Ellis Horwood Limited, Chichester, UK (1989)

Improving the Wi-Fi Channel Scanning Using a Decentralized IEEE 802.21 Information Service

Fabio Buiati[1], Luis Javier García Villalba[1], Delfín Rupérez Cañas[1], and Tai-hoon Kim[2,3]

[1] Group of Analysis, Security and Systems (GASS)
Department of Software Engineering and Artificial Intelligence
School of Computer Science, Office 431
Universidad Complutense de Madrid (UCM)
Calle Profesor José García Santesmases s/n
Ciudad Universitaria, 28040 Madrid, Spain
{fabio,javiergv,delfinrc}@fdi.ucm.es
[2] Department of Multimedia Engineering
Hannam University
133 Ojeong-dong, Daedeok-gu
Daejeon, Korea
taihoonn@hannam.ac.kr
[3] Department of Information Technologies
Global Vision School Australia (GVSA)
20 Virgina Court, Sandy Bay
Tasmania, Australia
taihoonn@gvsa.asia

Abstract. Today, the possibility of ubiquitous mobility for data transport is both a reality and a challenge. The access can be made through different wireless technologies, e.g. Wi-Fi, Wi-Max and 3GPP networks. In the heterogeneous wireless environment, the network information discovery phase has a significant effect on the handover latency, especially discovering Wi-Fi networks. In this paper, we propose a new network discovery scheme using the IEEE 802.21 Media Independent Information Service (MIIS). In the proposed scheme, a Mobile Node (MN) obtains channel information from neighbor networks from a MIIS server and performs a selective scanning. Our idea introduces the notion of regional mobility areas, managed by different MIIS servers, in a decentralized way. The simulation results show that the proposed scheme enhances the MN´s performance if compared with the traditional scanning schemes.

Keywords: Mobility, IEEE 802.21, Scanning, Heterogeneous Networks, decentralized.

1 Introduction

In the emerging heterogeneous wireless environments, the MN can move between networks or access points (AP) in which the network information discovery phase is

T.-h. Kim et al. (Eds.): MulGraB 2011, Part II, CCIS 263, pp. 290–294, 2011.

highly critical, especially in Wi-Fi networks. Usually, the MN listens to see if there is a wireless LAN within range. This process of listening is called scanning. The problem is that scanning all the channels (full scanning) is very time and battery-level consuming [1]. In a Wi-Fi network deployment, several channels are expected to be empty, to reduce the interference between adjacent APs. Skipping empty channels can reduce the Wi-Fi AP discovery delay. So, the scanning delay can be reduced by simple refining the scanning procedure to a limited set of channels, denoted selective scanning.

We propose the use of the IEEE 802.21 MIIS [2] to improve the Wi-Fi channel scanning procedure. The main goal of MIIS usage is to allow the MN to acquire a global view of all heterogeneous networks information within a geographical area.

The proposed solution considers the splitting of the network coverage in regional mobility areas, managed by different MIIS servers, in a decentralized way. Using such a technique, the MN receives detailed channel information only related to its general neighborhood, even without using any location service or Global Positioning System (GPS) equipment. Upon receiving the information from the MIIS server, the MN performs a selective scanning. The remainder of the paper is organized as follows. Section 2 provides a brief description of the related work. Section 3 presents the proposed scanning scheme. Then, a performance evaluation is described in Section 4. Finally, Section 5 concludes the paper.

2 Related Work

Several works have been published to reduce the scanning delays using the MIIS server [3-5]. In [3] the authors proposed a WLAN discovery scheme by exploiting channel and location information of the networks. [4] suggested an enhanced MIIS server in which channel conditions are estimated using spatial and temporal locality, with the objective of minimizing the channel scanning delays. Finally, in [5], a decision algorithm of target network and fast L2 handover scheme using the location information of MN is proposed.

However, in these previous works, one common assumption is that the MN and APs have a GPS or other location service equipment in order to communicate with the MIIS server and obtain channel-related information. Our overall idea differs from the existing works in point of that the MN without any location service equipment can obtain channel information from the MIIS server in a geographical area, taking the advantage of use of a decentralized MIIS architecture.

3 Proposed Wi-Fi Scanning Scheme Using a Decentralized MIIS

In order to reduce the Wi-Fi scanning delay, we specify a new selective scanning using a decentralized MIIS architecture, as illustrated in Fig.1. The architecture is composed by two important elements: regional mobility areas (RMA) consisting of several Wi-Fi APs and regional MIIS servers (RMIIS) that manage each one of the RMA. Detailed procedures are as follows.

1) In the bootstrapping, the MN connects to an available network and receives channel-related information about APs in the same RMA from the RMIIS.
2) In the movement from one network coverage to another, the MN receives a link detected trigger (since the MN monitors signal quality of associated Wi-Fi APs). Upon detecting a new AP, it looks inside the RMA information.
3) If the detected AP belongs to the same RMA, no additional channel information is necessary, because the MN stores enough channel information from the RMA, previously provided by the RMIIS server.
4) Belonging to a different RMA (MN is crossing two different RMAs), the MN sends a *MIH Get information request* message to the RMIIS server including the detected AP identifier. The RMIIS server is able to contact the target RMIIS that holds information from the detected AP. Then, it replies with *MIH Get Information response* message containing a list of channels currently used by nearby APs within the new RMA (where the MN is moving to). After receiving the response from the RMIIS server, the MN constructs a list of valid used channels.
5) If a handover is triggered (e.g. link going down), a selective scan in the channels provided in (1) or in (4) is performed.

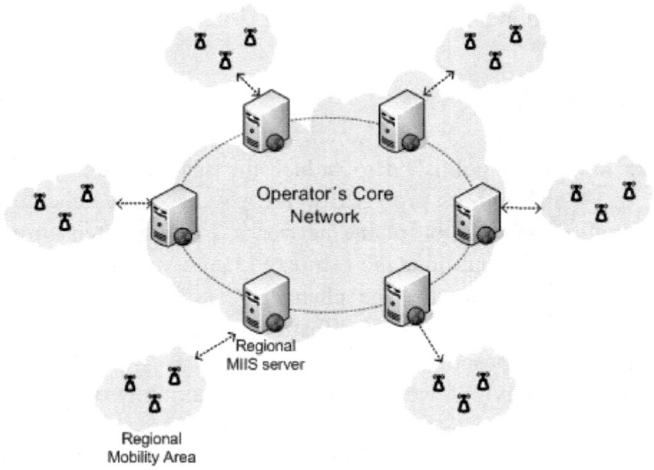

Fig. 1. A decentralized MIIS architecture

4 Performance Evaluation

We have evaluated our proposal using the NS-2[6]. The scenario is composed by four RMAs, with a variable number of APS (1 to 10). The used channel numbers are 1, 6 and 11. We compare three different scanning strategies (shown in Fig. 2):

1) Full Passive Scanning: expressed by (number of channels x beacon interval (around 100ms)). Therefore, scanning 11 channels might take 1.1s.

2) Full Active Scanning: the MN broadcasts probe requests messages and waits at least a *MinChannelTime* (set as 17ms). If any response arrives, the MN waits for a *MaxChannelTime* (30ms). This is done for each Wi-Fi channel. The MN needs 330ms to perform this scanning method.
3) RMA Selective Scanning: the MN requests information from the RMIIS server and only scans the used channels by the neighbors APs in the RMA. We also take in account the delay to get information from the RMIIS server, approximately 24ms. The RMA scanning delay varies from 54 ms up to 114ms, for the lowest and biggest number of APs in each RMA, respectively.

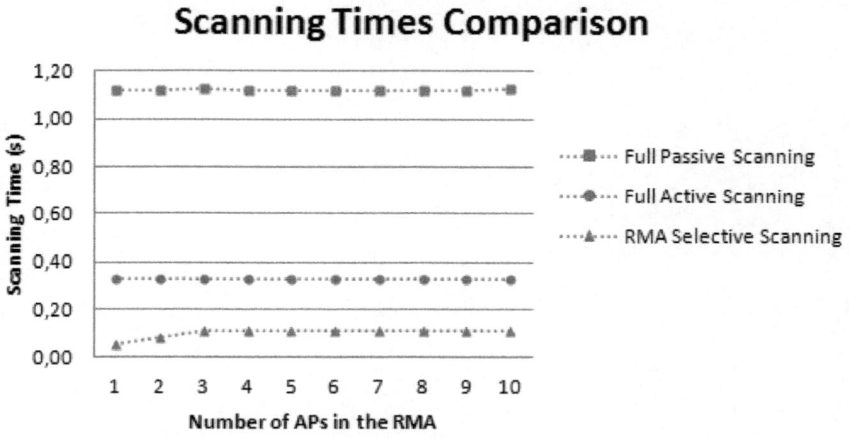

Fig. 2. Full scanning x Selective scanning times

5 Conclusion

This paper presented a scheme to reduce the Wi-Fi channel scanning using a decentralized MIIS architecture. The results show that the proposed can refine the traditional Wi-Fi scanning schemes.

Acknowledgments. This work was supported by the Ministerio de Industria, Turismo y Comercio (MITyC, Spain) through the Project Avanza Competitividad I+D+I TSI-020100-2010-482 and the Ministerio de Ciencia e Innovación (MICINN, Spain) through the Project TEC2010-18894/TCM. This work was also supported by the Security Engineering Research Center, granted by the Ministry of Knowledge Economy (MKE, Korea).

References

1. Murray, D., Dixon, M., Koziniec, T.: Scanning Delays in 802.11 Networks. In: International Conference on Next Generation Mobile Applications, Services and Technologies (NGMAST 2007). IEEE Computer Society (2007)

2. IEEE 802.21 Standard: Local and Metropolitan Area Networks – Part 21: Media Independent Handover Services (2009)
3. Lim, W.S., Kim, D.W., Suh, Y.J., Won, J.J.: Implementation and Performance Study of IEEE 802.21 in Integrated IEEE 802.11/802.16e Networks. Computer Communications (2009)
4. Kim, Y., et al.: An enhanced information server for seamless vertical handover in IEEE 802.21 MIH networks. Comput. Netw. (2010)
5. Kim, B., Jung, Y., Kim, I., Kim, Y.: Enhanced FMIPv4 Horizontal Handover with Minimized Channel Scanning Time Based on Media Independent Handover (MIH). In: IEEE NOMS Workshops, pp. 52–55 (2008)
6. NIST Mobility Package for Network Simulator-2 (2007)

Grid of Learning Resources in E-learning Communities

Julio César Rodríguez Ribón[1], Luis Javier García Villalba[2], Tomás Pedro de Miguel Moro[3], and Tai-hoon Kim[4,5]

[1] Programa de Ingeniería de Sistemas
Facultad de Ingenierías
Universidad de Cartagena
Campus de Ciencias Económicas e Ingeniería (Sede Piedra de Bolívar)
Cartagena de Indias, Colombia
jrodriguezr@unicartagena.edu.co
[2] Grupo de Análisis, Seguridad y Sistemas (GASS)
Departamento de Ingeniería del Software e Inteligencia Artificial (DISIA)
Facultad de Informática, Despacho 431
Universidad Complutense de Madrid (UCM)
Calle Profesor José García Santesmases s/n
Ciudad Universitaria, 28040 Madrid, Spain
javiergv@fdi.ucm.es
[3] Departamento de Ingeniería de Sistemas Telemáticos (DIT)
Escuela Técnica Superior de Ingenieros de Telecomunicación (ETSIT)
Universidad Politécnica de Madrid (UPM)
Avenida Complutense 30
Ciudad Universitaria, 28040 Madrid, Spain
tmiguel@dit.upm.es
[4] Department of Multimedia Engineering
Hannam University
133 Ojeong-dong, Daedeok-gu
Daejeon, Korea
taihoonn@hannam.ac.kr
[5] Department of Information Technologies
Global Vision School Australia (GVSA)
20 Virgina Court, Sandy Bay
Tasmania, Australia
taihoonn@gvsa.asia

Abstract. Virtual Learning Communities allow organizations to be more cooperative during training activities via the Internet, with the provision of their learning resource. However, today, such techniques are not being implemented optimally and efficiently. In this paper we present a description of the problems that would face the generation of the grid of learning resources. Currently little is known about the problems that prevent the formation of virtual learning communities, so, this work is important for community members (directors, teachers, researchers and practitioners) because it offers a conceptual framework that helps understand these scenarios and can provide useful design requirements when generating learning services (Grid of Learning Resources).

T.-h. Kim et al. (Eds.): MulGraB 2011, Part II, CCIS 263, pp. 295–299, 2011.

We also propose an experience in which virtual learning communities have been integrated in Cartagena (Colombia) obtaining an alternative solution to the current problems.

Keywords: E-learning, Grid, Learning Communities, Learning Resources.

1 Introduction

There are several unresolved problems that could prohibit the implementation communities [1] [2] [3] of e-learning in an appropriate, optimal, and flexible manner. Such problems could generate technological isolation. These issues are:

- Encapsulation of the Peers Expertise. The data sources of the Learning Management System – LMS [4] [5] that store the expertise of each peer (Organization) are heterogeneous (DBMS, files, etc.) and autonomous.
- Intellectual property rights of Expertise of Peers. Each peer brings expertise to form various e-learning communities. However, authors' rights of this expertise in the current scenes are not protected.
- Confidentiality of the expertise of Peers. Lack of mechanisms to access the expertise of the peers only through the community.
- Lack of architecture of community services. There is no architecture for describing the grid resources available to build communities of e-learning.
- Scalability of the expertise of peers. In the current scenarios, there remains the inability to add new expertise of new or existing peers to the learning communities and even impossibility to modify current experiences.
- Availability of the service. Lack of a descriptor of services that are available in the community.

Due to the above, we propose to solve these problems by modeling the grid of learning resources (peer expertise).

AMENITIES [6] has been chosen as the methodology for modeling the grid resources in e-learning communities.

This paper initially takes a conceptual model of e-learning communities viewed as a group or organization. The paper continues by describing the useful information (grid of learning resources) that forms communities, then it explains a case of application of the proposed model and finally, it outlines the conclusions.

2 Research Background: Grid of Learning Resources in E-learning Communities.

The organization view identifies the aspects related to e-learning communities seen as an organization or group. The groups are structured and organized based on roles, which identify stereotyped behavior in the environment [6].

Within the Joint Venture (conceptual design pattern) [6] the director has the ability to represent and manage the alliance (the e-learning community), i.e. the actor who is in charge of external relations of partnership and coordinating between cooperating entities. The teacher has to make strategic decisions during the development of the course and meet regularly with students, who are described as partners in the design pattern. The student can take the representation of their classmates at the time that he is designated by them or by the teacher (Fig. 1).

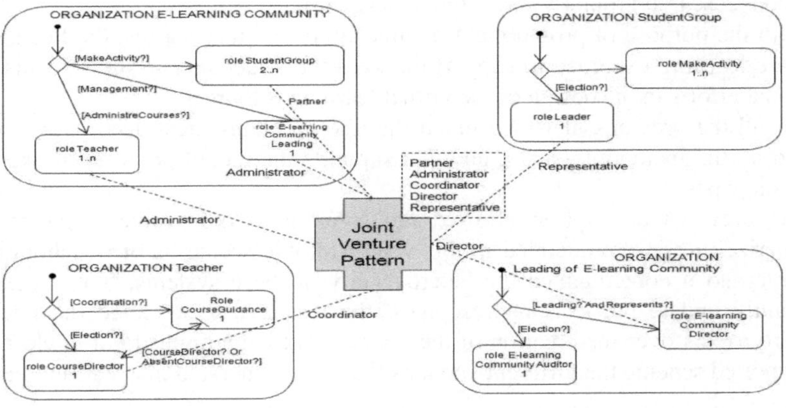

Fig. 1. Organization View: Application of the Joint Venture Pattern [6]

In the information view the most important elements which the system uses to work, in order to manage the collective knowledge, are the learning resources. They make reference to information that is used in the learning expertise and can be represented as presentations, tutorials, experiments, lessons, tools, tests, labs, course materials, etc. [7].

Each peer structures their expertise in a local scheme (Rx). These are encapsulated and labeled as expertise to share (Ex) within a framework that each peer has exported. Each E-learning Community is formed describing the federated schema with each of the expertise that conforms and those that are provided by the various peers (Fig. 2).

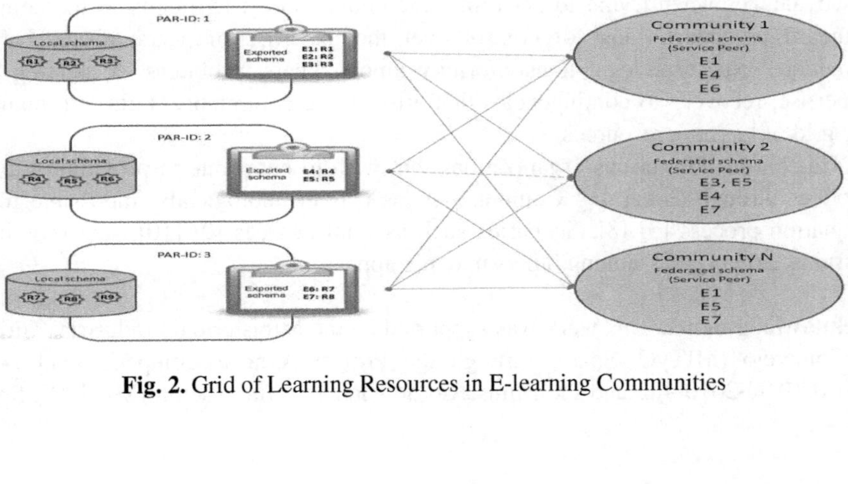

Fig. 2. Grid of Learning Resources in E-learning Communities

3 Case Study

The case of study is a learning virtual community that has been formed through the development of a virtual joint degree, named "Basic Informatics". Its course has been made between three peers: Peer ID1: the University of Cartagena (Colombia); Peer ID 2: the University of San Buenaventura – Cartagena (Colombia) and Peer ID 3: The E-Solutions research group (www.iesoluciones.com).

With the purpose of promoting academic cooperation scenarios, the Peers decided to share learning expertise to support the knowledge delivery to the students, and to share the efforts in the design of the virtual learning resources.

For all the previous, it was decided that the problems mentioned above could be solved by the methodological guide that supports the model proposed in the present research paper.

The previous description allowed the solution to the problems presented. To summarize, they were attended in this way: Multiple scenarios of collaboration was possible and it contemplated the heterogeneity of these systems, It was possible to constantly update the learning resources, the researchers protected the intellectual property rights over the creation of the courses and the administrator could notify in the exported scheme the different versions that were generated in a learning resource.

4 Conclusions

The proposed model serves as a reference for designing and implementing e-learning communities such as joint degrees between organizations through virtual technologies. It can also become a framework for generating design requirements of the expertise of peers that conform within the e-learning communities, in order that the LMS that support them in considering their architectures, their own characteristics, can form, maintain and access them.

You may continue with the e-learning communities as currently being developed, carrying learning resources between LMS or attempting to interoperate learning resources in one-to-one form (sharing resources between only two LMS), however, not attending the problems identified previously will bring the following disadvantages when trying to perform these communities: Difficulty in harmonizing standard procedures, loss of control over the expertise of peers, distrust of the provider's expertise, legal nonconformity among peers, problems in locating peer expertise, recovery to contingencies that arise in the community, failure to maintain the grid of learning resources.

This harms the various organizations that wish to cooperate in providing training services through E-learning Communities, as it is technologically impossible for its formation process [3] [8]. Scenarios such as joint degrees [9] [10], scenarios of E-learning 2.0 [11][12], among others may not appear.

Acknowledgments. This work was supported by the Ministerio de Industria, Turismo y Comercio (MITyC, Spain) through the Project Avanza Competitividad I+D+I TSI-020100-2010-482 and the Ministerio de Ciencia e Innovación (MICINN, Spain) through the Project TEC2010-18894/TCM. This work was also supported by the Security Engineering Research Center, granted by the Ministry of Knowledge Economy (MKE, Korea).

References

1. Cheon, E., Ahn, J.: Virtual community 101: know your virtual community and members. In: Proceedings of the 3rd International Conference on Ubiquitous Information Management and Communication, pp. 639–643. ACM, New York (2009)
2. Gordon, H.M., Stockdale, R.: Taxonomy of Online Communities: Ownership and Value Propositions. In: Proceedings of the 42nd Hawaii International Conference on System Sciences (2009)
3. Iriberri, A., Leroy, G.: A life-cycle perspective on online community success. ACM Comput. Surv. 41(2), 1–29 (2009)
4. Lonn, S., Teasley, S.D.: Saving time or innovating practice: Investigating perceptions and uses of Learning Management Systems. Computers & Education 53(3), 686–694 (2009)
5. McGill, T.J., Klobas, J.E.: A task-technology fit view of learning management system impact. Computers & Education 52(2), 496–508 (2009)
6. Isla, J.L., Gutierrez, F.L., Paderewski, P.: A Pattern-based Approach for Conceptual Modeling of Cooperative Systems. IEEE Latin America Transactions 5(4), 204–210 (2007)
7. Learning Technology Systems Architecture (LTSA), Draft Standard for Learning Technology (2001), http://ltsc.ieee.org/wg1/
8. Akram, A., Allan, R.: Organization of Grid Resources in Communities. In: Proceedings of the 4th International Workshop on Middleware for Grid Computing, vol. 194 (20), ACM, New York (2006)
9. Ribón, J.R., de Miguel, T.P., Ortíz, J.H.: Joint degrees in e-learning environments. In: Proceedings of the 2009 Euro American Conference on Telematics and information Systems: New Opportunities To increase Digital Citizenship, pp. 1–8. ACM, New York (2009)
10. Monroy, R.M., Ribón, J.R., de Miguel, T.P.: Federation of Academic Services Supported by Organizational and Design Patterns. In: Proceedings of the 2010 Euro American Conference on Telematics and Information Systems, Panamá (2010)
11. Ferretti, S., Mirri, S., Muratori, L.A., Roccetti, M., Salomoni, P.: E-learning 2.0: you are We-LCoME! In: Proceedings of the 2008 International Cross-Disciplinary Conference on Web Accessibility, Beijing, vol. 317, pp. 116–125 (2008)
12. Ribón, J.R., de Miguel, T.P., Monroy, R.M.: Web 2.0 Architecture for Services Federation in Virtual Learning Communities. In: Proceedings of the 2010 Euro American Conference on Telematics and Information Systems, Panamá (2010)

A Comparison Study between AntOR-Disjoint Node Routing and AntOR-Disjoint Link Routing for Mobile Ad Hoc Networks

Delfín Rupérez Cañas[1], Ana Lucila Sandoval Orozco[1],
Luis Javier García Villalba[1], and Tai-hoon Kim[2,3]

[1] Group of Analysis, Security and Systems (GASS)
Department of Software Engineering and Artificial Intelligence
School of Computer Science, Office 431
Universidad Complutense de Madrid (UCM)
Calle Profesor José García Santesmases s/n
Ciudad Universitaria, 28040 Madrid, Spain
{delfinrc,asandoval,javiergv}@fdi.ucm.es
[2] Department of Multimedia Engineering
Hannam University
133 Ojeong-dong, Daedeok-gu
Daejeon, Korea
taihoonn@hannam.ac.kr
[3] Department of Information Technologies
Global Vision School Australia (GVSA)
20 Virgina Court, Sandy Bay
Tasmania, Australia
taihoonn@gvsa.asia

Abstract. Routing in Mobile Ad Hoc Networks (MANETs) is complex problem because of the dynamic topology, limited process and storing capability, bandwidth constraints, and lack of a centralized system. The design of efficient routing protocols is a fundamental problem in MANETs. Researchers have proposed a number of routing protocols in literature. This survey treats about a bio-inspired routing protocol called AntOR for these networks. Thus, one of its key aspects is disjoint route property. The simulation results show that the disjoint-link property has a better performance than disjoint-node according to metrics such as average End-to-End Delay and Jitter.

Keywords: Ant Colony Optimization, AntOR, Mobile Ad Hoc Network, Routing Protocol.

1 Introduction

Mobile Ad Hoc Networks (MANETs) [1] are a collection of mobile nodes which have no fixed infrastructure. The nodes communicate through wireless network and there is no central control for the nodes in the network. Routing is the task of forwarding data packets from a source to a destination. Fundamentally, routing protocols based in

T.-h. Kim et al. (Eds.): MulGraB 2011, Part II, CCIS 263, pp. 300–304, 2011.

MANETs are composed into three categories: proactive, reactive and hybrid. Proactive routing protocols often need to exchange control packets among mobile nodes and continuously update their routing tables. Each node must maintain the state of the network in real time. Reactive routing protocols only seek a route to the destination when it is needed. Hybrid protocols are derived from a mixture of these two protocols. Another brand of classification is derived from behavior of the some special animals or insects. Within these bioinspired protocols are based on ants. Ant Colony Optimization (ACO) [2] is a set of applicable algorithms which focuses on Intelligence Swarm [3] can resolve complex problem in an efficient manner.

This article proposes AntOR [4], an innovative routing algorithm belonging to such bioinspired protocols and in where we realize a comparative of its two versions: disjoint-link and disjoint-node routes.

The rest of the paper is organized as follows. In Section 2, we present related work. In Section 3, we expose main characteristics of AntOR. The most relevant simulation results are shown in Section 4. The conclusions are presented in Section 5.

2 Related Work

In recent years a large number of routing algorithm MANET has been proposed. These algorithms all deal with the dynamic aspects of MANETs in their own way, using reactive or proactive behavior, or a combination of both.

In the MANET, the main classification is between proactive, reactive, and hybrid algorithms. But other classifications exist too. The bioinspired routing protocols have a really important and relevant. These protocols might belong to proactive like Probabilistic Emergent Routing Algoritm (PERA) [5], to reactive like improved Ant Colony Optimization algoritm for mobile ad hoc Networks (PACONET) [6]. Finally, as both advantages of theses ones approach we have AntHocNet [7], protocol which our proposal is based on.

3 Review of AntOR

AntOR [4] it is a hybrid ACO routing algorithm, based on AntHocNet that takes Ducatelle algorithm [7] as its starting point, and has the following differences a) Disjoint-link and disjoint-node protocol, b) Separation between the pheromones in the diffusion process, and c) Use distance metric in path exploration.

In this protocol there are two kinds of routes: disjoint-node and disjoint-link. The first ones correspond to routes that do not share nodes, and the latter are routes which do not share links. It is satisfied the property that all disjoint node are also disjoint link, but not vice versa. Both types of disjoint routes present the following advantages.

a) A node failure affects only one route.
b) It has better load balancing because of disjoint property.

However, the use of this kind of routes presents the disadvantage that more resources are needed because of not to share links and nodes.

4 Simulation Results

We have used the Network simulator 3 (NS) [8] to evaluate the performance of following two versions: AntOR-DNR (disjoint-node route version) and AntOR-DLR (disjoint-link route version). We compare these approaches varying pause time from 0 to 120 s. We have considered 100 moving within an area of 1000m x 1000 m using *Random Waypoint Model* (RWP). The maximum speed of nodes we have considered in simulation is 10m/s. In the simulation we use the traffic generator *Constant Bit Rate* (CBR), with bit rate of 2048 bit/s (4 packets of 64 bytes per second) and total simulation time is set to 120 s. We show the general simulation parameters in table 1.

Table 1. Simulation parameters according to routing protocol

Number of node: 100
Dimensions of area: 1000 x 1000
Transmission de range (open area): 300m
Physical layer: configured for IEEE 802.11b
Send data ratio: constant WiFi-6 mps
Simulation time: 120s
Number of trials: 5

The first metrics which we have has in consideration is the Average End-to-End Delay. It consists in measure of accumulative effectiveness of experienced delays by packets going from source to destination.

In Fig. 1 we can see that AntOR-DLR has a better performance than AntOR-DNR. The main reason is because of the disjoint-link route version has more alternative route than disjoint-node version and whether one route fails, the algorithm will use another alternative one.

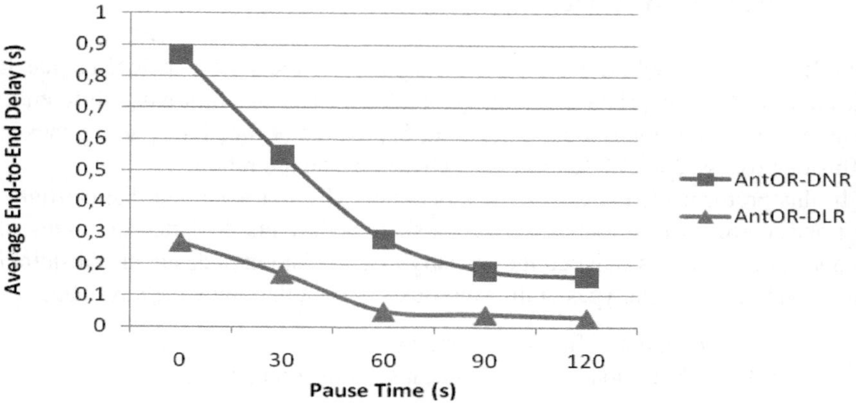

Fig. 1. Comparative AntOR-DNR against AntOR-DLR according to Average End-to-End Delay

In the Fig. 2 we can appreciate the same behavior than the Fig. 1. We see how the general performance of AntOR-DLR is better than AntOR-DNR according to Jitter. This metric takes into consideration the delay between consecutive delivered packets. We can see clearly that disjoint-link route version has a better performance to link/node failures because if a route that takes into account only the nodes and not the links, it could fails quicker and unsafely.

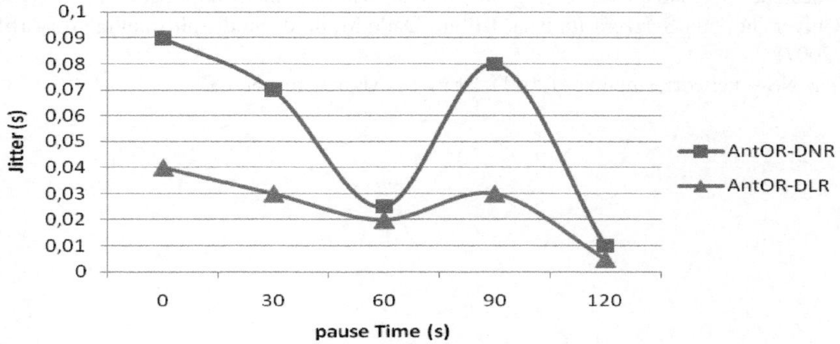

Fig. 2. Comparative AntOR-DNR against AntOR-DLR according to Jitter metric

5 Conclusions

We have presented a routing protocol for MANETs called AntOR that is classified as a bioinspired. The protocol is stable in the carried out simulations, which suggested its scalability. We can also observe the obtained results, which make the comparison in the two kinds of routes: disjoint-link and disjoint-node, where disjoint-link version has a better behavior than disjoint-node according average End-to-End delay and Jitter.

For the future, we can use these kinds of routes together from AntOR and compare results.

Acknowledgments. This work was supported by the Ministerio de Industria, Turismo y Comercio (MITyC, Spain) through the Project Avanza Competitividad I+D+I TSI-020100-2010-482 and the Ministerio de Ciencia e Innovación (MICINN, Spain) through the Project TEC2010-18894/TCM. This work was also supported by the Security Engineering Research Center, granted by the Ministry of Knowledge Economy (MKE, Korea).

References

1. Abolhasan, M., Wysocki, T., Dutkiewicz, E.: A review of routing protocols for mobile ad hoc networks. Ad Hoc Networks 2(1), 1–22 (2004)
2. Dorigo, M., Stützle, T.: Ant Colony Optimization. The MIT Press (2004)
3. Kennedy, J.: Swarm Intelligence. Morgan Kaufmann Publishers (2001)

4. García, L.J., Rupérez, D., Sandoval, A.L.: Bioinspired routing protocol for mobile ad hoc networks. IET Communication 4(18), 2187–2195 (2010)
5. Baras, J.S., Mehta, H.: A Probabilistic Emergent Routing Algorithm for Mobile Ad Hoc Networks, Modeling and optimization in Mobile Ad hoc wireless networks (2003)
6. Osagie, E., Thulasiraman, P., Thulasiram, R.K.: PACONET: imProved Ant Colony Optimization routing algorithm formobile ad hoc NETworks. In: 22nd International Conference on Advanced Information Networking and Applications, pp. 204–211 (2008)
7. Ducatelle, F.: Adaptive routing in ad hoc wireless multi-hop networks. PhD thesis, Universitá della Svizzera Italiana, Istituto Dalle Molle di Studi sull'Intelligenza Artificiale (2007)
8. The NS-3 network simulator (2011), `http://www.nsnam.org`

Comparing AntOR-Disjoint Node Routing Protocol with Its Parallel Extension

Delfín Rupérez Cañas[1], Ana Lucila Sandoval Orozco[1], Luis Javier García Villalba[1], and Tai-hoon Kim[2,3]

[1] Group of Analysis, Security and Systems (GASS)
Department of Software Engineering and Artificial Intelligence
School of Computer Science, Office 431
Universidad Complutense de Madrid (UCM)
Calle Profesor José García Santesmases s/n
Ciudad Universitaria, 28040 Madrid, Spain
{delfinrc,asandoval,javiergv}@fdi.ucm.es
[2] Department of Multimedia Engineering
Hannam University
133 Ojeong-dong, Daedeok-gu
Daejeon, Korea
taihoonn@hannam.ac.kr
[3] Department of Information Technologies
Global Vision School Australia (GVSA)
20 Virgina Court, Sandy Bay
Tasmania, Australia
taihoonn@gvsa.as

Abstract. In this paper we analysis a parallel approach of Ant-OR. This protocol is itself robust and susceptible to frequent topology changes, but with this approach called P-AntOR, which uses programming multiprocessor architectures based on shared memory protocol, we improve the behavior of AntOR, where the parallelization is applicable in the route discovery phase, route local repair process and link failure notification. The simulation results show that P-AntOR performs better than AntOR, considering metrics such as Throughput and Overhead in number of packets.

Keywords: AntOR, Mobile Ad Hoc Networks, Overhead, P-AntOR, Routing Protocol, Throughput.

1 Introduction

Mobile ad hoc networks (MANETs) [1] have had a large popularity because of their high flexibility in providing users with network access. MANET is a collection of mobile nodes that can establish quickly communication of civilian and military applications. As the size of MANET grows, the performance tends to decrease. One of the critical issues in ad-hoc networking is the lack of bandwidth and computation capability. So how to reduce the traffic overload and the pressure of computation is a very

T.-h. Kim et al. (Eds.): MulGraB 2011, Part II, CCIS 263, pp. 305–309, 2011.

important design in MANET. Many routing protocols have been proposed for efficient multi-hop routing. One of these brands consists in bioinspired protocols, existing a large variety. We focus on behavior of ants and we study the algorithms based on *Ant Colony Optimization* (ACO) [2] because of its relevance in this area. This group of algorithms or routing protocols is especially noteworthy in this kind of network due to the concept of Swarm intelligence [3]. It is based on the application of social behavior of insects and other animals to solve problems.

The routing is the handled issue in this article, so that we reference a bioinspired routing protocol in the literature called AntOR [4]. Since this starting point, we analysis an approach parallel of such protocol.

The rest of this paper is organized as follows. In Section 2 we discuss some related work. Then, we briefly present AntOR routing protocol in Section 3. This is followed by a description and results of our parallel approach in Section 4. Finally, the paper is concluded and possible future extensions in Section 5.

2 Related Work

Although ACO is itself a technique parallelizable, in this section we present most relevant parallelization techniques for ACO doing it more efficient.

One of the first one was introduced by [5], where this method can resolve difficult combinatorial optimization problems. Then, Stützle [6] applies a master/slave approximation to parallel the different searching methods from ACO solutions.

Finally, in [7] a parallelization hybrid system is shown. This method consists of evaluating the communication performance Message Passing Interface (MPI) multithreading. In this approach MPI across nodes and multithreading within a node is employed.

3 AntOR: Bioinspired Routing Protocol for MANETs

AntOR [4] has the following characteristics: a) is a protocol with the property of link/node disjoint, which provides a better distribution of packet traffic, b) has the property that separates the pheromone values in the diffusion process. Thus, a same route cannot have both a regular pheromone value and a virtual pheromone simultaneously, and c) uses the metric distance in the path exploration. This technique significantly reduces the protocol overhead.

4 Analysis of Parallel Approach of AntOR

To understand how the extension of AntOR works, it necessary to define three concepts:

a) Process: Program running. The processes are managed by the Operating System.
b) Thread: The basic unit of execution. Any program that executes at least has a thread.
c) POSIX Thread: Standard based in thread API for C / C++.

We specify a large-grained parallelization of AntOR-DNR protocol (node-disjoint version). This parallel technique launching a thread for each neighbor that is in the neighbor table of the node that starts one of the following phases: a) Routing Information Setup, b) Local route repair and c) Link Failure Notification.

These phases work as follows: The node, which initiates the process, looks for the possible neighbors in its update table and then this node sends an ant (agent) to each one through a thread. The essence of this parallelization is to substitute the *broadcast* messages by sent independent message using thread.

4.1 Simulation Results

We have executed several tests with network simulator NS-3 [8]. For the simulation we use 100 nodes configured according to IEEE 802.11b in an area of 1200 m $\times$1200 m, with a random distribution of the nodes. In the simulation we use the traffic generator *Constant Bit Rate* (CBR), with bit rate of 2048 bit/s and total simulation time is set to 120 s. In our experiment, that uses the Mobility Model *Random Wait Point* (RWP), we vary the node speed from 0 to 10 m/s with a pause time of 30 s.

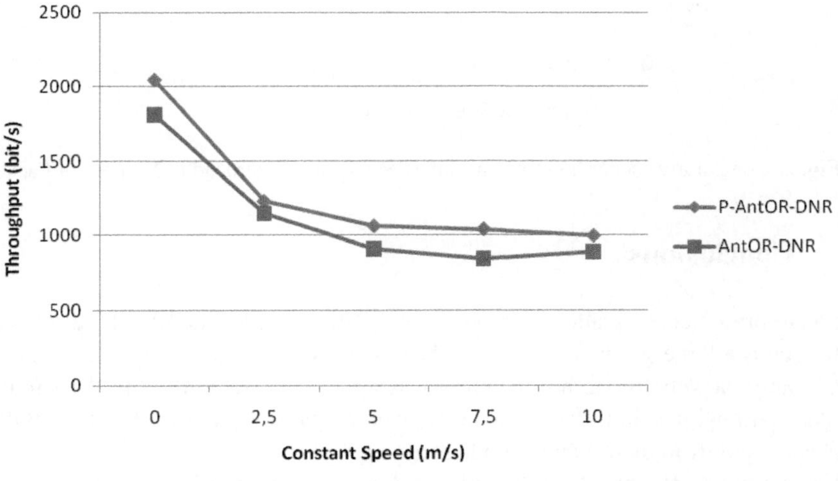

Fig. 1. Comparative according to Constant Speed against Throughput

In Fig. 1 we can see that Throughput in P-AntOR is better than its predecessor at all times, regardless of the speed of the nodes. We understand that throughput is the volume of work or information flowing through a system. It constitutes a relevant concept because of its relationship with delivered data packet ratio.

We have checked how the throughput improves with the decrease of sent packet number and we can also detect the influence of node speed.

On the other hand we analysis the overhead in number of packets in Fig. 2. It consists in relationship between the total numbers of transmitted control packets by the nodes of network and the number of delivered data packets to their destinations.

We appreciate how overhead is better in this parallel approach than Ant-OR and we show how the gap of overhead between P-AntOR and AntOR is significantly wide from 10 m/s. This improvement is due to limiting the number of sent messages, the overhead decreases.

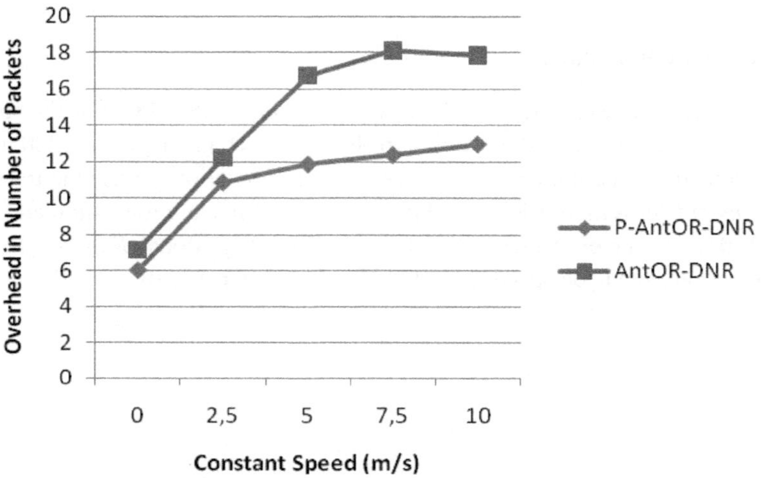

Fig. 2. Comparative according to Constant Speed against Overhead in Number of Packets

5 Conclusions

We have presented a parallel approach of AntOR, called P-AntOR. The used parallel technique is a large-grained approach. The essence of this parallel approach is to send specifically packets to one-hop neighbors using threads. According to the simulation results (Throughput and Overhead in number of packets) shows that P-AntOR improves to AntOR in their disjoint-node route version.

For the future, P-AntOR can be improved using multi-interfaces where each one of these may be handled with a multicore system. The main idea is that whether we have more "output" interface, we will send quickly more ants (agent) from each one according to parallel approach implementation.

Acknowledgments. This work was supported by the Ministerio de Industria, Turismo y Comercio (MITyC, Spain) through the Project Avanza Competitividad I+D+I TSI-020100-2010-482 and the Ministerio de Ciencia e Innovación (MICINN, Spain) through the Project TEC2010-18894/TCM. This work was also supported by the Security Engineering Research Center, granted by the Ministry of Knowledge Economy (MKE, Korea).

References

1. Royer, E., Toh, C.: A Review of Current Routing Protocols for Ad Hoc Mobile Wireless Networks. IEEE Personal Communications 6(2), 46–55 (1999)
2. Dorigo, M., Stützle, T.: Ant Colony Optimization. The MIT Press (2004)
3. Kennedy, J.: Swarm Intelligence. Morgan Kaufmann Publishers (2001)
4. García, L.J., Rupérez, D., Sandoval, A.L.: Bioinspired routing protocol for mobile ad hoc networks. IET Communication 4(18), 2187–2195 (2010)
5. Bullnheimer, B., Kostis, G., Strauss, C.: Parallelization strategies for the ant systems. In: High Performance Algorithms and Software in NonLinear Optimization Series: Applied Optimization, vol. 24 (1998)
6. Stützle, T.: Parallelization Strategies for ant Colony Optimization. In: Eiben, A.E., Bäck, T., Schoenauer, M., Schwefel, H.-P. (eds.) PPSN 1998. LNCS, vol. 1498, pp. 722–731. Springer, Heidelberg (1998)
7. Thakur, R., Gropp, W.: Test suite for evaluating performance of multithreaded MPI communication. Parallel Computing 35(12), 608–617 (2009)
8. The NS-3 network simulator (2011), `http://www.nsnam.org`

Location Acquisition Method Based on RFID in Indoor Environments

Kyoung Soo Bok, Yong Hun Park, Jun Il Pee, and Jae Soo Yoo*

Department of Information and Communication Engineering, Chungbuk National University, Cheongju, Chungbuk, Korea
{ksbok,yhpark1119,yjs}@chungbuk.ac.kr, junil.pi@gmail.com

Abstract. In this paper, we propose a new location acquisition method that reduces the computation cost of location acquisition and keeps the accuracy of the location. The proposed method performs the event filtering to selects the necessary reference tags and then computes the accurate locations of objects. If the locations of objects are changed then update the locations of objects. To show the superiority of our proposed method, we compare it with LANDMARC, which is the most popular localization method. It shows that the proposed system reduces the computation cost of location estimation 500 times more than LANDMARC.

Keywords: Location based service, RFID, Indoor, Location Acquisition.

1 Introduction

Through the development of sensor technology and communication technology, location based services have been developed. LBS provide information related certain locations or the locations of certain objects, has been highly increased [1, 2]. One of the most well known location-aware services is GPS. However, GPS has an inherent problem that accurately determines the location of objects inside buildings [1, 3]. LBS are important to the services for outdoor as well as indoor in Ubiquitous environments. The indoor location based service requires the accurate locations of objects less than number of meters. However, it is impossible to provide the indoor LBS because of the accurate locations because of the inaccuracy of the locations detected based on Global Positioning System(GPS)[4, 5].

Radio frequency identification (RFID) is an electronic identification technology for a real-time tracking and monitoring and is one of the core technologies for Ubiquitous services. RFID stream are generated quickly and automatically and then is a very large volume data. Since most of RFID stream sensed by reader are useless to the application, semantic event processing is required to detect more meaningful and interesting data to applications [7]. Recently, RFID based location systems are many researched in indoor environment. Generally, the location systems based RFID use

* Corresponding author.

T.-h. Kim et al. (Eds.): MulGraB 2011, Part II, CCIS 263, pp. 310–318, 2011.

the RSSI to measure the signal strength from each tag to readers. These systems are classified into two methods. The first method is that RFID tags are attached at certain fixed position and RFID readers are attached to the moving objects[9, 10]. In this method, there is a problem that the system requires too much cost to be constructed since the RFID readers are very expensive and the readers are attached to each object. [10] proposed an indoor location estimation system based on UHF based RFID. In [10], each tag has a unique ID number and is attached to the ceiling. RFID reader is attached to the person. The location of the person is calculated from the coordinates of detected tags. The second method is that RFID readers are attached at certain fixed position and RFID tags are attached to the moving objects [4, 8]. This method requires relatively low in price to construct the system. To increase the accuracy of detecting location of the objects, RFID readers are required as much as possible. In addition, since the readers are expensive, the methods to increase the accuracy and reduce the number of the readers have been researched.

LANDMARC is a prototype indoor location system based on active RFID [4]. LANDMARC uses the concept of reference tags to improve the overall accuracy of locating objects. Suppose we have *n* readers along with *m* tags as reference tags. Many studies have been studied to enhance a weakness of LANDMARC. LANDMARC does not work well in a closed area with sever radio signal multi-path effects. More, since the accuracy of localization relies on the placement of reference tags, more reference tags are need to improve location accuracy [3, 8]. Many studies have been studied to enhance a weakness of LANDMARC [3, 6, 8, 11]. VIRE used the concept of virtual reference tags to gain more accurate positions of tracking objects without additional tags and readers [11]. VIRE employ the concept of virtual reference tags to provide denser reference coverage in the sensing area instead of using many real reference RFID tags deployed in the sensing area. To alleviate the effects of uncharacteristic signal behavior, a proximity map is maintained by each reader. To estimate the possible position of an object, VIRE can eliminate those unlikely positions based on the information from different maps with certain design parameters. [8] used a sub-region selection mechanism to reduce the redundant calculation and proposed a nonlinear interpolation algorithm to calculate the RSSI values of virtual reference tags. To improve the accuracy of indoor localization in real environments, [6] used the method of curve fitting to construct the relationship between RSSI and distance from RF Reader to Tag. To calculate the moving object's position, [6] first obtain the *k* nearest reference tags and the moving object tag's position by LANDMARC algorithm. After that, [6] puts the *k* reference tags and the moving object' tag with the computed position in a set and repeats to calibrate the target coordinate by the error corrections which obtained by members of this set. The calibration will continue until the position of the moving object' tag tends to be a stable value.

In this paper, we propose a new location acquisition method using RFID tags that reduces the cost of computing the locations and guarantees the accuracy of the locations. The method classifies the RFID tags into object tags and reference tags. The reference tags and readers are attached at the fixed locations to recognize the object tags attached to the moving objects. The reference tags are used to correct the locations of the object tags as assistants. The reader records the information of both the reference tags and the object tags periodically. To save the cost of computing the locations of the objects, we adapt the filter phase that ignores unnecessary information of reference tags corrected from the un-relative readers.

The rest of this paper is organized as follows. Section 2 introduces our proposed method to detect the location of the RFID tags and update the locations efficiently. Section 3 shows the superiority of our proposed methods through performance evaluation. Finally, section 4 presents the conclusions and future works.

2 The Proposed System Method

2.1 The System Architecture

We propose a new indoor location acquisition method using active RFID tags to improve the computation cost and the location accuracy when RFID readers and reference tags are located in fixed location and only moving object attached tags moves in indoor environment. RFID tags are classified into reference tags and object tags. The reference tags served as reference points are placed in fixed location to reduce the number of RFID readers and to improve the location accuracy, and are similar to LANMARC. The object tags are RFID tags attached to the moving object and move about in indoor. To improve the computation cost and the location accuracy, we use an event filtering to rapidly determine the neighbor reference tag required to acquire the location of moving object and adopt a location update policy to minimize the management cost of updates.

Figure 1 shows the proposed system architecture. To rapidly acquire the location of object and enhance the location accuracy, our system consists of event filtering module and location tracking module, where the event filtering selects the necessary reference tags to compute the accurate location of an object tag and the location tracking calculates and updates the location of object tags. In the event filtering, data classification classifies the RFID stream transmitted from the middleware into objects tags and reference tags, and stores the RFID stream to each index structure according the kind of tags. The reference tags are used to assist deciding the locations of object tags by comparing the strength of the signal between the object tags and reference tags. The data filtering prunes the unnecessary reference tags to calculate the location of object tags. All the reference tags are not helpful to decide the locations of the object tags but only a few neighbor reference tags are used to calculate the location of object tag. The data filtering reduces the computation cost for calculating the locations of the objects using the reference tags. In the location tracking, the location generation calculates the real positions of objects based on the filtered RFID stream from data filtering. The location update decides whether the location of the object tag is updated according to the update policies or not. According to the decision, the locations of objects are updated and notify the service to update the locations. It reduces the communication cost between location management system and application.

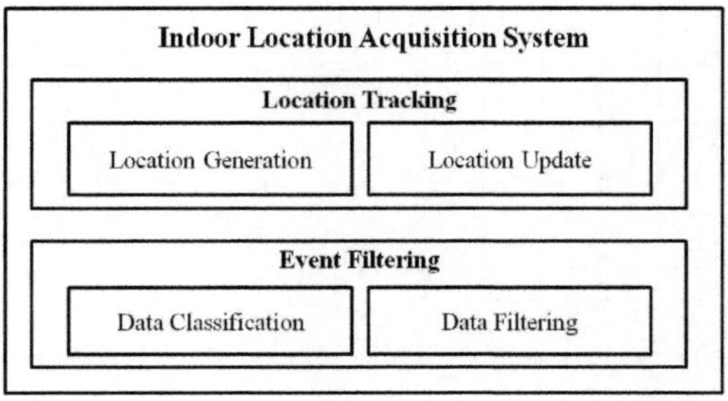

Fig. 1. The proposed system architecture

2.2 Event Filtering

To acquire the locations of moving objects, we manage an object tag table and a reference tag table that present RFID tag information sensed by RFID reader. The object tag table stores the tag information of moving objects and the reference tag table stores the information of the reference tag used in LANMARC. We have to register the moving objects monitored by applications to provide location based service. The registration of moving object means that it stores the physical identifier of RFID tag attached to the moving objet into the object tag table. After the registration, a logical identifier is assigned to the tag and stores into the moving object table. The tag information table is used to map the physical identifier to the logical identifier. The tag information table stores <*PID*, *LID*, *Info*> , where *PID* is a physical identifier which is EPC code of moving object, *LID* is a logical identifier, *Info* is a current location of moving object and initially is null. *Info* is consisted of $<t_i, (x_i, y_i), (v_{xi}, v_{yi})>$, where t_i is the time, (x_i, y_i) is the position of an object tag and (v_{xi}, v_{yi}) is a velocity vector. Initially, *Info* is null. *Info* stores the location information of object tag after the location generation module is processed. The reference tag table is similar to the object tag except *Info*. In the reference tag table, *Info* only stores the positions in which the reference tag is deployed.

To calculate the location of moving object, the data classification first classifies the RFID stream received from middleware into object tags and reference tags. We use two index structures such as *OR*(Object tag-Reader) index and *RR*(Reference tag-Reader) index. The index structures indicate the occurrences of the object tags and the reference tags sensed by readers. Figure 2 shows two index structures that is the grid based index structure to represent the relation of tags and readers, where OT_i is an object tag, R_i is a reader, and RT_i is a reference tag. Figure 2 (a) is the *OR* index which represent the occurrences of the object tags sensed by the multiple readers. Figure 2 (b) is the *RR* index which represent the occurrences of the reference tags sensed by the multiple readers. Initially, all the values of each cell in the two grid index structures set '0'. If the reader senses multiple tags, the reader transmits RFID streams to middleware. And then we classify the RFID stream into object tags and reference tags. If the physical identifier of a tag exists in the object tag table, we set '1' to the cell representing the reader and the object in *OR* index structure. If the physical identifier of a tag exists in the reference tag table, we set '1' to the cell representing the reader and the reference tag in *RR* index structure.

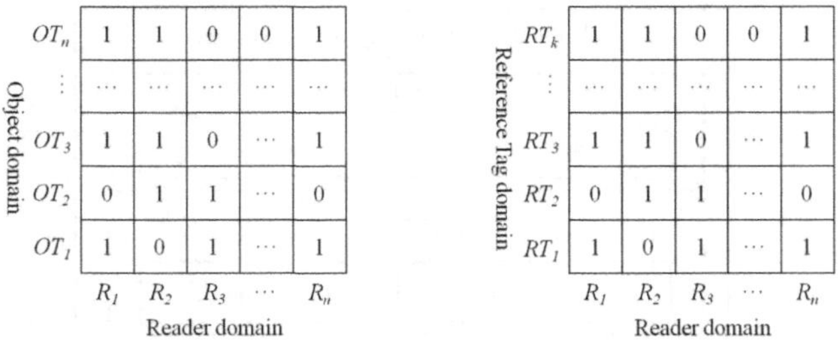

(a) *OR* index structure (b) *RR* index structure

Fig. 2. A grid-based index structure

To process data classification from RFID stream sensed by reader, the tag information table and gird based index structure is used. Figure 3 represents the procedure of data classification. The RFID stream transmitted from RFID middleware is defined as a tuple <*EPC*, *RID*, *TS, SS*>, where *EPC* is the unique identifier of tag defined by electronic product code standard, *RID* is the identifier of RFID reader, *TS* is a timestamp which represents the time when the tag is sensed by RFID reader, SS is the signal strength of the tag. If the RFID stream transmitted through RFID middleware exists at t_1 then we decide that the sensed RFID stream is classified through Tag information table and then the cell representing the sensed tag and the sending reader set '1' in two grid based index structure. For example, $<epc_1, r_1, t_1, 3>$ is the object tag because the PID of epc_1 exists in object tag table. Therefore, the cell $<1, 1>$ representing the sensed tag epc_1 and the sensing reader r_1 set '1' in OR index. The rest of the received RFID stream is processed in the same way as above.

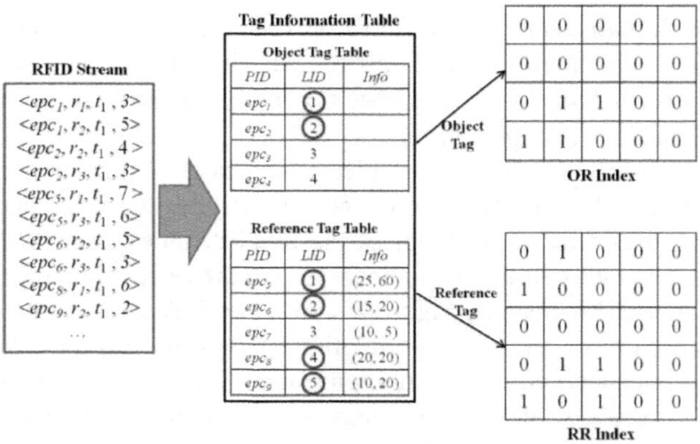

Fig. 3. An example for data classification process

We decide the set of reference tags and readers required to calculate the locations of object tags through a data filtering module. The data filtering module uses the *OR* index and *RR* index. First of all, we make the set of readers sensing object tags from *OR* grid structure. After the set of readers are made, In *RR* index structure, we find out the bit patterns that present the reference tags that the readers recognize. After that, we find the set of reference tag that is recognized by the readers in common through '*AND*' operation between the bit patterns of the readers.

Figure 4 presents the selection process of candidate reader from *OR* and *RR* index structure for an object OT_1. In *OR* index structure, a set of readers sensing an object OT_1 is $\{R_1, R_2\}$ at time t_1. The set of readers sensing an object OT_1 are the physically adjacent readers at time t_1. To find the reference tags simultaneously sensed by reader sensing an object, we examine the bit patterns of a reader R_1 and R_2 sensing an object OT_1. The bit patterns of R_1 and R_2 are '10011' and '11001'. As shown figure 4, we can obtain a set of adjacent reference tags commonly sensed by the readers through '*AND*' operation between the bit patterns of the readers sensing the object. Therefore, the reference tags found by the bit pattern of the readers in *RR* index structure are only the candidates used for calculating the location of the object.

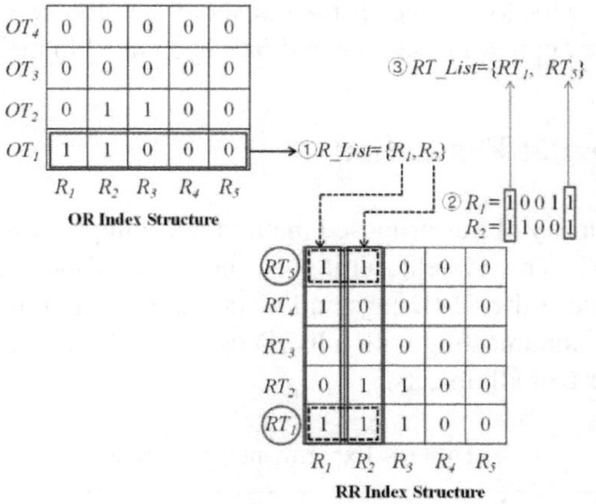

Fig. 4. Selection process of adjacent candidate objects

2.3 Location Tracking

To generate the location of an object, we use the adjacent readers and reference tags selected in previous steps. We suppose that n and m denote the number of the selected adjacent readers and adjacent reference tags respectively. The Euclidean distance in signal strengths between the object and the reference tag is equation (1) where S_i and θ_j denote the signal strength that the i-th reader receives from the object and j-th reference tag, respectively.

$$E_j = \sum_{i=1}^{n}((\theta_j)_i - S_i)^2, j \in (1, m) \quad (1)$$

We select k number of the reference tags that have minimum value $E=(E_1, E_2, \ldots, E_m)$ among the selected reference tags because we use only k number of reference tags is to increase the accuracy of the location to be estimated by using the reference tags that have the highest reliability. The E values of the k-selected reference tags are used to correct the location of the object with the weights according to the similarity of the signal strength between the object and the reference tags. The weight w_j is calculated by equation (2). Using the location information of the k-selected reference tags and their weights, we create the location of the object through equation (3).

$$w_j = \frac{1/E_j^2}{\sum_{j=1}^{m} 1/E_j^2} \tag{2}$$

$$(x, y) = \sum_{j=1}^{m} w_j(x_j, y_j) \tag{3}$$

To update the location information of an object, an application services can register and manage the update policies. First, we find the latest location information in the object tag table, and then compare the varieties between the latest location and the new locations of objects. The moving object table maintains the latest location information of objects from application services. If the distance between the current location and the new location exceeds the threshold then the new location information is transmitted to the application service and *Info* is updated in the moving object table.

3 Experimental Evaluation

To show the superiority of our proposed method, we compare our localization method with LANDMARC. The system setting is shown in Table 1. For the evaluation environment, we place the RFID tags and reader so that the minimum number of the adjacent readers communicating with a RFID tag is 3. We set the amount of objects to be monitored to 20% of all objects.

Table 1. Experimental parameters

Parameter	Value
Simulation area(SA)	50m×50m~200m×200m
Transmission range of a reader(TA)	20m
The total number of moving object(TMO)	100~400
The number of monitoring object(NMO)	20%
k	5

The comparison the computation cost according to the number of objects. To provide a real-time location based service in RFID systems, it is one of the most important factors to compute the location of objects. Table 2 shows the cost of computing the location of objects according to the number of objects from 100 to 400. The proposed method is about 500 times faster than LANDMARC. It is because the filtering step reduces the records to be used to computing the locations.

Table 2. The computation cost according to the number of moving object

TMO \ Method	LANMARC	The proposed method
100	3062500	6072
200	6125000	12222
400	12250000	24891

Table 3 presents the comparison of communication costs of our proposed method in various environments. When the size of simulation environment is increased, the computation cost is increased. It is because the number of reader and reference tags participated in the computation of vector E increases. However, the amount of computation is reduced in the proposed method because we just use smaller number of readers and reference tags affecting the objects to compute the location of objects than that of LANDMARC. Therefore, the proposed method detects and computes the location of objects for large scale environment in real time.

Table 3. The computation cost according to simulation area

Method / SA	LANMARC	The proposed method
50m×50m	30625	195.58
100m×100m	422500	163.58
150m×150m	2030625	199.88
200m×200m	6250000	183.18

To measure the accuracy, we compare the computed locations and the real locations of objects. Figure 5 presents the error distances of the proposed method comparing with LANDMARC during three time unit. The error distance of the proposed method is similar to that of LANDMARC. It means that the computed location of the proposed method guarantee the accuracy as that of LANDMARC even if smaller number of reader and reference tags then LANDMARC are participated in the computation. Therefore, the proposed method reduces the cost of computing the location of objects as well as keeps the accuracy of the locations.

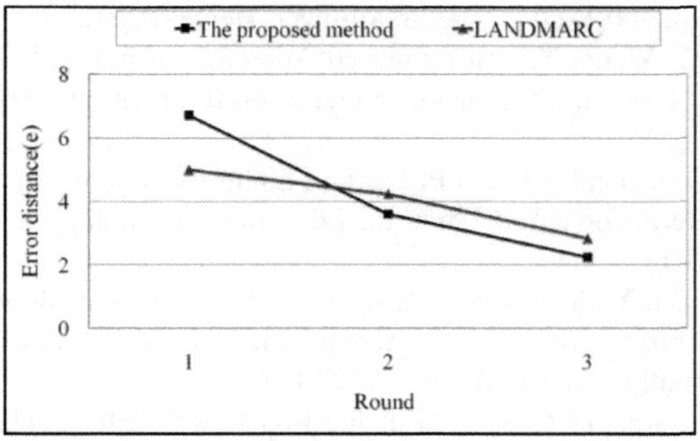

Fig. 5. The accuracy of the computed location

4 Conclusion

In this paper, we proposed a new location acquisition method to reduce the computation cost as well as the accuracy of the locations. We just use a small number of readers and reference tags for computing the location of objects through the event filtering. Through the performance evaluation, we prove that the computation cost is cut off about 50%~70%. The proposed system enhances the computation time about 500 times. For the further works, we will propose the method that detects the objects movement before computing the location of the objects to save the cost of computing the locations.

Acknowledgments. This work was supported by the Ministry of Education, Science and Technology Grant funded by the Korea Government (The Regional Research Universities Program/Chungbuk BIT Research-Oriented University Consortium) and Basic Science Research Program through the National Research Foundation of Korea(NRF) grant funded by the Korea government(MEST)(No. 2009-0089128).

Reference

1. Hightower, J., Borriello, J.G.: Location systems for ubiquitous computing. IEEE Computer 34(8), 57–66 (2001)
2. Gressmann, B., Klimek, H., Turau, V.: Towards Ubiquitous Indoor Location Based Services and Indoor Navigation. In: Proc. Workshop on Positioning Navigation and Communication, pp. 107–112 (2010)
3. Jin, H.Y., Lu, X.Y., Park, M.S.: An Indoor Localization Mechanism Using Active RFID Tag. In: Proc. the IEEE International Conference on Sensor Networks, Ubiquitous, and Trustworthy Computing, p. 4 (2006)
4. Lionel, M.N., Yunhao, L.: LANDMARC: Indoor Location Sensing Using Active RFID. Wireless Networks 10(6), 701–710 (2004)
5. Heo, J., Pyeon, M.-W., Kim, J.W., Sohn, H.-G.: Towards the Optimal Design of an RFID-Based Positioning System for the Ubiquitous Computing Environment. In: Yao, J., Lingras, P., Wu, W.-Z., Szczuka, M.S., Cercone, N.J., Ślęzak, D. (eds.) RSKT 2007. LNCS (LNAI), vol. 4481, pp. 331–338. Springer, Heidelberg (2007)
6. Jiang, X., Liu, Y., Wang, X.: An Enhanced Approach of Indoor Location Sensing Using Active RFID. In: Proc. International Conference on Information Engineering, pp. 169–172 (2009)
7. Liu, Y., Wang, D.: Complex Event Processing Engine for Large Volume of RFID Data. In: Proc. Second International Workshop on Education Technology and Computer Science, pp. 429–432 (2010)
8. Shi, W., Liu, K., Ju, Y., Yan, G.: An Efficient Indoor Location Algorithm Based on RFID Technology. In: 6th International Conference on Wireless Communications Networking and Mobile Computing (WiCOM), pp. 1–5 (2010)
9. Kim, S., Ko, D., An, S.: Geographical location based RFID tracking system. In: 2008 International Symposium on a World of Wireless, Mobile and Multimedia Networks, pp. 1–3 (2008)
10. Shiraishi, T., Komuro, N., Ueda, H., Kasai, H., Tsuboi, T.: Indoor Location Estimation Technique using UHF band RFID. In: Proc. International Conference on Information Networking, pp. 1–5 (2008)
11. Zhao, Y., Liu, Y., Ni, L.M.: VIRE: Active RFID-based Localization Using Virtual Reference Elimination. In: Proc. International Conference on Parallel Processing, pp. 57 (2007)

A Study on Compatibility between ISM Equipment and GPS System

Yong-Sup Shim and Il-Kyoo Lee

Department of Information & Communication Engineering, Kongju National University, Korea
besttla@kongju.ac.kr

Abstract. This paper describes radio interference analysis between Global Positioning System (GPS) and Industrial Scientific Medical (ISM) equipment. Due to increase of the usage of ISM equipment, the potential possibility of interference from ISM equipment to GPS system which used for safety life has been increasing. For the interference analysis between ISM equipment and GPS system, the scenario that GPS receiver operates in close to ISM equipment was set up. Then, protection distance between GPS receiver and ISM equipment was calculated in order to protect GPS system. The analysis result will be helpful for providing stable operation of GPS system.

Keywords: Interference analysis, GPS, ISM, Protection distance.

1 Introduction

GPS (Global Positioning System) is a constellation of 24 well-spaced satellites that make it possible for people with ground receivers to find their geographic location. Originally, GPS system is designed for military and since GPS is open to the public, GPS has become a widely deployed and useful tool for commerce, scientific uses, tracking, and surveillance. Such as automotive navigation, telematics, surveying, aircraft tracking, disaster relief service and so on.

Also, the equipment for using energy transmission has been increasing rapidly. Industrial Scientific Medical (ISM) equipment is representing the equipment for using the energy transmission. Especially, according to International Telecommunication Union-Radiocommunication (ITU-R), the ISM band that reserved internationally for the use of radio frequency energy for ISM equipment other than communication is assigned. Therefore, communications equipment operating in these bands must tolerate any interference generated by ISM equipment, and users have no regulatory protection from ISM equipment operation. So, many counties including Korea designated ISM band and encourage usage of ISM equipment in these band.

But, GPS system that is used for safety life has high priority than others even through in ISM band. So, in case that ISM equipment operates in close to GPS receiver, there is potential interference from ISM radiation power to GPS receiver. In order to remove interference, the protection method is needed for protecting GPS receiver.

T.-h. Kim et al. (Eds.): MulGraB 2011, Part II, CCIS 263, pp. 319–325, 2011.

In this paper, the scenario that ISM equipment is operating in close to GPS receiver was made and analyzed interference from ISM equipment to GPS receiver. Based on interference analysis, the protection distance that is separation distance between ISM equipment and GPS receiver is calculated in order to protect GPS receiver.

2 Interference Scenario

2.1 Interference Environment

GPS signal is transmitted by satellite and the signal is very weak due to the long distance between satellite and GPS receiver. Therefore, GPS received signal is sensitive from interference and can be generated positioning error due to interference. Fig. 1. shows the interference scenario that ISM equipments such as Arc welder, Signal generator, RF induction heater, etc operated in closed to GPS receiver.

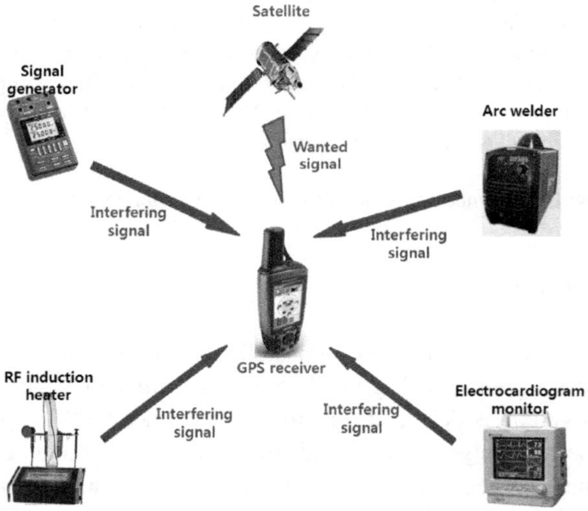

Fig. 1. Interference scenario that ISM equipments operate in close to GPS receiver

In the interference scenario, the protection distance that separation distance between ISM equipment and GPS receiver is needed in order to remove interference. As increasing the distance, the interfering signal can be attenuated by path loss.

2.2 ISM Equipment as Interferer

For setting up interfering signal for ISM equipment, International Special Committee on Radio Interference CISPR 11 limit was applied. CISPR was founded to set standards for controlling electromagnetic interference in electrical and electronic devices, and is a part of the International Electrotechnical Commission (IEC). Also, CISPR 11 gives a regulation on radiation limit that is allowable maximum radiation field strength for ISM equipment.

In the frequency band of 1575.42 MHz (GPS system), the radiation limit is 92 dBuV/m according to CISPR 11 [1]. Then, it is assumed that interfering signal of ISM equipment is continuous radiating in the entire GPS reception band. This assumption can be the worst case among interference scenario.

This field strength (dBuV/m) from CISPR 11 is can be converted into power (dBm) with equation 1 as following,

$$P(dBm) = E(dBuV\,/\,m) - 20\log F(MHz) - 77.2 \tag{1}$$

Here, P : interfering power, E : interfering field strength, F : frequency

From equation 1, -49.15 dBm/MHz of interfering power was calculated and was applied to set up the interfering signal of ISM equipment.

2.3 GPS System as Victim

A GPS receiver calculates its position by precisely timing the signals sent by GPS satellites high above the Earth. Each satellite continually transmits messages that include the information of time and orbit. In the case that interfering signal is received into GPS receiver, the distortion of information from GPS satellite is generated by interference signal then, positioning error is happen. Therefore, GPS receiver is needed to protection from interference in order to get accuracy position. For simulation, parameters of GPS system are summarized in table. 1[2]

Table 1. Characteristics of GPS system

Parameters	Value
Frequency	1575.42 MHz
Bandwidth	2.046 MHz
Sensitivity	-130 dBm
Rx antenna height	1.5 m
Rx antenna gain	0 dBi
Noise floor	-108 dBm
I/N	-12 dB
Propagation model	Free space

The parameters from Table 1 are used to get protection distance. For statistic method, the I/N is used instead of C/I as protection ratio.

3 Interference Analysis Method

3.1 Minimum Coupling Loss (MCL)

The MCL method is useful for an initial assessment of frequency sharing, and is suitable for fairly static interference situations. But, it is not considering the mobility of GPS receiver. So, the result of MCL is for fixed scenario that interfering signal is not variable. The MCL is defined as path loss that should be attenuated to prevent interference between interfering transmitter and victim receiver. In order to calculate Interfering power in the GPS bandwidth, equation 2 is needed as following [3],

$$P_{GPS} = P_{ISM} + 10\log(\frac{BW_{GPS}}{BW_{ISM}}) \tag{2}$$

Here, P_{GPS} : Power in the GPS bandwidth, P_{ISM} : Power in the 1MHz bandwidth

Then, the MCL is obtained with equation 3 as following [4][5],

$$MCL = P_{GPS} - Sen. + G - L + 10\log N \tag{3}$$

Here, Sen. : Sensitivity of GPS, G : Antenna gain, L : Cable loss, N : Number of interferer

Finally, protection distance can be calculated with equation 4 as following [6],

$$D = 10\text{^}[(MCL - 20\log(F) + 27.55)/20] \tag{4}$$

Here, F : Frequency, MCL : minimum coupling loss

Equation 4 is path loss from free space model. This model is used in the line of sight path with no obstacles nearby to cause reflection of diffraction.

3.2 Monte Carlo (MC)

The MC method is statistic analysis based on Monte Carlo technique and is considering mobility of GPS receiver. In many practical applications, MC method is useful to predict the statistical error. Fig. 2. Shows interfering link and victim link which include Interfering transmitter (It : ISM equipment), Victim receiver (Vr : GPS receiver), Wt (Wanted transmitter : Satellite)[7].

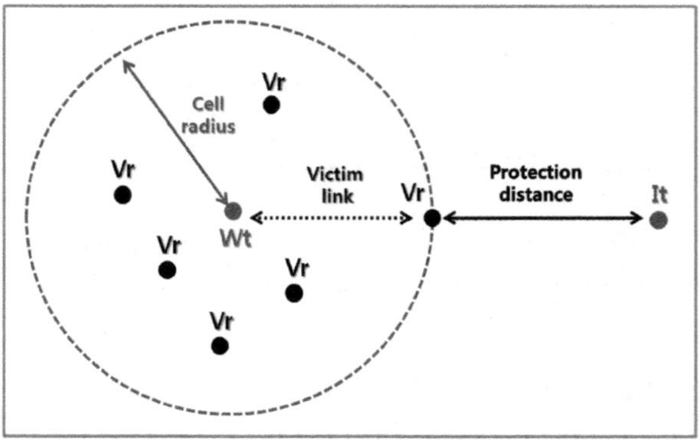

Fig. 2. The interfering link and victim link including It, Vr, Wt.

In this simulation, desired Received Signal Strength (dRSS) which is from Satellite and interfering Received Signal Strength (iRSS) which is from ISM equipment are different according to the location of Vr independently. So, statistic method such as probability was required.

Fig. 3 shows that how to calculate interference probability. The interference adds to the noise floor. The difference between the wanted signal strength and the interference signal is measured in dB, which is defined as the signal to interference ratio. This ratio must be more than the required C/I target if interference is to be avoided. The MC method is used to check over this condition and record whether or not interference is occurring [8].

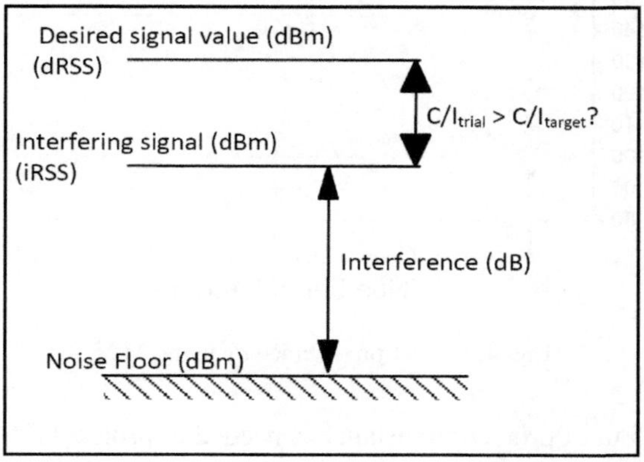

Fig. 3. The comparison between C/I and C/I target

The samples of C/I are compared against the C/I target to calculate the probability with the condition that the desired received signal strengths is greater than the sensitivity of the victim receiver with equation 5 as follow,

$$P = P(\frac{dRSS}{iRSS} > \frac{C}{I} \mid dRSS > Sensitivity) \tag{5}$$

Here, P : Probability that there is no interference.

Finally, interference probability of victim receiver is calculated with equation 6 as following,

$$P_I = 1 - P \tag{6}$$

Here, P_I : Probability of interference.

4 Interference Analysis Result

4.1 Protection Distance from MCL

In the static case, the protection distances were shown Fig. 4. according to number of interferer by using MCL. As increase of number of ISM equipment, higher protection distance is need to protect GPS system.

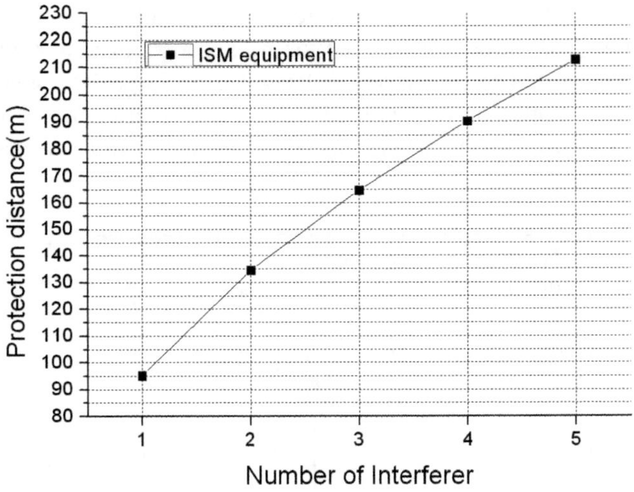

Fig. 4. Protection distance by using MCL

As in Fig. 4, 95 m of protection distance is needed to protect GPS system in case of one interferer. This protection distance can guarantee no interference from ISM equipment to GPS system.

4.2 Protection Distance from MC

In the statistic case, the Interference probabilities were shown in Fig. 5 according to number of interferer. As increase of number of ISM equipment, higher interference probability is calculated in the case that protection distance is fixed.

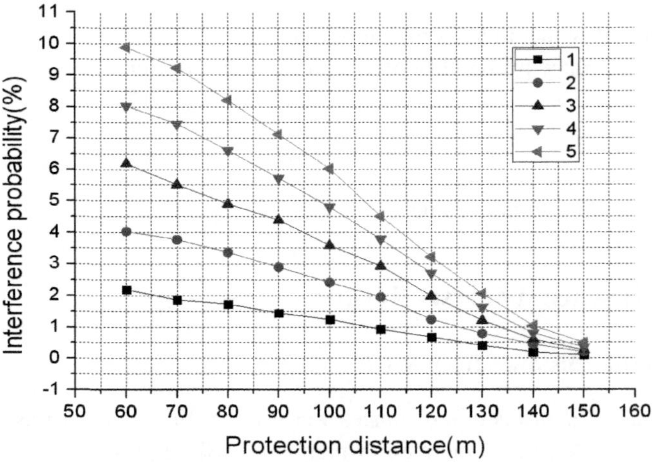

Fig. 5. Protection distance by using MC

Fig. 5. shows that the interference probability decreases as protection distance increases. According to the result, the protection distance is determined to meet 2 % of interference probability below. Therefore, in case of one interferer, 65 m of the protection distance is required to protect GPS system. GPS system has high importance. As regarding this, the 2 % of interference probability that is stricter than others is applied for GPS system.

5 Conclusions

This paper is about compatibility between ISM equipment and GPS system base on interference analysis from ISM equipment to GPS system. For the interference analysis, the scenario that ISM equipment is operated in closed to GPS receiver was set up. Then, protection distance is calculated by using MCL and the interference probability is calculated by using MC method in the scenario.

As a result, 95 m of protection distance was suggested by using MCL in the static case. And, 65 m of protection distance was suggested by using MC in statistic case. These protection distances will be helpful for the operation of stable GPS system.

References

1. CISPR : Industrial, scientific and medical (ISM) radio-frequency equipment-Electromagnetic disturbance characteristics limits and methods of measurement. CISPR Publication 11 (June 2004)
2. Borre, D., Akos, D.M., Bertelsen, N., Rinder, P., Jensen, S.H.: A Software-Defined GPS and Galileo Receiver, p. 54. Springer, Heidelberg (2005)
3. ERC Report 104, : Compatibility between Mobile Radio Systems operating in The range 450-470MHz and Digital Video Broadcasting-Terrestrial (DVB-T) System operating in UHF TV Channel 21 (470-478MHz), ECC within CEPT, p. 54 (June 2007)
4. ERC Report 101, : A comparison of the minimum coupling loss method, enhanced minimum coupling loss method, and the monte-carlo simulation, ERC, pp. 25–26 (May 1999)
5. Dafesh, P.A., Hanson, P., Yowell, R.: A portable UWB to GPS emission simulator. IEEE, 405–413 (April 2004)
6. Reynolds, M., Rhodes, A., Klein, J.: PMSE Spectrum Usage Right & Interference Analysis. SEAMCAT, 14 (June 2008)
7. CEPT Administrations, : Monte-Carlo Simulation methodology for the use in sharing and compatibility studies between different radio services or systems, ERC within the CEPT (February 2000)
8. ECO : SEAMCAT Handbook, CEPT, p. 56 (January 2010)

A Context Aware Data-Centric Storage Scheme in Wireless Sensor Networks

Hyunju Kim[1], Junho Park[1], Dongook Seong[2], and Jaesoo Yoo[1,*]

[1] Department of Information and Communication Engineering,
Chungbuk National University,
410 Seongbong-ro, Heungdeok-gu, Cheongju, Chungbuk, Korea
[2] Korea Advanced Institute of Science and Technology,
291 Daehak-ro, Yuseong-gu, Daejeon, Korea
{Hyunjuu,seong.do}@gmail.com,
{junhopark,yjs}@chungbuk.ac.kr

Abstract. In wireless sensor networks, a data-centric storage scheme (DCS) is one of representative researches to store sensor readings and to process a query efficiently. The DCS scheme assigns distributed data regions to sensor nodes and stores sensor readings to the sensor node which is responsible for the data region to process the query efficiently. However, the existing DCS schemes have some drawbacks that the sensor nodes have the fixed ranges to store sensor readings. Because the ranges of the sensor readings change periodically in real world applications, the existing DCS schemes have problems that they use storage space unevenly in entire sensors and their network lifetimes are reduced. To solve such problems, we propose a context aware data-centric storage scheme to store sensor readings equally in the entire sensor network. To show the superiority of our proposed scheme, we compare it with the existing DCS schemes. Our experimental results show that our proposed scheme improves about 377.7% network lifetime over the existing schemes on average.

Keywords: Wireless Sensor Networks, Data-Centric Storage Scheme, In-Network Query Processing.

1 Introduction

In recent, wireless sensor networks(WSNs) are widely used not only in natural phenomenon observation, military applications, industrial areas, disaster lookout and medical services but also in practical life with the leap of development in computing and communications hardware technologies[1]. WSNs are generally composed of at least hundreds of or even millions of sensor nodes. Such sensor nodes with the small size are characterized by the battery with a low capacity, the limited use of energy, and the limited data processing capability. Moreover, it is practically impossible to change or recharge the battery for each sensor node. Therefore, a data processing and storage scheme is absolutely required to maximize the lifetime of the sensor network[2].

* Corresponding author.

T.-h. Kim et al. (Eds.): MulGraB 2011, Part II, CCIS 263, pp. 326–330, 2011.

There are External Storage (ES), Local Storage (LS), and Data Centric Storage (DCS as typical ways to store the collected data and to process the query in the sensor network)[3,4,5]. To improve the performance of the query processing of the sensor network, many DCS schemes have vigorously been done to store the collected data and to efficiently process a query in the sensor network. In the DCS schemes, the collected data are classified by a hash function based on the data value or regional location. They are stored in specific sensor nodes according to the regions assigned to them. Therefore, when processing a query, the DCS schemes are effective because it is not distributed to the whole network but is processed in the nodes that store the data for it. However, the range of sensor readings changes periodically in real world applications according to the time (e.g. seasons) such as atmospheric temperature, water temperature distribution of the sea, and rainfall. In this environment, if the existing schemes store the data in the basis of the fixed data storage range, they generate inequality of storage space utilization for sensor nodes of the entire network and has reverse effects on network lifetime due to hot-spot[6].

In this paper, we propose a context aware data-centric storage scheme to store sensor readings equally in the entire sensor network. in order to solve these problems. The proposed scheme suggests an algorithm to effectively change the entire storage range of the sensor network by recognizing data generation patterns and to effectively utilize storage. By using this, the proposed scheme assures high storage utilization and improves the network lifetime.

2 The Proposed Context Aware Data-Centric Storage Scheme

Generally, wireless sensor networks are mainly used for natural phenomena with periodic data change. Fig. 1 shows the dead range that no data storage occurs according to data generation patterns. The wireless sensor networks are configured to store the data in a range of -20 ~ 40°C and generate the sensor readings in ranges A, B or C at individual cycles. The data are concentrated on the nodes to store data in these ranges but no data are stored in the nodes that are responsible for data storage in other ranges. Therefore, we suggest a novel data-centric storage scheme to increase the utilization of sensor network storage by minimizing the dead range.

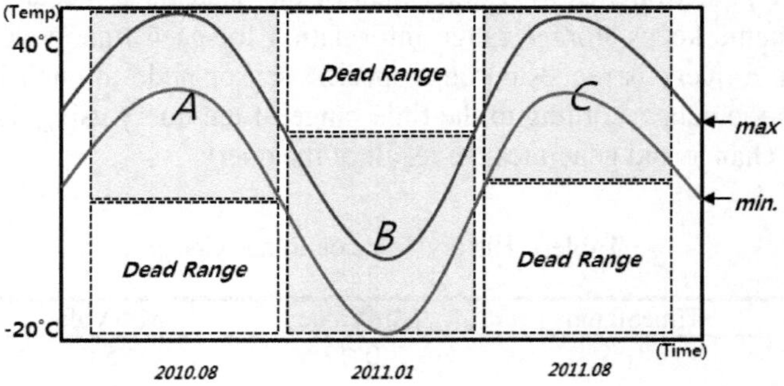

Fig. 1. The Graph of Temperature Change over Time

In the proposed scheme, it is necessary to change the entire storage range for the case with the outlier data out of the entire storage range and the case without data of storage range for a certain time or more.

First, in the case with outlier data as shown on Fig. 2-(a), as there are no sensor nodes to store outlier data on the sensor network, the entire storage range should be changed so as to include the values of the outlier data. Second, in the case with data of storage range for a certain time or more as shown on Fig. 2-(b), data are concentrated on specific range values and dead ranges occur. In order to minimize the dead ranges in the case in Fig. 2-(b), if a range without data for a threshold value(γ) or more occurs, it is required to change the entire storage range.

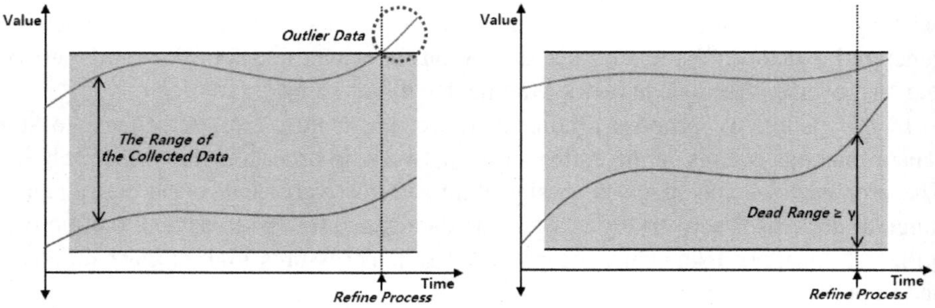

(a) The Occurrence of Outlier Data (b) The Occurrence of Dead Range

Fig. 2. The Graph of Temperature Change over Time

When each sensor node does not have data within their responsible storage range for more than time β, it sends a dead range generation message to the base station. If the range is larger than threshold, the sensor node determines the respective range as the dead range. The storage range determined as a dead range is required to be excluded from the entire storage ranges to calculate new entire storage ranges and distribute it to the entire sensor nodes to minimize the dead ranges.

The proposed scheme has different entire storage ranges according to individual time zones (e.g. seasons) as the outlier data of the dead range occur. Therefore, the proposed scheme keeps storage range information for each time zone in the sensor nodes. When a query is requested on a specific sensor node through it, each sensor node divides the data according to the time range of the query using the history table on the range change and generates the result of the query.

Table 1. History Table on Range Change

TimeStamp	MinValue	MaxValue
t_1	0℃	25℃
…	…	…
n	-20℃	10℃

3 Performance Evaluation

We have developed a simulator based on JAVA to evaluate our proposed scheme and the existing DCS scheme. We assume that 100 sensors are deployed uniformly in 100 x 100 (m) network field. The radius of communication is set to 18 (m) and the size of a data packet is set to 32 (Bytes). The model of the energy consumed for receiving the message from a sensor node is $\{MessageSize\} \times (\{TransmissionCost\} + \{AmplificationCost\} \times \{Distance\}^2)$, where the transmission cost is $50nJ/b$ and the amplification cost is set to $100pJ/b/m^2$. The model of the energy consumed for receiving the message from a sensor node is $\{MessageSize\} \times \{ReceiveCost\}$, where the receiving cost is set to $50nJ/b$. We used real datasets, which are temperature and humidity data measured in the Washington State [7].

Fig. 3 shows the rates of storage utilization and the ratio of survived nodes according to the execution time of network. The proposed scheme evenly distributes storage load to the entire sensor nodes by adjusting the entire storage range according to data generation patterns. However, because the existing scheme cannot evenly utilize the entire sensor nodes to store the data, storage load is concentrated on specific sensor nodes and the network lifetime is reduced. According to the execution time of network, the proposed scheme improves the storage utilization by 498% and the network lifetime by 377.7% over the existing DCS scheme.

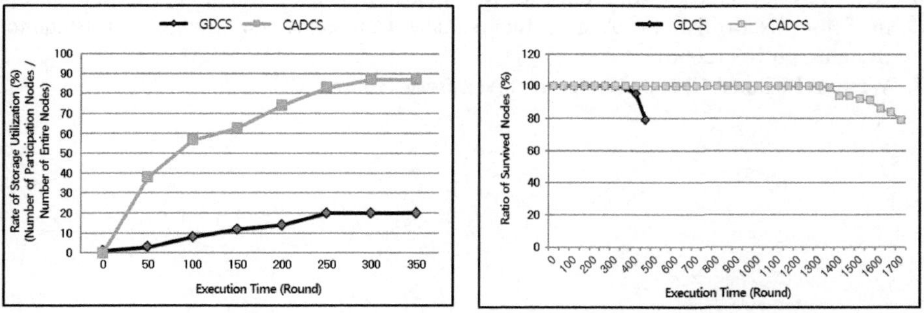

(a) Rate of Storage Utilization (b) Ratio of Survived Nodes

Fig. 3. Performance According to the Execution Time of Network

4 Conclusions

In this paper, we have proposed a novel data-centric storage scheme that solves the problems of the existing scheme. When data generation patterns change, this scheme resets the entire storage ranges to relieve the inequality of storage. Therefore, it is possible to store the data evenly and to increase the network lifetime. As the results of performance evaluation, the proposed scheme showed that storage utilization was improved by about 498% on average and the ratio of survived nodes was extended by about 377.7% on average over the existing DCS schemes. Therefore, it is very suitable for conserving energy and extending the lifetime of sensor networks.

Acknowledgments. This work was supported by the Ministry of Education, Science and Technology Grant funded by the Korea Government"(The Regional Research Universities Program/Chungbuk BIT Research-Oriented University Consortium) and Basic Science Research Program through the National Research Foundation of Korea(NRF) grant funded by the Korea government(MEST)(No. 2009-0080279).

References

1. Cerpa, A., Elson, J., Estrin, D., Girod, L., Hamilton, M., Zhao, J.: Habitat Monitoring: Application Driver for Wireless Communications Technology. In: ACM Workshop on Data Communications in Latin America and the Caribbean, pp. 20–41 (2001)
2. Culler, D., Estrin, D., Srivastava, M.: Guest Editors' Introduction: Overview of Sensor Networks. IEEE Computer 37(8), 41–49 (2004)
3. Li, X., Kim, Y., Govindan, R., Hon, W.: Multi-Dimensional Range Queries in Sensor Networks. In: ACM Conference on Embedded Networked Sensor Systems (SenSys 2003), pp. 63–75 (2003)
4. Aly, M., Pruhs, K., Chrysanthis, P.K.: KDDCS: a Load-balanced In-Network Data-Centric Storage Scheme for Sensor Networks. In: ACM Conference on Information and Knowledge Management(CIKM 2006), pp. 317–326 (2006)
5. Shin, J., You, J., Song, S.: GDCS: Energy Efficient Grid Based Data Centric Storage for Sensor Networks. Journal of the Korea Contents Association 9(1), 98–105 (2009)
6. Aly, M., Chrysanthis, P.K., Pruths, K.: Decomposing Data-Centric Storage Query Hot-Spot in Sensor Networks. In: Annual International Conference on Mobile and Ubiquitous Systems, pp.1–9 (2006)
7. Western Regional Climate Center, `http://www.wrcc.dri.edu`

A Continuous Query Processing Method in Broadcast Environments

Yonghun Park, Kyoungsoo Bok, and Jaesoo Yoo*

Dept. of Information and Communincation Engineering
Chungbuk National University, Korea
{yhpark1119,ksbok,yjs}@chungbuk.ac.kr

Abstract. To provide efficient location based services, various methods that process a query in broadcast environments have been proposed. In broadcast environments, a server broadcasts data periodically and a client receives the data and processes a query. Recently, several methods to process a continuous query for mobile objects in broadcast environments have been proposed. However, since clients process the query using the index of the past data that is already built before the broadcast in the methods, the accuracy of the query result is low. They also do not consider the mobility of the objects during the broadcast cycle. Therefore, the methods are not suitable for a continuous query over the dynamically moving objects. In this paper, we propose a new indexing method for a continuous query in broadcast environments. The proposed method uses the vector attributes of objects to reduce the error of the result during the broadcast cycle. To process the continuous query, clients receive the all data intersected with additional regions containing the objects affecting the query in the broadcast cycle as well as the query region. The proposed method also minimizes the additional search regions to save the costs of receiving the data and computing the query. To show the superiority of the proposed method, we evaluate the performance from various perspectives.

Keywords: Broadcast, Continuous query, Moving object.

1 Introduction

The interests of LBS(location based services) have been highly increased with the development of location aware technologies and the wide spread of smart phones. LBS is a kind of the services that provide the information related to the location to users. The typical examples of LBS are to find near gas stations, to provide the information of hotels, restaurants and hospital, and to get the locations of bus and taxi. Until now, most of the LBS services have been focused on static objects. However, the services over dynamically moving objects will have received much attention increased in the near future. Since the interests of LBS have been increasing all over the world, we expect that the core technologies of LBS will make it a higher value-added business.

* Corresponding author.

T.-h. Kim et al. (Eds.): MulGraB 2011, Part II, CCIS 263, pp. 331–337, 2011.

In wireless mobile computing environments, the data dissemination methods are classified by on-demand and broadcast accesses. In the on-demand access method, a mobile client submits a request to a server and the server locates the appropriate data and returns it to the mobile clients. In the broadcast access, data are broadcasted on a wireless channel open to the public. After a mobile client receives a query from the user, it tunes into the broadcast channel and filters out the data. The advantages of the on-demand access are that a client requests queries and receives the results in real time. However, the huge cost of processing a query is centralized to the server site when the number of clients is increased. Compared to the on-demand access, the broadcast access has the advantage of scaling up the services a huge number of clients without any additional costs at the server site [2].

Recently, several methods to process a continuous query for mobile objects in broadcast environments have been proposed. However, since clients process the query using the index of the past data that is already built before the broadcast in the methods, the accuracy of the query result is low. They also do not consider the mobility of the objects during the broadcast cycle. Therefore, the methods are not suitable for a continuous query over the dynamically moving objects.

In this paper, we propose a new indexing method for a continuous query in broadcast environments. The proposed method uses the vector attributes of objects to reduce the error of the result during the broadcast cycle. To process a continuous query, clients receive the all data intersect with additional search region containing the objects affecting the query result in the broadcast cycle as well as the query region. Then, the data is provided to users at the appropriate time in next broadcast cycle. The additional search region is estimated by projecting the vectors of the objects. The size of the additional search region depends on the maximum vector values of objects. As the size of the additional search region is increased, the cost of receiving the object data of the region at client site is increased. We also minimize the additional search region to save the cost of receiving the data. To minimize the additional search region, we change the baseline time of the index. The baseline time is the time that builds index based on the projected location of objects by their vector attributes. To show the superiority of the proposed method, we evaluate the performance from various perspectives.

The rest of this paper is organized as follows. Section 2 describes the related work. Section 3 proposes a new indexing method for a continuous query in broadcast environments. Section 4 shows the performance evaluation in the various points of view. Finally, section 4 presents the conclusions.

2 Related Work

A data dissemination method using R-tree structure on broadcast environments was proposed [1]. The method serializes the MBRs in the order of Hilbert-curve based on the center points of the MBRs and sends them on schedule. A parent node has the time to broadcast the children instead of the positions on disk so clients travel the serialized index in branch-and-bound manner. To improve the latency and tuning time, a data dissemination method using grid structure was proposed [2]. The method serializes the cells in the grid in the order of Hilbert-curve based on the center points of the cells and sends them on schedule. Since the size of the structural information on grid is smaller then that of tree-structure, the method cuts off the duration of the broadcast cycle and the latency and turning time to process queries.

Recently, several data dissemination methods to provide continuous queries over mobile objects on broadcast environments were proposed [3][4]. [3] provides the continuous queries over moving client and static objects. [4] provides the continuous queries over moving objects as well as moving objects. The method is based on the grid structure, and uses the dirty grid that is a bit-pattern and presents the updated cells in the grid. Every packet contains the dirty grid. The method figures out the cell to be searched in the broadcast cycle incrementally through the comparing the last result and dirty-grid. As other researches, [5] is a data dissemination method using multi-channels. [6] provides the search the shortest path on the broadcast environments.

3 The Proposed Method

Broadcast access method reduces the load to process queries at server site and shift the load to clients. It is because the clients analysis the broadcast data and compute the result of the queries. Therefore, latency and tuning time are used to evaluate the performance. Turning time is the amount of time spent by a client listening to the channel. This will determine the power consumed by the client to retrieve the request data. Latency is the time elapse from the time a client requests data to the point when the client downloaded all required data [2].

Index is important part in the data dissemination method. A Server disseminates the data on schedule and the schedule is presented by index structures. Figure 1 shows the relationship between index structure and dissemination schedule. Figure 1(a) presents a R-tree index structure and Figure 1(b) presents the serialized broadcast schedule in a broadcast cycle. In the broadcast schedule, a parent node has the time to broadcast the children instead of the positions on disk so clients travel the serialized index in branch-and-bound manner. As shown in Figure 1(b), after receiving the root node, client waits for the child node on broadcast cycle. It is continued until all request data are received.

(a) R-tree index (b) Serialized index for broadcast

Fig. 1. Serialized index structure on broadcast channel

The proposed method uses TPR-tree index structure to adapt the vector attributes into the index. The search manner is similar to R-tree but additional search region is required in TPR-tree according to the time of processing queries. For continuous queries, a client should receive all query result for the whole time of available time region for the broadcast data. Figure 2 shows the relationship between a query region and addition search region. The vertical axis presents one-dimensional data space and the horizontal axis presents one-dimensional time space. Q denotes the query region and R denotes the addition search region for the available time region T.

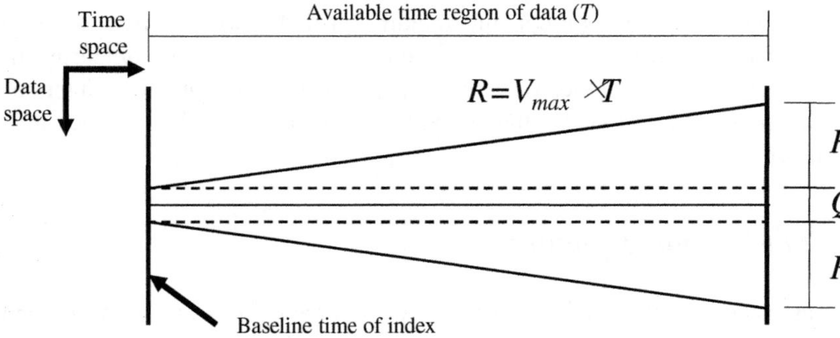

Fig. 2. Relationship between query region and additional search region

Available time region for the broadcast data is not the time duration for a broadcast cycle. We define that the available time region is the time duration from beginning of processing a query on this broadcast cycle to end of processing the query on next broadcast cycle. It is because the query result should be available until the query result is computed for next broadcast cycle. For the worst case, if the request data of a query is scheduled to the end of broadcast cycle, the query result should be available to the end of the next broadcast cycle. If T is the available time region and T_{bc} is the time duration for a broadcast cycle, we set T is $2 \times T_{bc}$.

The additional search region is decided by the vector attributes of objects and available time region. However, we change the baseline time of the index to minimize the additional search region. The baseline time is the time that builds index based on the projected location of objects by their vector attributes. The movement range of an object in the available time region is reduced by changing the baseline time. To minimize the additional search region, we decide the baseline time is the mid-point of the available time region of the broadcast data. Figure 3 shows the additional search region according to the baseline time of index. If the baseline time of index is the beginning of T, the total search region is $2R + Q$ and R is $V_{max} \times T$, where V_{max} is the maximum vector values of objects as shown in Figure 2. However, if the baseline time of index is set to the mid-point of T, R is $V_{max} \times (T / 2)$ because the movement range of an object from the baseline time is reduced as $T / 2$.

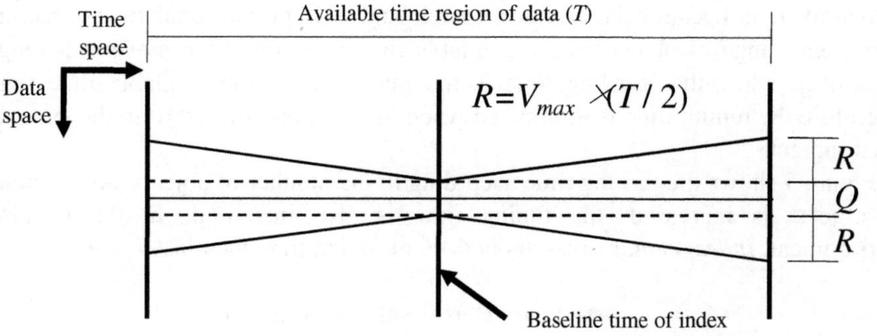

Fig. 3. Additional search region according to the baseline time of index

4 Performance Evaluation

To evaluate the performance, we measure the tuning time of the proposed method. Since it is difficult to limit the bandwidth in the simulation, we present the tuning time as the number of node access to shows accurate performance evaluation [1]. The proposed method is the first attempt to adapt the vector attributes on broadcast environments so we compare our proposed method according to the baseline time of index. *Index_start* denotes the index that the time baseline is set to beginning of the available time region and *Index_center* denotes the index that the time baseline is set to mid-point of the available time region. The index space is set to $10^3 \times 10^3$ and the broadcast period is set to 10 seconds. The number of client is set to 100 and each client request a continuous query that the region size is 20×20. The node fan-out of the index is set to 50. We measure the tuning time according to the number of objects from 10^5 to 10^6 and the maximum vector value of object from 1/s to 5/s. The default values of the number of objects and the maximum vector value are 6×10^5 and 3/s, respectively.

We, first, evaluate the tuning time according to the baseline time of the index. Since the broadcast period is 10, the available time region is 20. Figure 4 shows the result. As we expected, when the baseline time is 10, the tuning time has the smallest result. In addition, as the baseline time is far from the mid-point, the tuning time is

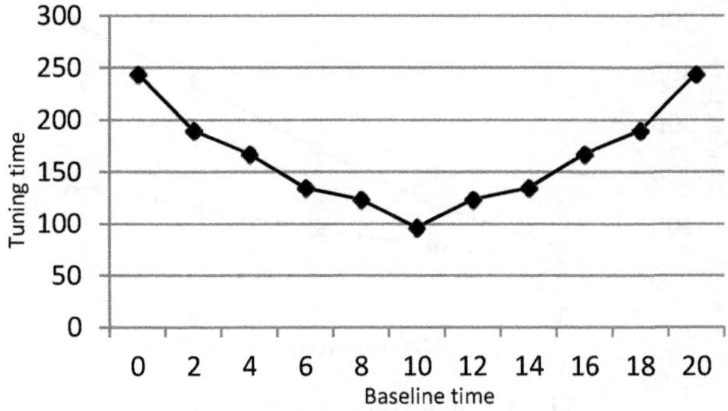

Fig. 4. Tuning time according to the baseline time of index

increased. It is because the addition search region is proportional to the maximum movement range of objects in the available time region and the movement range is minimized when the baseline time is the mid-point of the available time region. Therefore the tuning time is minimized when the baseline time is 10 in the simulation environment.

Figure 5 shows the turning time according to the number of objects. As the number of objects is increased, the tuning time is also increased. In the simulation environment, *Index_center* saves about 60% of tuning time then *Index_start.*

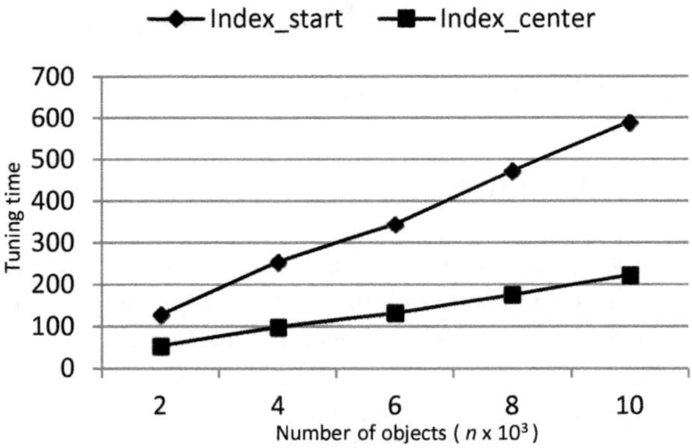

Fig. 5. Tuning time according to the number of objects

Figure 6 presents the tuning time according to the maximum vector value of objects (V_{max}). As V_{max} is increased, the tuning time is also increased. It is because the additional search range is proportional to V_{max}. *Index_center* is overall better then *Index_start* in terms of the tuning time. While V_{max} is from 1 to 5, *Index_center* saves about from 50% to 65% of tuning time. The simulation shows the benefit is increased as V_{max} is increased.

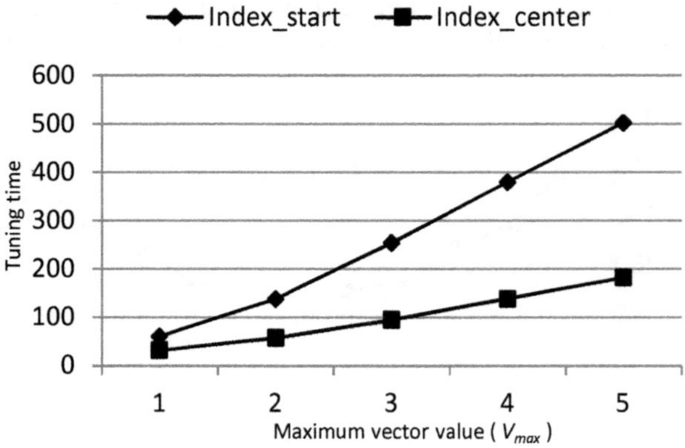

Fig. 6. Tuning time according to V_{max}

5 Conclusion

In this paper, we proposed a new indexing method for a continuous query in broadcast environments. The proposed method uses the vector attributes of objects to reduce the error of the query result during the broadcast cycle and minimizes the additional search regions to save the cost of receiving the data. To minimize the additional search regions, we change the baseline time of the index. To show the superiority of the proposed method, we evaluated the tuning time from various perspectives. Through the change of the baseline time of the index, we saved about 60% of tuning time in the simulation environments.

Acknowledgments. This work was supported by the Ministry of Education, Science and Technology Grant funded by the Korea Government (The Regional Research Universities Program/Chungbuk BIT Research-Oriented University Consortium) and Basic Science Research Program through the National Research Foundation of Korea(NRF) grant funded by the Korea government(MEST)(No. 2009-0089128).

References

1. Hambrusch, S., Liu, C.-M., Aref, W.G., Prabhakar, S.: Query Processing in Broadcasted Spatial Index Trees. In: Jensen, C.S., Schneider, M., Seeger, B., Tsotras, V.J. (eds.) SSTD 2001. LNCS, vol. 2121, pp. 502–521. Springer, Heidelberg (2001)
2. Zheng, B., Lee, W.C., Lee, D.L.: Spatial index on air. In: Proc. Intl. Conf. on Pervasive Computing and Communications, pp. 297–304 (2003)
3. Zheng, B., Lee, W.C., Lee, D.L.: Search continuous nearest neighbors on air. In: Proc. Intl. Conf. on Mobile and Ubiquitous Systems: Networking and Services, pp. 236–245 (2004)
4. Mouratidis, K., Bakiras, S., Papadias, D.: Continuous Monitoring of Spatial Queries in Wireless Broadcast Environments. IEEE Trans. on Mobile Computing 8(10), 1297–1311 (2009)
5. Amarmend, D., Aritsugi, M., Kanamori, Y.: An Air Index for Data Access over Multiple Wireless Broadcast Channels. In: Proc. Intl, Conf. on Data Engineering, p. 135 (2006)
6. Kellaris, G., Mouratidis, K.: Shortest path computation on air indexes. In: Proc. Intl. Conf. on Very Large Data Base (VLDB) Endowment, vol. 3(1), pp. 747–757 (2010)

An Adaptive Genetic Simulated Annealing Algorithm for QoS Multicast Routing

Bo Peng and Lei Li

Graduate School of Engineering, Hosei University, Koganei, Tokyo 184-8584 Japan

Abstract. As a result of the emergence of many kinds of high-speed communication systems and increasing demand of distributed multimedia applications, efficient and effective support of quality of service (QoS) has become more and more essential. Many service models and mechanisms have been put forward by IETF to meeting QoS requirement, multicast service is a key one of them and is becoming a key requirement of computer network supposing multimedia application.

Multicasting consists of concurrently sending the same information from a source to a subset of all possible destinations in a computer network. Multicast utilizes a tree delivery structure, on which data packets are duplicated only at fork nodes and are forwarded only once over each link. This approach makes multicast resource—efficient in delivering data to a group of member simultaneously and can scale well to support very large multicast group. This paper focuses on the algorithms to construct low cost multicast routing tree with QoS requirements.

In this paper, we study the bandwidth, delay, delay jitter, and packet loss constrained least cost multicast routing problem which is known to be NP-complete, and present a adaptive genetic simulated annealing algorithm (AGASA) to solve the problem. The proposed genetic algorithm has the following characteristics: (1) Tree structure coding scheme, by which we can use any data structure of the tree to describe the chromosome structure, is an effective solution to the algorithm in the coding and decoding. (2) Genetic algorithm is improved, and simulated annealing algorithm is combined with. Simulated annealing algorithm has stronger local search capabilities, which avoids a partial optimum during the search process. (3) The crossover and mutation probability of adaptive genetic algorithm is improved. The selection of the crossover and mutation probability is the key to the behavior and performance of the algorithm, which has the direct impact on the convergence of the algorithm.

The simulation results show that the algorithm has fast convergence and better performance. It is able to satisfy the changing network scale.

T.-h. Kim et al. (Eds.): MulGraB 2011, Part II, CCIS 263, p. 338, 2011.

A Quantified Audio Watermarking Algorithm Based on DWT-DCT

De Li[1], Yingying Ji[1], and JongWeon Kim[2]

[1] Dept. of Computer at Yanbian University, China
leader1223@ybu.edu.cn, ji_yingying@163.com
[2] Dept. of Copyright Protection at Sangmyung University, Korea
jwkim@smu.ac.kr

Abstract. An improved digital watermarking algorithm for audio was proposed based on DWT and DCT. Firstly, the binary watermark image which will be embedded to the audio convert signal was pre-processed; and the audio convert signal was divided evenly, the audio segments were selected from the divided audio, then by doing the DWT and DCT embedded the watermark to the low frequency coefficients of those audio segments which were selected; Finally, all of the audio segments were regrouped. The experimental results show that the proposed algorithm is more imperceptible and more robust against to the combinational attack.

Keywords: Audio Watermark, DWT, DCT, Scrambling, Quantization.

1 Introduction

With the rapid development of computer network, multimedia and information science, problems about copyright protection and integrity authentication of digital media have became more and more serious. Digital watermarking is an effective way to solve this kind of problem. Digital audio watermarking technology [1~3] is an effective means to protect the copyright of digital audio. Now it has become one of the hottest research points in the area of multimedia information processing and information security.

In this paper, we proposed a quantified algorithm of audio watermarking based on DWT-DCT. In Section 2, we introduced the proposed algorithm included the preprocessing, embedding and extracting process. Section 3 we did the experiments of attacking the watermarked audio, and examine the robustness against common attacks and combinational attack. A conclusion was drawn in the last section.

2 The Proposed Algorithm

2.1 The Basic Principle of Audio Watermarking Based on DWT-DCT

In this paper we used a binary image as a watermark. Divide the host audio into N segments evenly and do the DWT for each segment which we have selected, and then

T.-h. Kim et al. (Eds.): MulGraB 2011, Part II, CCIS 263, pp. 339–344, 2011.

do the DCT for the low frequency coefficients of which segment has been DWT transformed then get the coefficients. Then embed the watermark information into those coefficients quantitatively as follow method.

Where k denotes quantized interval. According to the value of k, we can divide those coefficients into A for 1 and B for 0 [4, 6] as equation (1):

$$A_i = 2ik + k/2$$
$$B_i = 2ik - k/2,\ i = 0, \pm 1, \pm 2, ... \tag{1}$$

If the value of watermark is 1, quantified as the midpoint of the nearest Class A; or quantified as the midpoint of the nearest Class B. Reassemble all the audio segments at last.

The basic principle shown as Figure 1:

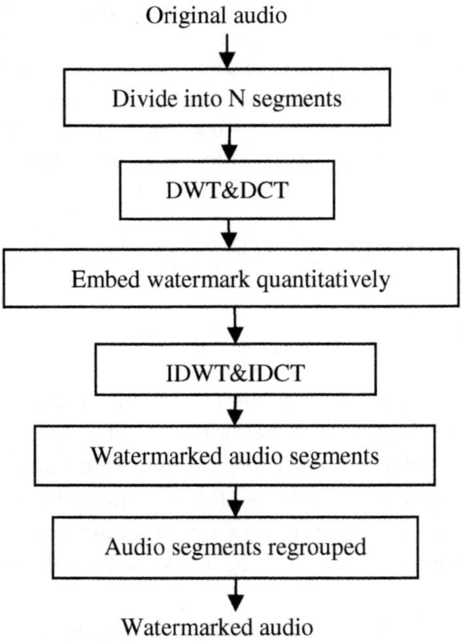

Fig. 1. Basic principle of audio watermark based on DWT and DCT

2.2 Watermark Preprocessing

In this paper, we chose meaningful binary image as watermark information. Watermark image w is a binary image of size M × N. In order to enhance the confidentiality of the watermark image and reduce its relevance, we used Arnold transform [5] to scramble watermark image firstly, which can disrupt an image regularly and making the image looks like random noise.

Suppose there is an image of size M × M and the gray value of the position (i, j) can be moved to the position (i', j') through a transformation. Equation (2) shows the relation.

$$\begin{bmatrix} i' \\ j' \end{bmatrix} = \begin{bmatrix} 1 & 1 \\ 1 & 2 \end{bmatrix} \begin{bmatrix} i \\ j \end{bmatrix} (\bmod M) \tag{2}$$

If we know the scrambling cycle it is very easy to descrambling because of the reversibility of the Arnold transform.

In this paper, the watermark image w is two-dimensional signal, and audio signal is one-dimensional signal, therefore we need to change the watermark image to one-dimensional signal as follow:

$$V = \{v(k) = w(i, j), 1 \le i \le M, 1 \le j \le N, k = i + j \times (M - 1)\}$$

Through processing, the element v(k) of the sequence V denotes the pixel w(i, j) of watermark w.

2.3 Watermark Embedding Algorithm

The embedding algorithm described as follows;

1) Read the original audio I of length LEN, and divided into segments Q (Q = LEN / piece) evenly and numbered each segment, where "piece" is the length of every segment.
2) Extract all the even-numbered segments of the original audio and renumbered. Do the H-level DWT for all the renumbered segments.
3) Do the DCT for the low frequency coefficients which selected from the DWT coefficients, and get the DC component and AC component.
4) Embed the watermark image (of size M × N) which has been preprocessed. Check the number of the renumbered segments, if its number is even then one bit will be embedded into DC component of the even segment quantitatively; if its number is odd then $\left\lceil \frac{M \times N \times 2}{\frac{Q}{2}} \right\rceil - 1$ bits will be embedded into AC components of this odd segment. After embedding the watermark information, we need to do the IDWT transform and IDCT transform for each segment.
5) Repeat step 4) until all the watermark information is embedded into the original audio segment.
6) Re-assemble the audio segments, and save as a new audio.

After processing all the steps, we can get the watermarked audio.

2.4 Watermark Extracting Algorithm

In this paper, we extracted watermark information without the original audio, it's a blind extraction. The extracting algorithm described as follows;

1) Read the watermarked audio I' of length LEN', and divided into segments Q (Q = LEN' / piece) evenly and numbered each segment.
2) Extract all the even-numbered segments of the watermarked audio and renumbered. Do the H-level DWT and then use the low-frequency coefficients to do the DCT for all the renumbered segments.
3) Extract the DC component of even segments and $\left\lceil \frac{M \times N \times 2}{\frac{Q}{2}} \right\rceil - 1$ bits AC components of odd segments.
4) According to the quantized algorithm, determine the watermark information of DC component and AC components which we have extracted is 1 or 0.
5) Repeat step 3), 4) until all the watermark information is extracted.
6) Transform the one-dimensional watermark information to two-dimensional watermark image, and get the watermark image after Arnold descrambling.

3 Experimental Results and Analysis

3.1 Evaluate the Performance of Watermark

Robustness and imperceptibility are very important for the copyright protection system of watermarking. In order to eliminate the subjective factors and reflect the fairness of copyright protection, we employed the normalized correlation coefficient (NC) to estimate the similarity between the original watermark and the extracted watermark. The normalized correlation coefficient (NC) is defined as equation (3):

$$NC(w, w') = \frac{\sum_{i=0}^{M-1}\sum_{j=0}^{N-1} w(i,j) \cdot w'(i,j)}{\sqrt{\sum_{i=0}^{M-1}\sum_{j=0}^{N-1} w^2(i,j)}\sqrt{\sum_{i=0}^{M-1}\sum_{j=0}^{N-1} w'^2(i,j)}} \tag{3}$$

Where w denotes original information and w' denotes the extracted information. The size of watermark is M×N.

We use SNR to measure not feeling intellectual of the watermarking.

3.2 Simulation Experiment

Through the simulation, we can verify the performance of proposed watermarking algorithm. In the experiment we chose the 10 seconds mono audio signal with the sampling frequency of 44.1 kHz and the resolution of 16 bits as original audio and chose the binary image "lena.bmp" of size 64×64 as watermark. DWT transform adopted the common wavelet "Daubechies-1" and level H = 3.

The waveform comparison of Original audio and watermarked audio as Figure 2:

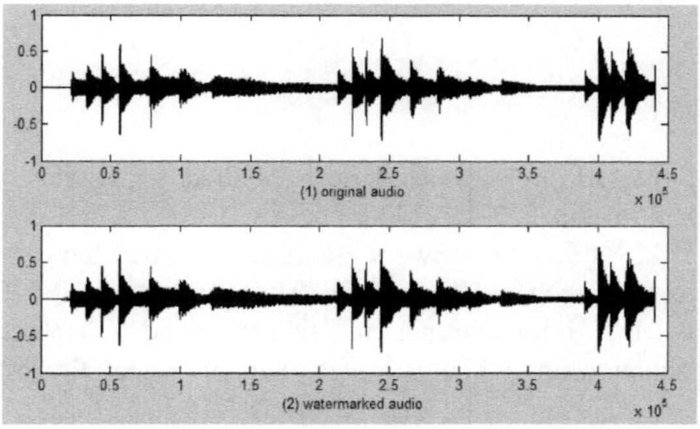

Fig. 2. Waveform comparison of original audio and watermarked audio

There is no significant difference between the two waveforms in Figure 2.

To evaluate the performance of watermark objectively, we did some common attacks to the watermarked audio [7], the experimental results were shown in table 1:

Table 1. Experimental results of proposed algorithm

	no attacks	compression	White noise	low-pass filter	combination attack
SNR (dB)	30.2285	19.7680	14.1989	23.6168	13.4854
NC	1.0000	0.9956	0.9647	0.9528	0.8948
Extracted watermark					

In table 1, it can be seen that using the proposed algorithm to embed watermark is inaudible. the combinational attack consists of compression, noise and low-pass filter. After the combinational attack, we still can extract watermark and it has good legibility.

4 Conclusions

This paper proposed an improved audio watermarking algorithm based on DCT and DWT. This algorithm is proved that it is robust to some common attacks like compression, noise and low-pass filter, etc. Moreover, it's also robust to the combination attack which is consist of compression, noise and low-pass filter. In future work we will further improve the processing efficiency and simultaneously improve the watermark embedding capacity of the algorithm.

Acknowledgements. This research project was supported by the Ministry of Culture, Sports and Tourism(MCST) and Korea Copyright Commission in 2011.

References

1. Nishimura, O., Suzuki, R.: Time-spread Echo Method for Digital Audio watermarking. IEEE Trans. on Multimedia, 212–221 (2005)
2. Yeo, I.K., Kim, H.J.: Modified patchwork algorithm: A novel audio watermarking scheme. IEEE Transactions on Speech and Audio Processing 11(4), 381–386 (2003)
3. Erelebi, E., Bataki, L.: Audio watermarking scheme based on embedding strategy in low frequency components with a binary image. Digital Signal Processing 19(2), 265–277 (2009)
4. Gao, H., Niu, X., Yang, Y.: Synchronous digital audio watermarking algorithm based on the quantitative wavelet domain. The Journal of Beijing post and Telecommunications University 28(16), 102–105 (2005)
5. Wu, F., Zhou, J.: The necessary conditions of two dimensions transform cycle digital image amold. The North University of Traffic 25(6), 66–69 (2001)
6. Chen, L., Yao, Z., Chen, L.: The project of audio frequency watermarking based on odd-even quantization fight synchronous attack. The Computer Engineering and Application 44(36), 112–114 (2008)
7. Steinebach, M., Petitcolas, F., Raynal, F., Dittmann, J., Fontaine, C., Seibel, S., et al.: Stirmark benchmark: Audio watermarking attacks. In: Proceedings of the International Conference on Information Technology: Coding and Computing, pp. 49–54 (2001)

Features Detection on Industrial 3D CT Data

Thi-Chau Ma[1], Chang-soo Park[2], Kittichai Suthunyatanakit[3], Min-jae Oh[3], Tae-wan Kim[3], Myung-joo Kang[2], and The-Duy Bui[1]

[1] Lab.of Human Machine Interaction, University of Engineering and Technology, Vietnam National University, Hanoi, Vietnam
[2] Dep. of Mathematical Sciences, Seoul National University, Seoul, Korea
[3] Dep. of Naval Architecture and Ocean Engineering, Seoul National University, Seoul, Korea

Abstract. Features are significantly used as design elements to reconstruct a model in reverse engineering. This paper proposes a new method for detecting corner features and edge features in 3D from CT scanned data. Firstly, the level set method is applied on CT scanned data to segment the data in the form of implicit function having two values, which mean inside and outside of the boundary of the shape. Next, corners and sharp edges are detected and extracted from the boundary of the shape. The corners are detected based on Sobel-like mask convolution processing with a marching cube. The sharp edges are detected based on Canny-like mask convolution. In this step, a noisy removal module is included. In the paper, the result of detecting both features is presented.

Keywords: Reverse Engineering (RE), Computed Tomography (CT), Corner and Edge Features Detection, Mask Convolution, Noise Removal.

1 Introduction

Features are significantly used as design elements to reconstruct a model in reverse engineering. Especially reconstructing a B-spline model from computed tomography (CT) scanned data, we needs a curve network including corners, sharp edges, ridges, etc. Fig.1 shows a scheme of CT to B-spline reverse engineering. Feature detection has been attracted lots of attention [1,4,5,6,7,8,9,14]. However, the existing methods either depend on mesh generation or take time to check every voxel data.

In this paper we propose a method to detect those features, i.e. corners and sharp edges, from CT scanned data. Firstly, the level set method (LSM) is applied on CT scanned data to segment the data in the form of implicit function having two values, which mean inside and outside of the boundary of the shape. Secondly, corners and sharp edges detection from the boundary of the shape is done. To detect corners, we apply Sobel-like mask convolution processing with a marching cube. To detect sharp edges, we apply Canny-like mask convolution. A noise removal model is included in the step of sharp edge detection as well.

T.-h. Kim et al. (Eds.): MulGraB 2011, Part II, CCIS 263, pp. 345–354, 2011.

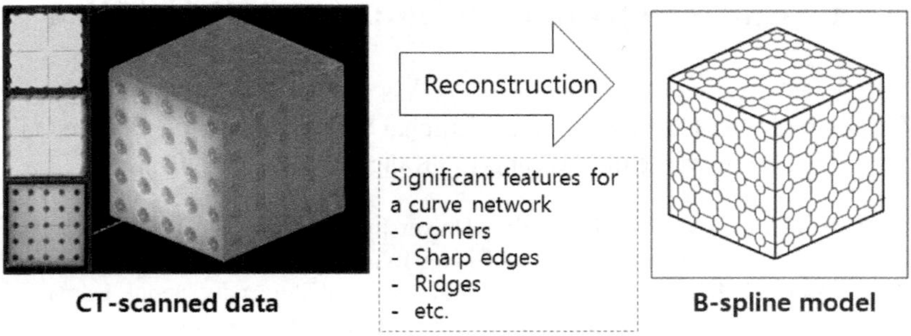

Fig. 1. Reverse engineering from CT scanned data to B-spline model

The paper is organized as follows. Section 2 shows related works and backgrounds. Section 3 presents our method to detect corner and sharp edge features. Experiments and results are provided in section 4.

2 Related Works and Backgrounds

2.1 Related Works

Feature detection methods can be classified into two groups: polygon-based methods and point-based methods. There exist many techniques for feature detection and extraction relying on polygonal meshes [1,5,7,9]. These techniques often include two steps: meshes generation and feature detection. In [7,9], discrete extremities to extract feature lines are used in regular triangles. Singular triangles are treated specially based on neighbors of singular or regular triangles. In [1], a normal-based classification operator was used to classify edges into different types by combining some of thresholds. In [5], Watanabe and Belyaev estimated the principle curvature extrema on dense triangle mesh. Then, these curvature extrema were used to form focal surface. The properties of focal surface were used to identify features.

Point based methods [4,6,8,14] are more interesting because of the lack of knowledge concerning normal and connectivity information. Gumhold et al. [14] considered the k-nearest neighbors for every data voxel. They used Principal Component Analysis (PCA) to analyze the neighbors of each point. Eigenvalues and eigenvectors of coefficient matrix were used to determine the probability of the voxel belong to feature lines, borders or corner points. Pauly et al. [8] extended the PCA approach to multiple neighborhood sizes. The algorithm recognized all kinds of features. In [4,6], Gauss map was built for each data voxel. Voxels are classified by clustering Gauss map. In [12], 3D filters were extended from 2D edge detection filters.

Those mesh-based methods require mesh generation and thus need relying on the accuracy of mesh generation; while those point-based methods require procedure running every data voxel and thus have high computational cost. For our method, we use LSM and mask convolution on voxels. The method can be applied to detect feature without normal and connectivity information, like mesh-based. In addition, the computational time is reduced.

2.2 Level Set Method

The level set method [2, 20, 21] is very popular in computational fluid dynamics, computer graphics, image processing because of its advantage of handling the complicated topology and implementing easily. It represents the contour or the surface as the zero level set of a higher dimensional signed distance function. We can explain the detail as follows. Let the region $\Omega(t)$ be enclosed by the closed surface $\Gamma(t)$. Then the level set method uses the level set function $\phi(x,t)$ to represent $\Gamma(t)$as the zero level set of $\phi(x,t)$ in Fig.2. i.e.

$$\begin{aligned} \phi(x,t) &> 0 \text{ in } \Omega(t), \\ \phi(x,t) &= 0 \text{ in } \Gamma(t), \\ \phi(x,t) &< 0 \text{ in } \overline{\Omega}^c(t), \end{aligned} \tag{1}$$

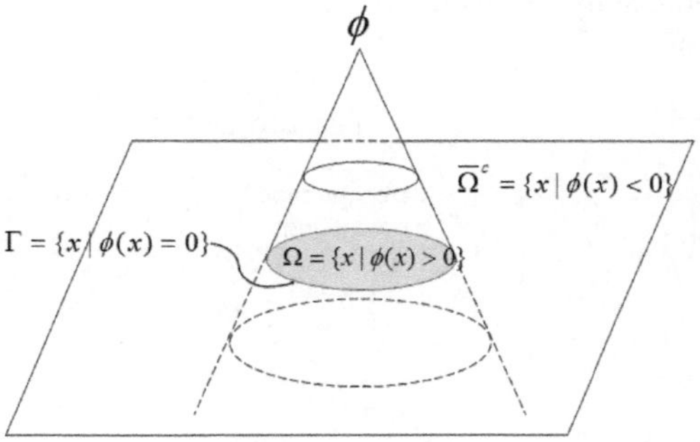

Fig. 2. Level Set Function

In the level set method, we discretize the domain into rectangular grids and have the value of $\phi(x,t)$ at each grid. As we solve some partial differential equation using finite difference method, we can evolve the surface $\Gamma(t)$.

We employ the segmentation model using the level set method. In image processing, the mathematical model of segmentation is introduced by Mumford and Shah [19]. For an image given, they decomposed the image into piecewise-smooth approximation by minimizing the following function:

$$F(u,C) = \mu L(C) + \lambda \int_{\Omega} (u_0 - u)^2 \, d\Omega + \int_{\Omega/C} |\nabla u|^2 \, d\Omega, \tag{2}$$

where $L(C)$ denotes the length of Cwhich is the boundary of object to be detected, $\lambda > 0$ and $\mu > 0$ are parameters. Usually in the boundary of C, the intensity of the image u_0 changes steeply. The first term makes the length of C as short as possible, that is, plays the role in reducing noises. The second term fits the image u to u_0 closely. The last term lets the regions except edges in the image make as smooth as it can. This term also helps to denoising.

After segmenting the 3D image directly by LSM, we can get the binary image of which value inside the object is -1 and value outside the object is 1.

With this LSM method, the computational time is $O(N)$, where N is number of input data.

3 Corners and Sharp Edges Detection

3.1 Overview

This section presents our corners and sharp edges detection method. The method is divided into two main steps, shown in Fig.3. The first step is applying the level set method (LSM) to segment the data in the form of implicit function. This data is used to detect corners and sharp edges in the second step by convolving with designed masks, i.e. Sobel and Canny, respectively.

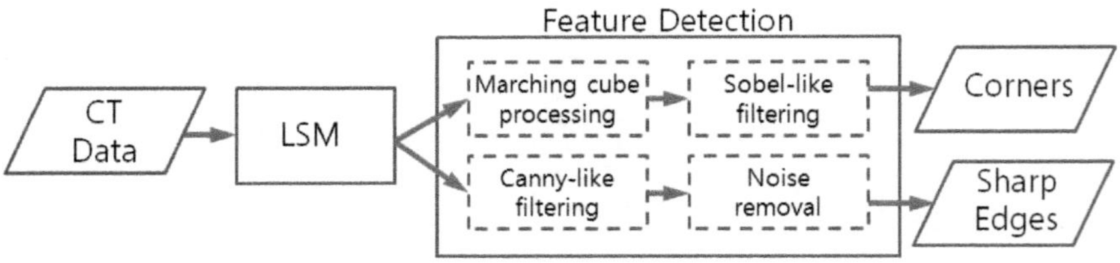

Fig. 3. Overview of Corners and Sharp Edges Detection

3.2 Corners Detection

In this step, marching cube is applied with each boundary voxel and Sobel-like mask is convolved in turn. Firstly, boundary voxels need to be filtered by processing a marching cube [17]. There are 15 configurations of a marching cube for polygonization, shown in Fig.4a. Only two configurations are considered to filter the boundary voxel, which is possibly a corner voxel – or candidate corner voxel. That is, cases 1 and 5 are the cubes containing the corner candidate, shown in Fig.4b. Instead of searching corners from the whole voxels, therefore, we only search corners from a set of corner candidates after processing a marching cube.

To detect a corner from the candidates, we use the method of 3D mask convolution. We invent a 3D mask in the pattern of Sobel, shown in Fig.5. There are three masks Sx, Sy and Sz provided in different directions, i.e. xy, yz, and xz-planes. We convolve these masks with a set of the corner candidates to estimate gradients in

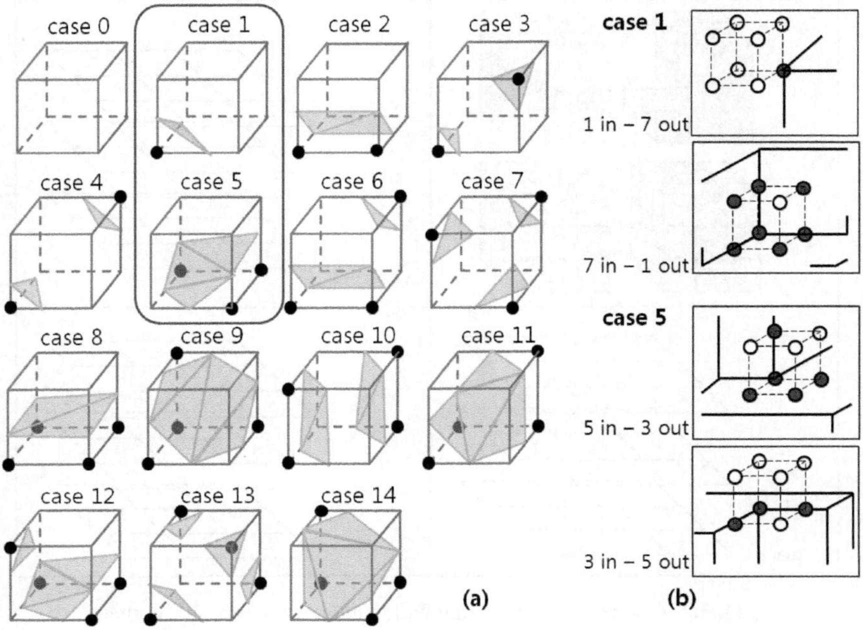

Fig. 4. (a) Configurations of a marching cube (b) Cases for corner candidate

those three directions. Corners are voxels having small changes in directions of gradients or having extreme gradient. Pseudo code of detecting a corner is provided below.

```
Procedure cornerDetect(CC,Sx,Sy,Sz,ts1,ts2)
    {
    Gx=Convolution(CC,Sx);
    Gy=Convolution(CC,Sy);
    Gz=Convolution(CC,Sz);
    Dxy=Gx/Gy ;
    Dyz=Gy/Gz ;
    Dzx=Gz/Gx ;
    For (i,j,k) in CC
    If((|Dx(i,j,k)-Dy(i,j,k)|<ts1 &&
    |Dy(i,j,k)-Dz(i,j,k)|<ts1&&
    |Dz(i,j,k)-Dx(i,j,k)|<ts1)   ||
    (|Gx(i,j,k)|+|Gy(i,j,k)|+|Gz(i,j,k)|<ts2))
        (i,j,k) is corner voxel.
    }
```

where CC is a set of the corner candidates, $ts1$ and $ts2$ are thresholds, Dxy, Dyz and Dzx are directions of gradients in 3 axis directions

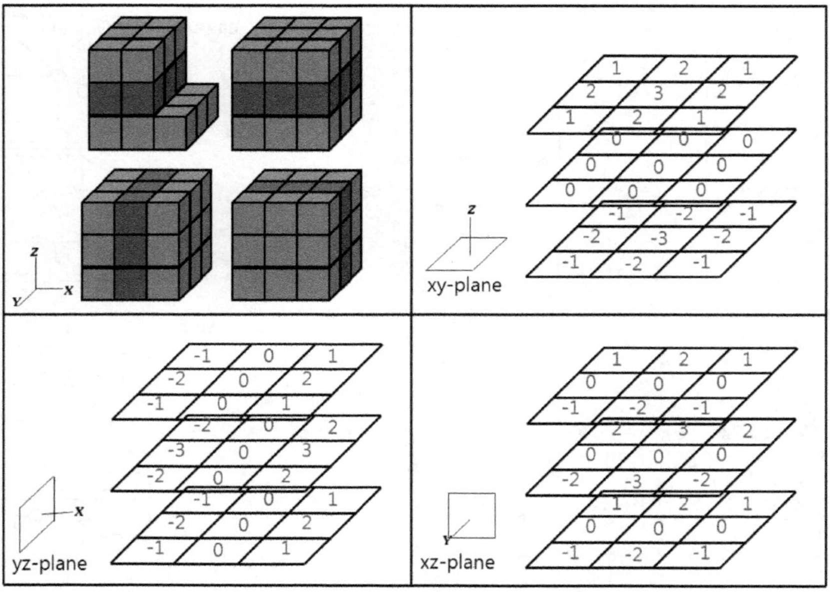

Fig. 5. Sobel-like pattern of convolution mask for detecting a corner

3.3 Sharp Edges Detection

Likewise, we invent a 3D mask to detect a sharp edge voxel. Like existing 3D edge detectors [10,12,16], this is used to approximate gradients or laplacians of 3D images by using mask convolution. In our case a 3D edge detector is inspired from Canny edge detector [3]. We design high pass filters to detect and extract sharp edge voxels by using a convolution mask. Three masks, Cx, Cy and Cz, are designed in three different directions, i.e. x-, y- and z-directions, shown in Fig.6. They can detect convex sharp edge voxels. To detect concave sharp edge voxels, however, other three masks, Cx_i, Cy_i and Cz_i are also designed. Fig.7 shown the masks of Cy and Cy_i. In addition, Pseudo code of detecting a sharp edge voxel is provided below.

```
Procedure edgeDetect(B,Cx,Cy,Cz,Cx_i,Cy_i,Cz_i, t1,t2)
    {
    Gx=Convolution(B,Cx);
    Gy=Convolution(B,Cy);
    Gz=Convolution(B,Cz);
    Gx_i=Convolution(B,Cx_i);
    Gy_i=Convolution(B,Cy_i);
    Gz_i=Convolution(B,Cz_i);
    For (i,j,k) in B
    If (Gx(i,j,k)<t1 || Gy(i,j,k)<t1 || Gz(i,j,k)<t1 ||
    Gx_i(i,j,k)>t2||Gy_i(i,j,k)>t2||Gz_i(i,j,k)>t2)
    (i,j,k) is a sharp edge voxel.
    }
```

where B is a set of the boundary voxel, $t1$ and $t2$ are thresholds.

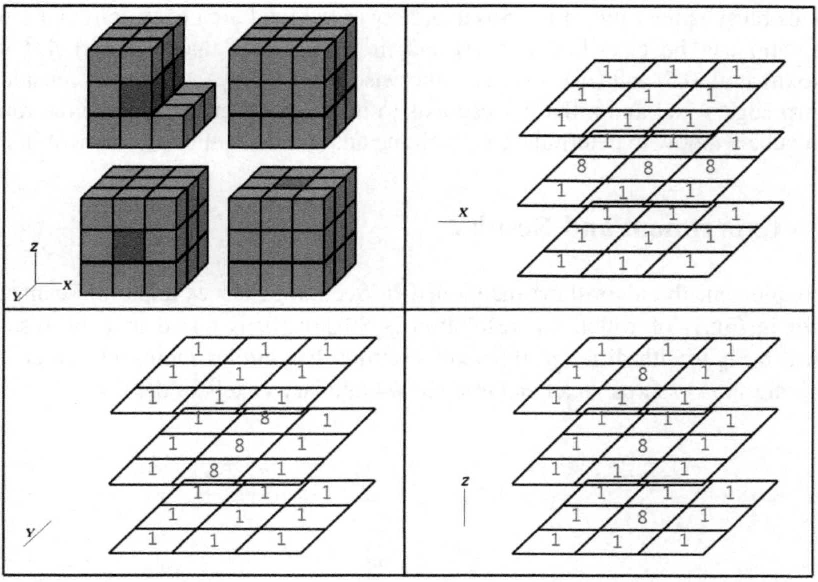

Fig. 6. Canny-like pattern of convolution mask for detecting a sharp edge

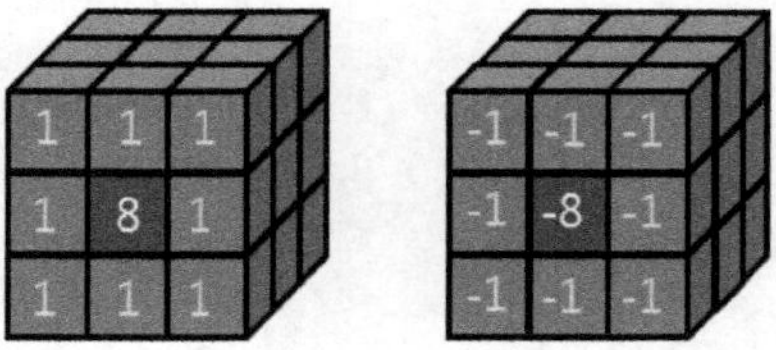

Fig. 7. *Cy* mask for convex sharp edge (left), *Cy_i* mask for concave sharp edge (right)

As well, this step includes a noise removal module. Because noise voxels and sharp edge voxels involve extreme gradients, we need to distinguish them. Susan method [15] is applied to solve this. This method is based on a circular window in which the central voxel, so-called nucleus, is the analyzed voxel. The operator

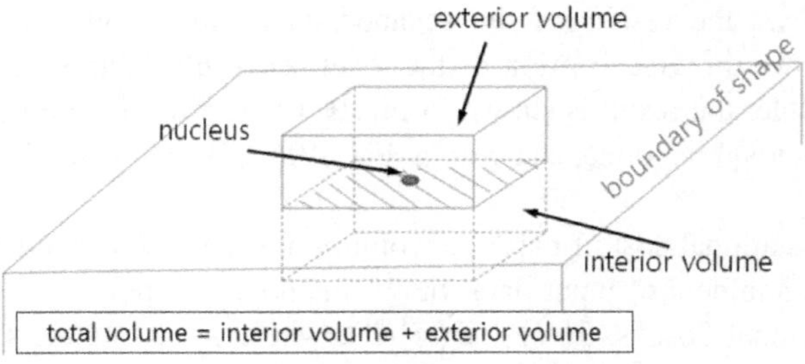

Fig. 8. A cube window for determining a Susan ratio

responsibility is the ratio of the Susan area over the total area of the circular window. This ratio can be classified into (i) *salient* if it is less than 0.5, (ii) *flat* if it is approximately 0.5, and (iii) *concave*, otherwise. In this way, a salient is considered to a sharp edge voxel and a flat corresponds to noise. In order to compute the ratio, we use a cube window to determine total volume and interior volume, as shown in Fig.8.

4 Experiment and Results

We implement the algorithms mentioned in Section 3. An example of scanned data shown in Fig.1, of which the resolution is 50x50x50, is tested and the results are shown in Fig.9 with different thresholds setting. Big circles represent corner voxels, small one show sharps voxel and grid show boundary voxels of the shape.

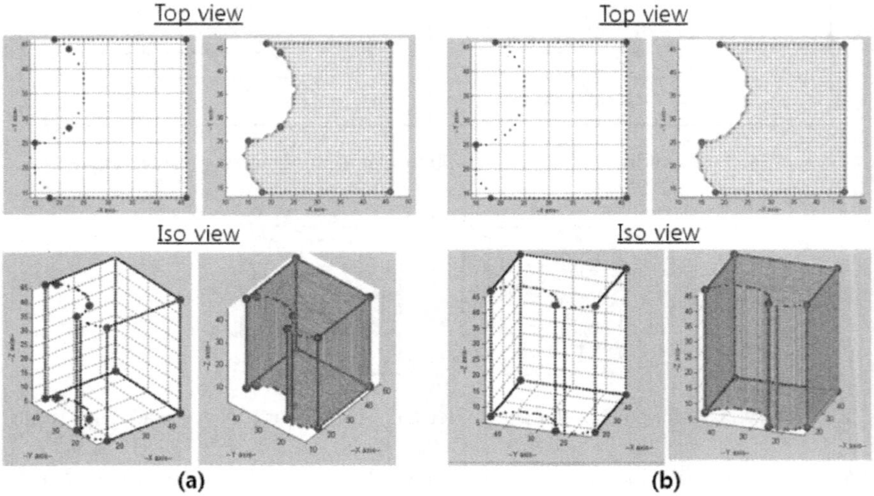

Fig. 9. (a) thresholds: t1 = 15, t2 =200, ts1 = 1.2, ts2 = 500, (b) thresholds: t1 = 15, t2 = 100, ts1 = 0.7, ts2 = 350

Fig.10 shows the results of the scanned data with resolution of 300x300x250. Fig.10(a) shows the visualization of the level set result. Without processing a noise removal module, the result is shown in Fig.10(b). The results are better if processing the noise removal is done, shown in Figs.10(c), 10(d) with different thresholds setting.

The computational cost of mask convolution is $O(n^3N)$, where $n \times n \times n$ is size of a mask, N is numbers of input data. In our method, we apply the LSM method, thus the computational cost is $O(N) + O(n^3N')$, where N' is numbers of the boundary voxels, instead of $O(n^3N)$. Because $N' \ll N$, the computational time with LSM is faster.

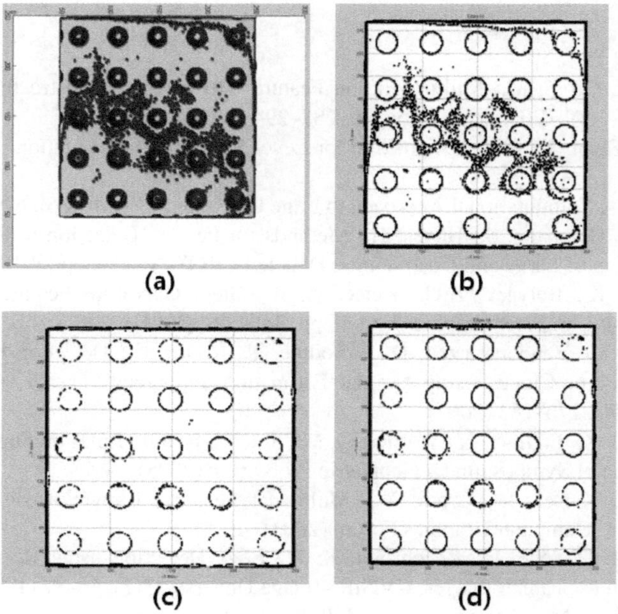

Fig. 10. Results of scanned data with resolution 300x300x125 with and without noise removal

5 Conclusions and Future Work

We propose a method of corners and sharp edges detection including two main steps. Firstly, the LSM method is applied to segment the boundary of the shape from 3D CT scanned data in form of implicit function. Secondly, Sobel-like mask convolution with processing a marching cube and Canny-like mask convolution including a Susan noise removal module are done to detect corner voxels and sharp edge voxels, respectively. Computational cost is $O(N) + O(n^3N')$, where N is numbers of input data, $n \times n \times n$ is size of a mask, and N' is numbers of boundary voxels. The computational time is faster if processing with LSM. The result is very good when including the Susan noise removal module.

For future work, we will develop a method for detecting other features such as ridges. Then we will develop how to construct a curve network from these resulting features and finally reconstruct a B-spline model.

Acknowledgments. We would like thank to the TRIG project at University of Engineering and Technology, VNU Hanoi and the project "Development of inspection platform technology based on 3-dimensional X-ray images" (Ministry of Knowledge Economy, Korea via Grant No 10035474. We also thank to Vietnam National Foundation for Science and Technology.

References

1. Hubeli, A., Gross, M.: Multiresolution Feature Extraction for Unstructured Meshes. In: Proceedings of IEEE Visualization, pp. 287–294 (2001)
2. Song, B., Chan, T.: A Fast Algorithm for Level Set Based Optimization. CAM-UCLA 68 (2002)
3. Canny, J.: A Computational Approach to Edge Detection. TPAMI 8(6), 679–698 (1986)
4. Weber, C., Hahmann, S., Hagen, H.: Methods for Feature Detection in Point Clouds. In: Visualization of Large and Unstructured Data Sets, IRTG Workshop (2010)
5. Watanabe, K., Belyaev, A.G.: Detection of Salient Curvature Features on Polygonal Surfaces. In: Computer Graphics Forum, pp. 385–392 (2001)
6. Demarsin, K., Vanderstraeten, D., Volodine, T., Roose, D.: Detection of Closed Sharp Edges in Point Clouds using Normal Estimation and Graph Theory. Computer-Aided Design 39(4), 276–283 (2007)
7. Hildebrand, K., Polthier, K., Wardetzky, M.: Smooth Feature Lines on Surface Meshes. In: Proceedings of Symposium on Geometric Processing (2005)
8. Pauly, M., Keiser, R., Gross, M.: Multi-scale Feature Extraction on Point Sampled Surfaces. In: Computer Graphics Forum (2003)
9. Monga, O., Deriche, R., Rocchisani, J.: 3D Edge Detection using Recursive Filtering: Application to Scanner images. CVGIP - Image Underst. 53(1), 76–87 (1991)
10. Morgenthaler, M.: Rosenfeld. A.: Multidimensional Edge Detection by Hyper-surface Fitting. In: PAMI-3, July 4 (1981)
11. Bentum, M.J., Lichtenbelt, B.B.A., Malzbender, T.: Frequency Analysis of Gradient Estimators in Volume Rendering. IEEE Transactions in Medical Imaging (1997)
12. Monga, O., Deriche, R., Malandain, G., Cocquerez, J.P.: Recursive Filtering and Edge Closing: Two Primary Tools for 3D Edge Detection. In: Faugeras, O. (ed.) ECCV 1990. LNCS, vol. 427, pp. 56–65. Springer, Heidelberg (1990)
13. Osher, S., Paragios, N.: Geometric Level Set Methods in Imaging, Vision and Graphics. Springer-Verlag, New York, Inc. (2003)
14. Gumhold, S., Wang, X., McLeod, R.: Feature Extraction from Point Clouds. In: Proceedings of 10th International Meshing Roundtable (2001)
15. Smith, S.M., Brady, J.M.: Susan - A New Approach to Low Level Image Processing. Int. J. Computer Vision 23(1), 45–78 (1997)
16. Zucker, S.W., Hummed, R.A.: A Three Dimensional Edge Operator. IEEE Transaction on Pattern Analysis and Machine Intelligence, 3 (1981)
17. Lorensen, W.E., Cline, H.E.: Marching Cubes: A High Resolution 3D Surface Construction Algorithm. Computer Graphics 21(4) (1987)
18. Pratt, W.K.: Digital Image Processing, 2nd edn. John Wiley and Sons, New York (1991)
19. Mumford, D., Shah, J.: Optimal Approximation by Piecewise Smooth Functions and Associated Variational Problems. Commun. Pure. Appl. Math. 42, 577–685 (1989)
20. Chan, T., Vese, L.: Active Contours without Edges. IEEE Transactions on Image Processing 10(2), 266–277 (2001)
21. Osher, S., Fedkiw, R.: Level Set Method and Dynamic Implicit Surfaces. Springer, Heidelberg (2003)

Author Index

GPSR Compliance

The European Union's (EU) General Product Safety Regulation (GPSR) is a set of rules that requires consumer products to be safe and our obligations to ensure this.

If you have any concerns about our products, you can contact us on ProductSafety@springernature.com

In case Publisher is established outside the EU, the EU authorized representative is:

Springer Nature Customer Service Center GmbH
Europaplatz 3
69115 Heidelberg, Germany

Batch number: 10682617

Printed by Printforce, the Netherlands